THE JAPANESE EXPERIENCE OF ECONOMIC REFORMS

The Japanese Experience of Economic Reforms

Edited by

Juro Teranishi
Professor of Economics
Hitotsubashi University, Tokyo

and

Yutaka Kosai
President
Japan Center for Economic Research, Tokyo

150th YEAR
M

St. Martin's Press

First published in Great Britain 1993 by
THE MACMILLAN PRESS LTD
Houndmills, Basingstoke, Hampshire RG21 2XS
and London
Companies and representatives
throughout the world

A catalogue record for this book is available from the British Library.

ISBN 0–333–57971–2

Printed in Great Britain by
Antony Rowe Ltd
Chippenham, Wiltshire

First published in the United States of America 1993 by
Scholarly and Reference Division,
ST. MARTIN'S PRESS, INC.,
175 Fifth Avenue,
New York, N.Y. 10010

ISBN 0–312–08560–5

Library of Congress Cataloging-in-Publication Data
The Japanese experience of economic reforms / edited by Juro Teranishi and Yutaka Kosai.
p. cm.
Includes index.
ISBN 0–312–08560–5
1. Japan—Economic policy—1945–1989. 2. Economic stabilization–
–Japan. I. Teranishi, Jūrō. II. Kōsai, Yutaka, 1933– .
HC462.9.J3297 1993
338.952—dc20 92–20307
CIP

Contents

Preface

This book provides a renewed investigation into the various aspects of economic reforms in postwar Japan. The process and impact of reform measures in such areas as industrial organization, finance, labour and landholding which took place immediately after the war are thoroughly examined. Policies for stabilization of postwar inflation and their relationship with structural reform are discussed. Some new light is also shed on the process of deregulation and liberalization implemented during the 1960s and 1970s.

The main purpose of this undertaking lies in its possible relevance to the ongoing attempt at structural reform and stabilization in the former socialist economies as well as less developed countries. Some of the specific institutional devices introduced during the period of postwar reform and depicted in this volume might be useful in these attempts. More importantly, the process of trial and error experienced by Japan is of considerable relevance to the formulation of policies of these countries. It is our sincere desire that this volume provide a useful reference-point for these countries as they develop policies and institutions tailored to the specific needs of their economies and societies.

Two other points with respect to the relevance of this book are also worth mentioning. First, we hope that these contributions will provide some insight into the economic success of Japan. The role of administrative guidance in industrial policy is frequently emphasized as one of the secrets of Japan's economic success. However, one must also be aware of the significance of the competitive environment prevailing in Japan. To a considerable degree this environment is attributable to the postwar reform measures analysed in this book, as well as the competitive atmosphere inherited from the prewar period. Second, this book is also expected to shed light on the origin and nature of the so-called Japanese model of capitalism. The origin of Japanese institutions such as the cooperative relationship between government and the private sector, between employer and employee as well as among firms and banks is no doubt rooted in the long historical process of modernization. But at the same time it is true that the various reform measures implemented after the Second World War are of considerable importance in explaining these characteristics.

This volume is the culmination of a project on Japanese experience of economic reform undertaken by the Japan Center for Economic Research (JCER) between September 1990 and December 1991. We are grateful to the more than ten economists, all leading figures in their fields, who participated in the project and kindly contributed papers to this volume. Akiko Oishi and Kumiko Mizutani of JCER have also played an essential part in the project. Their assistance and devotion have been critical to timely publication of the study. For a book written in English by Japanese, a good edition of English language is of vital importance. The assistance of Laurie A. Freeman and Robert W. Bullock is highly appreciated.

JURO TERANISHI
YUTAKA KOSAI

Notes on the Contributors

Kimihiro Etoh is an Economist with the International Department of the Bank of Japan.

Mitsuhiro Fukao is Principal Administrator in the Economics and Statistics Department of the OECD.

Akira Goto is Professor of Economics at Hitotsubashi University, Tokyo.

Toshihiko Kawagoe is Associate Professor of Economics at Seikei University, Tokyo.

Takao Komine is a Cabinet Councillor with the Economic Planning Agency, Tokyo.

Masahiro Kuroda is Professor of Economics and Director of the Keio Economic Observatory, Tokyo.

Yoshiro Miwa is Professor of Economics at the University of Tokyo.

Toru Nakakita is Associate Professor of Economics at Toyo University and Senior Economist at the Japan Institute of International Affairs, Tokyo.

Tetsuji Okazaki is Associate Professor of Economics at the University of Tokyo.

Masao Oumi is Chief of the Liaison Group for the International Department at the Bank of Japan.

Seiichiro Yonekura is Associate Professor of Business History at Hitotsubashi University, Tokyo.

Yoshie Yonezawa is Professor of Economics at Aoyama Gakuin University, Tokyo.

Hiroshi Yoshikawa is Associate Professor of Economics at the University of Tokyo.

1 Introduction: Economic Reform and Stabilization in Postwar Japan

Juro Teranishi and Yutaka Kosai*

1.1 AIM OF THIS VOLUME

The purpose of this volume is to offer a renewed investigation into the process of economic reform and stabilization in the postwar Japanese economy. The main focus is on economic reforms, structural changes and the stabilization of inflation rates during the years 1945–50, although the longer-term trend of deregulation and liberalization thereafter will also be taken into account.

The articles included in this volume are the outcome of a project on 'Japanese Experience of Economic Reforms' undertaken by The Japan Center for Economic Research between September 1990 and December 1991. The major aim of these articles is to provide a useful reference point and relevant materials for the former socialist countries currently making an attempt to move towards a market economy. It is hoped that the book will also prove useful for developing countries as they work to draw up policies for the structural adjustment and stabilization of their economies.

The study is composed of three parts. Part I, entitled 'Stabilization Policy', comprises four chapters on various aspects of stabilization policy in Japan in the immediate postwar period. The causes of inflation, which at one point was as high as 30 per cent per month, as well as various aspects of anti-inflation policy such as the role played by orthodox stabilization policies, the effects of price controls, the relationship between growth and stabilization, income distribution and the anchoring effect of adopting a single exchange rate, are among the issues discussed here. Part II, 'Economic Reform After the War', consists of four chapters examining structural changes and reforms during 1945–50, when drastic measures aimed at the democratization and rehabilitation of the economy were implemented under the guidance of SCAP (Supreme Commander for the Allied

Powers). Deconcentration policy, financial sector reform, land reform and labour–management relations are discussed here. Part III, titled 'The Role of the Government in the Postwar Growth Process', is composed of five chapters on the role played by the government in the process of deregulation. These chapters take a long-term perspective of postwar economic growth. Among the topics discussed are: industrial rationalization policy, the role of technology importation, economic planning, trade and capital liberalization policies as well as protectionism and deregulation in agriculture.

Before summarizing the articles contained in this volume (sections 1.5–1.7), we provide a historical overview of the Japanese economy since the late nineteenth century. It is hoped that this overview will serve to situate the following discussion of the role and impact of postwar reforms and stabilization measures. In section 1.2, after a brief review of the long-term growth of the Japanese economy, the characteristics of the economy immediately before the war (around 1936), as well as the degree of control during the Second World War and wartime destruction are examined. In evaluating the Japanese experience, it is important to note that prior to wartime regulation Japan had a well-developed market economy; wartime controls lasted only eight years, and after the Second World War most production facilities as well as a well-trained labour force were still in place.

Section 1.3 is devoted to a discussion of the basic characteristics of the stabilization and reform process in Japan. Based on examination of the external and internal factors of reform, we find it had three basic characteristics: (i) it was conducted with the primary aim of democratization and demilitarization, (ii) it was gradual, and (iii) strong emphasis was placed on the micro and supply side of the economy as opposed to the macro and demand side. Section 1.4 offers a brief discussion of the relevance of the Japanese experience for LDCs and the former socialist economies.

In order to facilitate understanding, a brief chronology of events immediately after the war is provided in the final Appendix at the end of the volume. In addition, three special chronological tables in the form of appendices to chapters will be useful in understanding particular topics; one related to inflation stabilization and international economic transactions (Chapter 5), one on trade and capital liberalization (Chapter 13) and one related to institutional changes in the financial sector (Chapter 7).

1.2 POSTWAR REFORMS IN AN HISTORICAL PERSPECTIVE

1.2.1 Patterns of Long-Term Growth

Modern Japan has known two periods of radical economic reform: that implemented in the years 1868–85 by the newly-established Meiji government and that carried out during the immediate postwar period, 1945–50. In the earlier period, reform measures were implemented in order to, among other things, provide the government with a sufficient power base from which to control the money supply, raise tax revenues and implement national development policy. In addition, the Meiji government had to cope with a serious inflation that resulted from deficit financing carried out in order to establish and nurture industries deemed necessary for economic growth and from debts incurred as a result of the civil wars preceding the formation of the new state.

By 1885 inflation was finally contained, the central government was firmly established and the Japanese economy was on a trajectory of sustained growth that would continue until 1937, the year war broke out with China. The annual average growth rate of real GNP during the years 1885–1936 was 3.11 per cent, considerably higher than that of other countries at that time, but certainly lower than the average growth rate of 9.53 per cent during the so-called period of high growth after the Second World War (1955–70). The rate of inflation of the GDP deflator was moderate except for the two periods mentioned above, at an annual rate of 3.13 per cent during the period 1885–1936 and 4.49 per cent during the period 1955–90. Although in 1885 Japan was predominantly an agrarian country with 70.1 per cent employed in agriculture (including fishery and forestry) accounting for 45.2 per cent of NDP (net domestic product), the share of agriculture had declined to 48.7 per cent in terms of number of employed and 18.1 per cent in terms of sectoral NDP by 1935, and to 19.4 per cent and 8.6 per cent respectively by 1970. These changes in the industrial structure are also clearly reflected in the composition of exports (Table 1.1). During 1882–91, 74.9 per cent of exports were made up of primary goods such as raw silk (36.8 per cent of total exports), rice, coal and copper. Owing to the development of light industries such as the modern cotton-spinning industry, the share of primary goods decreased to 38.5 per cent during 1922–31 and 19.9 per cent during 1930–9. Figures for the 1930s show a stagnation of

Table 1.1 Percentage composition of commodity export

	Primary goods			*Manufactured goods*			
	Raw silk	*Others*	*Total*	*Textile*	*Other light industries*	*Heavy and chemical industries*	*Total*
1882–1891	36.8	38.1	74.9	8.8	9.1	7.2	25.1
1892–1901	29.3	25.8	55.1	23.3	13.4	8.2	44.9
1902–1911	26.2	19.0	45.2	27.7	14.5	12.6	54.8
1912–1921	22.6	11.6	34.2	33.8	15.3	16.7	65.8
1922–1931	31.7	6.8	38.5	34.1	14.6	12.8	61.5
1930–1939	13.1	6.8	19.9	35.0	18.6	26.5	80.1
1931–1955	–	4.7	4.7	39.5	15.9	39.9	95.3
1956–1960	–	4.5	4.5	32.0	18.4	45.1	95.5
1961–1965	–	3.5	3.5	21.3	16.4	58.6	96.5
1966–1970	–	1.7	1.7	13.7	13.4	71.2	98.3

Note: Percentage of value of total exports.

Source: Yamazawa (1990).

exports of raw silk due, on the one hand, to the development of synthetic fibres and the depression in the United States, and on the other hand, to increased exports of the products of the heavy and chemical industries to colonial regions. After the Second World War this trend of replacing light industry with heavy and chemical industries became even stronger.

There are three major characteristics associated with the long-term growth pattern of the Japanese economy. First, the main engine of growth has been the active importation of foreign technology. Starting with cotton-spinning technology during the nineteenth century, leading technologies for the heavy and chemical industries were imported around the turn of the century and especially during and after the First World War. After the Second World War, new technology in the machinery, electronics and petro-chemical industries was vigorously introduced. The impact of these technology imports becomes clear in the growth accounting shown in Table 1.2. With respect to the growth rate of GDP of industry, about 50 per cent of growth, namely 2.89 per cent out of 6.94 per cent in the prewar, and 6.54 per cent out of 12.39 per cent in the postwar period, is explained by the rise in total factor productivity. Although the impact of domestic R&D should not be disregarded, it was mainly foreign technology

Table 1.2 Growth accounting (annual rate of growth, %)

	Prewar period (1889–1938)	*Postwar period (1955–1976)*
Agriculture		
GDP	1.34	2.09
Labour	–0.22	–3.90
Labour productivity	1.56	5.99
Total factor productivity	0.94	2.40
Industry	*(1908–38)*	*(1955–76)*
GDP	6.94	12.39
Labour	2.50	2.86
Capital	6.00	11.96
Labour productivity	4.44	9.53
Total factor productivity	2.89	6.54

Note: Figures in parentheses show time period under calculation. Agriculture includes forestry and fishery; industry comprises manufacturing and mining.

Source: Minami (1986).

that contributed to this high increase in productivity.

One important characteristic of the importation of technology to Japan was the relatively small role of foreign direct investment. During the prewar period, Japan was not a major target for Western multinational firms, mainly for geographical reasons, so that the predominant methods of introducing foreign technology were the purchase of foreign machines and the delegation of engineers to foreign countries.[1] After the Second World War, inbound foreign direct investment was strictly regulated, and in spite of *de jure* deregulation, *de facto* controls were imposed, so that the import of technology consisted mainly of the licensing and purchasing of machineries (see Chapter 11 by Goto in this volume).

Second, Japan's growth was mainly financed by domestic savings and the dependence on foreign capital was rather limited. This was due partly to increases in the saving rate over time and partly to the isolated geographical position of the country. Personal saving rates display a rising pattern from a 5 per cent level during the nineteenth century to a 20–25 per cent level in the 1970s (Minami, 1986). Moreover, compared with an active flow of funds across the Atlantic, capital movements across the Pacific were limited. One indicator of the degree of financial interdependence is the simple correlation

Table 1.3 Balance of payments (annual average)

	Current account				*Capital account*		*Official settlement balance*
	Trade account	*Non-trade account*	*Transfer*	*Total*	*Long-term*	*Short-term*	
1885–1889	–1.2	–1.0	1.0	–1.3	–0.7	4.2	2.2
1890–1894	–6.3	1.6	3.6	–1.1	–1.1	3.0	0.9
1895–1899	–56.8	–10.2	77.4	10.4	26.4	–30.5	6.3
1900–1904	–30.1	–10.3	10.9	–29.6	24.6	–1.4	–6.4
1905–1909	–55.7	–41.2	16.7	–80.1	185.9	–30.6	75.2
1910–1914	–44.4	–38.8	–3.3	–80.5	42.8	5.3	–32.4
1915–1919	266.8	321.3	29.9	618.0	–330.9	72.4	359.5
1920–1924	–546.1	190.9	34.6	–320.6	–114.6	348.1	–87.1
1925–1929	–338.7	172.8	14.3	–151.6	–102.2	224.2	–29.6
1930–1931	–156.7	136.9	–0.8	–20.1	–318.1	–67.6	–406.2
1932–1936	–77.4	128.7	64.6	115.9	–334.8	191.4	–27.5
1947–1951	–197.8	28.4	396.2	226.6	–15.8	2.2	230.8
1952–1956	–361.6	367.4	26.2	32.4	–35.0	20.6	19.0
1957–1961	7.8	–111.6	–62.8	–166.8	–29.2	3.6	–162.8
1962–1966	957.6	–708.6	–73.4	175.6	–95.4	64.6	137.8
1967–1971	3827.6	–1480.0	–198.8	2148.8	–775.8	810.4	2373.0

Note: Units: in million yen for the prewar period and in million dollars for the postwar period.

Source: Bank of Japan, *Nihon Ginko Hyakunen-shi: Shiryo-hen* (One Hundred-Year History of the Bank of Japan: Statistics).

coefficient of short-term interest rates. This figure was 0.11 for the US and Japan, 0.44 for the US and Germany, and 0.55 for the US and the UK, calculated on monthly data from September 1909 through March 1914; and 0.62, 0.77, 0.93 respectively during the period from January 1925 to December 1938 (Teranishi, 1991). However, a low dependence on foreign capital does not imply that Japan has not made use of foreign savings. Table 1.3 shows shifts in the balance of payments between 1885 and 1971. There were three instances in the prewar period when the official settlement balance recorded large positive values. In the first case of 6.3 million yen per annum recorded during 1895–9 reflects the receipt of reparation payments from China following the Sino-Japanese War (1894–5). Japan used this money to finance deficits of 6.4 million yen incurred during 1900–4, a period of rapid fiscal expansion for military and infrastructure build-up.

In the second case of 75.2 million yen recorded during 1905–9, this resulted from borrowings for the war with Russia (1904–5) and is reflected in the large positive value of long-term capital inflow. The annual rate of decrease in foreign reserves of 32.4 million yen during 1910–14 almost exactly corresponds to the estimated interest payments on foreign borrowing for the war (32.4 million yen per annum). Finally, in the third case an accumulation of 359.5 million yen during 1915–19 reflects windfall gains in the export boom following the First World War. It can be assumed that the foreign reserves accumulated during this period were later used to finance the deficits of 1920–9, a period of urbanization as well as import substitution from light to heavy and chemical industries. These considerations suggest that although Japan did not rely heavily on foreign borrowings for its development, it did benefit from fortuitous events which resulted in an inflow of foreign exchange. For example, the reparations from China of 138.9 million yen amounted to 6.0 per cent of GNP in 1899, and the total accumulation of foreign reserves during 1914–20 of 1837 million yen corresponded to 11.6 per cent of GNP in 1920. In other words, without these inflows of foreign exchange, Japan would have had to resort to foreign borrowings more heavily. (The same applies to the years after the Second World War, as will be discussed below.) However, it must be emphasized that Japan never tried to accomplish a rapid industrialization by relying mainly on foreign borrowings.

The third characteristic of the long-term growth pattern was a significant growth in agriculture either concurrently or prior to the growth of industry. In the prewar period, and especially before the First World War, the growth rate in agriculture was high, owing to the diffusion of high-yield crop varieties and new technology throughout the country. This not only facilitated the provision of food but also contributed to an increase in tax revenues and a redundant workforce which could be channelled into industry. The high rate of growth of 2.09 per cent (Table 1.2) during the postwar period was mainly due to rapid mechanization and the diffusion of new technology developed during wartime isolation. Mechanization and technology diffusion had also led to a reduction of the workforce at an annual rate of 3.9 per cent. Although population growth was rather slow (1.18 per cent during 1885–1936 and 1.00 per cent during 1955–70), it is widely believed there was a significant amount of Lewisian type excess labour in agriculture. The marginal productivity of labour in agriculture was considered to be lower than that in industry, and an elastic supply of cheap labour from agriculture comprised an important source for industrial growth along with the availability of foreign technology.

In sum, the long-term growth process of Japan during 1868–1970 has three outstanding features: (i) rapid absorption of foreign technology without significant reliance on foreign direct investment, (ii) limited dependence on foreign capital (even if there were occasional and significant inflows of foreign exchange), and (iii) elastic supply of labour from agriculture.

1.2.2 The Japanese Economy in the mid-1930s

By the 1930s, Japan already had a relatively developed market economy and a fairly competitive industrial sector.

The prewar Japanese economy basically operated on the principles of the free market. In 1936, the total population was 65.6 million and there were 87 500 incorporated firms (reporting to the tax bureau) together with numerous non-incorporated management-owned firms. The degree of concentration was low: the share in paid-in capital of the four big family-owned conglomerates (Zaibatsu) (Mitsui, Mitsubishi, Sumitomo and Yasuda) was 22.5 per cent in financial industries and 14.6 per cent in heavy and chemical industries. The involvement of the government in the economy was minimal and was certainly less than in the postwar period.[2] This is evidenced by the share of government expenditures (government consumption and capital formation) in GNP (Table 1.4): even when there is an increasing trend over time, the government share does not exceed 18.3 per cent until 1936. This is further substantiated by the fact that in 1936 government revenue from government enterprises as a percentage of GNP was only 1.7 per cent and tax revenues accounted for only 5.9 per cent of GNP.[3]

The monetary and fiscal system was relatively well developed. As of 1930, there were 872 commercial banks, 23 special banks, 37 trust companies, 92 insurance companies, 12 913 credit cooperative and 9954 postal offices (offering postal savings). Direct and indirect finance were well balanced. The private sector's portfolio comprised 35.5 per cent of deposits, 10.5 per cent of insurance and trust funds and 36.5 per cent of securities. Only 2.1 per cent of assets were held in cash (1931–5 average). The ratio of assets held by the private sector to GNP, which was 0.55 during 1886–90, climbed to 2.59 during 1931–5. In 1936, 67.0 per cent of central government revenues

Table 1.4 Percentage composition of real GNP

	Personal consumption	*Government consumption*	*Gross fixed capital formation*		*Inventory investment*	*Exports*	*Imports*
			Government	*Private*			
1888	80.0	6.7	2.4	11.3	–	7.2	7.6
1900	72.0	7.3	5.3	10.8	–	11.6	13.6
1910	76.0	8.2	6.1	11.4	–	15.1	16.3
1920	72.3	6.6	6.2	13.8	–	18.9	17.8
1930	73.0	11.0	5.3	9.0	–	18.3	18.5
1936	64.1	15.3	3.0	11.3	5.5	26.1	25.3
1944	34.0	35.4	5.1	19.4	6.8	11.2	11.8
1948	59.0	9.6	12.2	12.2	10.7	2.5	6.3
1960	60.2	12.7	6.5	17.6	2.4	8.0	7.4
1970	51.3	8.2	8.2	26.8	4.3	11.7	10.6

Note: Calendar year except for 1944 (fiscal year).

Sources: Ohkawa *et al*. (1965) (through 1930), and thereafter Somu-cho (Management and Coordination Agency) *Nihon Choki Tokei Soran* (Historical Statistics of Japan), vol. 3, Table 13–10.

were obtained through taxes, 20.5 per cent of which were personal and corporate income taxes, while 18.0 per cent came from state enterprises.

As Table 1.1 shows, during 1930–9, manufactured goods (of which textiles accounted for 35.0 per cent) constituted 80.1 per cent of total exports; although the share of the heavy and chemical industries made up 26.5 per cent. The international competitiveness of these industries was still insufficient. As of 1935, 69.6 per cent of the goods exported by the heavy and chemical industries went to colonial and semi-colonial regions. As for machine industries, although Japan could produce small- and medium-level machines domestically, most large and sophisticated machinery was still imported from Western countries. It was only during the postwar high growth era that these industries reached technological maturity and could accomplish full import and export substitution.

1.2.3 The Wartime Economy

Despite the so-called Manchurian Incident of 1931, the economy remained largely free, and it was not until 1937 when Japan entered the war with China that full-scale regulation of the economy was imposed. In 1937, the allocation of funds as well as foreign trade were put under government control, and the National Mobilization Law (Kokka Sodoin-ho) enacted in 1938 brought the allocation of labour and production equipment as well as prices and wages under government control. Many basic commodities were rationed at this time and the government even intervened in the determination of stock prices and dividends.

Concurrently, the share of government expenditures in GNP rose to 40.5 per cent in 1944 (Table 1.4), and in the same year, 39.6 per cent of outstanding lendings by the five largest commercial banks and the Industrial Bank of Japan (Nihon Kogyo Ginko:IBJ) were directed to the production of military equipment. The industrial structure itself underwent considerable changes at this time. Activities in non-military industries such as textiles and food processing were discouraged, while workforce and equipment were converted for military use. As a result, the share of light industries in the total production of the manufacturing sector declined from 66.3 per cent in 1931 to 24.1 per cent in 1945. The low ratio of remaining capacity to maximum capacity for cotton industries after the Second World War reflects the effects of this compulsory conversion (Table 1.5).

The physical destruction of the war also affected the economy. Marine vessels and residential housing in urban areas were heavily

Table 1.5 Productive capacity of industries

	Year of maximum capacity through the end of 1944	*Destruction due to bombing raid /maximum capacity*	*Capacity at the end of war/maximum capacity*
Hydroelectric power	1944	0.0	102.6
Thermal power	1941	23.5	53.3
Ordinary steel and steel products	1944	–	100.5
Aluminium	1944	23.9	75.2
Machine tools	1943	22.6	63.2
Soda ash	1941	17.8	59.3
Sodium hydroxide	1944	35.7	64.3
Sulphuric acid	1944	14.4	85.6
Cotton staple yarn	1941	5.0	20.4
Cotton textile	1941	5.1	31.5

Note: Figures in the second and third column show percentages to maximum capacity.

Source: Miyazaki and Ito (1989).

damaged. However, the loss of productive capacity due to bombing raids was relatively small for most industries except for the machinery industries and some chemical industries (Table 1.5).

In sum, the Japanese experience of wartime control was rather short, lasting only eight years. What's more most of the productive capacity and trained workforce were kept intact after the war together with the free market managerial know-how which prevailed before the war.

1.3 CHARACTERISTICS OF REFORMS AND STABILIZATION POLICIES

1.3.1 External and Internal Factors in Policy Implementation

A majority of the postwar reforms were carried out before the ratification of the Japan–US peace treaty in 1951, and thus Supreme Commander for the Allied Powers (SCAP) played an overwhelming role in determining the course of reform. Especially with respect to the most important and drastic reforms – land reform, the Zaibatsu dissolution and the labour reform – the Japanese government was given little opportunity to voice its opinions. Moreover, the more experienced SCAP became in dealing with Japan, the less dependent it grew on control by Washington. After 1947 most policy measures were decided under the guidance of SCAP (Nakamura, 1979).

The basic aim of SCAP and US government policy was the demilitarization and democratization of Japan. The prewar and wartime landlord system, the Zaibatsu and the labour management system were considered to have largely contributed to the military expansion of Japan, and drastic reform measures were introduced in order to 'educate' the Japanese towards democracy. At the same time that reform was being carried out in these areas, Japan had to fight severe inflation and seek ways to reconstruct its devastated economy. The Cold War, which started in 1948, brought important changes in occupation policy, and emphasis was shifted from demilitarization to the reconstruction and recovery of the economy in order to make Japan a stronghold against communism. This change in the basic stance became apparent in the suspension of the US requirement that Japan make reparations payments and in the deemphasis of deconcentration.

It is important to note that one reason why drastic policies such as land reform and Zaibatsu dissolution could be implemented relatively smoothly and quickly was that there had been a gradual weakening in the power of landlords and Zaibatsu families since the 1930s and during the war. Controls on rent, the protection of tenancy rights and the rationing of agricultural products during the war had considerably reduced the profitability and incentives for landlords to hold land (see Chapter 8 of this volume by Kawagoe). Likewise, while the Zaibatsu share in economic activity had increased significantly during the war (the share in paid-in capital of the four big Zaibatsu reached 49.7 per cent in financial industries and 32.4 per cent in heavy and chemical industries in 1945), at the same time, the public was permitted to hold stock in Zaibatsu firms owing to the necessity to raise outside funds. In addition, the activities of the Zaibatsu groups came under increasing control by the military government. The drastic reform measures implemented by SCAP were based on these conditions.

It is also important to note the economic thought prevailing at the time. There was a pronounced lack of faith in the working of the market mechanism, originating from Marxist theory and the general move toward the establishment of a welfare state since the turn of the century. Both were strengthened by the 'success' of the Soviet economy on the one hand and the Great Depression on the other. SCAP's economic bureaucrats were New Dealers, democrats but not liberals. They had strong anti-big-business sentiments, but at the same time firmly believed in the efficiency of economic planning (Nakamura, 1979). All this fit in well with the Keynesian justifications of government intervention that became the dominant theory behind economic policy, until the resurgence of neoclassical theory in the 1970s.

Foreign aid also played an important role in the postwar reform process. During 1946–52, Japan received US-$ 2114 million of aid (reflected in the average annual increase of the official settlement balance by US-$ 230.8 million during 1947–51 in Table 1.3). This accumulation of foreign reserves helped 'finance' the current account deficits that appeared after the termination of the Korean War boom: during 1952–6 the Japanese economy benefited largely from special procurements made by the US in the wake of the Korean War. The total amount of special procurements was US-$ 3527 million during 1950–5. Although this also brought about an increase in the import of materials, the net balance was still positive, as can be seen from the increase in foreign reserves by 19.0 million dollars per annum during 1952–6 (Table 1.3).

The total amount of aid received during 1946–52, US-$ 2114 million corresponded to 12.2 per cent of GNP in 1952, while the total accumulation of official settlement balance during 1952–6, 34.2 billion yen was 3.5 per cent of GNP in 1956. These figures are not as large as those of current developing countries, but seem to have been large enough to tide Japan over at the time.

1.3.2 Economic Reforms for Democratization and Demilitarization

One characteristic of the reform process during the years 1945–50 was that the primary purpose of reforms was the democratization and demilitarization of the socio-economic structure of Japan. In other words, unlike the structural adjustment policies currently undertaken by LDCs, SCAP did not pursue increased efficiency. Thus, land reform was conducted for the purpose of breaking up the traditional landlord–tenant relationship which was regarded as the hotbed of militarism in prewar rural Japan; 1828 ha of tenanted land, equalling 77.9 per cent of total tenanted land or 35.8 per cent of total farm land, was sold to tenantry at prices which, given the severe inflation, were so low that the land was virtually free. On the other hand, the Zaibatsu and big business firms were regarded as having collaborated with the military regime. Holding companies were dissolved and stocks were sold to the public, and 325 large firms were designated to be divided up into smaller companies; however, only 18 of these were actually restructured due to the start of the Cold War. There was a purging of 1535 top executives as well as 40 Zaibatsu appointees. New labour laws were promulgated in order to democratize the labour–management relationship, and workers were given the right to organize themselves and engage in collective bargaining.

There is no doubt that these reforms have attained their primary objective of democratizing Japanese society, but their effects on economic efficiency and economic growth are rather controversial. Putting aside their direct effects on the economy, two indirect effects are worth noting. First, income and assets were distributed more evenly. This was in part a direct effect of reform measures but it was also due to an inflation which wiped out all nominal contracts including debts held by small farmers. Second, a significant shift in the power structure of the economy occurred. Corporate control by stockholders and prewar business managers was weakened and given to new managers and, above all, to bureaucrats.

It has been generally assumed that these direct and indirect effects brought about fresh incentives as well as a stable and competitive economic environment, and thus provided a favourable framework for economic growth. However, although it is reasonable to argue that political stability, especially that resulting in rural society, was an important prerequisite to economic growth (Kosai, 1986), whether the reforms had significant incentive effects remains controversial. Kawagoe (Chapter 8 of this volume) shows that with respect to agriculture there is no difference between the production efficiency of owner-cultivators and that of tenants. Therefore, there is no reason to believe that farmers who had recently obtained land faced increased incentives. Instead, Kawagoe points out serious negative effects of land reform including illiquidity in the farm land market which prevented Japanese farmers from adopting new technologies based on large-scale mechanization (Chapter 14 of this volume by Kawagoe). A similar point is offered by Miwa (Chapter 6 of this volume) with respect to the manufacturing sector. Taking the machinery industry as an example, Miwa argues that the current competitive structure of the industry is not primarily a result of deconcentration policies such as Zaibatsu dissolution or the Law for the Elimination of Excessive Concentration of Economic Power (Kado Keizairyoku Shuchu Haijo-ho). Yonekura (Chapter 9 of this volume), in a case study of the steel industry, evaluates the positive effects of the privatization and break-up of the largest steel company (Japan Steel): but he argues that the success of this industry was the result not only of deconcentration policies, but also of the efforts of an innovative and well-educated managerial and labour force who gained experience through a process of trial and error.

In sum, the primary effect of the radical economic reform measures carried out from 1945 to 1950 was the democratization of the socio-economic structure as originally intended; as far as the effects on economic growth and efficiency are concerned, however, research results are not unequivocal.

1.3.3 Phased and Gradual Deregulation

A second characteristic of the postwar reform process was that it was carried out gradually and in phases.

In the long-term perspective of postwar economic growth, the reforms of the years 1945–50 can be regarded as the first of three phases in the transition to a market economy. Along with drastic reforms aimed at democratization, in the first phase various wartime controls on resource allocation were removed, although some measures such as commodity and credit rationing remained for a while in order to facilitate the fight against inflation and the resumption of production. However, the system that emerged after reform and decontrol was by no means a truly market-based system; instead, it was characterized by a substantial degree of government intervention. For example, foreign trade was controlled by means of quantity rationing, financial markets by interest rate regulation and segmentation of lending areas, private international financial transactions and inbound foreign direct investments were prohibited.

During the second phase, trade and foreign direct investment were deregulated. Japan joined the International Monetary Fund (IMF) in 1952 and General Agreement on Tariffs and Trade (GATT) in 1955, but joining the international economic community meant that Japan gained both rights and obligations. When Japan was promoted to a GATT Article 11 country in 1962, and an IMF Article 8 country in 1964, the liberalization of trade and capital became an international obligation. Japan's development strategy had relied on the protection of infant-industry, and liberalization was not necessarily a policy pursued positively by Japan. However, the necessity of liberalization was accepted and regarded as the price to be paid for joining the circle of developed nations (Nakakita's Chapter 13 in this volume). The import liberalization rate (one minus the share of commodities under quantity rationing in total value of imports) reached 92 per cent in 1963, and the liberalization of inbound direct investment carried out gradually beginning in 1967 was finally completed in 1975.

The third phase of liberalization came in the 1980s, after Japan had become an economic superpower and the world economy was rapidly moving towards integration. Financial markets were progressively deregulated and important state enterprises including the national railways were gradually privatized, while energy, communication and transportation industries faced deregulation.

There seem to be two major reasons for the gradual and protracted transition to a market economy. First, various markets were considered to be underdeveloped initially and, more importantly, it was thought that the development of a 'market' would take time and that intervention was needed in order to offset market inefficiencies. This understanding of the 'market' inefficiency was supported by the Keynesian and Marxist theories prevalent at the time, and provided the justification for government intervention. Second, during the long period of regulation and protection, interest groups increasingly gained political power, while bureaucrats, concerned about their own relative power positions, displayed strong resistance to all liberalization measures.

Whatever the reasons for the protracted nature of regulation, the so-called high growth era (HGE) corresponds to the period between the first and third phase mentioned above. This leads us to ask two questions; (i) Did regulation contribute to the high growth, or is it rather that high growth occurred inspite of the possible inefficiencies caused by regulation? (ii) If we assume that regulation had positive effects on growth, was this true only for a particular phase, and a particular economy, (namely, the Japanese economy) or can one claim generality or universality here? These questions may be too ambitious for this project and demand further research. However, one can consider the regulated system as having been conducive to growth in a particular phase of the Japanese experience (for example, Chapter 7 of this volume by Teranishi). At the same time, it is also true that the costs of the system in terms of inefficiency in resource allocation and adverse distributional effects were substantial. For example, in the case of agriculture, prolonged and inadequate intervention by the government has resulted in serious failures in structural adjustment by the industry (Kawagoe's Chapter 14 of this volume); similarly, deposit interest-rate regulation has had serious adverse distributional effects for holders of small assets (Teranishi, 1990).

1.3.4 Emphasis on Micro and Supply-Side Policies

A third characteristic of Japanese postwar reforms and stabilization was the preponderance of micro and supply-side policies as opposed to those on the macro and demand-side.

The emphasis placed on the supply side is particularly evident in inflation stabilization policy. Although there was disagreement over whether demand-management or supply-side policies should be implemented, the majority, including the Bank of Japan, the Ministry of Finance (Okura-sho) and the Economic Stabilization Board (Keizai Antei-honbu) favoured supply-side measures. As a result, the Priority Production System (Keisha Seisan Hoshiki : PPS) and active production subsidies, closely linked with price anchoring, were adopted, and these policies were financed by the printing of additional Bank of Japan notes. It is true that inflation was stopped by the orthodox demand-management policies prescribed by Joseph Dodge (the special adviser delegated by President Truman). However, one can argue that the inflation rate had already been considerably reduced as a result of supply-side measures introduced before the adoption of the 'Dodge Line'. Moreover, the tight monetary control introduced by Dodge may not have been very efficient: the money supply (M2) increased partly because of the active loan mediation by the Bank of Japan.

Throughout the years 1945–50, strong emphasis was put on the preservation of the integrity of micro production units, and the rehabilitation of business firms and financial institutions was given highest priority. For this purpose, the balance sheets of these economic units were divided in two (old and new accounts), and the losses incurred by the suspension of wartime compensations were placed under the old accounts heading, where they were ultimately offset by the reduction of equities and reserves, to the disadvantage of stockholders. At the same time, companies were encouraged to start rebuilding immediately based on the new accounts. In other words, these measures had the effect of rehabilitating firms and banks to the detriment of stockholders (Teranishi's Chapter 7 of this volume). In addition, price control and anchoring policies were implemented so as to support the maximizing behaviour of production units. Moreover, as is shown in Chapter 3, special attention was paid to the retention of idle labour force with firm-specific skills for higher levels of production. This policy, combined with the proper anchoring of the relative price system, was effective in bringing about inflation stabilization and real growth (Teranishi's Chapter 3 of this volume).

Needless to say, this emphasis on micro and supply-side measures was in a sense a double-edged sword. The excessive protection of production units almost certainly leads to serious moral hazard and rent-seeking activities, and this is exactly what happened in Japan. However, the Japanese economy at the same time succeeded in keeping intact a relatively competitive market. The main reason for this probably lies in the existence of a large pool of innovative entrepreneurs who had experienced cut-throat competition with foreign firms in prewar competitive markets, and on a well-developed banking system.[4]

1.4 IMPLICATIONS FOR DEVELOPING COUNTRIES AND SOCIALIST ECONOMIES

In order to discuss the implications for the structural adjustment of LDCs or the transformation of socialist economies, a careful interpretation of the Japanese experience is needed. First of all, differences in the initial conditions or phases of economic development have to be taken into consideration. Compared with most LDCs today, the level and type of existing and available production capacities and trained labour force was considerably higher in wartime Japan. Second, the duration of totalitarian controls of the economy was short and the degree of this control was probably less than that in the former socialist economies. Moreover, Japan at that time did not have an accumulated debt. Third, the international environment is not what it was forty years ago, when the degree of international integration was far lower and the global movement of capital and labour was limited. Finally, there is a marked difference in prevailing economic thought. Although there is an increasing trend towards accommodating the role of the government, the dominant view on government intervention is negative, and this is quite different from the atmosphere prevailing immediately after the war. Careful investigation on a case-by-case basis is required before one can derive any implications from the Japanese experience.

Among the three characteristics of the reform and stabilization process in postwar Japan, the second and the third – phased regulations and emphasis on micro and supply-side issues – seem to be particularly worthy of further investigation, because they have largely been neglected in the discussions of policies appropriate for developing and socialist economies. It is worth noting that the policies implemented in the immediate postwar period in Japan were quite different from the macro-based, one-shot therapy currently prescribed by the IMF and the World Bank or the so-called Harvard group. The caveat here, of course, is the double-edged sword nature of these measures. Due attention must be paid to costs and benefits. It is one thing to discuss the efficiency of the Japanese model in light of Japan's economic success, but it is quite another to claim the generality or universality of the model, even if it happened to be suitable for a particular phase in the historical development of Japan. It must be emphasized that the Japanese experience investigated in this volume can claim relevance for other countries only in the following two senses: (a) as a well-documented case of the process of tailoring an economic system to specific needs, and (b) as a specific model of reform that, when adjusted for differences in given conditions, phases of economic development and the like may serve as a useful reference. In other words, lessons from the Japanese experience cannot be distilled through an *ex post* positive evaluation of the characteristics of Japanese development, but rather through an examination of the process of trial and error in which the system was tailored to suit the specific needs of the economy at a given time.

1.5 PART I: STABILIZATION POLICY

In the following three sections, we summarize the chapters contained in this book in order to provide an overview of our findings.[5]

The Japanese experience of inflation stabilization has several interesting characteristics. First, although orthodox stabilization policies were employed in the final stage under the guidance of Joseph Dodge, the actual implementation of these measures was not faithful to orthodoxy: the money supply was increased despite Dodge's intention, and some authors consider the slashing of subsidies which fed wage–price spirals as an incomes policy of sorts. Second, incomes policy in the rigorous sense (direct control of prices and wages) was recommended by SCAP, but due to serious labour disputes and concerns over social unrest, wage controls were never implemented, though price controls were put into place. Third, the industrial production index showed a significant upward trend during and after the stabilization policy. Fourth, the so-called Priority Production System, or the policy of concentrating resources in bottleneck sectors, was utilized as an important measure for coping with inflation and the severe shortage of basic goods for living and production; however, this was financed by issuing new currency. Finally, price anchoring measures were extensively utilized. Price subsidies were one of the main instruments in controlling inflation in domestic as well as imported goods, and the adoption of a single exchange rate is considered to have had a significant anchoring effect for traded goods.

The four papers included in Part I of this book try to analyze these issues. Chapter 2 by Masahiro Kuroda gives a detailed description of the five-year process of fighting inflation by dividing the period into seven sub-phases. Various policy measures such as deposit freezes, the subsidies system for price adjustment, wage stabilization programmes and Dodge's stabilization line are examined within the context of the economic situation in which each of these policies was adopted. Special emphasis is put on two mechanisms which were bound to lead to a vicious spiral of inflation. The first is the possibility of a spiral from subsidies and budget deficits to money supply and inflation. The second is a possible interaction between wage hikes and price increases. Kuroda evaluates the orthodox Dodge measures as having been successful in avoiding a spiralling process in either of these. However, he also draws attention to the emergence of a political atmosphere which made possible the slashing of wage subsidies, and the effects that planning and control measures implemented prior to the Dodge Line had in providing the basic foundations for success.

Chapter 3, by Juro Teranishi, highlights the phenomenon of real growth under stabilization policy. Following a brief overview of the process of inflation, the paper first analyzes the effects of the Priority Production System (Keisha Seisan Hoshiki). Although Teranishi acknowledges the positive effects of this system on the growth of production, he is sceptical about its effects on inflation since the marginal propensity of expenditure was very high at that time. Instead of connecting the two, the paper emphasizes the role of price controls and anchoring. Through an examination of the methods of price control, Teranishi points to two important characteristics of the policy measures: first, price anchoring was designed to conform to relative price system of normal production; second, since price controls and subsidies took into account an idle labour force with firm-specific skills, a return to full capacity utilization was a realistic target. In other words, price controls were carefully aimed at inducing producers to return to the normal level of production. The paper concludes that this growth-oriented nature of price control was the main reason for the simultaneous attainment of stabilization and growth.

The paper by Hiroshi Yoshikawa and Tetsuji Okazaki, Chapter 4, raises three issues. First, it draws attention to the often-neglected aspect of income and asset distributional effect of inflation. The paper points out that there was a rise in the income share of farmers and the self-employed and a fall in that of the employed. This can be contrasted with the movement of effective wage rates analyzed in Chapter 2. Second, the paper emphasizes the effects of changes in income velocity of money holdings. Yoshikawa and Okazaki claim that when the production level exceeds the threshold minimum level, a reduction in income velocity follows, regardless of expectations; they suggest that the consequent increase in the demand for money works favourably for inflation stabilization. Although a theoretical model and empirical proof of a demand for money with minimum output seems necessary in order to sustain this proposition, it certainly is an approach worth further investigation. Third, Yoshikawa and Okazaki claim that there was an incomes policy aspect in Dodge's deflation measures. They regard the cutting of the subsidies which financed wage hikes to be a sort of incomes policy, because it was effective in breaking the wage–price spiral of the economy. Although this may be a rather 'heterodox' view of the Dodge policy, it is compatible with Kuroda (Chapter 2), who also evaluates the Dodge line in this way.

Chapter 5 by Mitsuhiro Fukao, Masao Oumi and Kimihiro Etoh emphasizes the international aspects of inflation stabilization. Since import subsidies were a significant source of the budget deficit, it is conceivable that the prohibition of import subsidies had a considerable impact on inflation. The authors consider the adoption of a single exchange rate as an essential element in inflation stabilization, because the new exchange rate closed the gap between international and domestic price levels. Through a detailed analysis of the relationship between trade subsidies and the government deficit, the authors show a link between internal convertibility and international convertibility, suggesting the impact that the adoption of a single exchange rate had on inflation stabilization. Although an evaluation of the relative contribution of this measure in comparison with other stabilization measures has yet to be conducted and remains an important area of further research, this aspect of stabilization bears significant relevance for the countries currently inflicted with inflation.

1.6 PART II: ECONOMIC REFORM AFTER THE WAR

This part discusses the removal of wartime controls and the process of economic reforms in postwar Japan until approximately 1955. As already noted, these changes yielded a new economic regime, which laid the foundation for the high economic growth of Japan after 1955. Each chapter in this part has two ultimate goals: (a) to explain the process of economic reform and decontrol; and (b) to evaluate their contribution to the new economic regime of the high growth period.

Policies for economic deconcentration are discussed by Yoshiro Miwa in Chapter 6 and Seiichiro Yonekura in Chapter 9. Miwa challenges the conventional view that decentralization policies were quite effective in bringing about a competitive economic system. Taking the case of the machinery industry, one of the most important sectors in the high growth period, as an example, he shows that the industry was not much affected by decentralization measures. This was because it consisted primarily of small-size business firms, so there were no big businesses to be decentralized in the first place. For the same reason, the direct effects of decentralization policies in terms of promoting competition and growth were also rather limited. While Miwa does not deny either the direct effects of the policy on iron and steel, pulp and paper and others, or the indirect effects of decentralization and economic reforms on the industrial organization in general, he draws attention to the difficulties of exact measurement and of discussing the causal chains of specific policy actions.

Financial industries were exempted from deconcentration policies in spite of their size and their relation with the Zaibatsu. However, because they suffered severely from losses due to wartime lendings, reorganization of the banking industry was an urgent task, and resulted in a banking structure strongly controlled by the government. Chapter 7 by Juro Teranishi compares the new structure with that of the wartime period and finds significant similarities as well as important differences. The dominance of indirect finance, government regulation in fund allocation, and the main bank system are among the similarities, while the direct control of bank lendings combined with market-determined interest rates of the wartime period was replaced by an indirect method of fund allocation through a specialization of business areas in banking combined with rigidly regulated interest rates in the high growth period. Teranishi examines the origins of the postwar system from various angles, such as the state of emergency which prevailed immediately after the war, ideologies and political power structures of that period, as the fundamental conditions of the real economy. In sum, this chapter underscores the importance of tailoring economic institutions to meet the specific needs of an economy, given its stage of economic development as well as its socio-political background.

Chapter 8 by Toshihiko Kawagoe sheds new light on the background and implications of the land reform carried out under the leadership of SCAP, which displayed strong idealism in regard to democratizing the rural communities. Based on a careful examination of the historical changes in the landlord system, Kawagoe first shows that the drastic reforms were possible because land was no longer an attractive source of income for landlords, because it was subject to the various controls on rents and wholesale prices, which had been introduced in the wartime period. Also, comparing the differences in productivity between landowner farmers and tenant farmers before the war, he offers a convincing argument against the view that reforms were effective in bringing about growth in agriculture based on incentives for cultivators who had recently acquired land. It is also shown that the scale of landholding by landlords was already low before the introduction of the reforms and that the various legislations introduced in relation to land reform had the effect of reducing the market liquidity of farmland and thus worked instead as a serious impediment on agricultural growth. Kawagoe concludes his chapter by showing the dangers in a programme that is based on ideological preconceptions but not on proper considerations of resource allocation.

Chapter 9 by Seiichiro Yonekura examines the effects of decentralization policies and the purge of wartime business leaders on the iron and steel industry. This paper concludes that these policies had a positive effect in that they helped destroy the oligopolistic regime which had existed in this industry during the prewar and wartime periods. At the same time, the paper emphasizes that educational levels, training as well as the entrepreneurship that existed among management were of crucial importance in exploiting the opportunity opened up by these policies, leading to higher competition and innovation. Even though the emergence of a competitive and innovative steel industry in Japan cannot be explained by these policies alone, they certainly initiated and triggered the process. It is also interesting to note that the process of tailoring the system to meet the specific needs of the industry is also important in labour–management issues. The democratic labour movement, which was encouraged by SCAP, gave rise to the so-called Japanese-style labour-management relations with characteristics such as lifetime employment, a seniority wage system, cooperative enterprise-based labour unions, more or less equal treatment of white- and blue-collar workers, and the like. All of these were not necessarily originally intended by the reformers, but they reflect the concept of democracy and human rights as interpreted by the Japanese at the time. Yonekura offers a detailed discussion on how these characteristics emerged as the result of 'councils and struggles' between labour and management especially during the turbulant years of the late 1940s.

1.7 PART III: THE ROLE OF THE GOVERNMENT IN THE POSTWAR GROWTH PROCESS

The five chapters in Part III discuss policies which derive not from the Occupation but from domestic issues. The authors analyze various aspects of the Japanese economic development from a long-term perspective and cover the whole postwar period. Government–business and public sector–private sector relations are one of the most important common topics.

In Chapter 10 Yoshie Yonezawa reviews the evolution of industrial policy placing particular emphasis on the Industrial Rationalization Policy (Sangyo Gorika Seisaku : IRP) of the early 1950s. The IRP can be viewed as the prototype of Japanese industrial policy, because many of its features, including target selection, cooperation between government and firms for a common goal, and policy instruments (preferential tax treatments and lendings from government-affiliated financial institutions) were also incorporated into the industrial policy of the high growth period. Successful and unsuccessful cases of rationalization are cited, and the main reason given for differences in outcome is the degree of interaction between government intervention and private initiatives. Yonezawa also compares alternative 'mercantilistic' policies with IRP and tries to find specific circumstances where IRP was successful.

Chapter 11 by Akira Goto analyzes the process of technology importation and identifies the reasons behind the successful transfer of foreign technology. After showing the strength of the existing technological base (well-trained engineers, the backlog of R&D during the war, and the existence of a structure in which the importation of advanced technology was essential for competition), Goto stresses the interaction between government and industry. First, restrictions on trade and foreign direct investment comprised the essential part of technology policy. Such restrictions meant that the only access foreign producers had to the Japanese market was through the selling of technology licences. Goto suggests that this had the positive effect of promoting foreign technology importation, although he carefully avoids assessing the overall effects on national welfare. Second, the government utilized various measures to control the import of technology such as the Ministry of International Trade and Industry (Tsu-sho Sangyo-sho : MITI) review of individual cases based on foreign exchange rationing, taxation, and intervention by the Fair Trade Commission (Kosei Torihiki-iinkai). The conclusion here is that although these measures were effective in controlling the timing of technology importation, they did not change the overall pattern of technology transfer.

Chapter 12 by Takao Komine analyzes the role of economic planning, with special emphasis on the evolving nature and changing goals, methods, and missions of economic planning according to the phases of economic development. In the reconstruction period, economic plans were imperative in that the government needed to control production, distribution, and the prices of major commodities. However, direct control was regarded as a temporary measure and was gradually abolished as the economy recovered. Economic plans after 1955 assumed that the market would act as the main allocative mechanism; also, the plans now became indicative, based on forecasts and general policy orientations rather than planning. Komine claims that while overstressing the role of economic planning in Japan is misleading, the process in which economic plans *per se* are formulated is very important in bringing about consensus, transmitting information as well as inducing commitment by all parties involved.

While such sectors as agriculture, transportation and energy were still under strict government control, the other segments of the economy were gradually deregulated after the 1960s. As a typical example, Toru Nakakita in Chapter 13 gives a comprehensive picture of the process of deregulation of international trade and capital transactions. Although there had been a shift in the trade system from state trade to private trade before 1950, strict controls in the form of import quotas as well as foreign exchange rationing remained in place until the early 1960s. Trade liberalization accelerated in the beginning of the 1970s, while gradual deregulation of inbound foreign direct investment was carried out in the mid-1960s. Nakakita gives an overview of the process, and also depicts Japan's rise to economic superpower status after the first oil shock of 1973. He finds that the Japanese authorities considered the liberalization of trade and foreign direct investment to be the price they had to pay to become a full member of the international economic community, and that this meant the sacrifice of MITI's protectionist policies. In this sense, the aims of trade liberalization were different from those pursued with the deregulation and privatization of finance, transportation or communication in the 1980s, where efficiency as well as equity were the main aims of policy. However, there is no doubt that Japan has benefited greatly from the effects of trade liberalization and the development of free trade in the world.

Chapter 14 by Toshihiko Kawagoe deals with an important case of the failure of structural adjustment and increasing intervention. In the case of agriculture, excessive government intervention resulted in a level of protection which is still among the highest in the world. The postwar land reform, although effective in bringing about political stability in the farm sector, changed neither the pattern of production nor the structure of agrarian society. Government efforts to modernize agriculture failed for various reasons, such as a lack of correspondence between reforms and technical progress in farm mechanization, strict regulation on the market for land and inadequate methods for compensating farmers, based on the introduction of price controls instead of subsidies. The result of this policy failure was the increasing inefficiency and backwardness in production, which in turn resulted in the demand for more protection of the farm sector, and thus further reduced international competitiveness. This chapter offers a clear example of what happens when government intervention exceeds its initial goals of establishing equality or protecting infant industries.

Notes

* The authors are greatly indebted to the contributors of this volume for helpful comments, and especially thankful to Akira Goto and Ulrike Shaede for extensive comments on an earlier draft.

1. However, this does not mean that we can neglect the role of foreign direct investment in such areas as electric machinery, especially during the interwar period.
2. See Teranishi (1990) for a comparison of regulation in the financial market between the prewar and postwar periods.
3. Compare these figures with those for developing countries reported in Sachs (1987).
4. Another relevant point might be that restrictive as well as supportive policies were applied as a rule equally to all eligible firms. If instead there had been discretionary choice of target firms, the result might have been considerably different.
5. During the course of this project, the authors and editors have met together on numerous occasions to deliberate and exchange views on the postwar Japanese experience. Nevertheless, as might be expected with a study of this nature, differences in interpretation of the data still remain. Miwa (Chapter 6) and Yonekura (Chapter 9), for example, differ from each other in their evaluation of the role played by the Anti-Monopoly Law (Dokusen Kinshi-ho). Likewise, Fukao, Oumi and Etoh (Chapter 5) and Nakakita (Chapter 13) argue that the account balance for the Trade Fund Special Account (Boeki Shikin Tokubetsu Kaikei) was in the red during he period 1946–8. Yoshikawa and Okazaki (Chapter 4), however, assert that, on the whole, the Fund maintained an equilibrium between revenue and expenditures during this period. This difference in interpretation is due to the complexity of the system of Trade Fund Special Account as well as to the scarcity of data on the immediate postwar period. Therefore, it is not easy to compromise the conflicting views. The

editors have taken the stance of paying respect to the view of each author on these points.

References

Kosai, Yutaka (1986) *The Era of High-Speed Growth: Notes on the Postwar Japanese Economy* (Tokyo: University of Tokyo Press). Translation of *Kodo Seicho no Jidai* (Tokyo: Nihon Hyoron-sha, 1981).

Minami, Ryoshin (1986) *The Economic Development of Japan: A Quantitative Study* (London: Macmillan). Translation of *Nihon no Keizai Hatten* (Tokyo: Toyo Keizai Shinpo-sha, 1981).

Miyazaki, Masayasu and Osamu Ito (1989) 'Senji, Sengo no Sangyo to Kigyo' (The Industry and Firm in the Wartime and Postwar Periods), in *Nihon Keizai-shi*, vol. 7, ed. by Takafusa Nakamura (Tokyo: Iwanami Shoten).

Nakamura, Takafusa (1979) 'SCAP to Nihon (SCAP and Japan)', in *Senryoki Nihon no Keizai to Seiji*, ed. by Takafusa Nakamura (Tokyo: Tokyo University Press).

Ohkawa, Kazushi, Miyohei Shinohara and Mataji Umemura (eds.). (1965) *Choki Keizai Tokei* (Long-term Economic Statistics), vol. 1 (Tokyo: Toyo Keizai Shinpo-sha).

Sachs, Jeffrey D. (1987) 'Trade and Exchange Rate Policies in Growth-Oriented Adjustment Programs', in *Growth-Oriented Adjustment Programs*, ed. by Vittorio Corbo, Morris Goldstein and Mohsin Kahn (IMF and the World Bank).

Teranishi, Juro (1990) 'Financial System and the Industrialization of Japan: 1900–1970', *Banca Nazionale del Lavoro Quarterly Review*, no. 174, September, pp. 309–41.

Teranishi, Juro (1991) *Kogyoka to Kiny'u Shisutemu* (Industrialization and Financial System) (Tokyo: Toyo Keizai Shinpo-sha).

Yamazawa, Ippei (1990) *Economic Development and International Trade – The Japanese Model* (Honolulu: East-West Center).

Part I

Stabilization Policy

2 Price and Goods Control in the Japanese Postwar Inflationary Period

Masahiro Kuroda*

2.1 INTRODUCTION

Japan began efforts to restore its economy, totally destroyed by the Second World War, immediately after accepting an unconditional surrender in 1945. These efforts would take time to bear fruit. Per capita real GDP (Gross Domestic Product) in 1946 was less than 55 per cent that of the prewar peak level in the 1934–6 period. The manufacturing production index in 1946 recorded only one-fifth of its peak level in 1944. Moreover, the rice harvest was the worst since 1903 and people were forced to live at the minimum subsistence. Economic woes were compounded by galloping inflation. The wholesale price index recorded nearly a 300 per cent increase in 1946 and continued to rise more than 100 per cent for the next several years.[1] The consumer price index also recorded more than a 200 per cent increase in 1946.[2]

This hyper-inflation was in part due to the imbalance between supply and demand. The supply of goods was severely curtailed by shortages of raw materials and damaged production capacity, while the demand for goods increased with the rapid expansion of the domestic population.[3] Increases in the money supply also contributed to inflation; these rises accompanied growing government expenditure to settle wartime accounts. In order to deal with inflation, the Economic Stabilization Board (Keizai Antei-honbu: ESB) was set up in August 1946, initially tackling the inflation problem with price controls and the rationing of commodities. Soon, however, the ESB began to implement the 'Priority Production System (Keisha Seisan Hoshiki: PPS)', channeling limited resources into specific basic industries such as coal mining and the iron and steel industry. Specifically, the ESB first allocated resources to the coal industry, with increased coal output then allocated to the iron and steel industry. Finally, increased iron and steel output was allocated back to coal mining in order to further increase output in that industry. By utilizing Japan's limited resources to create this virtuous production circle, the ESB hoped to ease inflation as well as promote Japanese economic independence.

In spite of price controls and the Priority Production System, inflation continued at somewhat lower but still very high rates until 1949, when it was dramatically halted by Joseph Dodge's deflationary policies, the so-called Dodge Line. Dodge, a subscriber to classical economic beliefs, cited as causes for Japan's economic problems its over-dependency on foreign aid from the US and the over-protection of private sectors by government subsidies. By slashing subsidies, increasing government revenues, and cutting expenditures, Dodge's disinflationary policies rapidly halted inflation.

Figure 2.1 denotes four different types of price indices for consumer goods during the 1945–52 period: (A) the free market price index of consumer goods constructed by the Bank of Japan (BOJ); (B) the effective market price index of consumer goods constructed by the Prime Minister's Office, which represents a weighted average of free market prices and official retail prices; (C) the official retail price index constructed by BOJ; and (D) the estimated official retail price index constructed by the Ministry of Finance (Okura-sho: MOF). These indices are comparable with each other at any given moment and also across time.[4] Figure 2.2 represents four types of price indices for producer goods; (E) the free market price index of producer goods constructed by BOJ; (F) the effective market price index of producer goods constructed by BOJ; (G) the official wholesale price index constructed by BOJ; and (H) the estimated official wholesale price index constructed by MOF.[5] These two figures highlight several characteristics of trends in price indices during the inflationary period. Firstly, official prices as shown in (C), (D), (G) and (H) are shifted up intermittently at the time of revisions to official prices. There were large-scale revisions of official prices in March 1946, July 1947, June 1948 and April 1949 respectively. Secondly, the official retail price of consumer goods increased almost 21 times during the period from February 1946 to its peak in September 1949, while the official wholesale price index for producer goods increased by only 19 times during approximately the same period. In other words, the official prices of producer goods were maintained relatively below prices for consumer goods during the period of price controls. This bias gradually disappears by June 1951, when both consumer and producer prices were stabilized.

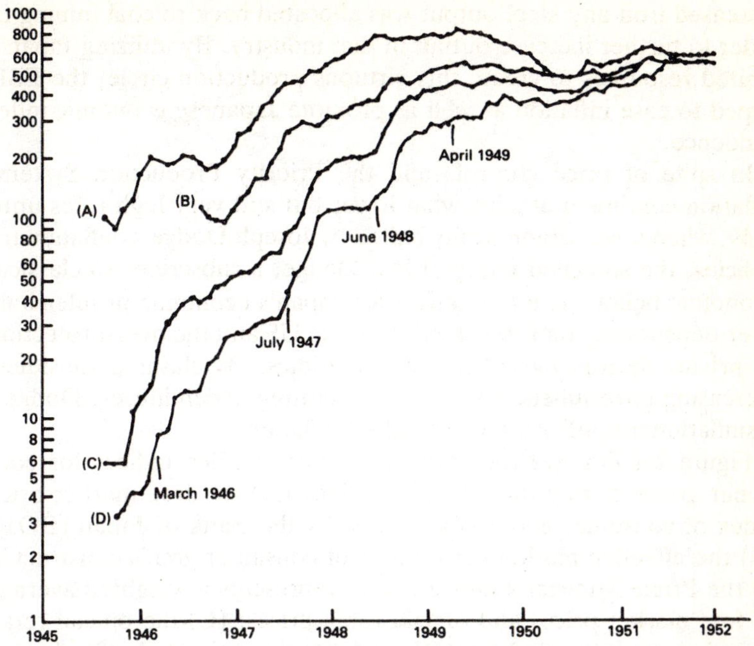

Figure 2.1 Four types of price indices of consumer goods during the period 1945–52

(A) Black-market price index of consumer goods constructed by BOJ.
(B) Effective market price index of consumer goods constructed by the Prime Minister's Office.
(C) Official retail price index constructed by BOJ.
(D) Estimated official retail price index constructed by Ministry of Finance.

Other features of price trends are also apparent from these figures. Revised differences between the old and new official prices were narrowed as the prices were revised. Differences between official prices and free market prices also gradually disappeared, partly because of increases in official prices during revisions and partly because of the growing stability of prices. These differences had almost disappeared by May 1950, immediately before the outbreak of the Korean War. Free market prices of consumer goods and producer goods had largely stabilized by June 1948; consumer good prices tended to decrease after April 1949 and producer good prices tended to fall after February 1949. Interestingly, measures for free market prices show stability prior to the introduction of the Dodge Line and

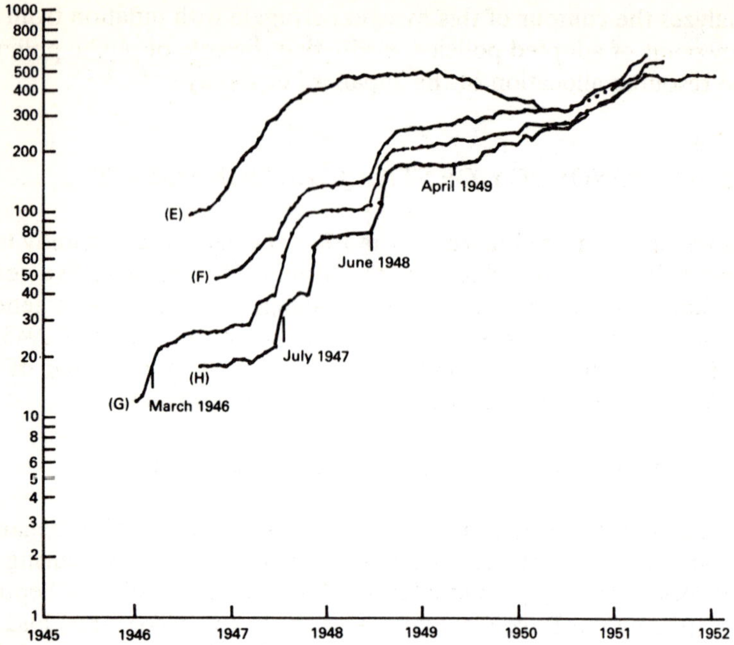

Figure 2.2 Four types of price indices of producer goods during the period 1945–52

(E) Black-market price index of producer goods constructed by BOJ.
(F) Effective market price index of producer goods constructed by the BOJ.
(G) Official wholesale price index constructed by BOJ.
(H) Estimated official wholesale price index constructed by MOF.

the fourth large upward revision of official prices. Finally, we can observe that trends in the market prices for producer goods are more closely correlated with changes in corresponding official prices than are market prices for consumer goods correlated with official consumer good prices. This indicates that the government was more effective at controlling producer rather than consumer prices.

As we can see in the above figures, the struggle with inflation continued for almost five years. It was a major long-term effort, and adopted policies were not necessarily uniform or consistent, especially since they represented the combined effort of the Japanese government and the staff of the Supreme Commander for the Allied Powers (SCAP) and the two sometimes disagreed. This chapter analyzes the contour of this five-year struggle with inflation from the viewpoint of adopted policies, evaluating the role of public policy in the resource allocation of the Japanese economy.

2.2 CHRONOLOGY OF STABILIZATION POLICY

As we can see from Figures 2.1 and 2.2, the Japanese economy took almost five years to achieve price stability. During these five years, the implementation of policy often changed as did Japan's general economic circumstances. These changes serve to divide the 1945–52 period from Japan's unconditional surrender to the closing of the ESB into six sub-periods which are summarized below.[6]

2.2.1 Initial Condition: August 1945–February 1946

On 21 August 1945, just after the end of the war, MOF began to reconsider its recent experience with economic controls. During the war, prices and wages had been anchored at the level of 18 September 1939 by the Price Control Order (Kakaku-to Tosei-rei) and the Ordinance on Emergency Measures for Wages (Chingin Rinji Sochi-rei). Also, production and consumption were controlled under the rationing systems set up by the Goods and Materials Control Ordinance (Busshi Tosei-rei). Even during the war, however, these regulations had not necessarily succeeded. This lack of success was particularly noticeable just before the end of the war, when huge differences between controlled and market prices together with a complex regulatory system dramatically undermined the government's ability to regulate prices and ration goods.

Because of this failure, MOF originally intended to decontrol almost all goods and services in postwar Japan, excepting necessities, favouring liberalization by market forces. On the other hand, SCAP insisted that it was essential to control prices and ration commodities as emergency measures because of severe supply shortages.[7] In November 1945, the Price Division (Bukka-bu) was established as an administrative office in MOF. At the same time, the Committee for Emergency Measures for Prices (Sengo Bukka Taisaku-iinkai) was established as an advisory committee. The Price Division in MOF tried to forge a framework for anti-inflationary policy in collaboration with this advisory committee. Groping for concrete policy measures while narrowing the perception gap between SCAP and the Japanese government about price controls, the government finally wrote 'An Outline of Policy Measures on Prices in the Postwar Period' (*Sengo Bukka Taisaku Kihon Yoko*) in February 1946. This outline focused on the construction of policy measures dealing with (i) excess purchasing power, (ii) price controls, (iii) food shortage, (iv) expansion of production capacity, (v) rationing and (vi) employment. However, measures were not implemented until after February 1946.

During the initial period characterized by policy indecision, wholesale prices jumped sharply, increasing almost 17 per cent monthly during August–December 1945. Inflation was partly due to the rapid increase in the money supply related to the postwar expansion of government expenditure,[8] and partly due to a sharp fall in production caused by the destruction of production capacity and the shortage of raw materials.[9]

2.2.2 Freezing Deposits and the 3.3 Official Price Setting: March 1946–July 1946

The government issued a programme on Emergency Measures for the Economic Crisis (Keizai Kiki Kinkyu Taisaku) in February 1946. This represented the first systematic and concrete government response to the problems facing the postwar economy. Central to these emergency measures were (i) the freezing of bank deposits, (ii) the redenomination of the yen,[10] (iii) the imposition of a new property tax and (iv) a new system of official prices. Under this programme, the yen was redenominated on 3 March 1946 subject to the following: (a) an individual could change only 100 yen of the old currency into the new currency, (b) all deposits were frozen, (c) the withdrawal of deposits was forbidden excepting certain amounts for living and production activities, and (d) the government recommended that wages in new yen be limited to 500 yen per month, a wage level that was consistent with the new system of official prices. The new system of official prices was enforced from 3 March 1946, the same day that the Price Control Ordinance (Bukka Tosei-rei) was implemented to replace the wartime price control. Under this 3.3 system, so named because of the date it was implemented, all official prices were decided according to linkages with the basic prices of rice, wages and coal products. The basic price of rice was set at 300 yen per 150 kg for producers, and the government purchased rice at this price. On the other hand, the rice price for consumers, or the price at which the government sold rice to consumers, was set at 250 yen per 150 kg. At that time, the government calculated monthly living costs per household at 526.2 yen.

The government set the basic price of coal at 250 yen per ton for producers and 150 yen per ton for users, also consistent with the rice prices and wages. Although other related official prices were decided by their linkages with these three basic components, rice prices, coal prices, and wages, the government intended to set the average level of official prices eight times higher than the regulated wartime price levels. The gaps between producer prices and purchaser prices in this official price system were filled with subsidies, paid out of the government budget. In 1946, these price subsidies totalled 9 billion yen, 7.8 per cent of total government outlays under the central government budget. These price subsidies, officially named the System of Subsidies for Price Adjustment (Kakaku Chosei Hokyukin: SSPA), were originally intended to halt the spiral between prices of materials and final goods. However, the subsidies themselves led to increases in government spending and growth in the money supply in the postwar economy.[12]

In spite of the lower levels for consumer prices, considerable differences between official prices and free market prices remained.[13] The 3.3 official price system really reflected expectations about economic recovery, growth, prices, and income: the government expected that real national income would recover to 1937 levels in 1949, that prices in 1949 would be eight times the level of 1937, and that the foreign exchange rate would be 20 yen per dollar. These expectations were unrealistic, undermining the efficacy of pricing policy. The government found it difficult to continue its financial reform programme, including the freezing of deposits, under rapidly increasing prices, and it suspended the deposit freeze in July 1947. However, while operative, the deposit freeze did help to absorb the excess supply of money, decreasing potential demand pull in the short run and thus working to control inflation. As we can see in Figures 2.1 and 2.2, the free market price of consumer goods was stable for much of 1946, increasing again only from the end of the year. Prices for producer goods picked up earlier.

Although these postwar emergency measures did not succeed in stabilizing the economy instantaneously, they at least reveal the government's *attitude* towards economic controls. Moreover, Japan's initial experience with policy also indicates that orthodox policy measures such as financial reform[14] are not necessarily effective when people are existing at a minimum subsistence level and when there are enormous supply shortages in the market.

2.2.3 Birth of the Economic Stabilization Board and the Price Bureau: August 1946–May 1947

The Economic Stabilization Board (ESB) and the Price Administration Agency (Bukka-cho: PAA) were established in August 1946 as respectively, a planning agency and an administrative office for price policy in order to unify policy in the government.[15] Although the government felt that it urgently needed to reduce potential purchasing power through emergency financial reform in order to stem hyper-inflation, it also felt that it needed to plan the next step of restoring production capacity to reduce the gaps between demand and supply. The ESB began formulating a complete plan of emergency economic measures, focusing on the following three basic problems: (i) increasing the level of production of basic producer commodities, (ii) reducing excess purchasing power through fiscal and financial policy, and (iii) strengthening the rationing system for commodities. Tanzan Ishibashi, Minister of Finance (May 1946 through May 1947), insisted that it was more important to restore production, even if this meant reducing control over prices. He stated, 'The inflation resulted from economic destruction at that time. In order to overcome this type of inflation, the revival of economic activities was more important than a deflationary policy. To this end, fiscal deficits as well as an increase in currency circulation could be allowed.'[16] Ishibashi did not advocate expanding effective demand due to the fiscal deficit, but he did argue for support of certain basic industries in order to restore production capacity. However, his ideas were totally opposed by SCAP, who insisted on the strong regulation of quantity and price.[17] It should be noted that SCAP policy at that time was based on ideas of regulation and planning, reflecting in part the influence of the New Dealers in the Occupation. Early SCAP policy was not based upon orthodox fiscal and monetary stabilization measures and differed radically from the market-oriented emphasis of the late Dodge Line. Given SCAP's faith in rationing and planning, they strongly pushed for laws to regulate commodities and hence control prices. Hence, the government established the Temporary Law for Adjusting the Demand and Supply of Materials (Rinji Busshi Jukyu Chosei-ho) in October 1946. Under this law, 34 producer goods and

52 consumer goods were designated as rationed commodities and were rationed uniformly according to the ESB.

The ESB used this law not only to try to stabilize prices but also to actively promote the recovery of production in certain industries. The ESB designated basic industries such as coal mining, the chemical fertilizer industry, and the iron and steel industry as targets for development and specifically rationed materials to these industries. This was the 'Priority Production System' (PPS), under which the government offered not only financial support to select industries but also rationed commodities in such a way as to stimulate recovery. In order to enforce smoothly the rationing system, the ESB proposed to establish eight public corporations (*kodan*) to carry out the necessary administration. At the same time, three public corporations were set up for reconstruction of industry, price adjustment and maritime credit, and four were set up to handle the administration for foreign trade.

2.2.4 Emergency Economic Measures and the Revision of Official Prices: June 1947–June 1948

After the stabilization programme of February 1946 failed, prices began to increase again in the fall of 1946, despite efforts by the ESB to break the inflationary trend. Free market consumer prices increased by almost 80 per cent from September 1946 through March 1947. This forced the government to revise official prices for both producer and consumer goods; these revisions amounted on average to 65 and 85 per cent from March through September in 1946, and 20 and 40 per cent from September 1946 through March 1947, respectively. On the other hand, the level of production also stagnated further due to the shortage of material goods in the fall of 1946, where the production index (= 100.0 in 1935) fell to 38.0 in November 1946 and 34.5 in February 1947.

After the general election for the House of Representatives, Tetsu Katayama, the leader of The Japan Socialist Party (Nihon Shakai-to: JSP), was elected as Prime Minister. The Katayama Cabinet concentrated on countermeasures to halt inflation, and the ESB in June 1947 announced policy changes emphasizing the establishment of order over resource allocation and a revision of official prices. To that end, the rationing system was strengthened and a major revision of official prices, the second largest in the postwar period, was implemented in July 1947. In revising prices, the ESB introduced Price Stabilizing

Zones (Kakaku Antei-Tai: PSZs), where maximum price levels were fixed. Initially, the levels were set about 65 times higher than 1934–6 prices. Goods subject to this system were called Price Stabilized Commodities (Antei-tai Busshi: PSC). PSZs were established in order to adjust imbalances in production costs arising from differences in utilization rates and to stabilize relative purchaser prices. For example, if the producer price had been increased by more than the PSZ, producers were subsidized and the purchase price was decreased to the level set by the PSZ, with subsidies provided by the SSPA. The number of Price Stabilized Commodities was expanded from already regulated basic commodities (rice, coal and basic foods) to other important commodities including coal, iron, non-ferrous metal, chemical fertilizer, and caustic soda. Subsidies in 1947 amounted to 22.5 billion yen, which was 10.7 per cent of the general government budget.

In addition to establishing PSZs, the ESB determined appropriate levels for producer prices for basic manufacturing commodities based principally on the cost of production, where the cost of production included not only variable and fixed costs, but also normal profit margins. Prices for agricultural products were generally decided by the parity method, where price increases for agricultural products paralleled those of material goods used in agricultural production.[18] The new ESB measures also did not attempt to control wages directly, although there were certain guidelines for wage levels by industry and occupation. These guidelines were consistent with the cost of living based upon the new system of official consumer prices.

Table 2.1 presents the system of official prices in this revision. The new official producer prices differed widely compared to 1934–6 averages. For example, prices for coal, pig iron, ammonium sulphate, caustic soda, transportation fees and electricity were increased 127, 136, 80, 67, 23 and 10 times respectively. Prices for commodities which were selectively subsidized under the Priority Production System such as coal, pig iron and fertilizer were increased much more than the average, while prices of consumer goods including agricultural products and services such as transportation fees showed increases smaller than the average. Despite this wide variation in producer prices, the introduction of PSZs was intended to stabilize the price system and offset imbalances by setting the purchase price for commodities at levels 65 times those in 1934–6. For example, the producer price of pig iron was set at 6370 yen per ton, which was 135.9 times the price of 1934–6, while the purchaser's price was set at

Table 2.1 Price of important commodities constructed by price system, July 1947

		New official price (yen) (A)	Average price (1934–6) (yen) (B)	(A)/(B)
Coal (ton)	producer price	956.08	7.50	127.5
	public consumer price	1 208.58	12.43	97.2
	specific consumer price	600.00	12.39	48.4
Oil (Kl)	crude oil price	3 461.00	70.00	49.4
	consumer price	6 539.64	116.18	56.3
Coke (ton)	producer price	2 240.38	46.00	48.6
	consumer price	2 710.25	46.00	58.9
Pig iron (ton)	producer price	6 370.00	46.87	135.9
	consumer price	3 050.00	46.98	64.9
Steel thin:1.6mm (ton)	producer price	14 220.00	108.10	131.6
	consumer price	8 690.00	133.70	65.0
Lead (ton)	producer price	33 000.00	253.00	130.4
	consumer price	23 000.00	253.00	90.9
Sodium ash (ton)	producer price	10 000.00	–	–
	dealer sales price	6 562.00	100.00	65.6
Sodium hydroxide (ton)	producer price	8 600.00	127.93	67.2
	dealer sales price	11 051.00	170.00	65.0
Ammonium sulphate (ton)	producer price	8 000.00	100.00	80.0
	consumer price	6 500.00	101.11	64.4
Cement (ton)	wholesale price	1 649.25	19.00	86.8
	retail price	1 714.25	20.00	85.7
National railway fare	passenger(Km b))	0.35	0.015	23.3
	transportation(t/Km)	0.25	0.015	16.7
Gas(m^3)	standard rate	3.50	0.084	41.7
Electricity	electric light(c)	8.00	0.67	11.9
	power rate (Kilowatt/month d)	40.00	4.21	9.5
Barber charge		20.00	0.50	40.0
Rice	producer price(1 rock)	1 700.00	27.16	62.6
	consumer price(10Kg)	99.00	2.47	40.0

continued on p. 42

Table 2.1 Continued

		New official price *(yen) (A)*	*Average price (1934–6)* *(yen) (B)*	*(A)/(B)*
Potato	producer price(10kg)	87.00	1.58	55.1
	consumer price(10kg)	85.00	2.36	35.9
Bread	consumer price(45g)	1.91	0.08	31.8
Sake 1st class (1.8l)	retail price	132.00	1.70	77.7
Beer (standard bottle)	retail price	23.00	0.33	69.7

Source: Okura-sho (Ministry of Finance), *Showa Zaisei-shi* (The Fiscal History of the Showa Era), vol. 10, p. 347.

3050 yen per ton, which was almost 65 times the price in 1934–6. Differences between the producer and purchaser prices were subsidized by SSPA.

Revisions of official prices may not have accelerated inflationary trends. In fact, by reducing excess purchasing power, they helped alleviate inflation. The rate of increase in the issuance of BOJ notes was fairly stable from the beginning of 1947, and manufacturing production recovered to two-thirds the prewar peak level by June 1948. Hence, free market prices for consumer and producer goods became more stable from the beginning of 1948, and these prices actually decreased in September 1948 compared to the levels of the previous year. As a result, differences between official prices and free market prices gradually shrank. The gap between official prices and free market prices for consumer goods, which was 30–40 times just after the war, fell to 23.7 times in March 1946, 10.4 times in July 1947, and 7.6 times in June 1948, while that for producer goods was reduced from 9.2 times in July 1947 to 5.9 times in June 1948. However, increases in wages continued unabated: in the year following the revision of official prices, wages rose from 1800 yen per month to 4300 yen. As a consequence, official prices again lost consistency, necessitating another revision. As hyper-inflation abated, the government focused increasingly on ways to promote a full-scale economic recovery. Two plans were presented to the Katayama Cabinet almost simultaneously: The Economic Reconstruction Plan (Keizai Fukko Keikaku) and the Intermediate Stabilization Plan (Chukan Antei

Keikaku). Although neither of these was adopted, they helped promote the concept of economic planning as a policy tool. The Economic Reconstruction Plan was a five-year economic plan, wherein production was expected to recover to prewar peak levels, a balance of payments equilibrium was to be achieved, and inflation was gradually to fall through 1949–50. After initial discussion, the Economic Reconstruction Plan was subject to intense debate, revised in the end in May 1949 under the second Yoshida Cabinet. The economy at this time was suffering from the initial impact of the Dodge deflation, one result being that the Economic Reconstruction Plan was generally ignored.

Discussions of the Intermediate Stabilization Plan began in early 1948. The Intermediate Stabilization Plan did not support orthodox stabilization measures such as tight monetary and fiscal policy to stabilize the economy. Rather, it advocated measures such as increased foreign aid to temporarily ease inflation, and the recovery of production thereafter to permanently break the wage–price spiral. On the other hand, SCAP insisted that wages be controlled directly under the May 1948 Wage Stabilization Programme (Chingin Antei Keikaku) in order to stabilize the economy. However, the Ashida Cabinet which followed Katayama was reluctant to implement wage controls, worrying that guidance of nominal wages would cause turmoil in labour markets because of real wage instability. In place of direct controls, the government attempted to introduce indirect control measures, at the same time requesting increased US aid to stabilize the economy.

During this period of policy debate, there was an interesting discussion between advocates of the one-shot stabilization policy (*ikkyo antei-ron*) and those of the gradual stabilization policy (*chukan antei-ron*). The one-shot stabilization policy essentially consisted of monetary tightening according to institutional monetary theory; it was proposed by an economist with Marxist training. They considered that it was most effective not only to control money supply by the monetary or financial policies, but also to introduce certain reforms for the monetary system directly, in order to stabilize the inflation. In contrast, the gradual stabilization theory, backed by economists at MOF and BOJ, emphasized the recovery in production as a prerequisite for stabilization. The one-shot stabilization policy encouraged monetary reform based on the gold bullion standard, while the gradual stabilization policy opposed rapid reform of the monetary system for fear of a stabilization crisis. While advocates of the gradual stabilization policy did believe that the increasing money supply stemmed from the government deficit and its overlending as a financial intermediary, they believed that restoring production was the first priority in alleviating inflation. Although elements of both of these policies can be found in the Dodge Line (i.e., emphasis on the uniform exchange rate and the belief that government deficits lay behind the rising money supply), this policy debate did not really shape the adoption of Dodge's deflationary policies.

2.2.5 Third Revision of Official Prices and Wage Stabilization Programme: August 1948–March 1949

During this period of policy debate, nominal wages rose rapidly, as shown in Table 2.2. The average wage in June 1948 was 4395 yen, almost 2.5 times higher than that of the previous year. This implied some inconsistencies in the July 1947 revision of official prices, necessitating further revisions which were implemented in June 1948. This third large-scale revision in official prices since 1945 can be summarized as follows: (i) transportation fees for passengers and freight on the National Railways were raised 3.5 times while telecommunication fees were increased 4.0 times the current level; (ii) the average monthly wage was set at 3700 yen, estimated to keep constant living standards under the new price system; (iii) the purchaser prices of Price Stabilized Commodities were set at 110 times the level of 1934–6; (iv) the purchaser prices for basic producer goods and con-

Table 2.2 Average industrial wages (in yen)

	Year	
Month	*1947*	*1948*
1	964	2951
2	1022	2981
3	1083	3219
4	1233	3670
5	1425	3761
6	1689	4395
7	1835	4872
8	2031	5459
9	2181	5975
10	2309	6574
11	2536	6921
12	3517	9038

sumer goods were fixed at 1.7 times and 1.8 times the current maximum levels, respectively; (v) differences between purchaser and producer prices were subsidized by SSPA; (vi) the producer prices of mining and manufacturing commodities were mainly estimated on the basis of production costs, while prices for agricultural commodities were estimated by the parity method (the parity index of rice was anchored at 1.32 times the level of 1934–6); (vii) the average exchange rate (yen/dollar) was assumed to be 300 yen. At this exchange rate, official prices were compared with US domestic prices. Gaps were adjusted by setting separate exchange rates for certain commodities. This marks the first time that the exchange rate level and comparison with international market prices were considered when the official prices were determined.

After this third revision of official prices, nominal wages continued to increase. As can be seen from Table 2.2, nominal wages rose almost 59 per cent between May and September 1948. However, real wages also increased, gaining 24 per cent, because consumer prices rose only 22 per cent during this period. Moreover, real wages after tax increased more than 30 per cent because of a reduced income tax rate on labour compensation. Despite these encouraging developments, subsidies soared further: subsidies on SSPA amounted to 62.5 billion, 13.2 per cent of the general government budget. These figures included not only subsidies for price adjustment, but also special subsidies such as wage payments and compensation for company deficits.[19] Subsidies to compensate for increases in nominal wages when real wages were rising tended to promote the over-compensation of workers, generating demand on pull inflation. These subsidies also undermined economic efficiency since they supported loss-making firms. It might be difficult to recognize that these special subsidies as wage payments and company deficits were the direct cause of the inflation, because of their small size. On the other hand, however, we may be sure that several experiences of the revision of official prices easily created the certain expectation on the part of the public of a rise in official prices at the next revision and thus induced its dependence on government subsidies. Inflation was also fuelled by the floating of Bank of Japan notes caused by the government deficit associated with price subsidies; the surge in credits through the Reconstruction Finance Bank (Fukko Kin'yu Kinko: RFB) also increased note issue since BOJ discounted RFB bonds.

SCAP suggested three principles to break the spiral between subsidies, lending to the deficit firms, and increases in official prices.

The Three Principles for Wages (Chingin San Gensoku) proposed in November 1948 advocated the following: (i) subsidies to compensate for increased wages would be permitted only as long as new government funds were available, (ii) lending would not be permitted to firms which aimed to compensate for deficits generated by increased wages, (iii) wage increases which might generate a rise in the general price level were not permitted. These three principles were designed to break firms' dependence on the government. These three principles acted as a sort of indirect control on wages, differing from SCAP's earlier demand for direct wage controls.

In addition, SCAP also considered the introduction of a uniform exchange rate to halt inflation and stabilize the economy. *The Young Report*, released June 1948, stressed the need for such a uniform exchange rate to replace the multi-tiered exchange rate structure in place at the time.[20] Exchange rates were set individually for each export and import. The average rate for exports was 330 yen per dollar; that for imports, 130 yen per dollar. Hence, even though the dollar-denominated trade balance was in deficit, yen-denominated exports actually exceeded yen-dominated imports. It was partly true that this system of exchange rates contributed to stabilize prices domestically due to the over-appreciation of the yen. These 'hidden subsidies' to importers and domestic produces, however, were financed by the Bank of Japan through the government's special accounts. Consequently, the multiple exchange rate structure contributed to the increase in Japan's money supply and inflation.[21] In an attempt to respond to SCAP recommendations, the Japanese government tried to reorganize its stabilization policies, proposing the Outline of New Economic Policies (Shin Keizai Seisaku Taiko-an) in November 1948. In the Outline, the government showed willingness to adopt a new system of prices, one based on internationally accepted standards, once a uniform exchange rate was set. Firms were not to be dependent on the government, although government protection would be used to guarantee economic stability. This outline marked Japan's first step towards an open economy.

With these efforts to stabilize the economy, inflation did abate somewhat. The ratio of the free market price of consumer goods to the official price fell from 7.5 in June 1948 to 2.8 in March 1949, while the ratio for producer goods declined from 5.9 to 2.8. The rate of increase in free market prices for consumer goods had fallen to an annual rate of 20 per cent and prices for producer goods were rising only 5 per cent. It was during this period of declining inflation that the Dodge Line was implemented.

2.2.6 Dodge's Stabilization Policy and Deregulation of Price and Commodities: April 1949–July 1952

The desirability of a single, general exchange rate was again asserted in a directive to SCAP from the US government in December 1948.[22] A single exchange rate was expected to be set at about 300 yen per dollar. As such, the exchange rate for exports would appreciate (from an average of 330), while that for imports would depreciate (from an average of 130). The subsequent increase in prices for imported goods would have an inflationary impact on the economy, but the reduction of hidden subsidies would be disinflationary. The Japanese government expected that any trade deficit caused by the single exchange rate could be covered by US foreign aid, which would also be used to help subsidize prices for imported goods. Joseph M. Dodge reached essentially the same conclusions in drawing up his stabilization policy for the Japanese economy.

Dodge had served as director of the financial division in the US occupation government in Germany in 1946 and later was president of the Detroit Bank. US President Truman requested that he lead US efforts to reform the Japanese economy. Dodge, a believer in classical economics, focused on two weaknesses in the Japanese economy: over-dependence on aid from the US and over-protection of the private sector by government subsidies. Intending to restore the market mechanism, he slashed subsidies and constructed a balanced government budget. In fact, the government budget in 1949 was not only balanced but showed a surplus of 15.76 billion yen. Dodge addressed inflation not only through this over-balanced budget but also through tight control of the money supply. He also set a single yen–dollar exchange rate of 360.

Although these policies, known collectively as the Dodge Line, are generally evaluated as orthodox measures, Dodge recognized at the same time that it was also highly important to restore production, not through subsidies but by management efforts of firms. As such, Dodge refused to allow the Japanese government to use subsidies funded by BOJ note issues to compensate for the import price hikes which accompanied the yen depreciation. Instead, special accounts for collateral funds, the so-called US Aid Counterpart Fund

(Mikaeri Shikin), were established. These funds did not necessarily generate a rise in the money supply, since fund sources were revenues from the sale of government purchases of foreign aid commodities to the public as well as other funds from the general government accounts. Subsidies for exports were prohibited.[23] Dodge also decided to gradually abolish subsidies for Price Stabilized Commodities, in place since 1947. Direct wage controls were not used, and special wage subsidies such as those for deficit firms were also abolished.

Corresponding to the policy reform of the Dodge Line, official prices were again revised on a large scale. Although revisions were divided into several stages according to commodity group, changes were intended to abolish controls and restore the free market. Official producer prices were partly decreased and official purchaser prices partly increased to reduce the gaps between them. Higher import prices also had some impact on general price increases. However, after the revisions, official price rises were smaller than expected, with increases of only 10–20 per cent for the period of April 1949–January 1950. Free market prices for consumer goods, non-rationed consumer goods and producer goods actually began declining from the beginning of 1949. Declines were caused partly by the drop in demand, which was brought about by the Dodge Line as well as a gradual recovery in production. Gaps between free market and official prices also fell: whereas free market prices for both consumer and producer goods were 2.3 times official prices in March 1949, these ratios had fallen to 1.2–1.3 by June 1950.

Commodities had been rationed under the Temporary Law for Adjusting the Demand and Supply of Materials since October 1946, while prices had been regulated under the Price Control Ordinance since March 1946. To accomplish commodities rationing, the government established fifteen public corporations (*kodan*) in 1946. Under the deregulation policy of the Dodge Line, eight of these were abolished in March 1949 and the remaining seven by March 1951. The number of rationed commodities also fell, from a high of 252 producer goods and 64 consumer goods to 48 and 15, respectively, by April 1950. The outbreak of the Korean War in June 1950 stimulated the Japanese economy tremendously, and the Dodge deflation gave way to a boom driven by special procurements by the US government. This growth in demand put pressure on Japanese prices again, as did tightness in international markets for commodities which increased import prices. The government, however, did not change its basic policy of deregulating the economy. Deregulation, such as the abolition of the System of Subsidies for Price Adjustment, reduced differences between prices in the domestic and the international market, effectively linking the two.

In June 1951, the government released a statement on economic policy which reconfirmed that prices would be controlled only as long as necessary to stabilize the economy. This step marked the end of focusing on price and commodity regulation to quell inflation. Afterward, inflation policy centred on indirect fiscal and monetary policy to halt price increases. The Price Administration Agency and the Economic Stabilization Board, which both fulfilled important roles in the period of direct controls, were closed in March and July 1952, respectively.

2.3 PLANNING AND CONTROL

The discussion of inflation policies in section 2.2 reveals that measures adopted to combat price rises differed from the orthodox use of tight monetary and fiscal policies. Rather, adopted measures included direct plans and controls mixed with certain orthodox stabilization measures. Plans and controls were used as micro-policy instruments. Within a legal framework, prices of selected goods were officially controlled and these commodities were rationed by designated organizations. However, the impact of these measures was not only limited to the micro level but also influenced the macro economy. Hence, to assess these measures, it is necessary to look at their effect on both individual behaviour (the micro level) as well as the money supply and the government budget (the macro level).

The series of monetary reforms enforced in February 1946 through the Emergency Measures for the Economic Crisis constituted a form of orthodox stabilization policy. One objective was to reduce the purchasing power of consumers. The public was prohibited from withdrawing money from bank deposits exceeding set amount for living and production activities. Monthly wages per person of 500 yen, were set as the maximum level permitted under the new currency system, a figure which was low in relation to actual living costs. According to statistics of MOF's Price Division, the level of 500 yen was consistent with standard living expenses for the average-sized household, assuming an eightfold increase in prices from those in 1934–6 (see first two columns, Table 2.3). However, price increases were in fact much greater. Table 2.3 also shows observed monthly expenditure

Table 2.3 Monthly standard of living cost per household in 1946 (yen)

	Assumed standard of living in 3.3 system		*Observed standard of living in 1946*		*Observed standard of living in 1937*		*Consumer price index in 1946*
	(yen)	*(%)*	*(yen)*	*(%)*	*(yen)*	*(%)*	*(1935=1.0)*
Food	260.47	49.5	543.12	73.6	29.02	39.9	78.0
Housing	52.65	10.0	31.50	4.3	11.97	16.5	23.1
Clothing	35.00	6.6	37.00	5.0	7.22	9.9	81.7
Light & fuel	31.58	6.0	35.00	4.7	3.94	5.4	18.7
Miscellaneous	146.32	27.9	91.26	12.4	20.60	28.3	16.5
Total	526.02	100.0	737.88	100.0	72.75	100.0	48.7

Source: Okura-sho (Ministry of Finance), *Showa Zaisei-shi* (The Fiscal History of the Showa Era), vol. 10, p. 260, and vol. 19, pp. 52–3.

totals and breakdown for 1946 and 1937. According to these data, the standard living costs in the 3.3 system of official prices were assumed to be about 70 per cent of actual living costs in 1946 (0.712 = 526.02 yen/737.88 yen) and about seven times that of the prewar level (7.23 = 526.02 yen/72.75 yen). Yet, the consumer price index shown in the last column of Table 2.3 reveals that the average rise in consumer prices between 1935 and 1946 was almost 50 times. Price increases for food and clothing were particularly great, rising 78 and 82 times respectively. Hence, if households intended to maintain their 1937 living standards in 1946 prices, they would need at least 3540 yen per month, almost seven times the assumed living costs under the 3.3 system of official prices. Figures for living expenses in 1946, shown in column 3 of Table 2.3, also imply that the observed living standards in 1946 were only 20 per cent of those in 1937; for food alone, 1946 was at best 30 per cent of the 1937 level. Hence, the observed living standards in 1946 represent expenses for barely a subsistence level. This analysis suggests that households could not survive on the maximum monthly payment of 500 yen but needed to withdraw funds from their bank deposits. Furthermore, households found it necessary to supplement rationed foods with purchases on the black market. Since black-market transactions were conducted only in the new currency, the new yen appreciated against the old much beyond their official exchange rate. This appreciation increased the purchasing power of the new currency. Consequently, controlling deposit withdrawals and wages under the Emergency Measures did not much reduce the purchasing power of households, nor did such measures suppress inflation. Monetary policy, not unexpectedly, failed to suppress consumption below minimum subsistence levels, and the appreciation of the new currency generated effective excess demand in the black market.

In the chaotic situation immediately following the war, fiscal and monetary policies alone did not suffice to halt inflationary trends in the economy. Inflation arose not only because of monetary reasons, but also because of supply shortages caused by the destruction of production capacity and the interruption of raw-material imports. Price and wage controls attempted to address these supply-side issues, as distinct from the demand management of monetary and fiscal policy. The government intended to increase production incentives in fixing prices and subsidizing differences between producer and consumer prices. Also government rationing of commodities attempted to channel raw materials to selected industries in order to raise output. Under the subsidy system, producers were guaranteed at least full recovery of their production costs. Were they to reduce these costs below the government estimates used to set official producer prices, then their profits rose.

At the time of the 1947 price revision, the System of Subsidies for Price Adjustment (SSPA) was expanded both in size and in scope. Price subsidies focused increasingly on three important industries, coal, iron and steel, and fertilizer. These industries, which were designated under the Priority Production System (PPS), also received priority in obtaining raw materials and benefited from other financial support provided by the Reconstruction Finance Bank (RFB). Table 2.4 shows the importance of these three industries: they received a majority of government subsidies after 1946, and government subsidies rose almost twelve times between 1946 and 1949. Subsidies were directed at three important industries in particular: coal, steel and fertilizer. The sharp rise in output of these industries during this period indicates the effectiveness of price subsidies.[24] Together with other measures (e.g., directing raw materials to selected industries[25] under the PPS), price subsidies, by offering incentives to producers, helped to promote recovery in production and thus helped to restore a balance between supply and demand. Price subsidies also need to be differentiated from other special subsidies such as those for wage payments, firms in deficit, and imported goods. These other special subsidies, which also rose after 1947, did not necessarily act as a direct incentive to raise output. Infact, they may have somewhat

Table 2.4 Subsidies for price and wages (100 million yen)

Price subsidies	*Year* 1941	1942	1943	1944	1945
Food	144	201	440	545	413
Coal	95	207	428	1 021	1 919
Iron	–	–	134	261	545
Non-ferrous metal	2	3	21	117	1 145
Electricity	20	7	32	71	86
Petroleum	3	4	18	7	9
Others	3	–	–	87	219
Total (A)	267	422	1 073	2 109	4 330
General government expenditure(B)	8 134	8 276	12 552	19 872	21 496
A/B (%)	3.3	5.1	8.5	10.6	20.1
Increase in claims on government(C)	7 769	9 634	10 742	16 243	28 986
A/C (%)	3.4	4.4	10.0	13.0	14.9

Table 2.4 Continued

Price subsidies	*Year* 1946	1947	1948	1949
Food	6 480	5 542	–	–
Coal	2 531	9 957	18 119	21 675
Iron	–	3 873	21 372	46 375
Non-ferrous metal	–	808	2 392	1 803
Chemical fertilizer	–	1 815	10 470	25 625
Caustic soda	–	159	1 433	2 450
Electricity	–	–	–	–
Petroleum	25	–	–	–
Textile	–	–	–	–
Others	–	–	–	–
Total(C)	9 036	22 154	53 786	97 928
Other special subsidies(D)[1]	0	356	8 713	72 286
Total(C)+(D)	9 036	22 510	62 499	170 214
General government expenditure(E)	115 207	206 523	462 956	699 598
(C+D)/E (%)	7.8	10.9	13.5	24.3
Increase in claims on government(F)	16 910	107 800	171 000	–120 000
(C+D)/F (%)	53.4	20.9	36.5	–

Note: 1. Other special subsidies after 1948 included special wage subsidies and subsidies for company deficits.

Source: Okura-sho (Ministry of Finance), *Showa Zaisei-shi* (The Fiscal History of the Showa Era), vol. 19, pp. 230–529.

discouraged production by over-protecting industries.

Unfortunately, the macro-economic impact of the SSPA was not as favourable as its impact on the production levels of individual industries. As shown in Table 2.4, subsidies totalled more than 10 per cent of general government expenditures. They increased claims on the government and led to an increase in the issue of BOJ notes. Table 2.5 shows sources of issuance of BOJ notes during 1945–50. After the financial reforms dictated by the Emergency Measures in spring 1946, new issuance of BOJ notes again began to increase. This trend continued until the Dodge policy in 1949. BOJ note issues increased by 125.7 billion yen in 1947 and 136.1 billion yen in 1948, largely to fund increased subsidies. Although in 1949 new issuance of BOJ notes was reduced rapidly by the Dodge reforms, BOJ credit to the private sector was at the same time increased, and cancelling out decreases in claims on government. As shown in Table 2.5, while the increases in claims on government decreased by 108.4 billion yen in the first quarter of 1949, claims on the private sector (lending to commercial banks and purchases of government bonds from them) increased by 20.8 billion yen in the same quarter. This sharp rise in the money supply caused inflation to accelerate, creating new pressures to raise wages. However, these higher wages led to excess demand, generating further inflationary pressures. Moreover, since differences between official price and cost were subsidized by the government, they also generated higher money supply growth, which again acted to fuel inflation. This vicious spiral between subsidies, the money supply, inflation and prices, apparent since 1947, might have been broken by direct wage controls, which were in fact recommended by SCAP. Controls could have ensured that wage increases did not outstrip productivity gains, and the continued use of price subsidies could have acted to promote productivity increases. However, the Japanese government was reluctant to introduce direct wage controls, choosing instead to seek greater foreign aid as a means to break inflation. However, higher foreign aid did not accomplish this goal: the government used this aid to increase subsidies for imported goods, thus raising 'hidden subsidies' to almost 100 billion in 1948. This increase then raised the money supply and further exaggerated inflation.

This chapter has outlined trends of production, employment and real monthly wage rates during the period 1944–50 for selected industries. According to the production index shown in Table 2.6 almost all industries had been damaged enormously by the war where the

Table 2.5 Sources of issuance of BOJ notes (billion yen)

Quarterly	Total issuance of BOJ notes (B+C+D)	Increase in claims on government	Increase in other claims	Increase in claims on private sector (E+F)	Increase in Deposit at BOJ by private sector	Increase in BOJ credit to private sector (G+H+I+J)	Lending to commercial bank	Purchase of government bonds	Purchase of TB	Purchase of RFB bonds
1945.1	2.8	2.9	–0.1	0.0	–0.5	0.5	5.5	–5.2	0.2	0.0
4	5.7	5.2	0.8	–0.3	–1.3	0.9	6.5	–5.6	0.0	0.0
7	15.2	11.8	8.0	–4.5	–0.1	–4.4	2.6	–7.0	–0.1	0.0
10	14.0	9.2	–1.7	6.5	–0.3	6.9	14.2	–7.5	0.1	0.0
1946.1	–32.1	–14.3	0.4	–18.3	–3.9	–14.4	–9.2	–5.4	0.2	0.0
4	19.4	14.1	–0.2	5.5	–0.6	6.1	3.4	1.5	1.2	
7	21.7	6.6	6.9	8.2	–1.9	10.1	10	0.1	0	
10	29	10.5	3.5	15	–0.3	15.3	8.4	1.1	5.8	
1947.1	22.3	10.1	–0.6	12.8	–0.4	13.2	1.5	2.2	7	2.5
4	20.6	10	–0.2	10.8	–0.2	11	–4.9	0.3	8.2	7.4
7	20.1	22.1	2.1	–4.1	–5.1	1	–10.3	0.6	–2.7	13.4
10	62.7	65.6	6.3	–9.2	–4.4	–4.8	–4.4	1.3	–10.7	9
1948.1	–0.4	–24.7	–5.9	30.2	2.7	27.5	25.7	0.6	–8.9	10.1
4	11.8	20.8	–1.8	–7.2	2.5	–9.7	–5.8	0	–12.9	9
7	31.6	37.4	2.5	–8.3	–6.5	–1.8	10.9	1.5	–14.5	0.3
10	93.1	137.5	6.6	–51	–0.4	–50.6	–11.2	1.2	–20.9	–19.7
1949.1	–42.7	–108.4	45.3	20.4	–0.4	20.8	16	4.8		
4	–11.9	–21.6	–3.9	13.6	1.7	11.9	1.8	8.9		1.2
7	–2.4	–39.6	2.8	34.4	1.7	32.7	20.8	7		4.9
10	57.1	49.6	4.2	3.3	–2.5	5.8	–1.9	7.7		
1950.1	–44	–73.2	–4.4	33.6	1.3	32.3	20.2	12.1		
4	–0.2	–36	1.9	33.9	3.8	30.1	21.3	8.8		
7	17.6	–25.5	4.1	39	–1.2	40.2	25.9	14.3		
10	93.3	138.9	6.3	–51.9	–6.8	–45.1	–41.5	–3.6		
Yearly										
1945	37.695	28.986	7.029	1.68	–2.247	3.927	28.895	–25.234	0.266	
1946	37.957	16.91	10.622	10.425	–6.71	17.135	12.592	–2.632	7.175	
1947	125.7	107.8	7.6	10.3	–10.1	20.4	–18.1	4.4	1.8	32.3
1948	136.1	171	1.4	–36.3	–1.7	–34.6	19.6	3.3	–57.2	–0.3
1949	0.1	–120	48.4	71.7	0.5	71.2	36.7	28.4		6.1
1950	66.7	4.2	7.9	54.6	–2.9	57.5	25.9	31.6		

… Bank of Japan Statistics), pp. 396–411

Table 2.6 Production and productivity

Industry	*1944*	*1947*	*1950*
	Real wage index		
Mining	1.0285581	1.0527048	0.9500812
Foods	1.2274325	1.4079718	1.4419695
Textile	1.3132307	1.0535384	1.5169230
Wood mfg.	1.2926023	0.9088507	0.8672391
Chemical	1.2790621	1.1260175	1.4705307
Stone	1.2581860	1.1370617	1.1286583
Steel	1.2008753	–	1.4402211
Machinery	1.2805369	1.0265771	1.0928859
	Employment index		
Mining	1.3010033	1.1153846	0.9882943
Foods	0.7915742	1.0221729	1.7184035
Textile	0.6265822	0.8306962	0.8750000
Wood mfg.	0.7995283	1.6910377	1.1533018
Chemical	0.9526627	1.7721893	1.1597633
Stone	0.7920792	0.7623762	0.9174917
Steel	1.1729428	0.9609483	0.8270571
Machinery	1.1597883	1.1851851	0.3714285
	Production index		
Mining	0.9705676	0.4751226	0.7112824
Foods	0.5313283	0.3132832	0.6207184
Textile	0.2453488	0.2116279	0.5186046
Wood mfg.	0.8277425	0.7262012	0.8848594
Chemical	0.5501930	0.2168597	0.6447876
Stone	0.3976744	0.2360465	0.5848837
Steel	1.2951205	0.1434450	0.7142857
Machinery	2.2199329	0.2850982	0.5874460
	Productivity index		
Mining	0.7460147	0.4259720	0.7197070
Foods	0.6712298	0.3064874	0.3612180
Textile	0.3915668	0.2547569	0.5926910
Wood mfg.	1.0352885	0.4294411	0.7672401
Chemical	0.5775318	0.1223682	0.5559648
Stone	0.5020639	0.3096194	0.6374811
Steel	1.1041633	0.1492744	0.8636473
Machinery	1.9140844	0.2405516	1.5815856

Note: Base year(1940) in index = 1.0.

Source: Okura-sho (Ministry of Finance), *Showa Zaisei-shi* (The Fiscal History of the Showa Era), vol. 19.

Table 2.7 Trends of efficiency wages

Industry	*1944*	*1947*	*1950*
Mining	1.37874	2.47130	1.32009
Food	1.82863	4.59390	3.99196
Textile	3.35378	4.13542	2.55938
Wood mfg.	1.24854	2.11636	1.13034
Chemical	2.21470	9.20188	2.64501
Stone	2.50603	3.67245	1.77050
Steel	1.08759	1.20000	1.66760
Machinery	0.66901	4.26760	0.69101

Note: Base year (1940) in index = 1.0

Source: Okura-sho (Ministry of Finance), *Showa Zaisei-shi* (The Fiscal History of the Showa Era), vol. 19.

production of foods, textiles, chemicals, stone, steel and machinery in 1947 had decreased by 31, 21, 21, 23, 14 and 28 per cent respectively from 1940 levels. During the period 1947–50, certain industries such as chemicals and steel were restored rapidly. On the other hand, the employment index shows that employment in these industries did not necessarily suffer from the economic collapse at the end of the war. It implies that almost all industries employed excess labour and its utilization obliged to be lowered with the over-employment because of the shortage of raw materials and energy. Although the range of industries covered here is limited by the lack of data, we can observe trends of efficiency wages from 1944 to 1950. An increasing trend of more than unity in Table 2.7 implies that the real wage rate was higher than the productivity increase. In all the industries listed in the table, the efficiency wage increased rapidly during 1944–7 and decreased gradually during the next three years. In other words, the rate of increase in the real wage was higher than that of productivity before 1947, the period of higher inflation. Although the efficiency wage after 1947 decreased gradually in almost all the industries in the table, it has still been more than unity. These figures imply that inflation was caused by the demand-pull effect due to the increase in the real wage relative to productivity increase, as well as by the cost-push effect due to the rise in production costs.

Dodge's stabilization strategy in 1949 was largely orthodox, consisting primarily of tighter monetary and fiscal policy. This was the second attempt in the postwar period to introduce orthodox stabilization measures, but the economic situation in 1949 differed greatly from that of 1946. Most important, inflation was abating, not accelerating. From autumn 1948, free market prices for producer and consumer goods became fairly stable, implying that excess demand had eased. Another difference was that growth in the money supply prior to the implementation of the Dodge Line was largely the result of government subsidies. It was against this backdrop that Dodge balanced the government budget, introduced a uniform exchange rate and slashed subsidies. Although the outbreak of the Korean War makes difficult a complete evaluation of Dodge's policies, they were more successful at stabilizing the economy than were policies in 1946. What success the Dodge Line enjoyed arose from the more favourable economic situation at the time his policies were implemented, and this more favourable economic environment was at least partially created by government planning and control policies from 1946 to 1949. Although price controls alone did not succeed in eliminating inflation, they did lay the foundation for successful stabilization.

Notes

* I would like to express my appreciation for the valuable comments and advice provided by Juro Teranishi of Hitotsubashi University, and James E. Vestal and Sumi Tani, both of Keio University. Of course the usual caveat applies: any remaining faults are solely my own.

1. Refer to the wholesale price index computed by the Bank of Japan in *Showa Zaisei-shi* (The Fiscal History of the Showa Era), vol. 19, pp. 38–9.
2. Refer to the consumer price index computed by the Prime Minister's Office in *Showa Zaisei-shi*, pp. 47–8.
3. The labour force increased rapidly with the demobilization of soldiers and repatriation from abroad. The population increased by 5 million persons during 1944–7, increasing the labour force by 1.5 million. More than 4 million workers were absorbed by the primary sector due to the deterioration of the manufacturing sector.
4. Price indices (A), (B) and (C) are estimated figures based upon officially published price indices for each organization. They were originally not comparable because of differences in commodities or regions covered. However, MOF has adjusted for these differences. Refer to *Showa Zaisei-shi*, vol. 10, pp. 585–6.
5. Price indices (E), (F) and (G) are also adjusted figures based upon officially published price indices. Again, MOF has made adjustments to make the different series comparable.
6. Nakamura suggested dividing the period into three sub-periods: August 1945–February 1946, March 1946–August 1946, and September 1946–

April 1949 in *Showa Zaisei-shi* vol. 12, p. 149. Here, we tried to divide his third period into four sub-periods, in order to clarify policy development over time.

7. Refer to 'Directive No. 3' by the Office of the Supreme Commander, 22 September 1945.
8. The new issuance of Bank of Japan notes in 1945 amounted to 37.7 billion yen. This was almost 14 times the average annual issue of 1940–4.
9. The manufacturing production index in 1946 was only one-fifth of the peak level in 1944. The rice crop was the worst since 1903. Imports of coal and iron ore were decreased to 12 and 2 per cent of the 1935 level in 1945.
10. Precisely speaking, this should be called 'the issuance of new yen currency', since it was not intended to revalue the 'yen' by the denomination policy.
11. 150 kg is equal to 1 *koku* in the Japanese measure.
12. SSPA was originally enforced in 1940 as subsidies for coal. During consideration of price control measures just after the end of war, the Japanese government originally intended to suspend SSPA. In the Price Control Ordinance, the government also wanted to reduce its own burden by setting up special accounts, in which subsidies for price adjustment were combined with the disposition of marginal profits arising from the setting of official prices. These ideas were not realized.
13. For example, the purchase price of rice in the free market was 6500 yen per 150 kg, which was almost 26 times the official price.
14. It might be questionable to classify the Emergency Measures in February 1946 as a purely orthodox measure. However, in the sense that it was intended to suppress the excess demand created by the earlier reforms of the financial and fiscal ordinances, we have tried to evaluate it as a type of orthodox measure.
15. ESB and Price Administration Agency correspond to the US Office of Economic Stabilization and the US Office of Price Administration.
16. Refer to Adams and Hoshii (1972) and Bronfenbrenner (1975).
17. Refer to *Essentials of the ESS Economic Stabilization Program* (*Keizai Antei Keikaku no Gaiyō*), Economic and Scientific Sections (ESS), SCAP, May 1947.
18. For rice, price increases of 71 goods used in rice production were estimated at about 62.55 times the level of 1934–6. Thus, the producer price of rice was calculated as 62.55 times the rice price in 1934–6 which was 27.16 yen per 150kg. This came to 1700 yen per 150 kg.
19. Special subsidies included compensation for deficits of firms such as private railway companies, passengers' traffic companies, and coal mining companies and compensation for wage payments in coal mining and electric companies. Special subsidies were less than the total subsidies in 1948.
20. 'Report of the Special Mission on Yen Foreign Exchange Policy', June 1948.
21. This point was emphasized by Young who used the phrase 'hidden subsidies' (*miezaru hojokin*).
22. 'Nine-Point Stabilization Program' (Keizai Antei Kyu Gensoku).

23. According to MOF estimates, hidden subsidies amounted to more than 100 billion yen in 1948. Adding these to the conventional figures brought total subsidies to almost 30 per cent of government expenditures and 6 per cent of GNP. Subsidies were largely funded by BOJ lending.
24. For example, output of crude steel by 1948 had more than doubled from the 1946 level of 0.56 million tons.
25. Although the production of coal mining products in 1946 had dramatically decreased almost 37 per cent from the peak level during the war and rationed coal products were reduced from 60.522 million tons in 1943 to 22.389 million tons in 1946, rationing of coal products was continued from mid 1947 to benefit selected industries such as steel, chemical, electricity and gas.

References

Adams, T. F. M. and Iwao Hoshii (1972) *A Financial History of the New Japan* (Tokyo: Kodan-sha International).

Arisawa, Hiromi (1948) *Infureshon to Shakaika* (Inflation and Socialization) (Tokyo: Nihon Hyoron-sha).

Bank of Japan (eds) (1985) *Nihon Ginko Hyakunen-shi* (One Hundred-year History of the Bank of Japan) (Tokyo: Toyo Keizai Shinpo-sha).

Bronfenbrenner, M. (1975) 'Inflation Theories of the SCAP Period', *History of Political Economy*, vol. 7, no. 2.

Iida, Tsuneo *et al.* (eds) (1976) *Gendai Nihon Keizai-shi* (Economic History of the Postwar Japan) (Tokyo: Chikuma Shobo).

Keizai Antei-honbu (Economic Stabilization Board) (1947) *Keizai Jisso Hokoku-sho* (The Real State of the National Economy).

Keizai Kikaku-cho (Economic Planning Agency) (eds) (1973) *Shiryo: Keizai Hakusho Nijugo-nen* (A Survey: Economic White Papers since 1947) (Tokyo: Nihon Keizai Shinbun-sha).

Keizai Kikaku-cho (Economic Planning Agency) (1976) *Gendai Nihon no Tenkai: Keizai Kikaku-cho Sanju-nen-shi* (The History of the Economic Planning Agency).

Kosai, Yutaka (1981) *Kodo Seicho no Jidai* (Tokyo: Nihon Hyoron-sha). Translated as *The Era of High-Speed Growth* (Tokyo: University of Tokyo Press, 1986).

Kosai, Yutaka and Yoshitaro Ogino (1980) *Nihon Keizai Tenbo* (Tokyo: Nihon Hyoron-sha). Adapted and translated as *The Contemporary Japanese Economy* (London: Macmillan, 1984).

Kuroda, Masahiro (1985) 'Keizai Seicho to Zen'yoso Seisansei no Suii' (Economic Growth and Productivity), *Mita Shogaku Kenkyu*, vol. 282, no. 2.

Nakamura, Takafusa (1968) *Sengo Nihon Keizai: Seicho to Junkan* (Postwar Japanese Economy: Growth and Cycle) (Tokyo: Chikuma Shobo).

Nakamura, Takafusa (1970) *Keizai Seicho no Teichaku* (Stable Economic Growth) (Tokyo: University of Tokyo Press).

Nakamura, Takafusa (1978) *Nihon Keizai: Sono Seicho to Kozo* (Tokyo: University of Tokyo Press). Translated as *The Postwar Japanese Economy* (Tokyo: University of Tokyo Press, 1981).

Nakamura, Takafusa (ed.) (1989) *Nihon Keizai-shi* (Japanese Economic History), vol. 7 (Tokyo: Iwanami Shoten).

Nakamura, Takafusa and Konosuke Odaka (eds) (1989) *Nihon Keizai-shi* (Japanese Economic History), vol. 6 (Tokyo: Iwanami Shoten).

Ohkawa, Kazushi and Henry Rosovsky (1972) *Nihon no Keizai Seicho: Nijusseiki niokeru Susei Kasoku* (Tokyo: Toyo Keizai Shinpo-sha). Translated as *Japanese Economic Growth: Trend Acceleration in the Twentieth Century* (Stanford: Stanford University Press, 1973).

Ohkawa, Kazushi and Ryoshin Minami (eds) (1975) *Kindai Nihon no Keizai Hatten* (Economic Development in Modern Japan), (Tokyo: Toyo Keizai Shinpo-sha).

Ohkawa, Kazushi, Miyohei Shinohara and Mataji Umemura (eds) (1967) *Choki Keizai Tokei* (Long-term Economic Statistics) (Tokyo: Toyo Keizai Shinpo-sha).

Okura-sho (Ministry of Finance) (1980) *Showa Zaisei-shi* (The Fiscal History of the Showa Era), vol. 10 (Tokyo: Toyo Keizai Shinpo-sha).

Suzuki, Takeo (1952) *Gendai Nihon Zaisei-shi* (Fiscal History of Modern Japan) (Tokyo: University of Tokyo Press).

Teranishi, Juro (1991) 'Inflation Stabilization with Growth – Experience of Japan during 1945–1950', conference paper on the Role of Government in Economic Development.

Uchino, Tatsuro (1978) *Sengo Nihon Keizai-shi* (Economic History in the Postwar Japan) (Tokyo: Kodan-sha).

Yasuba, Yasukichi and Takenori Inoki (eds) (1989) *Nihon Keizai-shi* (Japanese Economic History), vol. 8 (Tokyo: Iwanami Shoten).

3 Inflation Stabilization with Growth: The Japanese Experience, 1945–50

Juro Teranishi*

3.1 INTRODUCTION

For an economy inflicted with high inflation and low economic growth, it is often suggested that successful stabilization is an essential prerequisite for transition to sustained growth. Most of the recent experience in developing economies, however, seems to belie this proposition. In the case of Bolivia, the stabilization programme introduced in 1985 brought down the rate of inflation almost instantaneously, but production levels and the economic growth rate have to date failed to show any signs of upsurge. While the Bolivian economy relied mainly on orthodox stabilization measures such as fixing exchange rates and fiscal tightening (Morales and Sachs, 1990), the situation in economies that adopted more heterodox measures, including incomes policy, is not much different. This is clear if we look at the stabilization programmes in Argentina in 1985 (Dornbusch and de Pablo, 1990), Israel in 1985 (Bruno and Piterman, 1988) or Poland in 1990 (Lipton and Sachs, 1990). In all cases, while the programmes were highly successful in bringing down the rate of inflation, no significant increase in the level of real production and employment or a shift to a sustained growth path was observed.[1]

There are various conceivable reasons for such unsatisfactory results. First, the mix of stabilization and structural policies may have been inappropriate. Though the generally accepted view (McKinnon, 1982; Edwards, 1984) supports a sequencing of policies with stabilization preceding structural adjustment, depending on prevailing conditions, sequencing in reverse order or parallel implementation may be quite adequate. Second, one may question the method of stabilization itself. Stabilization measures that are too harsh may destroy the incentives and motivation for individual production units to expand. Stabilization policies may also prove detrimental to investment decisions if they lead to social and political instability. Third, the structural adjustment measures undertaken subsequent to stabilization may be problematic. Slow adjustment in state-run enterprises may be a serious obstacle to growth. The timing and manner of injecting new money, as real interest rates soar following the introduction of stabilization measures, may also be crucial (Dornbusch and Fisher, 1986) A sufficiently long period of time may be necessary before implementing structural adjustment policies (Sachs, 1987).

The purpose of this chapter is to shed light on the relationship between stabilization and growth by examining the functioning of the Japanese economy in the immediate postwar period. This exercise is worthwhile because the Japanese economy showed a strong upward movement in the level of production and real economic activity not only after the successful implementation of the stabilization programme but also during the period of implementation. It is suggested here that the, rather exceptional, performance of the Japanese economy during the 1945–50 period was due to the growth-oriented nature of stabilization measures.

The Japanese economy utilized four stabilization measures:

(1) Deposit freezes were used between February/March 1946 and July 1947.
(2) A Priority Production System (Keisha Seisan Hoshiki: PPS) was used to break production bottlenecks during the period between mid-1947 and March 1949.
(3) Price controls with subsidies and anchoring were first implemented in March 1946 and extensively applied from July 1947 through March 1951.
(4) Orthodox stabilization measures such as fiscal tightening and a shift to a single fixed exchange rate were carried out beginning in April 1949.

Of these, the first was effective in mitigating the rate of inflation but it had a limited role to play due to its temporary nature. Nothing conclusive can be said about the effect of the second measure. Though it has been argued that the Priority Production System was effective in increasing the production of 'bottleneck goods', our preliminary analysis does not indicate a close relationship between increased credit and increased production. Moreover, the effect of increased production on inflation stabilization is also uncertain, partly because the effect on excess demand would have been small as the marginal propensity to spend out of incremental income, given the severe shortages of goods, must have been very high. Besides, an increase in production accompanied by an expanded money supply resulting from subsidized credit would have fuelled inflation. Orthodox stabilization measures played an important role in finalizing the stabilization process. Especially important was the anchoring effect of the fixed exchange rate. The effect of fiscal tightening, however, should not be overly exaggerated due to the following three reasons. First, since price subsidies were the main source of fiscal deficits, these would have declined automatically once the third measure achieved its objectives (see discussion in section 3.3). Second, though budget deficits were drastically cut and the issuance of the Bank of Japan (BOJ) notes reduced, there was an offsetting increase in commercial bank credit leading to a rise in the money supply (M2). Third, as discussed later, the rate of inflation was in a declining phase even before this measure was introduced.

We consider that the pricing and anchoring systems, brought into action under the third and fourth measures referred to above, were extremely important in bringing down the rate of inflation and raising the level of production simultaneously. It is argued that these measures owed their success to the following four factors. First, price anchoring aimed not only at stabilizing the nominal price level but also at establishing or attaining a relative price system suited to 'normal' times. Second, price subsidies were closely linked to the level of capacity utilization and were used to guide production levels. Third, price subsidies were determined at a level that would make it possibile for production units to retain idle human resources with firm-specific skills in anticipation of higher activity levels in the future. Fourth, multiple anchoring was adopted to retain integrity of control and avoid spill-over effects.[2] Although wage rates were to be determined by the market, the standard wage for each industry was linked closely to price subsidies and, after April 1949, the fixing of the exchange rate served as a powerful anchor for tradable prices.

It may be discerned that the control and anchoring system summarized above is strongly geared to recovery of and efficiency in production. We believe that this growth- or production-oriented policy was the key to the Japanese experience of stabilization with growth. In the next section we discuss the process of inflation stabilization, while section 3.3 considers why the process functioned without stifling the growth potential of the economy.

3.2 THE PROCESS OF INFLATION STABILIZATION

3.2.1 The Inflationary Process[3]

Though an increase in the money supply was the direct cause of postwar inflation in Japan, a sharp fall in production after the war provided the backdrop for rising prices. With foreign trade under the complete control of the Supreme Commander for the Allied Powers (SCAP), the import of goods, especially raw materials like coal and oil, was kept to a minimum. As a result, industrial production gradually declined reaching a trough in January/February 1947 as inventories of basic materials ran out. The import/GNP ratio in 1946 (Table 3.1) stood at less than a quarter of the 1934–6 average (normal prewar level) and, consequently, the index of industrial production was less than a third of its prewar level. Moreover, agricultural production, especially rice, recorded a historical low in 1945 at less than two-thirds of its prewar level due to bad weather and input shortages (fertilizers and labour). Nationwide starvation was a realistic scenario at that time.

Table 3.1 Macro indices

Year	*Production index*[1]		*Imports*[3] */GNP (%)*	*Budget*[3] *deficits/GNP (%)*	*Growth rate of real GNP*
	Industry[2]	*Agriculture*			
1935–9 average	125.8	108.3	23.1	15.6	8.2
1940–4 average	156.4	102.9	12.1	46.9	0.0
1945	60.2	65.5	–	–	–
46	30.7	78.2	5.1	18.3	–
47	38.3	80.1	6.2	9.8	8.4
48	58.5	92.1	7.2	8.4	13.0
49	78.2	96.2	9.7	4.1	2.2
1950	93.8	100.4	9.2	–2.5	11.0
51	127.8	106.0	12.8	2.0	13.0
52	136.4	122.7	11.5	3.6	11.2

Table 3.1 continued

Year	*Production index*[1] *Industry*[2]	*Agriculture*	*Imports*[3] */GNP (%)*	*Budget*[3] *deficits/GNP (%)*	*Growth rate of real GNP*
53	166.5	133.0	12.3	0.4	7.0
54	180.5	144.0	11.3	1.4	3.7

[1] 1934–6 (1933–5 for Agriculture) = 100.
[2] Estimates by the Economic Stabilization Board (Keizai Antei-honbu) until 1952, and the Ministry of International Trade and Industry for 1953 and 54.
[3] Budget deficits are increments in central government debt. Government debt refers to debts at the end of the fiscal year. GNP and imports for 1946–51 and real GNP after 1945 are for fiscal years (April–March).

Sources: Okura-sho (Ministry of Finance) *Showa Zaisei-shi* (The Fiscal History of the Showa Era), vol. 19; Bank of Japan *Honpo Keizai Tokei* (Economic Statistics Annual); Somu-cho (Management and Coordination Agency) *Nihon Choki Tokei Soran* (Historical Statistics of Japan), vol. 3.

In contrast to low production levels, nominal demand soared due to an increased money supply. First, immediately after the end of the war in August 1945, the money supply expanded substantially as the government tried to meet its war-related commitments (payments against retirement allowances to soldiers and for wartime procurement) financed by notes issued by the BOJ. As depicted in Table 3.2, the total issue of notes by the BOJ in 1945 amounted to 37.7 billion yen compared to an annual average of 2.8 billion yen during 1940–4. Wholesale prices doubled between August and December 1945 (Table 3.3). Second, the Priority Production System adopted by the cabinet in December 1946, was fully implemented in mid-1947. Since price subsidies for producers and imports and subsidized credit through the Reconstruction Finance Bank (Fukko Kin'yu Kinko: RFB) were the main tenets of this system, it became necessary to issue an increasingly large number of new BOJ notes beginning in 1947. The large increase in claims on the government in 1947 and 1948 (Table 3.2) reflects government deficits resulting from such subsidies. In 1947 alone, the BOJ purchased as much as 32.3 billion yen worth of RFB bonds.[4] Total new issue of BOJ notes in 1947 and 1948 was 125.7 and 136.1 billion yen respectively, more than four times as high as in 1945–6.

Table 3.2 Methods for issuing Bank of Japan (BOJ) notes

Calendar Year	(1) Increase in claims on government	(2) Increase in claims on private sector		(3) Other net claims	(4) Total issue of Bank of Japan notes = ((1) + (2) + (3))
		Lending to commercial banks	Purchase of RFB bonds		
1935–9 average	2.9	–2.4	–	0.1	0.4
1940–4 average	9.8	–6.8	–	0.2	2.8
1945	29.0	3.9	–	–4.9	37.7
46	16.9	17.1	–	4.0	38.0
47	107.8	–11.9	32.3	–2.5	125.7
48	171.0	–34.6	–0.3	–0.3	136.1
49	–120.0	71.2	6.1	48.9	0.1
1950	4.2	57.5	–	5.0	66.7
51	–24.4	122.1	–	–13.4	84.3
52	69.0	2.2	–	–1.1	70.1
53	–12.5	78.8	–	–12.9	53.4
54	84.4	–65.1	–	–27.1	–7.8

Note: 'Other net claims' are deposits at agency banks minus deposits at the Bank of Japan by commercial banks. Lending to commercial banks includes the purchase of government bonds from them.

Source: Bank of Japan, *Nihon Ginko Hyakunen-shi* (One Hundred-Year History of the Bank of Japan) (Statistics Volume).

The inflationary process is depicted in Table 3.3. Two characteristics of this process need to be mentioned. First, stabilization was quite protracted. Deposits were frozen during the period February/March 1946 to July 1947 and the head-on attack on inflation using PPS and price controls became effective only from mid-1947. Monthly inflation rates as revealed by market prices, however, did not decline to less than 5 per cent (89 per cent annual rate) until after mid-1948. This 12-month lag required to achieve the stabilization of prices seems quite long compared with the almost instantaneous slowdown of inflation in the countries mentioned in the opening paragraph. Second, during the period when inflation was running high and stabilization measures were being implemented as well as after stabilization was achieved, the index of industrial production, as depicted in Table 3.1, increased steadily. The average real rate of growth in GNP, though somewhat low at 2.2 per cent in 1949, was fairly high at 8.4 per cent per annum during the 1947–54 period.

In sum, though it took longer, compared to other countries, for Japan to fight inflation after the Second World War, the process was accompanied by positive and high rates of growth in production.

3.2.2 Stabilization Measures

Let us now examine the implementation of the stabilization measures and their ultimate effects.

(a) Deposit Freeze

This was an emergency measure to cope with the runaway inflation caused by bloating government expenditures as the government tried to meet its war-related commitments. In view of a sharp increase in the supply of BOJ notes, the government, in February 1946, (a) ordered that all BOJ notes above a certain denomination be deposited, and (b) forbade withdrawals of deposits except for the minimum needs for living and production activity. Old bank notes were invalidated and new notes issued at the time of withdrawal of deposits.[5] However, as economic activity gradually recovered, limitations on deposit withdrawals were relaxed and the measure was formally suspended in July 1948. All deposits, except for the large corporate deposits that were eventually used to compensate for war-related losses, were freed.

Table 3.4 indicates that the introduction of this measure halved the outstanding currency balances (mostly in the form of BOJ notes) and

Table 3.3 Monthly price levels

	(1) Consumer price index (1950=100)	(2) Wholesale price index (1950=100)	(3) Monthly rate of increase in market prices	(4)	(5) Market/ official price	(6)
			Consumption goods	Production goods	Consumption goods	Production goods
1945						
Aug.	–	1.4	–	–	–	–
Sept.	–	1.5	–	–	–	–
Oct.	–	1.5	–8.0	–	28.7	–
Nov.	–	1.6	21.7	–	31.8	–
Dec.	–	2.7	14.3	–	29.7	–
1946						
Jan.	–	3.2	32.8	–	40.1	–
Feb.	–	3.5	17.6	–	39.8	–
March	–	4.8	–2.0	–	23.7	–
April	–	6.2	–4.6	–	21.3	–
May	–	6.3	2.1	–	15.1	–
June	–	6.6	5.2	–	20.6	–
July	–	7.0	–0.5	–	14.7	–
Aug.	5.11	7.4	–7.0	–	13.5	–
Sept.	4.62	8.0	–7.5	–	9.0	5.6
Oct.	4.39	8.1	4.7	3.7	8.8	5.9
Nov.	4.26	8.8	7.8	10.3	7.7	6.4
Dec.	4.89	9.1	14.4	13.4	8.3	7.2
1947						
Jan.	5.56	9.4	14.4	22.3	9.3	8.3
Feb.	6.14	9.6	8.3	12.6	9.9	9.3

March	6.81	9.8	10.5	12.5	10.3	11.1
April	7.08	12.3	14.5	10.8	11.2	11.1
May	8.34	12.9	6.3	17.7	11.7	12.5
June	9.77	13.3	13.2	7.7	13.1	12.7
July	11.61	19.4	8.8	12.8	10.4	9.2
Aug.	12.28	24.2	–0.9	10.0	8.3	9.3
Sept.	13.09	27.0	5.8	5.6	8.1	9.1
Oct.	12.55	29.9	6.3	4.7	6.6	9.8
Nov.	12.55	32.6	2.2	1.7	5.1	5.6
Dec.	13.72	33.8	7.5	2.5	5.1	5.3
1948						
Jan.	13.76	34.5	6.8	5.2	5.4	5.6
Feb.	14.84	34.9	3.5	3.9	5.5	5.8
March	15.83	35.1	4.7	3.5	5.8	5.9
April	16.18	35.2	4.3	1.4	6.0	6.0
May	16.81	35.7	5.3	–0.5	6.3	6.0
June	17.13	38.0	7.0	0.5	7.3	5.9
July	18.87	54.5	2.2	0.2	5.7	4.2
Aug.	21.02	63.8	–4.2	1.1	4.6	3.0
Sept.	20.94	69.1	0.0	1.3	3.5	2.9
Oct.	20.22	70.3	0.0	–0.5	3.1	2.8
Nov.	21.07	75.1	0.3	1.7	2.9	2.8
Dec.	22.24	75.9	2.7	0.5	2.9	2.9
1949						
Jan.	23.22	77.0	0.8	–0.6	2.7	2.8
Feb.	23.67	79.5	0.5	1.1	2.8	2.8
March	24.39	79.8	1.5	–1.8	2.8	2.8
April	24.66	83.5	3.7	–2.2	2.6	2.7
May	24.93	85.2	–1.6	–1.8	2.6	2.6
June	24.08	84.8	–0.7	–1.9	2.6	2.5
July	24.57	85.0	–1.9	–4.8	2.5	2.4

continued on p. 70

Table 3.3 continued

	(1) *Consumer price index (1950=100)*	(2) *Wholesale price index (1950=100)*	(3) *Monthly rate of increase in market prices*	(4)	(5) *Market/ official price*	(6)
			Consumption goods	*Production goods*	*Consumption goods*	*Production goods*
Aug.	24.57	86.4	−2.7	−4.5	2.1	2.1
Sept.	24.48	87.9	−4.2	−4.3	2.0	1.9
Oct.	23.90	88.8	−4.0	−5.0	1.8	1.7
Nov.	22.91	88.8	−2.7	−1.8	1.8	1.7
Dec.	23.26	88.7	−4.4	−0.6	1.8	1.7
1950						
Jan.	23.6	92.5	−4.6	−0.2	1.7	1.5
Feb.	22.64	91.9	−8.3	−3.0	1.5	1.5
March	22.28	92.1	−7.0	−7.2	1.5	1.3
April	21.65	92.4	−7.7	−2.9	1.4	1.2
May	22.06	92.9	−2.2	−1.2	1.3	1.2
June	21.61	93.3	−0.2	0.7	1.3	1.2
July	22.19	98.6	4.2	3.9	1.3	1.2
Aug.	22.64	103.3	13.8	9.1	1.4	1.2
Sept.	22.73	105.7	−3.3	7.0	1.3	1.2
Oct.	22.10	109.3	1.3	5.7	1.3	1.2
Nov.	22.24	113.1	3.8	3.5	1.3	1.2
Dec.	23.18	115.3	0.3	2.9	1.3	1.2

Note: Consumer and wholesale price indexes are for the country as a whole, and indicate effective price (including market and official prices). Market price covers black market prices for rationed goods and prices of commodities not rationed, and refers to Tokyo area.

Source: Okura-sho (Ministry of Finance) *Showa Zaisei-shi* (The Fiscal History of the Showa Era), vol. 19, pp. 42–5, p. 49, pp. 657–8 and pp. 64–5.

Table 3.4 Effects of deposit-freeze

	(1) Currency in circulation	(2) Deposits	(3) Deposits frozen	(4) Currency and deposits not frozen =((1)+(2)−(3))
1946				
Feb.	55.6	166.5	–	222.0
March	24.6	185.3	144.8	65.2
June	44.1	197.2	146.7	94.6
Sept.	65.8	200.2	143.0	123.0
Dec.	94.8	198.9	128.7	164.9
1947				
March	117.2	203.0	113.7	207.2
June	137.9	199.2	99.4	244.6
Sept.	158.1	236.8	92.8	302.1
Dec.	220.9	286.9	87.9	419.9
1948				
March	220.5	312.1	60.6	472.0
June	232.1	349.8	53.4	528.5
Sept.	263.5	456.0	–	719.5

(1) In billions of yen.
(2) Deposits are the sum of postal savings and total deposits at All Banks (Zenkoku Ginko).
(3) Amount of frozen postal savings is assumed to be constant at 23.6 billion yen, based on information in *Honpo Keizai Tokei* (March 1948 edition) p. 62.

Source: Bank of Japan, *Honpo Keizai Tokei* (Economic Statistics Annual).

reduced the sum of currency and deposits (a rough measure of M2) to one-third. As a result, hyper-inflation, which had been running at almost 40 per cent per month, was cut by half, as evidenced in Table 3.3. It is, however, also true that outstanding currency returned to its original level in the summer of that year and began expanding again. M2 shows a similar pattern though with a lag. It may be said that deposit freezing helped only in converting near hyper-inflation into high inflation.[6]

(b) The Priority Production System (PPS)

It is well known that despite the severe damage to urban housing in the bombing raids, most of the production equipment was unimpaired. The ratio of production capacity available in 1945 to the maximum capacity attained before 1944 was 78 per cent for electricity, 100.2 per cent for steel, 89 per cent for nonferrous metals, 52.2 per cent for machinery, 68.9 per cent for chemicals and 31.2 per cent for textiles.[7] The low figure for machinery is the result of large damages incurred during bombing while that for the textile industry reflects the compulsory diversion of equipment for military use during the war. Thus, the decline in production after the war was primarily the result of raw-material and energy shortages (Keizai Antei-honbu (Economic Stabilization Board), *Keizai Jisso Hokokusho* (Economic White Paper), 4 July 1947). PPS aimed at breaking this bottleneck by concentrating scarce materials, energy and manpower in key industries. Initially, the coal and steel industries were targeted with fertilizers, electricity and railway transport being added later on. A mechanism resembling the reproduction schedule of Marxist economics was utilized in the production of coal and steel. The government envisaged a snowballing effect in the production of coal and steel by allocating coal resulting from an increase in the production of coal to the steel industry in order to increase production there. This increase was, in turn, allocated preferentially to coal mining. Three measures were adopted in this regard: (i) rationing of strategic commodities based on the Temporary Law for Adjusting the Demand and Supply of Materials (Rinji Busshi Jukyu Chosei-ho) promulgated in October 1946; (ii) establishment of the RFB in January 1947 to channel investment funds to priority industries;[8] and, (iii) compulsory rationing of 50 per cent of the new funds of commercial banks to priority industries based on the Emergency Financial Measures Ordinance (Kin'yu Kinkyu Sochi-rei) adopted in February 1946. The rationing of commodities was implemented through eight domestic distributors and three government-owned foreign trade agencies established after April 1947. Rationed commodities included such goods as industrial materials, coal, crude oil, fertilizers, food, textiles and so on. The RFB was most active during 1947 and 1948 and was dismantled in March 1949 with the introduction of the orthodox stabilization policies of Joseph M. Dodge. The rationing of commercial bank loans was gradually reduced and virtually abolished in August 1949. In may be noted here that we do not mention subsidies as a tool of PPS. This is a delicate issue since both coal as well as steel were the major recipients of price subsidies (Table 3.5). But, while PPS aimed at increasing the production of bottleneck goods by means

Table 3.5 Domestic price subsidies (million yen)

Fiscal year	*1946*	*1947*	*1948*	*1949*	*1950*	*1951*
Coal	2 531	9 957	18 119	21 675	–	–
Steel	–	3 873	21 372	46 375	162	–
Nonferrous metals	–	808	2 392	1 803	–	–
Fertilizers	–	1 815	10 470	25 625	793	–
Soda	–	159	1 433	2 450	–	–
Crude oil	25	74	–	–	–	–
Foods	6 840	5 671	714	–	–	–
Others	–	154	7 999	3 700	–	–
Total	9 030	22 511	62 699	109 627	34 774	955
Percentage to total government expenditure (general accounts)	7.8	10.9	13.5	15.67	5.5	0.1
Percentage to GNP	1.9	1.7	2.3	3.3	0.9	0.0

Source: Okura-sho (Ministry of Finance), *Showa Zaisei-shi* (The Fiscal History of the Showa Era), vol. 19.

of input–output interaction, price subsidies to producers were geared towards lowering the purchase price of the goods as a means of rehabilitating production consistent with a realistic system of relative prices. In this sense, the subsidies were not directly related to expansion of production and hence we assume, in this chapter, that subsidies were not an essential tool of PPS.

An immediate consequence of PPS was the continuation of inflation, as evidenced in Table 3.3. As much as 70 per cent of RFB funds were raised via BOJ credit; the commercial banks also relied heavily on borrowing from the BOJ and budget deficits arising from price subsidies also resulted in new note issues by the BOJ. Tables 3.6 and 3.7 provide a basis for a cursory analysis of the effects of PPS. Column 4 in Table 3.6 presents figures for change in credit supplied by the RFB and commercial banks between September 1947 (the first month for which figures are available) and March 1949 (when the RFB was dismantled). It is readily seen that the rate of increase of credit was large for industries like coal, steel, fertilizers, electricity and gas, and transport. This seems to correspond to the priorities of the PPS discussed above. The figure for food processing is also substantial, reflecting, probably, the profit-seeking behaviour of com-

Table 3.6 RFB and commercial bank lending to industry

	Total lending (billion yen)				
	1947 Sept. (1)	*1949 March (2)*	*1950 June (3)*	*(2)/(1)*	*(3)/(2)*
Mining	11.5	74.9	77.3	6.47	1.03
(Coal)	10.0	67.2	65.9	6.75	0.98
Metals	3.9	28.6	52.8	7.25	1.85
(Steel)	1.3	21.8	39.3	17.00	1.80
Machinery	11.2	66.6	92.8	5.95	1.39
Ceramics	1.3	8.5	16.0	6.50	1.88
Chemicals	8.8	56.2	102.2	6.40	1.82
(Fertilizer)	1.7	15.1	11.3	8.70	0.75
Textiles	12.9	68.8	141.8	5.32	2.06
Wood processing	4.1	13.8	17.8	3.34	1.27
Food processing	2.3	25.0	41.6	10.66	1.67
Other manufacturing	1.7	6.7	12.1	4.02	1.79
Construction	6.1	13.8	19.1	2.25	1.39
Electricity and gas	3.0	26.4	27.3	8.90	1.04
Transportation	3.7	30.2	44.8	8.20	1.49
Commerce	18.4	72.4	178.5	3.94	2.47
Total	107.4	540.2	896.9	5.02	1.66

Note: Total includes lending to other areas, and hence listed items do not add up to total. Commercial banks are All Banks (Zenkoku Ginko).

Source: Bank of Japan, *Honpo Keizai Tokei* (Economic Statistics Annual).

mercial banks.[9] Column 4 in Table 3.7, on the other hand, shows changes in production index for the same period. The rate of increase is high for four industries: steel, nonferrous metals, machinery and food processing. The increase in coal production was not exceptionally large compared to production increases in other industries.[10] However, since coal was a bottleneck commodity, the effects of an increase in coal production on other sectors would have been larger than the reverse. The 1947 *Keizai Jisso Hokoku-sho* (Economic White Paper) noted that the 'doubling of coal production is expected to result in a quadrupling of manufacturing production' (Keizai Antei-honbu (Economic Stabilization Board), *Keizai Jisso Hokoku-sho*, 4 July 1947). The high rate of increase in machinery production and the low rate for chemicals does not correspond to changes in the credit supply. The rate of expansion in production, however, is

Table 3.7 Production indexes by industry

	Production index[1] *(1955 = 100)*				
	1947 Sept. (1)	1949 March (2)	1950 June (3)	(2)/(1)	(3)/(2)
Mining	56.9	85.6	82.0	1.50	0.96
(coal)	67.1	102.2	91.9	1.52	0.90
Steel	14.3	34.9	53.0	2.44	1.52
Nonferrous Metals	32.5	53.7	56.5	1.65	1.05
Machinery	21.5	44.9	37.5	2.09	0.84
Ceramics	23.5	42.1	50.4	1.79	1.20
Chemicals	18.3	30.2	43.0	1.65	1.42
Textiles	20.6	31.0	42.4	1.50	1.37
Wood processing	57.8	72.6	54.6	1.26	0.75
Food processing	23.9	48.8	43.0	2.04	0.88
Electricity	51.9	71.5	74.0	1.38	1.03
Gas	22.5	39.7	39.7	1.76	1.00
Total	25.1	42.9	47.6	1.71	1.11

[1] Estimates by the Ministry of International Trade and Industry.

Note: Total includes mining, manufacturing and public utilities.

Source: Okura-sho (Ministry of Finance), *Showa Zaisei-shi* (The Fiscal History of the Showa Era), vol. 19.

dependent not only on the credit supply but also on a number of other factors such as the availability of imported materials[11] and *initial conditions*. Though there seems little doubt that PPS had a positive effect on production, our cursory analysis is inconclusive.

It should be pointed out that even if PPS had a positive effect on production, its effect on inflation stabilization is not expected to be large since its main instrument – RFB credits – was dependent on a supply of new currency. Likewise the marginal propensity to spend as a result of increased income may have been quite high due to a severe shortage of goods.

(c) Price Controls and Anchoring

The rationing of goods and price controls, that had been initially introduced during the war, were reintroduced in a new form in March

1946 with the promulgation of the Price Control Ordinance (Bukka Tosei-rei) and were widely used after July 1947. Basic industrial goods and food were rationed through public corporations and official prices were set. The purchasers' or consumer price was set at a fixed multiple of the prewar (1934–6) level. Since the multiplicand was the same for all basic goods, it implied that the relative prices were anchored to the 1934–6 relative price structure. There were four large-scale revisions of official prices. The March 1946 revision set the multiplicand at 8 which was revised up to 65 in July 1947 and 110 in the June 1948 revision. This period (1934–6) was chosen as the norm since this was the last peaceful and prosperous period before the war as the Sino-Japanese War began in 1937.[12] The real GNP growth during the period was 5.6 per cent per annum and the GNP deflator was rising at an annual rate of 2.5 per cent. The current account to GNP ratio stood at 0.5 per cent and the ratio of new openings to applicants at employment centre was 1.45 indicating near full-employment conditions.

The sellers' or producers' prices were set so that they equalled the estimated total average cost of each basic good. Production cost was calculated at the current level of capacity utilization,[13] and was comprised of the following: (i) fixed cost (including interest cost but excluding depreciation on unused capacity); (ii) variable costs (including wages for idle labour);[14] and, (iii) normal profits (positive for firms with more than average efficiency). Since production costs reflected market prices, they normally were higher than the purchasers' price and the difference was met by providing subsidies. (Table 3.5 presents the amount of subsidies by industry.)

Table 3.3 provides data on the ratio of the free-market price to the official purchasers' price. One can easily discern that every large-scale revision of official prices (March 1946, July 1947, June 1948 and April 1949), indicated by an upward movement of the wholesale price index (WPI) series in column 2 combining the market and official prices, is accompanied not only by a fall in the free market to official price ratio (columns 5 and 6) but also by a decline in the rate of inflation in market prices (columns 3 and 4).[15] Incidentally, it should be noted that in the case of the June 1948 revision, all changes (rise in WPI, fall in the rate of increase in market prices and decline in the ratio of free-market to official price ratio) occur not in June but in July. This reflects the fact that this revision was carried out in two parts, on 23 June and 10 July. In all other cases, the changes were implemented at once and during the earlier part of the month and, hence, the impact was felt in the same month.

(d) Orthodox Stabilization Measures[16]

The orthodox stabilization policy was implemented under the guidance of Joseph M. Dodge (special economic adviser sent by President Truman) after April 1949. This policy had three pillars: (i) an extremely stringent budget for fiscal years 1949 and 1950; (ii) the introduction of a single exchange rate; and, (iii) suspension of RFB activities. The first measure had a strong contractionary impact on the economy. Together with measure (iii), it caused a drastic reduction in the currency supply (Table 3.2). However, the impact on the rate of growth of the total money supply (M2) was small, as commercial banks were expanding credit, and hence deposits, significantly under BOJ guidance[17] to alleviate the deflationary impact on production. The annual rate of M2 growth, 75.2 per cent and 85.4 per cent in fiscal years 1947 and 1948, fell to 35.6 per cent and 37.55 per cent during fiscal years 1949 and 1950 (calculated from materials presented in Asakura and Nishiyama, 1979).

Budgetary tightening was accomplished mainly through a reduction in price subsidies, domestic as well as international. The reduction in domestic price subsidies restored the relative price structure of the economy to that of 'normal' times, as shown below. The reduction in international price subsidies, especially for imports, helped anchor tradable prices to the international price structure.[18] Since there was a shift to a single fixed exchange rate in April 1949 and a significant increase in foreign trade in the private sector after July 1948, the effect of such anchoring on inflation *should have been substantial* (see Chapter 5 of this book). In fact, the effect on price stability was in line with the expectations outlined in the Young Mission Report which was the first to recommend adoption of a fixed exchange rate.[19]

It should be noted here that the figures in Table 3.3 indicate that both consumer price index as well as wholesale price index had stabilized by mid-1948 and the monthly rate of increase in market prices had already declined substantially. At the same time, the margin between the free-market and official price also narrowed significantly. Moreover, it is also well known that the government budget during the high growth period (approximately 1955–73) consistently showed a significant surplus. This was not because expenditure was reduced but was due to an increase in tax revenue as a result of a high rate of income growth. Since the economy was growing rapidly even before orthodox stabilization measures were introduced, the argument – that inflation could have been stabilized without recourse to the deflationary policy implemented by Dodge (Nakamura, 1978; Nanto, 1980) – does seem to carry some weight.

Prior to the introduction of the Dodge policy, a controversy developed between supporters of the one-shot stabilization argument (*ikkyo antei-ron*), mainly economists with Marxist leanings, and supporters of the gradual stabilization argument (*chukan antei-ron*) such as the Ministry of Finance, the BOJ and SCAP who emphasized production recovery as a prerequisite for stabilization. Though confusing in some respects, the Dodge policy was different from the former viewpoint in that the money supply was not necessarily reduced and the international anchoring of prices played an important role. As we explain later, the method used to anchor domestic prices was closely related to an increase in production and therefore it is possible to argue that the latter viewpoint was reasonable to a certain extent.

Another interesting point was Dodge's opposition to credit expansion by the BOJ. However, there was a sharp disagreement between Dodge and SCAP which advocated the *chukan antei-ron* and it may be conjectured that SCAP endorsed the BOJ policy (Kosai, 1986).

3.3 GROWTH ORIENTED STABILIZATION POLICIES

This section closely examines the system of price controls and anchoring to explain why it was growth-inducing. Let us envisage an industry operating at a certain point of time within an inflationary environment such as that existing in July 1947. Also assume that real conditions – the shape of the demand and cost functions – were the same as those obtained in the 1934–6 period, that nominal prices were fixed at a level *n*-times (say 65-times) higher than the 1934–6 level and, finally, that prices in the normal period, 1934–6, were equal to the minimum average total cost as a result of free entry.[20]

Figure 3.1 depicts the situation of a representative production unit in this industry. The horizontal axis plots quantities and the vertical axis prices as a multiple of 1934–6 price. *Ok* is the maximum production capacity and equals the level of production in 1934–6. Let us

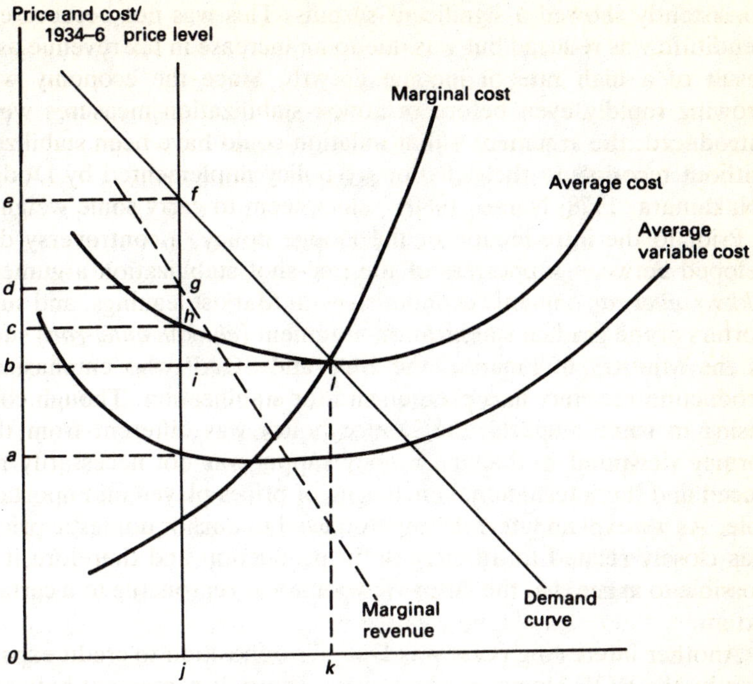

Figure 3.1 Price regulation and cost

assume that actual production in July 1947 was *Oj* due to severe industrial materials and energy shortages.

It is easy to interpret the pricing system discussed in the previous section as follows: The purchasers' or consumer price is set at *Ob* (65-times the 1934–6 level). The estimated unit cost, including the cost of idle labour as discussed in the previous section, is *Od* (average cost *Oc* plus the cost of idle labour *cd*) such that the rectangle *bdgi* shows the amount of price subsidy given to the producer. Apparently, there are other possible solutions. Let us consider two alternatives. A competitive solution or the solution without government controls would result in prices being set at *Oe*. An incomes policy-based solution where prices as well as wages are frozen, on the other hand, may result in prices being set at some intermediate level between *Oc* and *Oa*.[21] However, in the competitive solution, there is no guarantee that the firm will cover the cost of idle labour (excess profit, *ec*, would either be retained within the firm or distributed to shareholders). In the incomes policy-based solution, even if prices cover the variable cost, they may fail to cover not only the cost of an idle workforce but also the cost of some fixed factors of production. In the process of implementing this policy, the fixed factors of production would deteriorate and workforce with firm-specific skills would leave the industry. This makes the return to normal production, once stabilization has been achieved, quite difficult assuming that factor markets are imperfect, which was the case in Japan in the immediate postwar period. Even if the price level *Ob*, corresponding to minimum average costs, is targeted, a return to production at point *1* is not assured.

The growth-oriented nature of anchoring and pricing is clear. By gradually reducing the rate of subsidy, *bd*/*Ob*, as the rate of capacity utilization rises, the margin between the purchasers' and producers' price narrows and the subsidy eventually vanishes (though the rate of subsidy declines, the reduction in total subsidy is not necessarily monotonic as revealed by actual data in Table 3.5). The targeted level, or the anchor, is realistic for two reasons. First, since fixed factors as well as firm-specific skills are retained, it is possible to return to production at *1*. Second, since all basic goods are assigned the same multiplicand, the relative price structure is geared to the attainment of normal and efficient production levels. It can be assumed that when every industry in the economy follows this scheme of subsidy control, input–output interaction works itself out, and a move toward point *i* from point *l* is actualized. Although the shortage of imported materials still resulted in bottlenecks, this impediment was gradually removed as private trade resumed.

The actual response of production units to this policy was impressive. Table 3.8 shows that the rate of capacity utilization rose even during the deflationary period of 1949. The *Keizai Genkyo Hokoku* (Economic White Paper) of 30 June 1950 remarks that the necessity of cost reductions signalled by the future reduction in subsidies was so imperative that firms increased production even if it meant stockpiling inventories. Incidentally, the wage level was not controlled by the government in Japan due to frequent labour disputes (Okura-sho, 1982). However, the government did try to influence the wage level by stipulating a standard wage for each industry, estimated in a manner consistent with other production costs. This, together with the fixed exchange rate introduced in April 1949, may be considered to constitute the multiple nominal anchoring system.

Table 3.8 Rate of capacity utilization (%)

	1946 Dec.	*1948* Dec.	*1949* Dec.
Steel	1.7 – 26.1	14.5 – 41.4	24.1 – 56.9
Light metal rolling	44.9	62.9	72.9
Ammonium sulphate	66.8	55.9	76.2
Soda	3.8 – 37.4	25.3 – 47.5	37.5 – 74.5
Cement	22.3	52.3	81.6
Rubber	23.9	26.0	36.1

Note: Estimates by *Keidanren*. Calculated by dividing the amount of production by the estimated maximum production capacity for the month.

Source: Keizai Antei-honbu (Economic Stabilization Board), *Keizai Genkyo Hokoku-sho* (Economic White Paper), 30 June 1950.

3.4 CONCLUDING REMARKS

We believe that the Japanese experience of inflation stabilization with growth was the result of a deliberate growth-oriented stabilization policy. Since the price controls and anchoring system relied on subsidies financed by BOJ credit, the policy itself was inflationary. However, the proper anchoring of both nominal as well as relative prices, together with a policy to induce firms to retain a productive capacity corresponding to targeted price structure, enabled the reduction in the rate of subsidy. Eventually subsidies disappeared and the money supply stabilized.

It is difficult to find an economic system providing benefits without any costs attached to it. It must be emphasized here that price controls and anchoring had serious drawbacks as well. Since the system relied basically on subsidies, there was a considerable possibility that corruption and moral hazard would occur. For example, there is evidence that subsidies provided an incentive for coal mining companies to deliberately work inferior mines leaving more efficiently workable mines for future exploitation (Nakamura, 1989, p. 50). The estimation of *costs for calculating an adequate level of subsidies* has also been criticized. At the time of the June 1948 price revision, the degree of capital utilization was assessed at an extremely low level and costs were assessed at a level that was too high. This resulted in excess profits to producers (Kosai, 1986).

We have, in effect, argued that the Japanese policy during this period was primarily geared towards preservation of the organizational efficiency of microeconomic units. It was believed that recovery allowing them was possible if these units were allowed to pursue rational maximizing behaviour. Let us conclude by touching upon a related anecdote. With the suspension of wartime compensation by order of SCAP, every medium- and large-scale firm, and hence financial institution, suffered huge losses. To cope with this, the balance sheet of each company was quickly separated into two parts – old accounts containing the losses and new accounts showing the minimum assets and liabilities necessary for day-to-day operation. The firms and financial institutions were encouraged to start afresh on the basis of new accounts. (After some years, the wartime losses were offset, mainly through a reduction in equity capital and the disposition of frozen deposits, and old accounts were merged with the new (see Chapter 7 of this book).)

Notes

* The author is greatly indebted to comments by Dr Yutaka Kosai and members of the Research Group on Money and Banking of the Tokeikenkyukai, a non-profit research organization in Tokyo.

1. Khan (1990) found a negative effect on growth immediately after the implementation of adjustment programmes supported by the IMF for a sample of 69 developing countries.
2. The importance of multiple nominal anchoring is emphasized in Bruno and Piterman (1988).
3. A detailed chronological description of the inflationary process and policy implementation is given in Chapter 2 by Kuroda.
4. RFB issued 167 billion yen worth of bonds during fiscal years 1946–8 of which 115.6 billion yen worth were bought by the BOJ.
5. In practice, however, no new notes were printed. The new notes were in fact the old notes stamped with an official seal.
6. Nakamura maintains that deposit freezing postponed the explosion of inflation by six months (Okura-sho (1976), p. 164). The importance of the difference between high and hyper-inflation is highlighted in Morales and Sachs (1990). Dornbusch and de Pablo (1990) also emphasize the institution-melting phenomenon under hyper-inflation.
7. Calculated as an average of the figures for sub-categories in each industry. Based on Miyazaki and Ito (1989).
8. As of March 1949, 75 per cent of RFB loans were for investment purposes as compared to only 7 per cent of commercial bank (*zenkoku ginko*) loans.

9. Towards the end of 1947, commercial bank credit to non-priority sectors increased (Okura-sho (1976), p. 247; and Industrial Bank of Japan, *Kogyo Ginko Goju Nen-shi*, p. 680).
10. The same applies to the period before September 1947. Change in the production index for coal and total manufacturing between January 1946 and September 1947 was 93.3 per cent and 164.4 per cent respectively.
11. For example, it is argued that the emergency import of crude oil and iron ore was effective in bringing about recovery in steel production. Cf. Miyazaki and Ito (1989) and Kosai (1986).
12. Yamamoto states in his essay on prewar Japan (1987, p. 10), 'For a while after the war, people talked about the price index for the year 1933 (*Showa 8 nen*). Those over fifty will now remember that the economic and social situation of 1933 was considered to be an ideal to which economy and society should return.'
13. Any expected changes in rate of capacity utilization in the near future were also taken into account.
14. Wage cost per output is estimated as wage rate multiplied by labour–output ratio, which is calculated as existing labour force in the firm divided by current level of output. Therefore, whenever output falls as a result of a lower rate of capacity utilization, idle labour arises, and their cost is taken into account.
15. Shionoya in Okura-sho (1980) also emphasizes this point (p. 369).
16. Although we consider Dodge's policy as an orthodox stabilization policy of sorts, Kuroda in Chapter 2 as well as Yoshikawa and Okazaki in Chapter 4 see some similarities between this policy and incomes policy. They claim that the slashing of subsidies which partly financed wage hikes had effects similar to the direct control of wages.
17. The BOJ helped in the expansion of commercial bank credit using the credit mediation system (*yushi assen seido*). Cf. Chapter 7 by Teranishi.
18. Total import subsidies in fiscal year 1949 amounted to 68 586 million yen (Okura-sho (1980), p. 231) or 63 per cent of the domestic subsidies which amounted to 109 627 million yen (Table 3.5). Figures for other years are unavailable.
19. See 'Report of the Special Mission on Yen Foreign Exchange Policy (Young Report)' in Okura-sho (1982).
20. This situation corresponds to the free-entry equilibrium in a market with product differentiation, as discussed in Chamberlain (1933), chapter 5.
21. At prices below *Oa*, production will not be undertaken.

References

Asakura, Kokichi and Chiaki Nishiyama (1979) *Nihon Keizai no Kahei-Bunseki* (A Monetary Analysis and History of the Japanese Economy) (Tokyo: Sobun-sha).

Bruno, Michael and Sylvia Piterman (1988) 'Israel's Stabilization: A Two-Year Review', in *Inflation Stabilization – The Experience of Israel, Argenti-*

na, Brazil, Bolivia and Mexico, ed. by Michael Bruno, Guido Di Tella, Rudiger Dornbusch and Stanley Fisher (Cambridge, Mass.: MIT Press).

Chamberlain, Edward H. (1933) *The Theory of Monopolistic Competition* (Cambridge, Mass.: Harvard University Press).

Dornbusch, Rudiger and Stanley Fisher (1986) 'Stopping Hyperinflations, Past and Present', *Weltwirtschaftliches Archiv*, Bd. 122, H. 1. pp. 1–47.

Dornbusch, Rudiger and Juan Carlos de Pablo (1990) 'Debt and Macroeconomic Instability in Argentina', in *Developing Country Debt and Economic Performance*, vol. 2 (Country Studies – Argentina, Bolivia, Brazil, Mexico), ed. by Jeffrey D. Sachs (Chicago: University of Chicago Press).

Edwards, Sebastian (1984) *The Order of Liberalization of the External Sector in Developing Countries*, Essays in International Finance no. 156 (Princeton: International Finance Section, Department of Economics, Princeton University).

Khan, Mohsin S. (1990) 'The Macroeconomic Effects of Fund-supported Adjustment Programs', *IMF Staff Papers*, vol. 37, pp. 195–231.

Kosai, Yutaka (1986) *The Era of High-Speed Growth: Notes on the Postwar Japanese Economy* (Tokyo: University of Tokyo Press). Translation of *Kodo Seicho no Jidai* (Tokyo: Nihon Hyoron-sha, 1981).

Lipton, David and Jeffrey D. Sachs (1990) 'Creating a Market Economy in Eastern Europe: The Case of Poland', *Brookings Papers on Economic Activity*, 1, pp. 75–147.

McKinnon, Ronald (1982) 'The Order of Economic Liberalization: Lessons from Chile and Argentina', in *Economic Policy in a World of Change*, Carnegie-Rochester Conference Series on Public Policy 17.

Miyazaki, Masayasu and Osamu Ito (1989) 'Senji, Sengo no Sangyo to Kigyo' (Industry and Firms in the Wartime and Postwar Periods), in *Nihon Keizai-shi*, vol. 7, ed. by Takafusa Nakamura (Tokyo: Iwanami Shoten).

Morales, Juan Antonio and Jeffrey D. Sachs (1990) 'Bolivia's Economic Crisis', in *Developing Country Debt and Economic Performance*, vol. 2 (Country Studies – Argentina, Bolivia, Brazil, Mexico), ed. by Jeffrey D. Sachs (Chicago: University of Chicago Press).

Nakamura, Takafusa (1978) *Nihon Keizai: Sono Seicho to Kozo* (The Japanese Economy: Its Growth and Structure) (Tokyo: University of Tokyo Press). Translated as *The Postwar Japanese Economy* (Tokyo: University of Tokyo Press, 1981).

Nakamura, Takafusa (1989) 'Gaisetsu: 1937–54' (An Overview: 1937–54), in *Nihon Keizai-shi*, vol. 7, ed. by Takafusa Nakamura (Tokyo: Iwanami Shoten).

Nanto, Dick K. (1980) 'The Dodge Line: A Revaluation', in *The Occupation of Japan: Economic Policy and Reform* (The proceedings of a symposium sponsored by the MacArthur Memorial, 13–15 April 1978) (Norfolk, Va.: MacArthur Memorial).

Okura-sho (Ministry of Finance) (1976) *Showa Zaisei-shi* (The Fiscal History of the Showa Era), vol. 12 (Tokyo: Toyo Keizai Shinpo-sha).

Okura-sho (Ministry of Finance) (1980) *Showa Zaisei-shi* (The Fiscal History of the Showa Era), vol. 10 (Tokyo: Toyo Keizai Shinpo-sha).

Okura-sho (Ministry of Finance) (1982) *Showa Zaisei-shi* (The Fiscal History of the Showa Era), vol. 20 (Tokyo: Toyo Keizai Shinpo-sha).

Sachs, Jeffrey D. (1987) 'Trade and Exchange Rate Policies in Growth-Oriented Adjustment Programs', in *Growth-Oriented Adjustment Programs*, ed. by Vittorio Corbo, Morris Goldstein and Mohsin Kahn (IMF and the World Bank).

Yamamoto, Natsuhiko (1987) *Senzen to yu Jidai* (The Prewar Period) (Tokyo: Bungei Shunju).

4 Postwar Hyper-Inflation and the Dodge Plan, 1945–50: An Overview

Hiroshi Yoshikawa and Tetsuji Okazaki

In this chapter, we describe the difficulties the Japanese economy faced immediately after the war (1945–50), and how it overcame those difficulties. In doing so, we place particularly emphasis on an oft-neglected but extremely important aspect of the economy, that is income distribution, and also attempt to evaluate the government's various economic policies.

4.1 THE DIFFICULTIES THE JAPANESE ECONOMY FACED

4.1.1 The Real Economy

The Japanese economy faced two major difficulties on the real side immediately after the war: the destruction of capital stock and the continued interruption of imports of raw materials from abroad.

It is estimated that capital stock decreased by 25 per cent in 1945 relative to the wartime peak, and was roughly equal to the 1935 level. It is not clear, however, how much of the kind of capital stock necessary for domestic production was really destroyed. For example, 24.6 per cent of structures, 7.5 per cent of ports, 3.5 per cent of bridges, 7.0 per cent of railways, and 80.6 per cent of civilian ships were destroyed. With the exception of the damages suffered by marine transport, those to the domestic transportation system as a whole were relatively small. Production capacity, in the iron and steel industry was kept almost intact and in the textile industry decreased only by 10 per cent. However, in the machinery and chemical industries it decreased by 25 per cent and 30–50 per cent respectively. Production equipment in consumer goods industries was severely damaged not only by the strategic bombing, but also by the Japanese government itself, which scrapped and used such equipment as material for steelmaking.[1] One consequence of the severe damage in the chemical industry was a shortage of fertilizer for agricultural use and this aggravated the food problem after the war.

Many Japanese economists believe, however, that the interruption in the import of raw materials from abroad was much more damaging to the Japanese economy than the destruction of capital stock. Table 4.1 shows that the amount of imports in 1946 was one-eighth of the 1935 level in real terms. Moreover, the recovery of imports was very slow: it took a decade for them to return to the prewar peak level. In addition to the decrease in imports, the domestic production of coal also decreased substantially because Korean and Chinese coalminers, most of whom were drafted during the war, left the mines. As a consequence the number of coalminers suddenly dropped, from 460 000 (1944) to 270 000 (1945), or by 40 per cent. This process also created chaotic situations such as frequent strikes and even riots at many coal mines.[2]

Since capital stock substantially decreased and availability of raw materials was interrupted, it is no wonder that production fell dramatically. Table 4.1 shows that real GNP in 1946 fell by 50 per cent relative to 1939. In line with the slow recovery of imports, it also took a decade for real GNP to return to the prewar peak level.

It should be noted that the basic problems the Japanese economy faced in those days were supply-side issues and not the result of aggregate demand deficiency. High unemployment, for example, was caused by shortages of capital stock and raw materials rather than a lack of demand. There was also a misallocation of resources among sectors most notably caused by a radical shift of demand from military to civilian use.[3]

Despite the serious difficulties confronting the economy, during the first five years after the war real GNP increased by 40 per cent. Most of this increase was, however, absorbed by consumption (Table 4.1). In contrast, investment increased very little. It was only natural that per capita consumption recovered after having fallen to the minimum subsistence level in this period. At the same time, we must note that output increased by 40 per cent without a corresponding increase in capital stock. This fact in turn suggests a sharp increase in capacity utilization in this period, and therefore that the drop in capacity utilization due to shortages in raw materials and/or intersectoral misallocations of resources was much more serious than the war-time destruction of capital stock.[4]

Table 4.1 Gross national expenditure at constant prices (1934–6 calendar year base, in millions of yen)

Year	Total	Private consumption	Government consumption	Gross domestic capital formation	Surplus of current account	Exports etc.	Imports etc.
CY 1935	16 631	10 726	2 611	3 140	154	4 205	4 051
1936	17 157	11 003	2 618	3 405	131	4 471	4 340
1937	21 220	11 540	4 247	4 572	861	5 407	4 546
1938	21 935	11 382	5 491	4 745	317	4 978	4 661
1939	22 117	10 839	4 688	6 007	583	5 255	4 672
1940	20 796	9 723	4 896	5 967	210	5 684	5 474
1941	21 130	9 410	6 134	6 415	–559	4 433	4 992
1942	21 405	8 956	6 460	6 557	–568	3 246	3 814
1943	21 351	8 469	7 445	5 857	–420	2 910	3 330
1944	20 634	7 006	7 301	6 462	–135	2 310	2 445
FY 1946	11 594	6 826	1 123	4 077	–432	102	534
1947	12 573	7 410	828	4 845	–510	247	757
1948	14 211	8 391	1 360	4 987	–527	362	889
1949	14 524	9 297	1 619	4 041	–433	753	1 186
1950	16 115	10 077	1 838	3 893	307	1 614	1 307
1951	18 207	11 040	2 022	4 715	430	2 187	1 757

Note: CY denotes calendar year, while FY denotes fiscal year.

Source: Somu-cho (Management and Coordination Agency) (1987).

Table 4.2 Postwar inflation

Calendar Year	*WPI*	*Ratio of black market prices to official prices*
1945	100	n.a.
1946	464	7.2
1947	1375	5.3
1948	3651	2.9
1949	5961	1.7
1950	7045	1.2

Source: Okura-sho (Ministry of Finance) (1978).

4.1.2 Inflation

The Japanese economy suffered from hyper-inflation along with a sharp decline in real output (Table 4.2). This hyper-inflation was certainly not as bad as the historically notorious hyper-inflation experienced by Germany after the First World War. Still, even the official wholesale price rose seventy times between 1945 and 1950.

What were the major effects of this hyper-inflation? As is well known, if all the nominal values including wages, assets and debts change in exactly the same proportion, it is conceivable that inflation would leave all the real variables intact no matter how high the rate of inflation. Of course, in reality, most inflation affects the real economy. We can point out two problems associated with hyper-inflation. First, severe hyper-inflation makes money essentially useless as a medium of exchange, and results in a return to a barter economy. This entails a substantial loss in efficiency in the real economy. Second, inflation, if it does not destroy the monetary system altogether, is almost certainly not neutral to the real economy. Nominal prices and wages vary at different rates and as a result relative prices change. Also, not all assets and liabilities are perfectly indexed against inflation. Therefore in the course of inflation, incomes and assets are redistributed among groups of people and/or factors of production. We emphasize that this second effect of inflation on the real economy is, as a first approximation, a distribution effect rather than a loss of macroeconomic efficiency, although it is certainly possible that the redistribution of income and wealth in turn has a macroeconomic impact on the real economy.

In the case of postwar Japanese hyper-inflation, the monetary system did not collapse. Of course, barter exchanges took place in certain cases but only marginally. During the course of inflation, the official and black-market prices diverged significantly (Table 4.2). In 1946, the black-market prices of investment and consumer goods were respectively more than seven and eight times the official prices. The black-market exchanges, perhaps sometimes even barters, certainly involved macroeconomic inefficiency. Still, we argue that under conditions of hyper-inflation, the monetary system operated with little macroeconomic inefficiency. The major real effect of inflation was therefore distributional.

High inflation redistributed both income and wealth. On the asset/liability side, there were three major effects: First, the value of national government bonds in real terms dropped to nearly zero. As a result of the large-scale issue of war bonds, the government became the largest net debtor after the war (see Table 4.3). Second, and in a similar fashion, the real value of deposits was reduced significantly. In March 1946 the government implemented Emergency Financial Measures (Kin'yu Kinkyu Sochi) in an attempt to force citizens to deposit all circulating currency into banks and in principle to forbid withdrawals of such deposits except for the minimum amount necessary to survive. During 1946 over 70 per cent of total deposits were frozen and, in the interim, inflation reduced the real value of the deposits to less than one-quarter.[5] As a result of these measures financial institutions, seriously damaged by the reduction in real terms of their national and corporate bonds, were able to recover. Lastly, within the private sector the real value of debts held by tenant farmers also declined. In the amended Agricultural Land Adjustment Law (Nochi Chosei-ho) of 1946, land owners were forced to sell a certain portion of their tenant lands to the government, which subsequently sold this land (80 per cent of the total acreage of tenant land) to the tenant farmers. Thus, the tenant farmers were in debt to the government for the purchase price of such land. However, because the purchase price was determined based on prices as of November 1945, these debts were reduced to nearly zero due to subsequent inflation. It was as if the transfer of tenant acreage was in fact implemented without compensation.[6]

In addition to the substantial redistribution of assets and liabilities, incomes were also significantly redistributed. Table 4.4 shows the distribution of national income. We can observe that income distribution drastically changed from the prewar period (1934–6) to 1946.

First of all, employees' compensation fell, from 39.3 per cent to

Table 4.3 Financial assets and liabilities by sector (end of Dec. 1946) (millions of yen)

	A *B–C*	B *Assets*	C *Liabilities*
Financial institutions	–32 480	342 469	374 949
Government	–175 429	74 114	249 543
Private	201 510	380 574	179 064

Note: Local governments are included in 'Government'. Public companies are excluded.

Source: Okura-sho (Ministry of Finance) (1978).

Table 4.4 Distribution of national income (per cent)

	1934–6 C.Y.	*1946 F.Y.*	*1947*	*1948*	*1949*	*1950*
Total	100.0	100.0	100.0	100.0	100.0	100.0
Compensation of employees	39.3	31.8	33.2	29.2	43.5	42.6
Incomes of owners of unincorporated enterprises	32.4	64.0	65.1	54.5	47.4	45.9
Agriculture	14.5	28.6	26.8	23.1	20.8	19.1
Manufacturing	3.8	8.8	11.8	10.2	9.5	12.2
Commerce	8.3	9.3	12.9	11.4	9.1	4.8
Rent	10.3	1.1	0.8	0.7	0.7	0.8
Farm rent	4.4	0.3	0.2	0.1	0.1	0.1
Interest	6.9	2.0	0.9	0.8	1.1	1.4
Corporate reserve	8.3	1.0	1.0	2.4	5.1	9.1

Source: Keizai Shingi-cho (Economic Deliberation Agency) *Sengo Nihon no Kokumin Shotoku* (National Income of Postwar Japan).

31.8 per cent by 7.5 per cent. Rent and corporate income also fell by 9.2 per cent and 7.3 per cent, respectively. In contrast, the relative share of the self-employed increased by 31.6 per cent. This increase in the share of the self-employed partly reflected the land reform of 1946. That is not, however, the whole story. The effect of the land reform should be roughly equal to the decline in the share of the agricultural rent, which was only 4.1 per cent. Therefore the rest of the increase in the share of the self-employed in agriculture, namely 11 per cent, must be accounted for by other factors such as changes in relative prices in favour of agricultural products. It is also interesting to note that in 1947 the share of the self-employed in agriculture fell slightly while the share of the self-employed in manufacturing and trade (retail and wholesale) kept rising to 11.8 per cent and 12.9 per cent from their prewar levels of 3.8 per cent and 8.3 per cent, respectively.

In short, the effects of the land reform on the income share was substantial, but it is clear that aside from the land reform, the economic conditions very strongly favoured the self-employed. Specifically, the divergence between the official and black-market prices was basically taken advantage of by the self-employed. Employed workers and corporate firms, however, suffered in 1946–8, the period of high inflation.

4.2 ECONOMIC POLICIES

In this section, we explain economic policies in the turbulent period under consideration.

4.2.1 Imports

After the war, real output fell to such a low level that per-capita consumption fell to a minimum subsistence level. It was therefore imperative that the government secure enough food in order to avoid famine. In this respect, food imports were absolutely necessary: roughly a quarter of the food consumed in those days was imported. The government controlled imports so as to give the top priority to food. In fact, SCAP (Supreme Commander for the Allied Powers) entirely controlled the Japanese international trade. The United States government ruled that exports and imports be permitted only under the approval and supervision of SCAP, and that only essential goods could be imported ('The United States Initial Post Defeat Policy Relating to Japan': SWNCC-150/3).[7] The prewar Japanese economy depended heavily on imports for raw materials: the ratio of raw materials to total imports was as high as 60 per cent. After the war, however, it fell to 20–30 per cent, while food imports increased dramatically in accordance with the above-mentioned policy of SCAP. Foreign aid, particularly by the US, was also crucial in this respect. Japan sustained large trade balance deficits in the latter half of the 1940s, that were met with United States aid (Table 4.5). Most of the aid received directly after the war came mainly from the budget account of the US Department of Army named GARIOA (Government and Relief in Occupied Areas).

Table 4.5 Balance of payments (millions of dollars)

	1946 C.Y.	*1947*	*1948*	*1949*	*1950*
Current balance	–78.1	46.4	74.8	207.1	476.3
Trade balance	–238.0	–267.4	–284.3	–194.8	34.4
Exports	65.3	181.6	262.3	533.3	920.3
Imports	303.3	449.0	546.6	728.1	885.9
Net transfers	194.5	404.8	461.6	513.5	429.4
Others	–34.6	–91.0	–102.5	–111.6	12.5

Source: Okura-sho (Ministry of Finance) (1978).

The trade policy of SCAP surveyed above was revised as the objectives of the Occupation shifted from disarmament and democratization to economic recovery.[8] An early example is the permission given by SCAP for the importation of heavy crude oil for steel production. This eventually became the starting-point for the Priority Production System (Keisha Seisan Hoshiki) mentioned later. The clear turning-point however was the Johnston Report (*Report on the Economic Position and Prospects of Japan and Korea*, 26 April 1948).[9] The Johnston Report stated explicitly that imports should be permitted not only for the maintenance of a minimum standard of living but also for economic reconstruction. The source of most of the aid for economic reconstruction was EROA (Economic Rehabilitation in Occupied Areas), a part of GARIOA. With this shift in trade policy Japanese imports, heavily dominated by foodstuffs directly after the war, gradually saw an increase in raw materials (Table 4.6).

4.2.2 Fiscal Policy

Although the government cancelled all wartime debts to the private sector except for the government bonds, it still ran huge deficits. The budget deficits relative to GNP are shown in Table 4.6. For three years beginning in 1946 the budget ran an extremely large deficit though in 1949 suddenly it became balanced turning to a surplus in 1950. This surplus had been brought about by an abrupt and drastic fiscal tightening known as the Dodge Plan, which will be discussed in more detail in section 4.3.

The budget deficits in this period, particularly beginning in 1947, consisted mainly of transfers and subsidies. For example, in 1947 more than 80 per cent of the deficits resulted from payments to special accounts, two-thirds of which were used to provide subsidies

Table 4.6 Increase of central government debts (millions of yen)

Fiscal year	*Total*	*Ratio to GNP (%)*	*General account total*	*Special account total*	*Foodstuff control*	*Trade*	*Communication*	*Railways*
1946	65 888	13.9	99 437	–33 551	3 280	1 400	3 406	9 487
1947	95 286	7.3	15 542	79 744	33 700	5 200	6 861	18 562
1948	163 781	6.1	28 578	135 204	78 000	18 400	13 004	20 624
1949	112 877	3.3	150 354	–37 477	0	5 400	9 723	–53 580
1950	–83 278	–2.1	–44 029	–39 249	0	–30 400	0	0
1951	91 455	1.7	728	90 727	6 000	70 000	15 999	0

Source: Okura-sho (Ministry of Finance) (1978).

for rice, railway travel and the like (Table 4.6).

In this period the relative price of rice (relative, for example, to labour service) sharply increased. Rice is such a basic food, that the government purchased all the rice at the official price and distributed it under regulation to consumers at a lower price.[10] Since the official price was lower than the black-market price, there was a strong incentive for farmers to hide and sell rice on the black market. Still, the regulated consumer price was almost equal to – and in 1945 and 1946 even lower than – the official purchase price. Thus official transactions in rice incurred deficits for the government: all the costs such as transportation and storage were basically borne by the government. In effect, this part of the government deficits mitigated the drastic change in income distribution by guaranteeing a certain amount of food to everyone at a low price. The same goes for deficits in the national railway accounts: the government offered benefits by reducing the cost of the transportation service.

4.2.3 Monetary Policy

These public deficits were mainly financed by government bonds and the Bank of Japan's lending to the government. Since most government bonds were directly or indirectly purchased by the Bank of Japan, the two means mentioned above were essentially the same: up to 1949, the government deficits were financed by high-powered money created by the Bank of Japan (Table 4.7).

In 1949, for example, the Bank of Japan's lending to the government was four times as large as its lending to commercial banks. Evidently, this sharp increase in the high-powered money financing the government deficits was a major cause of an increase in the money supply which in turn brought high inflation. In 1949, the

Table 4.7 Accounts of the Bank of Japan (millions of yen)

		1945 C.Y.	*1946*	*1947*	*1948*	*1949*	*1950*
Assets	Loans to private sector	37 838	50 431	32 301	51 901	88 645	269 025
	Loans to govt.	11 220	7 600	53 201	83 509	100 004	63 014
	Govt. bonds	7 156	34 761	145 866	247 718	188 900	136 787
Liabilities	Bank notes	55 440	93 397	219 141	355 280	355 311	422 063
	Private deposits	4 159	10 869	20 953	22 660	22 126	25 062
	Subtotal (HPM)	59 599	104 266	240 094	377 940	377 437	447 125
	Govt. deposit	17 776	6 463	6 703	14 002	12 036	47 757

Source: Okura-sho (Ministry of Finance) (1978).

Table 4.8 Quantity equation of money (%/year)

	Nominal GNP	*Real GNP*	*Deflator*	*M2*	*Velocity*
C.Y. 1939	21.1	0.8	20.3	27.6	–6.5
1940	17.5	–6.2	23.6	22.7	–5.3
1941	13.1	1.6	11.5	19.7	–6.6
1942	19.2	1.3	17.9	20.5	–1.3
1943	16.0	–0.3	16.3	21.6	–5.6
1944	15.5	–3.4	18.9	36.5	–21.0
F.Y. 1947	101.6	8.1	93.5	65.8	35.8
1948	71.1	12.2	58.9	61.9	9.2
1949	23.6	2.2	21.4	26.9	–3.3
1950	15.7	10.4	5.3	30.4	–14.7

Source: Somu-cho (Management and Coordination Agency) (1987).

money supply (defined as currency plus deposits) was about five times as large as that in 1946. As we saw in the previous section, in parallel to this increase in money supply, the official wholesale price index increased from 464 in 1946 to 5941 in 1949.

On the other hand, from Table 4.8 we can also observe that an increase in the money supply was not the only cause for high inflation in this period. The table shows the 'quantity equation' in terms of the rate of change. In 1947 and 1948, an increase in velocity substantially contributed to inflation. During the war, when most commodities were rationed and money hoarding was encouraged by the government, the velocity continued to decline. In sharp contrast, in 1947 and 1948 the velocity increased substantially. A standard explanation for an increase in velocity is that people anticipate a depreciation of the real value of money during a period of high inflation. However, in addition to this expectation effect it is possible that velocity increases when real output falls to the minimum subsistence level. When the standard of living falls to the minimum subsistence level, people cannot afford to hold money as a store of value, for only commodities that serve for immediate consumption are valuable. In such situations, even the transaction demand for money, a kind of inventory stock for contingent transactions, will also be kept to a minimum. Basically whenever people obtain money, they quickly exchange it for the commodities they need for their survival. After all, one cannot eat money, and velocity naturally increases. In sum, a sharp increase in high-powered money to finance the government budget deficits, an increase in velocity and a drop in production to the minimum subsistence level all contributed to the postwar Japanese hyper-inflation.

4.2.4 Direct Control

In the postwar period, economic policies were not confined to standard monetary and fiscal policies. The government exerted direct control on almost every aspect of the economy.

During the Second World War, the Japanese government produced a wide range of economic controls in order to manage the war economy.[11] Even after the war these controls were kept in place in order to deal with the problems faced by the war-torn economy. Price controls were first implemented in 1939. From then on prices were officially set by the government based on the National Mobilization Law (Kokka Sodoin-ho). After the war ended, there were discussions within the government to limit the range of prices to be controlled. However, in March of 1946 the government established a new statute called the Price Control Ordinance (Bukka Tosei-rei), which allowed price controls to continue for important commodities.[12] As noted above, a widespread black market was in existence but transactions conducted with prices exceeding the official rate were considered illegal. In conjunction with the incorporation of this act, a systematic official price scheme was established. Cost calculations for each commodity were conducted based on wages and prices for rice and coal; using these base costs, official prices were calculated to make possible production on a commercial basis.[13] However, increases in wages and the prices of non-regulated commodities made these official rates untenable and the government revised its official price scheme based on new cost calculations, in July 1947. To avoid sharp price increases, the official prices were to be maintained by setting a ceiling for basic-materials costs that was 65 times the prewar price and by subsidizing the difference between actual costs and the ceiling.[14] Subsequent to the revision of the official price scheme, the amount of subsidies paid for price adjustment increased.

Since the official prices were set lower than those prices which cleared the market, a second form of economic regulation was seen in the form of quotas. The government was authorized to set quotas by the Temporary Law for Adjusting the Demand and Supply of Materials (Rinji Busshi Jukyu Chosei-ho) of November 1946, having lost that authority with the abolition of the National Mobilization Law. According to the 1946 Act, purchasers of specified goods were to present a Demand Request Form to the government; after taking into consideration the total amount demanded by the Request and forecasted supply, the government was to allot goods according to the importance each purchaser had to the recovery of the economy.[15] This quota system was called the Materials Supply and Demand Plan (Busshi Jukyu Keikaku) and public corporations called *kodan* were established for actual handling and distribution of the allotted goods to the purchasers.

This planning and rationing system was used to recover the production of Japanese mining and manufacturing industries beginning in the end of 1946, and is known as the Priority Production System (PPS) (the policy giving first priority to coal and steel industries). The primary purpose of the policy was to input as much steel as possible in to the coal mines and then, in return, send coal back to the steel industry to make a kind of virtuous cycle between two industries.[16] Because the Japanese economy faced at that time a serious shortage of raw materials, this policy was essentially an attempt to substitute domestic production of coal for interrupted imports and made sense, at least in theory. How successful the policy actually was still remains a controversy today.

4.3 DISINFLATION – THE DODGE PLAN

In the early stages of the occupation the United States government and SCAP were interested exclusively in the disarmament and democratization of Japan. However, they became increasingly interested in the reconstruction of the Japanese economy, as the Cold War became more intense. The shift in the priority of occupational policy to economic reconstruction was confirmed finally by the United States government in October 1948 ('NSC Recommendations with Respect to U.S. Policy Toward Japan': NSC-13/2). The basic strategy for economic reconstruction chosen by the United States government was to stop inflation in the first place.

In 1949, Joseph Dodge, an American banker, came to Japan as an economic advisor to SCAP. Japan, which was still occupied by the Allied Forces, had no power to veto the Dodge Plan which urged the government to drastically cut the deficit and to attempt to turn the budget to surplus. The Japanese government carried out this plan and was actually able to achieve a budgetary surplus by 1950 (Table 4.6).

Reflecting a drastic fall in the government budget deficit, the Bank of Japan's lending to the government, including the Bank's direct purchase of government bonds, declined by about one-third in 1950. The policies prescribed by Dodge soon severely damaged many industries, and the rate of unemployment began to rise in 1949. In order to alleviate the deflationary effect of the Dodge Plan, the Japanese government and the Bank of Japan eased monetary policy.[17] Consequently, the Bank of Japan's lending to commercial banks increased from 89 billion yen in 1949 to 269 billion yen in 1950 (Table 4.7). In short, the drastic tightening of fiscal policy based on the Dodge Plan was matched by an easing of monetary policy in 1950.

This policy mix successfully achieved the goal of fast disinflation. What was the mechanism for bringing about successful disinflation? The years 1946–9 was a period when labour's income share significantly decreased and accordingly labour conflicts intensified.[18] In this economic climate, firms accepted any wage increase workers demanded.[19] Losses caused by wage increases were then compensated for through all kinds of public subsidies and transfers which in turn caused a government budget deficit. And as we observed above, this government deficit was the heart of high inflation.

The Dodge Plan urged the government to abolish most public subsidies and transfers. In this respect, one of the most important policies in this period was the establishment of a single exchange rate of 360 yen to the dollar in April of 1949. Whether the 360 yen rate was an overvaluation or undervaluation of the yen at the time still remains an issue today.[20] If one emphasizes the fact that there was a recession in 1949, one may subscribe to the overvaluation theory. On the other hand, relative to the 330 rate which at the time was widely held to be the 'equilibrium' rate, the 360 yen was an undervaluation.

At any rate, the Japanese economy did not get stuck in a period of prolonged stagnation in subsequent years. Therefore the 360 rate seems to have been in the neighbourhood of the 'equilibrium' rate. What was really important at the time was the establishment of a single exchange rate. This in effect meant that the government abolished numerous subsidies relating to foreign trade.[21]

To understand the relationship between the establishment of a single exchange rate and subsidies, it is necessary to keep in mind the way trade was conducted up to 1948.[22] During this time Japanese trade was implemented through the yen-denominated Trade Fund Special Account (Boeki Shikin Tokubetsu Kaikei) that was managed by the Japanese government on the one hand, and the dollar-denominated accounts controlled by SCAP on the other. For instance, when a Japanese importer wanted to import a good, it would pay the domestic yen-denominated official price to the Trade Fund Special Account of the Japanese government, and SCAP would purchase the good from abroad at international prices using dollars from its dollar-denominated account. In the case of exports, the Japanese government would purchase the good based on the domestic official price; payment from abroad would be in international prices and would be made to SCAP account. Thus, an exchange rate in the normal sense did not exist: the yen–dollar rate would be determined *post hoc* with each trade transaction. Looking at an average of such rates for exports and imports respectively, it can be seen that the yen rate for exports was significantly lower than for imports (see Table 4.9). This method is equivalent to a subsidy whereby the relative yen prices that Japanese nationals could receive for selling their exports abroad was high, and prices for purchasing imports was relatively low. The size of the implicit subsidy can be estimated from the difference between the dollar-denominated trade balance and the so-called yen-denominated trade balance calculated from the Trade Fund Special Account (see Table 4.10). While the dollar-denominated trade balance maintains a significant deficit as noted above, the Trade Fund Special Account are roughly in balance. The difference between the two data can be interpreted as the amount of implicit subsidy. If we take the average yen rate for exports and imports to recalculate the dollar-denominated balance and take the difference, the amount is almost half of the price adjustment subsidy paid from the General Government Account. It may thus be said that the *de facto* subsidy expended for trade due to the lack of a unified exchange rate was quite substantial.

Table 4.9 Average exchange rates (yen per dollar)

Calendar year	Export	Import
1946	21.9	13.3
1947	58.5	38.5
1948	328.8	88.1
1949	333.2	314.4
1950	363.4	357.4

Note: Export or import in terms of yen divided by that in terms of dollar.

Source: Okura-sho (Ministry of Finance) (1978).

Table 4.10 Estimation of subsidies by multiple exchange rates (millions of yen)

		1946	1947	1948
A	Deficit of trade balance	3 684	11 623	33 877
B	Surplus of trade fund special account	–7	1	818
C	A–B	3 690	11 622	33 060
D	Subsidies for price control	10 216	26 557	70 472
	C/D	0.36	0.44	0.47

Note: A is based on calendar year; B and D are on fiscal year. 'Deficit of trade balance' is converted into yen by the average exchange rate (the total trade in terms of yen divided by that in terms of dollars).

Source: Okura-sho (Ministry of Finance) (1978).

When the government subsidies and transfers were abolished, high wage increases would have pushed firms to the edge of bankruptcy. In effect, the Dodge Plan meant forceful incomes policy, and cut the vicious cycle of wage and price increases. Before the Dodge Plan the Japanese government attempted to implement an incomes policy; for example in the calculation of official price schemes in July 1947, nominal wages were assumed to be only 28 times higher than the prewar level, whereas the general price level was assumed to be 65 times higher. However, the government could not force effective wage control, because SCAP still kept a pro-labour standpoint at that time. In December 1948, SCAP issued a memorandum on wage stabilization to the Japanese government, prohibiting wage increases by means of subsidies. We emphasize that a cut in the budget deficit *per se* would not have been enough to curb high inflation and that the incomes policy aspect of the Dodge Plan was instrumental to disinflation. We can also trace this disinflationary process in terms of the quantity equation in Table 4.8. The money supply certainly declined to a considerable degree from 61.9 per cent in 1948 to 30.4 per cent in 1950. But at the same time, velocity also declined from 9.2 to −14.7. To some extent, a decline in velocity is the result of disinflation through the standard expectation effect, but it can also be a *cause* of further disinflation. A possible reason for a decline in velocity independent of expectations is that output recovered sufficiently to get the economy out of the minimum subsistence level. As explained in the previous section, when output falls to the minimum subsistence level, velocity increases. Conversely, velocity will decrease, independent of expectations of disinflation, when output rises above the minimum subsistence level. We argue that an increase in output – a real factor – contributed to disinflation as well as a deceleration of the money supply and the effective 'incomes policy' in the Dodge Plan period. The relative importance of real and monetary factors in the process of disinflation remains a very important and yet unresolved problem.

4.4 CONCLUDING REMARKS

After the war, real output inevitably fell due to the destruction of capital stock and the interruption of imports of raw materials from abroad. There was absolutely no way to avoid this economy-wide decline in real output. The question then was how this burden was to be shared among the people. Obviously, the preferred solution to minimize social instability in a turbulent economy where per-capita consumption has fallen to a minimum subsistence level is to make the burden of the wealthy greater than that of the poor. The Japanese government basically attempted to achieve this goal through the implementation of various economic policies.

In particular, the government put rice, the basic foodstuff, under its control and subsidized it at a low price. This subsidy for rice as well as numerous other subsidies resulted in a huge budget deficit. This budget deficit was subsequently financed by the Bank of Japan, and thus brought about high inflation. High inflation wiped out the debts of tenant farmers and also the nominally denominated assets of the wealthy such as bank deposits or government bonds. Therefore inflation tended to equalize asset/debt distribution.[23]

On the other hand, in the course of high inflation the official and black-market prices substantially diverged and this divergence was taken advantage of by farmers and other self-employed merchants and entrepreneurs. The income share of employed workers significantly declined while that of the self-employed dramatically increased in this period.

The subsidies and transfers which were the major cause of the government budget deficit, and therefore ultimately of inflation, made wage hikes easy and discouraged producers from pursuing efficiency. By abolishing many subsidies and transfers, the Dodge Plan restrained wage increases and inflation on the one hand, and encouraged producers' efforts to enhance efficiency.

We argued that real factors, notably a recovery of real output, also contributed to disinflation (1949–50) together with a severe budget cut which resulted in a sharp decline in the money supply. The relative importance of real and monetary factors in the process of disinflation awaits further investigation. In any case, both a recovery of output from the minimum subsistence level and disinflation gave the Japanese economy a favourable environment for further growth.

Notes

1. Miyazaki and Ito (1989) pp. 174–9.
2. Hokkaido Tanko Kisen (1958) pp. 617–32.
3. Therefore 'products conversion into civillian uses' (*minju tenkan*) was an important task for the government and the enterprises. See Tsusho Sangyo-sho (Ministry of International Trade and Industry) (1991).
4. Kosai (1981) pointed out the low marginal capital coefficient in the postwar period (p. 3).
5. Okura-sho (Ministry of Finance) (1976b) pp. 116–18.
6. Mori (1990) pp. 196–202.
7. Keizai Kikaku-cho (Economic Planning Agency) (1962) pp. 19–23.
8. Miwa (1989); Okura-sho (Ministry of Finance) (1976a) ch. 4.
9. Keizai Kikaku-cho (Economic Planning Agency) (1962) pp. 27–8.
10. Shokuryo-cho (Food Agency) (1969) part 2, ch. 3.
11. As to the Japanese wartime economic control, see Okazaki (1987) and Okazaki (1991).
12. Okura-sho (Ministry of Finance) (1980) pp. 213–18, 272–82.
13. Ibid, pp. 247–66.
14. Ibid, pp. 334–63.
15. Ibid, pp. 294–313.
16. Kosai (1981) pp. 44–53.

17. Nakamura (1978) pp. 165–6; Kosai (1981) pp. 68–9.
18. Yamamoto (1990).
19. This problem can be identified with 'softening of the budget constraint', as in the case of firms in socialist economies. See Kornai (1980) pp. 299–322.
20. Shinohara (1987) pp. 127–36; Fujino (1988).
21. Kosai (1981) pp. 66–7.
22. Keizai Kikaku-cho (Economic Planning Agency) (1962) pp. 64–7.
23. By the way, the income distribution of Japan was substantially equalized in the 1940–50s. The Gini coefficient fell from 0.4 level to 0.3 level. See Mizoguchi (1986) and Minami and Ono (1987).

References

Asakura, Kokichi and Chiaki Nishiyama (1974) *Nihon Keizai no Kaheiteki Bunseki* (A Monetary Analysis and History of the Japanese Economy) (Tokyo: Sobun-sha).

Fujino, Shozaburo (1988) 'Sengo Nihon no Kokusai Shushi' (Balance of Payments in Postwar Japan), *The Economic Review*, vol. 39, no. 2.

Hokkaido Tanko Kisen Kabushikigaisha (1958) *Sekitan Kokka Tosei-shi* (History of Public Control of the Coal Mining Industry), (Tokyo: Nihon Keizai Kenkyu-jo).

Keizai Kikaku-cho (Economic Planning Agency) (1962) *Sengo Keizai-shi* (Economic History of Postwar Japan) (Tokyo: Okura-sho Insatsu-kyoku).

Keizai Shingi-cho (Economic Deliberation Agency) (1953) *Sengo Nihon no Kokumin Shotoku* (National Income of Postwar Japan), (Tokyo: Gakuyo Shobo).

Kornai, János (1980) *Economics of Shortage*, (Amsterdam: North Holland).

Kosai, Yutaka (1981) *Kodo Seicho no Jidai* (The Era of High-Speed Growth) (Tokyo: Nihon Hyoron-sha). Translated as *The Era of High-Speed Growth* (Tokyo: University of Tokyo Press, 1986).

Minami, Ryoshin and Akira Ono (1987) 'Senzen Nihon no Shotoku Bunpu' (Income Distribution in Prewar Japan), *The Economic Review*, vol. 38, no. 4.

Miwa, Ryoichi (1989) 'Sengo Minshuka to Keizai Saiken' (Democratization and Economic Reconstruction in Postwar Japan) in *Nihon Keizai-shi*, vol. 7, ed. by Takafusa Nakamura (Tokyo: Iwanami Shoten).

Miyazaki, Masayasu and Osamu Ito (1989) 'Senji Sengo no Sangyo to Kigyo' (Industries and Firms in the Wartime and Postwar Periods) in *Nihon Keizai-shi*, vol. 7, ed. by Takafusa Nakamura (Tokyo: Iwanami Shoten).

Mizoguchi, Toshiyuki (1986) 'Nihon no Shotoku Bunpu no Choki Hendo' (Long-term Trends in the Distribution of Income in Japan), *The Economic Review*, vol. 37, no. 2.

Mori, Takemaro (1990) 'Senryoki no Keizai' (The Japanese Economy under the Occupation), in The Historical Society of Japan (ed.) *Nihon Dojidai-shi* (History of Contemporary Japan), vol. 1 (Tokyo: Aoki Shoten).

Nakamura, Takafusa (1978) *Nihon Keizai: Sono Seicho to Kozo* (The Postwar Japanese Economy) (Tokyo: University of Tokyo Press). Translated as *The Postwar Japanese Economy* (Tokyo: University of Tokyo Press, 1981).

Nakamura, Takafusa (1986) *Showa Keizai-shi* (Economic History of the Showa Era) (Tokyo: Iwanami Shoten).

Okazaki, Tetsuji (1987) 'Senji Keikaku Keizai to Kakaku Tosei' (Wartime Economic Planning and Price Control), in Kindai Nihon Kenkyukai (ed.), *Kindai Nihon Kenkyu Nenpo* (The Annual Report of Modern Japan Studies) (Tokyo: Yamakawa Shuppan-sha).

Okazaki, Tetsuji (1991) Senji Keikaku Keizai to Kigyo (Japanese Firms under Wartime Economic Planning), in Institute of Social Science, Univ. of Tokyo (ed.), *Gendai Nihon Shakai* (Contemporary Japanese Society), vol. 4, (Tokyo: University of Tokyo Press).

Okura-sho (Ministry of Finance) (1978) *Showa Zaisei-shi* (Fiscal History of the Showa Era), vol. 19, (Tokyo: Toyo Keizai Shinpo-sha).

Okura-sho (Ministry of Finance) (1976a) Ibid., vol. 3.

Okura-sho (Ministry of Finance) (1976b) Ibid., vol. 12.

Okura-sho (Ministry of Finance) (1980) Ibid., vol. 10.

Shinohara, Miyohei (1987) *Sekaikeizai to Nihon* (The World Economy and Japan) (Tokyo: Chikuma Shobo).

Shokuryo-cho (Food Agency) (1969) *Shokuryo Kanri-shi* (History of Food Control) vol. 1 (Tokyo: Shokuryo-cho).

Somu-cho (Management and Coordination Agency) (1987) *Nihon Choki Tokei Soran* (Historical Statistics of Japan), vol. 3 (Tokyo: Japan Statistical Association).

Tsusho Sangyo-sho (Ministry of International Trade and Industry) (1991) *Tsusho Sangyo Seisaku-shi* (History of Industrial Policies), vol. 2, (Tokyo: Tsusho Sangyo Chosa-kai).

Yamamoto, Kiyoshi (1990) 'Sengo Nihon no Rodo Sogi' (Labour Disputes in Postwar Japan) in Rodo Sogi-shi Kenkyukai (ed.), *Labour Disputes in Japan* (Tokyo: University of Tokyo Press).

5 Japan's Experience in the Immediate Postwar Period: Moving Toward a Single Exchange Rate and Denationalization of Trade

Mitsuhiro Fukao, Masao Oumi and Kimihiro Etoh

5.1 INTRODUCTION

After defeat in the Second World War, Japan was occupied by the Allies, mostly Americans. For some time, all international transactions were effected through the Japanese government and SCAP (Supreme Commander for the Allied Powers). International prices and domestic prices had little relationship with each other, the latter being strictly controlled against the background of a thriving black market. In the immediate postwar period, the yen was not freely usable (almost all products were rationed) even within Japan.

Through the reconstruction period, the Japanese economy gradually recovered from the devastation of war and the yen regained its position as the nation's currency. Thus the postwar history of the yen is also a process of the yen's recovery of domestic and international convertibility. Since many currencies of East European and less-developed countries are not convertible, it is perhaps instructive to review this experience and consider what lessons might be drawn.

Although 'convertibility' usually means the general acceptance of a currency in international economic transactions, the general acceptance of a currency for *domestic* transactions is a prior condition for international convertibility. The following section explains the concept of convertibility. We then review the widespread restrictions on the domestic use of the yen after the war and examine the initial process of reestablishing international convertibility through the harsh policy measures of the Dodge Line.[1]

5.2 CURRENCY CONVERTIBILITY

Currency 'convertibility' is an ambiguous concept with several meanings. Therefore, when one describes a currency as convertible, it is necessary to specify (a) convertible to what, and (b) convertible for whom.

5.2.1 Convertibility for Current International Transactions

Convertibility often means that a currency is convertible for current international transactions. McKinnon (1979, p. 6) provides a clear definition of this usage:

> Domestic nationals wishing to buy foreign goods and services, not specifically restricted, can freely sell domestic for foreign currency in a unified market at a single but possibly variable exchange rate covering all current transactions inclusive of normal trade credit; whereas foreigners (non-residents) with balances in domestic currency arising from current transactions can sell them at the same foreign exchange rate or purchase domestic goods freely at prevailing domestic currency prices.

This concept corresponds to the definition of a convertible currency under Article VIII of the International Monetary Fund (IMF). Once this level of convertibility is achieved, domestic residents can freely buy foreign goods and services with the domestic currency at known prices. Therefore, achievement of convertibility greatly facilitates the international exchange of goods and services.

5.2.2 Convertibility for International Financial Transactions

Today, the currencies of the United States, Canada, West European countries, and Japan enjoy a higher level of convertibility for international transactions than those of other countries. In these countries, besides international current transactions, the following transactions can be carried out with little restriction:

(a) Residents of these countries can freely sell domestic currency for foreign currency to buy foreign deposits and financial assets in a unified foreign exchange market. They can also sell foreign financial assets to buy the domestic currency in the same market.
(b) Non-residents can freely sell foreign currencies to buy the currencies of these countries to acquire deposits and financial assets.

5.2.3 Currency Convertibility in the Domestic Economy

An important necessary condition for the establishment of currency convertibility for current international transactions is that the currency concerned be generally accepted for domestic transactions. In other words, residents of a country issuing a particular currency should be able to buy and sell goods and services in exchange for it. If prices are government-controlled or quantitative rationing is in force for a wide range of goods, it is not possible to achieve international convertibility for current transactions. Indeed, foreigners cannot freely buy goods and services in this country at domestic currency prices under such circumstances.

We refer to the absence of price controls and rationing in a domestic economy as 'internal convertibility of a currency'. The maintenance of such internal convertibility is a necessary precondition for external convertibility. Internal convertibility is essentially equivalent to the establishment of a market economy. As will be shown later, there were extensive price controls and rationing in Japan during the immediate postwar period. Parallel with the control system in the domestic economy, international transactions were tightly regulated by the government. In order to establish convertibility for international current transactions, Japan had to dismantle the domestic price control system and restore a nationwide market economy.

5.3 THE JAPANESE ECONOMY AFTER DEFEAT

5.3.1 Wartime Destruction

Japan accepted the Allies' ultimatum and surrendered unconditionally on 15 August 1945. In addition to the enormous loss of life, Japan suffered heavy physical damage from the war.[2] According to an

Table 5.1 Physique of Japanese Children

	Height(cm)		*Weight(kg)*	
	Age 6	*Age 12*	*Age 6*	*Age 12*
1930	108.1	137.1	17.9	31.8
1940	109.7	142.0	18.4	35.3
1946	**107.4**	**137.5**	**17.8**	**31.5**
1950	**108.6**	**136.0**	**18.5**	**31.5**
1960	111.7	141.9	19.1	34.6
1970	114.5	147.1	20.1	38.5

Sources: Originally from a survey conducted by the Ministry of Education. This table is quoted from Takafusa Nakamura, ed., *Nihon Keizai-shi*, vol. 7, (Tokyo: Iwanami Shoten, 1989), p. 42.

estimate by the Economic Stabilization Board (Keizai Antei-honbu: ESB), 34 per cent of industrial machinery and equipment and 25 per cent of buildings were destroyed. In total, Japan lost one-quarter of all reproducible national wealth during the war. Compared with the average for 1934–6, which is often selected as the final period of normalcy prior to the war, per capita real GNP in 1946 was only 55 per cent, and industrial production 39 per cent. Moreover, the rice crop in 1944 and 1945 was poor and large-scale famine was feared. Severe food shortages continued until 1947 and their impact can be seen in the poor physique of Japanese children (Table 5.1).

5.3.2 Inflation and Price Controls

The budget deficit during the war was accumulated as cash and government bonds and central government debt had reached over 200 per cent of annual nominal GNP by the end of 1944 (see Table 5.7). Although expenditures were tightly regulated during the war, the control system fell apart after defeat. Moreover, immediately after the war, a surge of military expenditures such as retirement allowances for ex-servicemen and compensation to the munitions industry for cancelled contracts were paid in cash. Such payments were financed by the Bank of Japan (BOJ) through the purchase of government bonds and loans to the government. Because of these expenses, the balance of Bank of Japan banknotes increased by 50 per cent during the single month of August 1945. Inflation flared up immediately. Poor statistics make it impossible to measure the effective inflation rate. However, even the WPI (wholesale price index)

Table 5.2 Japan's production, prices, and interest rates

Year	*Industrial production index* *1934–6=100*	*Wholesale price index (Official)* *1934–6=100*	*Wholesale price inflation (Official)* *%*	*Consumer price index (Tokyo)* *1934–6=100*	*Consumer price inflation (Tokyo)* *%*	*Average of highest loan rate provided by each bank* *%*
1943	159.7	2.05				6.21
1944	176.2	2.32	13.3			n.a.
1945	63.2	3.50	51.1			9.09
1946	39.2	16.3	364.5	50.6		10.90
1947	47.6	48.2	195.9	109.1	115.6	10.95
1948	67.1	127.9	165.6	189.0	73.2	14.60
1949	86.6	208.8	63.3	236.9	25.3	14.24
1950	101.9	246.8	18.2	219.9	–7.2	14.60
1951	133.9	342.5	38.8	255.5	16.2	18.25
1952	143.2	349.2	2.0	266.1	4.1	9.18
1953	172.9	351.6	0.7	286.2	7.6	8.97
1954	187.4	349.2	–0.7	301.8	5.5	9.00
1955	201.4	343.0	–1.8	297.4	–1.5	8.91

Source: Okura-sho (Ministry of Finance) (1978), pp. 28, 40, 52, 90, 473.

based on official controlled prices exactly doubled between August and December 1945. According to the same index, the price level increased 7000 per cent (70 times) between 1945 and 1950, when at last the gap between official prices and black-market prices largely disappeared. (Table 5.2).

The use of BOJ credit to finance budget deficits continued until 1949, when the deflationary Dodge Line policies were implemented. Yet the real balance of government debt declined sharply due to inflation and the debt/GNP ratio decreased to 20 per cent by 1948.

Interestingly, the Japanese government wanted to limit price controls and rationing to several key sectors because of the poor performance of the controlled war economy. However, SCAP insisted on price controls and its opinion prevailed. As a result, general price controls and rationing continued into the early postwar period. Because of price controls and the severe shortage of food and other essential goods, the black market flourished and its prices were extremely high. At the end of 1945, the average black-market price of consumer goods was about 30 times the official price. Although both official and black-market prices rose, successive increases in official prices gradually reduced the gap between the two, but not until 1950–1 did the gap essentially disappear (Table 5.3).

Table 5.3 Gap between official prices and free (black) market prices

Year	Free market wholesale price index 1946/Aug =100	Free-official price ratio (end of period)	Free market consumer price index Tokyo 1945/Sept=100	Free-official price ratio (end of period)
1945/Dec			128	29.7
1946/Sept–Dec	115.9	7.2	192	8.3
1947	304.3	5.3	412	5.1
1948	479.2	2.9	711	2.9
1949	444.1	1.7	758	1.8
1950	371.3	1.2	543	1.3
1951/Jan–April	549	1.1	642	1.1

Source: Okura-sho (Ministry of Finance) (1978), pp. 57, 64.

5.3.3 Japan's Postwar Trade and Production

During the immediate postwar period, Japan was not allowed to engage in international trade. Only limited imports of food and other indispensable goods, and exports to pay for them, were allowed. All international trade was effected through the Board of Trade (Boeki-cho: a ministry of the Japanese government) and SCAP. This restriction reduced the volume of exports and imports significantly. As a percentage of the 1937 level, Japan's trade volume was only 8 per cent in 1946 and 17 per cent in 1947.[3]

From September 1945 to the end of 1946, food was the biggest import item accounting for 54 per cent of total imports. If we add fertilizers and heavy oil for fishing boats, the share increases to almost 70 per cent; in 1947, the same three items accounted for over 80 per cent of imports. Other non-food related imports included raw cotton, heavy oil for steel production, and coal. The import of raw materials was restricted by SCAP to restrict heavy industry production. This trading structure was obviously very different from that of the prewar period. Even before the war, Japan was already highly industrialized and its imports mostly consisted of raw materials such as cotton, petroleum, and coal, along with machinery. Food accounted for only about 25 per cent of the total.

Among postwar exports, silk was shipped to the United States with high expectations but results were disappointing because of intensified competition with nylon. Subsequently, the export of cotton goods was encouraged. Moreover, inventories of scarce raw materials such as coal, tin, lead, natural rubber, copper and wool were exported to pay for food imports.

Restrictions on the import of raw materials for industrial production continued until the spring of 1948. Thus, Japan's production recovered little until that time. The industrial production index (1934–6=100) compiled by the ESB hit a peak of 176 in 1944, reflecting the high production levels of military industries (Table 5.2). However, with the disruption of shipping routes and decline in raw materials imports as the war intensified, production then fell sharply, reaching 63 in 1945. Production declined further after the war. Due to the termination of military production and raw material imports, the production index reached 39 in 1946. The import of raw cotton resumed that year and the production of cotton for export quickly resumed. Steel and shipbuilding production began to expand rapidly only from 1948.

5.3.4 Implementation of Urgent Measures for Financial Stabilization

Amidst rampant inflation and general uncertainty about the economy, the Emergency Financial Measures Ordinance (Kin'yu Kinkyu Sochi-rei) was implemented in February 1946. All banknotes in denominations of over five yen were required to be deposited at banks. Those not deposited became invalid. Subsequently, all deposits were 'blocked' and withdrawal of new notes limited. Also, a one-time wealth tax was imposed.

These measures were designed to absorb excess liquidity and restrain inflation, but several loopholes remained. While the payment of tax using blocked deposits remained possible, government expenditures were carried out with new notes or unblocked deposits that could be freely withdrawn. Because of this asymmetry, blocked deposits were gradually transformed into new banknotes or unblocked deposits. As a result, the balance of new banknotes increased 68 per cent in 1946. Inflation was moderated for only about six months.

5.3.5 Measures to Increase Industrial Production

The Japanese government worked desperately to increase coal production, as it was the only domestic energy source besides hydroelectric power. Until the end of the war, monthly coal production had been about 5 to 6 million tons. In the fall of 1945, however, production declined to only one million tons because Korean and Chinese workers, who were forcibly brought to Japan, refused to work after the defeat and began to return to their own countries. The labour shortage paralyzed Japanese mines, generating a severe shortage of fuel even for the railroads. Prime Minister Shigeru Yoshida urgently requested SCAP to approve the import of heavy oil in the fall of 1946 and made efforts also to increase coal production. This Priority Production System (Keisha Seisan Hoshiki: PPS) prioritized resource allocation to coal and steel production.[4]

Under the Priority Production policy, all imported heavy oil went to increase steel production, which was used to increase the production of coal. Greater coal output further enhanced steel production. Through this cyclical process, the production of both was expanded and allocated to other sectors. From 1947, many workers were recruited to produce coal, drawn in part by special access to food and other consumer goods. To supplement this policy, heavy subsidies for coal and steel were also introduced in July 1947.[5] The Priority Production System was financed by the newly created government-owned Reconstruction Finance Bank (Fukko Kin'yu Kinko: RFB), whose bonds were bought largely by the Bank of Japan.

These policies were, in a sense, a desperate move by the Japanese government in response to SCAP-imposed constraints on the import of industrial materials. However, the policy of the United States toward Japan began to change in 1947 because of the escalating Cold War with the Soviet Union. US subsidies to Japan were increased and war reparations, expected to be very severe, were minimized. The US did an about-face and adopted new policies to promote the speedy reconstruction of the Japanese economy. SCAP began liberalizing the import of raw materials and industrial production increased rapidly. The ESB's industrial production index increased 41 per cent in 1948 and 29 per cent in 1949. By the end of 1949, the index recovered to 92 (100 being the 1934–6 level).

As production recovered, inflation moderated somewhat. The effective price index of producer goods, which took into account black-market prices, increased 2.7 times in 1947 (the level in December 1947 over December 1946) and 1.9 times in 1948. The gap between black-market prices and official prices also narrowed. Black-market prices were about five times official prices at the end of 1947 but three times one year later (Table 5.3). However, rationing continued for most goods and the yen was not really a currency because it could not be used freely to buy goods.

5.3.6 Inflation and the Budget Deficits

Rapid inflation continued largely due to the expanding balance of banknotes to finance budget deficits.[6] Official prices of critical inputs such as steel, coal, fertilizer, fuel gas, and electricity were set below production costs, with the difference covered by government subsidies. Also, the government supplied a huge amount of import and export subsidies through nationalized international trade (see section 5.4).

Tax revenues were not sufficient to cover government expenditures, the remainder of which was mostly financed by credit extended by the Bank of Japan. Total BOJ assets increased from 79.1 billion yen at the end of 1945 to 405.1 billion yen at the end of 1948. Of the increase, 312.9 billion yen constituted loans to the central government, government bonds, and bonds of the Reconstruction Finance Bank. In correspondence to asset increases, BOJ notes increased from 55.4 billion yen at the end of 1945 to 355.3 billion yen at the end of 1948, an increase of more than 500 per cent.

5.4 SETTING A SINGLE EXCHANGE RATE AND THE DODGE LINE

5.4.1 Adjustment Toward a Single Exchange Rate

From the time of surrender until April 1949, when a uniform 360 yen per dollar exchange rate was established, the exchange rates of the yen and foreign currencies were in total disarray. The yen prices of goods for export were set at officially regulated levels and they were purchased by the national government budget (Trade Fund Special Account). When these goods were sold abroad at market prices, proceeds were deposited in SCAP foreign currency accounts. On the other hand, imports were bought by SCAP at market prices and paid for out of foreign currency accounts. Imports were sold domestically at official prices with proceeds deposited in the Trade Fund Special Account (Boeki Shikin Tokubetsu Kaikei). The upshot is that the ratio of yen price to foreign currency price for each traded commodity could only be calculated *ex post*. Japan had neither a single unified exchange rate nor systematic multiple exchange rates. In other words, the domestic price system and the international price system were almost completely independent, separated by state control of international trade.

As export and import volumes grew, the role of the private sector began to grow. From August 1948, Japanese producers and traders were allowed to meet with foreign buyers directly. And as early as the end of 1947, the introduction of a unified exchange rate was being discussed officially. It was recognized that the domestic and international price systems had to be aligned by a single and stable exchange rate.[7] Given the high inflation rate, however, most Japanese policymakers though it would be impossible to maintain a single, stable exchange rate.

Although the domestic purchase prices of exported goods were supposedly set at official prices, there were many exceptions. In fact, most exported goods were purchased by the government at high yen prices to subsidize production and sold at market prices abroad. As a result, yen exchange rates for exported goods were set at depreciated levels. Imported consumer necessities such as food were sold at low official yen prices to benefit consumers. Imported raw materials were also sold at low official yen prices to aid domestic production. Thus, the implied yen exchange rate (ratio of international prices to domestic yen prices) for imported goods was set at an appreciated level.

Japan's external trade balance showed large deficits during this period (Table 5.4). Under a single exchange rate system, when external trade accounts show a deficit, the corresponding domestic accounts should show a surplus because the sales proceeds of imported goods would be larger than the expenditures on exported goods. Instead, the Trade Fund Special Account showed yen deficits due to the low sales prices of imported goods and high purchase prices of exported goods in yen. These yen deficits were financed by loans from the Bank of Japan. On the external side, SCAP-managed

Table 5.4 Japan's balance of payments ($ mil)

	Exports	*Imports*	*Trade balance*	*Freight & insurance*	*Military procurements*	*Transfers*	*Current balance*
1946	65	303	−238	−36	0	195	−78
1947	182	449	−267	−88	0	405	46
1948	262	547	−285	−120	19	462	75
1949	533	728	−195	−164	49	514	207
1950	920	886	34	−90	63	429	476
1951	1354	1645	−291	−226	624	171	329

Note: The 1946 figure includes September 1945 to December 1946.

Source: Okura-sho (Ministry of Finance) (1978), pp. 120–1.

dollar accounts also showed deficits and were financed by the US aid. Thus the budget deficits caused by the national trading system were financed by two means – US aid and BOJ loans.

In May 1948, Ralph A. Young of the US Federal Reserve visited Japan. He made the following recommendations:

(a) The lack of a single and unified exchange rate is an important cause of inflation in Japan. The establishment of a single exchange rate will promote exports, a prerequisite for the economic independence of Japan.
(b) In order to maintain a single exchange rate, strong anti-inflationary policy is required; – a large cut in fiscal expenditures and increased tax revenues by reforming the tax system are essential.
(c) Borrowing by the Trade Fund Special Account from the Bank of Japan must be prohibited.
(d) The exchange rate of the yen must be set at a level that can maintain the current level of exports and possibly promote exports in the future. This exchange rate should induce high-cost industries to become more efficient and should cushion a possible surge of inflation for a few months following establishment of the exchange rate.

Based on these positions, he recommended a single yen–dollar exchange rate of 300 yen per dollar plus or minus 10 per cent.

Despite Young's report, SCAP opposed any hasty moves toward a single exchange rate because the resultant sharp increase in prices of imported goods and fall in exports could induce social unrest in Japan. However, because Washington hoped to reduce the cost of aiding Japan by encouraging economic independence, it instructed SCAP to establish a single yen exchange rate as soon as possible.

As a step in this direction, the Price Computing System was introduced in 1948. This was a quasi-multiple exchange rate system – for each category of exported goods, a minimum dollar price was set as well as a dollar–yen conversion rate. For goods sold at the minimum dollar price, the yen amount was determined as the product of this dollar price times conversion rate. For goods sold above the minimum price, a yen bonus of up to 25 per cent was paid to the exporter.

According to a Ministry of Finance (Okura-sho) estimate, in October 1948, the average exchange rate for exported goods was about

Table 5.5 Exchange rates for export commodities in late 1948: examples of price computing system rates (yen/dollar)

Agar (Japanese gelatin)	150
Sodium hydroxide	200
Rubber belts	250
Dried aquatic products	280
Pearls	300
Silk textiles	315
Woollen yarn	240–370
Fertilizers	390
Sewing needles	400
Explosives	420
Toys	500
Artificial flowers	500
Pencils	500
Cameras	500
Cast iron products	530
Radios	550
Phonographs	550
Printing ink	550
Ceramic ware	500–550
Flat glass	600

Note: Although cotton products were an important export item, imported raw cotton was processed by producers for a fee and ownership of the cotton was retained by the Japanese government. This seems to be the reason for not setting an exchange rate for cotton products.

Source: Okura-sho (Ministry of Finance) (1976), pp. 362–4.

350 yen per dollar, while that for imported goods was 150 yen. The exchange rates of exported goods varied heavily with the category of goods. For internationally competitive ones, the rate was set at 150 yen per dollar; for less competitive goods, it was as high as 600 yen per dollar (Table 5.5).

Anticipating the establishment of a single exchange rate, the Japanese government successively lowered yen prices of foreign currencies with respect to exported goods. In other words, the yen was appreciated. Under the Price Computing System, the weakest yen rate for exported goods was set at 450 yen per dollar after February 1949 and at 425 yen after April 1949. Also, the yen price of imported raw cotton was raised. However, the upward adjustment of yen prices of imported goods was grossly inadequate. When the single yen exchange rate was established at 360 yen per dollar in April 1949, increases of more than 100 per cent in the yen prices of imported goods was necessary.[8]

5.4.2 Implementation of the Dodge Line

In February 1949, the president of the Detroit Bank, Joseph M. Dodge, visited Japan as an Economic Adviser to SCAP. He recommended fundamental changes in fiscal and monetary policy, policies which came to be known as the Dodge Line and which were in step with Young's earlier recommendations. Dodge advocated immediate balancing of the budget by eliminating widespread subsidies. On 23 April 1949, SCAP prescribed a single and unified yen exchange rate of 360 yen per dollar, effective 25 April. As a result, export and import subsidies were eliminated. Dodge also criticized the Reconstruction Finance Bank as a source of inflation and directed the Japanese government to close it down. Instead, the government was directed to establish the 'US Aid Counterpart Fund (Mikaeri Shikin)', a new account to ensure that US aid to Japan was not used for subsidies but for constructive investment. The government was required to accumulate in this fund yen proceeds from imported goods purchased with the US aid. The public sector was streamlined as well: the national railway and telegraph and telephone systems were reorganized as public corporations (*kosha*) and each laid off 100 000 and 20 000 workers respectively (Nakamura, 1981, p. 166).

A balanced budget and termination of new loans from the Reconstruction Finance Bank (in October 1949) effectively halted the runaway growth of Bank of Japan notes. The annual growth rate declined from 62 per cent in 1948 to zero in 1949. In spite of sharp price increases in imported and producer goods, inflation was reduced dramatically. The effective consumer price index, which took account of black-market prices, rose 50 per cent year-to-year in March 1949 but posted a 9 per cent drop a year later. But production suffered as well, its growth rate falling from 48 per cent in March 1949 to zero in March 1950. Employment also declined. In the end, real GNP growth declined from 13 per cent in fiscal 1948 to 2 per cent in fiscal 1949.

Extremely tight macro policy and the elimination of subsidies reduced the gap between official and black-market prices. Seizing the deflationary opportunity, price controls on many goods were abolished between May 1949 and early 1950. By the end of 1950, the black-market prices of the remaining regulated consumer goods were only about 1.3 times official prices. For wholesale prices, they fell to about 1.2 times. By 1951, the gap virtually disappeared (Table 5.3). Thus while Dodge Line policy caused economic contraction, inflation was wiped out and the market economy greatly expanded.

5.4.3 Macro-economic Implications of the Dodge Line and Internal Convertibility of the Yen

In the late 1940s, the following reforms were essential to revive the market economy:

(a) Elimination of government subsidies for production, imports and exports. The elimination of subsidies on imports and exports was the other side of the coin to the establishment of a single, unified exchange rate.
(b) Elimination of price controls and rationing.
(c) Reduction in the Bank of Japan financing of budget deficits and Reconstruction Financing Bank loans to halt the increase in money supply and inflation.

Thus, the establishment of a single exchange rate was closely related to the recovery of internal convertibility of the yen. Prior to the recommendations of Young and Dodge, the Japanese government and SCAP both considered that cutting inflation through the reduction of budget deficits and the recovery of production was an important precondition for establishing a single yen exchange rate. However, Young and Dodge regarded the establishment of a single yen exchange rate as a key factor to eliminating budget deficits and consequent inflation. As we shall explain below, the judgement of Young and Dodge indeed proved correct.

The value of import and export subsidies in yen via the multiple exchange rate system was at least about 5 per cent of GNP in the late 1940s. That of the imported goods and services was about 10 per cent of GNP. Given that the introduction of the 360 yen single exchange rate led to a more than 100 per cent increase in the yen sales prices of imported goods, import subsidies in yen had been at least one-half the total value of imported goods and services. In addition as Table 5.6 shows, transfers from the US constituted about 5 per cent of Japan's GNP in the 1947–9 period. In other words, the Japanese government had to cover dollar deficits in the external transaction of goods and services amounting to about 5 per cent of GNP through external borrowings without US aid.

Table 5.6 Macro-economic indicators in postwar Japan

Fiscal year	*Nominal GNP ($100 mil)*	*Balance of payments transfer balance ($100 mil)*	*Balance of payments transfer (% of GNP)*	*Special military procurements ($100 mil)*	*Special military procurements (% of GNP)*	*Central government deficits (% of GNP)*
1946	62.5	1.95	3.12	0.00	0.00	13.9
1947	76.6	4.05	5.29	0.00	0.00	7.3
1948	92.6	4.62	4.99	0.19	0.21	6.1
1949	93.8	5.14	5.48	0.49	0.52	3.3
1950	109.6	4.29	3.91	0.63	0.57	-2.1
1951	151.2	1.71	1.13	6.24	4.13	1.7
1952	169.9	0.34	0.20	7.88	4.64	3.0
1953	196.8	0.21	0.11	8.03	4.08	0.3
1954	207.4	0.29	0.14	6.02	2.90	1.1
1955	228.8	0.22	0.10	5.05	2.21	1.5

Note: Nominal GNP in US dollars before 1949 is calculated by converting nominal GNP in yen with an estimated purchasing power parity exchange rate from GNP deflators of Japan and the US.

(GNP in $) = (GNP in ¥) * US deflator/(JP deflator * 360)

In effect, ¥360/$ at 1949 is used as a base.

On the yen side, the Japanese government was running huge deficits. The increase in the nominal debt of the central government was 14 per cent of GNP in 1946 and 6–7 per cent in 1947 and 1948 (Table 5.6). However, the debt–GNP ratio of the central government was declining (Table 5.7), indicating the huge 'inflation tax' on national debt. The US wanted to reduce aid to Japan during this period. If both the aid from the US and the 'inflation tax' had disappeared, the budget deficits of the Japanese government would have reached almost 10 per cent of GNP. Therefore, the elimination of trade subsidies via a single exchange rate and the substitution of explicit taxation for the inflation tax were indispensable for balancing the budget and wiping out inflation. Even if US aid continued, it was necessary to reduce budget deficits by at least 6–7 per cent of GNP. In fact, the Dodge Line dictated that Japan should eliminate trade subsidies and set aside yen proceeds from aid for investment purposes (US Aid Counterpart Fund). By increasing tax revenues, yen budgets could be balanced.

By current macro policy standards, the Dodge Line was an extremely restrictive package of fiscal and monetary policy. Under the Line, Japan could carry out painful adjustment and eliminate price

Table 5.7 Japan's GNP and government debts

CY: Calendar year *FY: Fiscal year*		*Nominal GNP (¥100 mil)*	*Real GNP (¥1 mil)*	*GNP deflator (1934–6=1.0)*	*Government debts (¥100 mil) (end of FY)*	*Debt (% of GNP)*
CY	1943	638	21351	2.99	851	133.4
	1944	745	20634	3.61	1520	204.0
	1945	n.a.	n.a.	n.a.	1995	n.a.
FY	1946	4740	11594	40.9	2653	56.0
	1947	13087	12573	104.1	3606	27.6
	1948	26661	14211	187.6	5244	19.7
	1949	33752	14524	232.4	6373	18.9
	1950	39467	16115	244.9	5540	14.0
	1951	54442	18207	298.9	6455	11.9
	1952	61180	20238	302.3	8267	13.5
	1953	70848	21657	327.2	8511	12.0
	1954	74657	22456	332.5	9327	12.5
	1955	82355	24967	329.9	10572	12.8

Source: Okura-sho (Ministry of Finance) (1978), pp. 27–8, 302.

controls and rationing. At the same time, the policies induced severe recession, increased unsold inventories and under-employment, and heightened social tension.

The recession was cut short by the outbreak of the Korean War in June 1950. While US aid sharply declined after 1951, the surge in US military procurements amounted to 4–5 per cent of GNP in 1951–3 (Table 5.6). The effect of the tight macro policy of the Dodge Line was more than offset by the military procurements and production entered steady growth.

5.5 FOREIGN EXCHANGE CONTROL SYSTEM AFTER THE DODGE LINE

The yen regained internal convertibility during the 1950–1 period through implementation of the Dodge Line. International trade was also denationalized. However, external current transactions remained tightly regulated. Below, we review the exchange control system after the implementation of the Dodge Line, relying heavily on Fukao (1990).

In March 1949, the administration of overseas transaction controls and foreign exchange reserves was transferred from SCAP to the Foreign Exchange Control Board (Gaikoku Kawase Kanri Iinkai), which was established as part of the Japanese government. That April, a unified exchange rate of ¥360/US$ was also established. The Foreign Exchange Control Board was abolished in 1952, with responsibility for foreign exchange reserves and control being transferred to the Ministry of Finance. Responsibility for foreign trade was returned to the private sector for exports in December 1949, and for imports in January 1950.

Parallel to this change was the reorganization of foreign exchange controls. In December 1949, the Foreign Exchange and Foreign Trade Control Law (Gaikoku Kawase oyobi Gaikoku Boeki Kanri-ho) was promulgated (also known as the 'old' Foreign Exchange Law, in effect until its complete overhaul in December 1980). Under this 1949 law, foreign exchange transactions were generally prohibited with exceptions granted only according to directives and notifications by government ministries. Under this system, while exports could be carried out relatively freely, imports of goods and services and international financial transactions were heavily regulated. A policy of foreign exchange concentration was adopted which, in principle, forbade the holding of foreign exchange by private parties (this system was introduced in June 1950 and continued in modified form until May 1972). Residents who obtained foreign exchange were required immediately to sell it to the monetary authorities through authorized 'foreign exchange banks'.

At first, exchange rates between clients and banks as well as those between banks and government were fixed, meaning that all foreign exchange holdings were concentrated in the government at the official rate. This system obviously left no room for a foreign exchange market. In June 1952, however, domestic foreign exchange banks were newly permitted to hold foreign exchange deposits in overseas banks up to certain limits. The settlement of export and import transactions was carried out through these accounts (this was a shift to concentration only of banks' net foreign exchange balances rather than gross balances).

Together with these developments, the Tokyo foreign exchange market was reopened as the venue for foreign exchange banks to adjust their overall foreign exchange balances. The rate of exchange between the government and foreign exchange banks was set at ¥360.35/US$ for sales and ¥359.65/US$ for purchases (from the viewpoint of the government). This very narrow ¥0.70 differential was also maintained for interbank transactions, and amounts transacted were very, very small.[9] At this time, the government only engaged in passive transactions at the official rate and did not actively intervene in the market.

Once private parties were permitted to engage in exports and imports, it was possible for rather large sums of money to move across borders by varying the time of payment for imports and receipt of proceeds from exports. In order to control such leads and lags, a regulation was promulgated in November 1950 to set time limits on the settlement of import and export proceeds. This system was gradually relaxed over time.

The foreign exchange holdings that the government built up under this system were allocated for foreign payments on a quarterly basis starting in January 1951 through the Foreign Exchange Budget System (semi annual basis from fiscal 1952 and abolished in April 1964; see Appendix A for details). The conversion of yen held by non-Japanese into foreign exchange was severely restricted so that the holding of yen-dominated assets by non-residents (such as yen cash and deposits) was very limited. In May 1950, the Foreign Investment Law (Gaishi-ho) was adopted which regulated inward investment in forms such as direct investment and the introduction of technology (this law was abolished in 1980 and related provisions incorporated in the New Foreign Exchange Law (Shin Gaikoku Kawase Kanri-ho) of 1980).

Under these circumstances, private sector capital movements were effectively prohibited. Moreover, foreign monetary authorities held almost no yen in their foreign exchange reserves because of its extremely limited convertibility. Thus, current account imbalances were almost entirely financed by changes in Japan's official foreign exchange reserves.

Exports were freely allowed under this exchange control system. However, it was necessary to obtain a special allocation from the foreign exchange budget to import foreign goods. In this respect, the yen was not convertible for current transactions. As Japan's economy grew, use of the foreign exchange budget was gradually liberalized. Yet the yen did not achieve convertibility for current external transactions until 1964, when Japan became an IMF Article VIII country and abolished the Foreign Exchange Budget System.

APPENDIX A: THE MECHANISM OF FOREIGN EXCHANGE BUDGET SYSTEM

The government first estimated foreign exchange obtained from exports and special military procurements during the next budget period, which was then allocated to meet estimated demand for imports. These estimates were made for each category of goods and for each currency region. Estimates for each currency region were necessary because of the inconvertibility among currencies (e.g. the US dollar and British pound).

There were two allocation mechanisms for individual importers under the Fund Allocation System, foreign exchange was allocated to each importer depending on its past imports, exports, and other factors. Under the Semi-Automatic Approval System, foreign exchange was allocated following application by importers so long as budgeted funds remained. In order to avoid speculative applications for foreign exchange, importers applying had to put up bonds, which were confiscated if an importer failed to import goods within a specified period. The bond level required in the Semi-Automatic Allocation System was high, reaching 15 to 20 per cent of proposed imports in cash.

Until 1952, budgets were generous due to the high level of special procurements for the Korean War by the US military. But in 1954 and in 1955, budgets were tight and imports restricted. The Foreign Exchange Budget System changed its character after this period (Okura-sho, 1976, p. 263). Gradually, the allocation system came to be manipulated to protect Japanese Industries from foreign competition.

APPENDIX B: A CHRONOLOGY OF MAJOR IMMEDIATE POSTWAR EVENTS RELATED TO STABILIZATION AND INTERNATIONAL TRANSACTIONS

1945	August	End of the Second World War.
1946	February	Introduction of 'Emergency Measures for the Economic Crisis' (including freeze on bank deposits).
	August	Establishment of Economic Stabilization Board.
	December	Introduction of Priority Production System.
1947	January	Establishment of Reconstruction Finance Bank.
	August	Limited resumption of private trade.
1948	May	Ralph Young visits Japan.
1949	February	Joseph Dodge visits Japan.
	March	Declaration of Dodge's economic policy for Japan, the 'Dodge Line'.
		Establishment of FECB [Foreign Exchange Control Board (transfer of international transactions and foreign reserve management from SCAP to FECB)].
	April	Establishment of single Y360/$ rate by FECB.
	November	Permission of foreign exchange operation granted to 11 Japanese banks.
	December	Introduction of Foreign Exchange and Foreign Trade Control Law.

		Liberalization of private sector exports. Ten foreign exchange banks granted permission to engage in foreign exchange operations.
1950	January	Introduction of Foreign Exchange Budget (FEB). Liberalization of private sector imports subject to budget constraints under FEB.
	June	Outbreak of Korean War. Introduction of foreign exchange concentration (external claims acquired by residents must be sold to foreign exchange banks at fixed official rate).
1952	January	Liquidation of Reconstruction Finance Bank.
	April	Permission to have dollar holdings granted to foreign exchange banks.
	May	Admission of Japan to the IMF and World Bank.
	July	Tokyo foreign exchange market re-opened.
	August	Abolition of FECB and transfer of its activities to the Ministry of Finance.
1953	February	Foreign exchange banks granted permission to have sterling pound holdings.

Notes

1. Fukao (1990) reviews Japan's history of exchange controls and effects on the balance of payments.
2. Our account of general postwar economic conditions draws from Kanamori (1990), Nakamura (1981), and Nakamura (ed.) (1989).
3. See Bank of Japan (1983), pp. 189–95.
4. See Nakamura (1980), pp. 148–9, 158–9.
5. For example, while the government guaranteed 13 590 yen per metric ton to producers of pig iron, it sold at 3600 yen, the difference of 9990 yen being subsidized by the government.
6. Although the March 1947 law explicitly prohibited issue of long-term government bonds, the government continued to issue short-term bills. Special government accounts were also running deficits.
7. See Bank of Japan, Institute for Monetary and Economic Studies (1983), pp. 318–26.
8. *Ibid*, pp. 338–9.
9. In January 1953, the band was widened from ¥0.70 to ¥1.60, with limits of ¥360.80 and ¥359.20. In September 1959, it was widened again to 0.5 per cent above/below IMF parity.

References

Bank of Japan (1985) *Nihon Ginko Hyakunen-shi* (One Hundred-year History of the Bank of Japan), vol. 5 (Tokyo: Toyo Keizai Shinpo-sha).

Bank of Japan, Institute for Monetary and Economic Studies (1983) *Nihon Kin'yu-shi Shiryo, Showa Zokuhen*, vol. 13 (Tokyo: Okura-sho Insatsu-kyoku).

Fukao, Mitsuhiro (1990) 'Liberalization of Japan's Foreign Exchange Controls and Structural Changes in the Balance of Payments', *Bank of Japan Monetary and Economic Studies*, vol. 8, no. 2.

Inuta, Akira (1981) 'Wagakuni Sengo no Gaikoku Kawase Kanri to Gaishi Kisei: Dai 2-sho' (The Exchange Control System and Regulations on Direct Investment into Japan After the War: chapter 2, Foreign Exchange Budget System), in *Keizai Ronshu*, vol. 7, no. 1–2 (Tokyo: Toyo Daigaku Keizai Kenkyu-kai).

Kanamori, Hisao (1990) 'Sengo-Keizai no Gaikan' (Overview of the Postwar Economy), in *Sairon Keizai Hakusho: Sengo Keizai no Kiseki*, ed. by Hisao Kanamori (Tokyo: Chuo Keizai-sha).

McKinnon, Ronald (1979) *Money in International Exchange* (New York and Oxford: Oxford University Press).

Okura-sho (Ministry of Finance) (1976) *Showa Zaisei-shi* (The Fiscal History of the Showa Era), vol. 15 (Tokyo: Toyo Keizai Shinpo-sha).

Okura-sho (Ministry of Finance) (1978) *Showa Zaisei-shi* (The Fiscal History of the Showa Era), vol. 19 (Tokyo: Toyo Keizai Shinpo-sha).

Nakamura, Takafusa (1981) *Nihon Keizai: Sono Seicho to Kozo* (The Japanese Economy: Its Growth and Structure) (Tokyo: University of Tokyo Press). Translated as *The Postwar Japanese Economy* (Tokyo: University of Tokyo Press, 1981).

Nakamura, Takafusa (ed.) (1989) *Nihon Keizai-shi* (Japanese Economic History), vol. 7 (Tokyo: Iwanami Shoten).

Part II

Economic Reform After The War

6 Economic Effects of the Anti-Monopoly and other Deconcentration Policies in Postwar Japan

Yoshiro Miwa

6.1 INTRODUCTION

The purpose of this chapter is to identify the effects on the Japanese economy of a series of postwar reform policies, especially the 'Deconcentration Policies'. These were executed in Occupied Japan under the force and supervision of the Allied Powers, following the end of the Second World War in August 1945. My main and ultimate focus is to evaluate their efficacy as development policies and their transferability to other countries. In order to do this, I must of course also provide an overview of the nature of these policies.

I discuss two sets of deconcentration policies. The first is 'Zaibatsu Dissolution (Zaibatsu Kaitai)', and other related policy interventions. These include (a) the Zaibatsu Dissolution, which included the dissolution of the Zaibatsu holding companies, the public sale of their stock holdings and the elimination of interlocking directorships, (b) the Law for the Elimination of Excessive Concentration of Economic Power (Kado Keizairyoku Shuchu Haijo-ho; hereafter, the Excessive Concentration Law), (c) the Economic Purge, and (d) the Enterprise Reconstruction and Reorganization Law (Kigyo Saiken Seibi-ho) and the Financial Institutions Reconstruction and Reorganization Law (Kin'yu Kikan Saiken Seibi-ho).

The second is the Anti-Monopoly Law (Dokusen Kinshi-ho) of 1947 and the enforcement of it and related policies. The common view is that the Zaibatsu Dissolution policies had a tremendous impact, while the Anti-Monopoly Law was introduced in order to maintain their long-run effect. However, as I will discuss below, even though the law has some articles of this character (for example, article 9 which prohibits the establishment of holding companies), its fundamental character is quite different and it should be treated separately.

There is increased interest worldwide in Japan's postwar reforms, especially the Deconcentration Policies and other economic reforms. I believe this interest has two sources. First, given Japan's industrial success, many people are interested in what underlay this growth and how it was attained. What roles were played by the government? Can we find any lessons for the developing economies? In the preceding periods there was also wide interest in Japanese industrial policy, which presupposed that it was one of the main engines of industrial success. However, today the standard view is that industrial policy's contribution, if any, was not so large. Instead it played a supporting role, while the main engines and mechanism were large numbers of active and competitive firms operating in fiercely competitive markets. From this perspective, interest centres on the relationship between the economic reforms and the emergence of active firms and competitive markets.

Second, in addition to its success in industrialization, the Japanese economy experienced sustained growth at a then historically unprecedented rate, which started just after the 15-year period of war and Occupation. During the war, production, sales, materials allocation, prices and investment were all under the control of the government. Many firms and industries were forced to merge and reorganize, under what is sometimes called the 'planification' (*keikakuka*) of the economy. Ultimately, much production capacity was destroyed. In the postwar period the character of government controls changed greatly during the transition period from the war economy to the normal peacetime economy. Rapid growth began just after this brief period of confusion, recovery and revitalization. It is the challenge of going as speedily and smoothly as possible from a 'socialist' command economy to a market economy that motivates this research project.

As mentioned above, the focus of interest and research on Japanese industrial policy has changed greatly. As we will see below, the same changes ought to occur in examining Japan's postwar economic reforms. To date most research on this period has been conducted by historians (especially economic historians) and political scientists. In my view there is a clear tendency to accept without question the facts and interpretations found in the memories and subsequent testimonies of those who were 'on the spot' during the reforms.[1] Various kinds of material are now available and cool and scientific discussion and assessment are now possible. Therefore, what follows is not a mere survey of previous research, because my perspective is fundamentally different from the dominant view.

6.2 THE CHARACTER OF THE PROBLEMS TO BE DISCUSSED

The task of identifying and evaluating the impact of a policy is seldom easy. The Deconcentration Policies were executed in a period of transition. Not only was there the recovery from wartime destruction, but at the same time there were other kinds of economic reforms together with political and cultural changes. In such a period of major change, it is quite difficult, indeed almost unimaginably difficult, to identify the impact of a single policy.

Even when we limit our attention to economic aspects, so many events took place in this period that the task of identification is still not easy. For example, the controls over production, materials allocation, prices, investment, employment and financial funds were abolished step by step. Similarly, the production capacity and human resources devoted to the war itself and to war-related production were freed up and could be used to enter new markets. Other economic reforms, such as the Farm Landholding Reforms and Labour Relations Reforms (hereafter, Land Reform and Labour Reform, respectively) were implemented.

Ideally, the task of identification can be accomplished by finding the deviations between the actual state of affairs and the hypothetical state without the policy actions. The difficulty lies in how to model such a state, that is, what the Japanese economy would have looked like in 1955 without the Deconcentration Policies.

One readily conceivable scenario is that the traditional type of Zaibatsu would not have survived the rapidly changing period, even had the Deconcentration Policies not been executed. Therefore, it may not be appropriate to conclude that, just because many Zaibatsu disappeared, it was due to these policies. Many make such illogical conclusions, in ignorance of the *post hoc*, *ergo propter hoc* fallacy.

I would thus like to caution readers on the following three points. First, I will limit my attention to the identification of 'policy' effects. Even if we find the disappearance of Zaibatsu, changes in the structure of stock holdings and shifts in the composition and characteristics of boards of directors, these may not all be due to policy actions.

Second, I will inevitably try to identify the effects of policies one by one. These will include the Zaibatsu Dissolution, the Excessive Concentration Law, the Economic Purge and the introduction of the Anti-Monopoly Law. But we should pay attention to the possibility that summing up the effect of each policy separately may not provide an appropriate assessment of the total effect of postwar reform. The fact that a series of reforms were executed simultaneously in such a transition period might play an important role. We should also keep in mind the possibility that important variables are missing, such as intellectual atmosphere and/or social tension.[2]

Third, the following discussion will not try to look directly for lessons to help the former 'centrally' planned economies tide over the difficulties of their transition period. The policies in Japan were not implemented with that purpose in mind. I will not include these aspects in the standards of policy evaluation, but will try to evaluate policies in terms of their own stated goals.

An additional difficulty in identifying the impact of a policy is that we may focus our sights too narrowly. Economic agents are mutually interdependent, and the effects of changes in policy variables appear in so many areas that we cannot take all the effects into account. As is usual, we must choose to limit our span before we begin, in selecting the economic variables on which our policy evaluation will depend. In my view, most of the previous research on the postwar economic reforms did not choose or clearly state their criteria for evaluation. I thus trace below the general criteria utilized by prior studies, and then present my own standards. While I begin with the postwar Deconcentration Policies (and, within those, the Zaibatsu Dissolution), all related policies will be evaluated along the same line.

At the beginning of the Japanese Occupation, General MacArthur was instructed that, under US policy, 'you will require . . . to submit, for approval by you, plans for dissolving large Japanese industrial and banking combines or other large concentrations of private business control'.[3] We can see the typical view underlying the Zaibatsu Dissolution policies in the following statement of Corwin D. Edwards, the Head of the State-War Mission on Japanese Combines, which submitted its report to the two departments in March 1946. (Note that this was expressed in 1964 for another occasion).

> A big firm has advantages over a smaller rival just because it is big. Money is power. A big firm can outbid, outspend, and outlose a small firm. It can advertise more intensively, do more intensive and

extensive research, buy up inventions of others, defend its legal rights or alleged rights more thoroughly, bid higher for scarce resources, acquire the best locations and the best technicians and executives. If it overdoes its expenditures, it can absorb losses that would bankrupt a small rival.[4]

So far as the objectives of the Deconcentration Policies were of this kind, the standards for policy evaluation should be as follows. For example:

(a) How many and what kinds of Zaibatsu were listed up and analysed, and how many were actually dissolved? How were these dissolution decisions made, and what was the standard for discrimination?
(b) What was the final extent of 'Dissolution', and was this satisfactory? For example, how did the stock holding structure change? How about interlocking directorships? Did the selection system for directors change? Did the manner and process of corporate decision-making change?
(c) As a symbolic and easier way to check (b) above, there are many reports that count the number of purged executives (especially Zaibatsu appointees), and calculate the value of shares disposed of through the Holding Company Liquidation Commission (Mochikabu Gaisha Seiri-iinkai: HCLC), Fair Trade Commission (Kosei Torihiki-iinkai FTC) and other institutions. (See Table 6.2, p. 141.)

As can be easily seen, it is almost impossible to draw from these studies information that can be used to directly answer questions such as the extent and nature of the relationship between these Deconcentration Policies and postwar economic growth. (For a more detailed discussion, see below.)

In addition, the Deconcentration Policies, together with the Land and Labour Reforms, were executed under the almost irresistible slogans of 'democratization' (*minshuka*) and 'modernization' (*kindaika*). This had the effect of prohibiting or at least discouraging attempts to question the desirability of these policies. Even efforts to identify the impact of each policy were discouraged, and it is not too extreme to say that such attempts were seen as challenges to taboos. Only recently have people begun to have an interest in this period, and researchers begun to seek factors that might explain the rapid growth of the following period.[5] Still, the initial attempts to dispassionately identify and evaluate the relation between these policies and economic growth leads us to question their efficacy.

Let me refer to Masamura (1985) for a concrete example. He begins his section on Zaibatsu Dissolution and the Anti-Monopoly Law with the following statement:

> Zaibatsu Dissolution and the policy for the Elimination of Excessive Concentration of Economic Power had a great impact on the economic system of postwar Japan. (p. 90)

The evaluation that follows deserves our attention:

> When the Occupation was over, some of the dissolved firms reunited and managers of some of ex-Zaibatsu firms formed their own clubs (presidents' clubs, *shacho-kai*). Banks that had been exempt from dissolution and revived general trading companies (*sogo shosha*) began to function as the centers of industrial groups (*kigyo shudan*), in which there are many subordinate 'keiretsu' firms.
>
> However, the Occupation policies such as the Zaibatsu Dissolution, the Excessive Concentration Law, the Anti-Monopoly Law and the Economic Purge greatly changed the industrial organization of Japan, along with the constitution and character of Japanese firms. These reforms destroyed the monopolistic and exclusive character of dominant firms, and thus provided the basis for the development of competition. All of these worked as stimuli for the rapid growth of the Japanese economy. Moreover, in return, the high rate of growth and the speedy change in industrial structure by themselves raised the barrier to the revival and reinforcement of their former monopolistic and exclusive character. (p. 99)

The important points for us to clarify are the empirical grounds for Masamura's contention about the nature of industrial organization and corporate behaviour. On what grounds do his judgements depend? What aspects of change does he find significant? How important do the effects appear to him? Among the series of reforms, which in his judgement are the most important? We cannot find satisfactory answers to such questions in Masamura's study.

6.3 STANDARDS OF EVALUATION

It is impossible to take on all these questions in a short paper. The focus of the following sections is thus of necessity limited to one specific industrial group, industrial and consumer machinery. I am not so bold as to claim that this provides an overall evaluation of the effects of the Deconcentration Policies.[6]

The machinery industries were selected for two reasons. First, the most visible side of Japan's postwar success is in machinery. This is true in terms of productivity increases, weight in GNP and importance as exports. Therefore, it is natural to investigate these industries first when we try to evaluate the importance of the Deconcentration Policies. Within machinery, different actors came upon the main stage successively, (a) starting with electric fans, sewing machines and binoculars, (b) then cameras, radio receivers, monochrome TVs, and bicycles, clocks and watches, (c) or motorcycles and three-wheeled vehicles, ships, (d) or passenger cars, various kinds of electrical machinery and industrial machinery. Furthermore, the roles played by these main actors changed rapidly from scene to scene. (Part of this history can be seen in Table 6.1).

Second, for the first 25 years, from the era of reforms until around 1970, Japan always suffered from a foreign currency shortage.[7] This strictly limited the scope and conditioned the nature of economic policies, in terms not only of trade policies but also of monetary and fiscal policies. Since imports, especially of raw materials and energy, are crucial for the Japanese economy, foreign currency shortages and the economic policies to counter them have deeply influenced the activities of Japanese firms. For this reason, exporting industries have held a special place, and machinery has been the star performer. It is hardly an exaggeration to say that, without the increased export of machinery, Japan would not have been able to import the materials and energy that were necessary for her survival and economic development.[8]

What was the effect of the Deconcentration Policies on the successful development and remarkable performance of these industries? Let me state my conclusion in advance. In all the machinery industries, competition has been fierce. One of the main objectives of so-called 'industrial policy' at the earlier stage was to limit or cool down competition, which government officials were fond of calling excessive competition (*kato kyoso*). As the standard view of industrial organization suggests (and this was in fact the case), such a

Table 6.1 Production of selected goods, 1935–53

Year/Unit	*Sewing machines*	*Electric fans*	*Radios*	*Ships (tons)*	*Three-wheel automobiles*	*Binoculars*	*Bicycles*	*Cameras*	*Clocks and watches*
1935	12 301	43 562	153 974	174 067	9 837	81 700	903 000	95 326	4 183 000
1936	40 924	42 228	427 287	274 784	12 557	79 200	1 055 000	154 648	4 864 000
1937	53 133	46 918	406 753	483 548	15 233	99 500	1 090 000	178 321	5 114 000
1938	104 204	43 575	604 463	464 679	10 450	45 600	1 080 000	187 569	3 814 000
1939	132 997	58 302	740 356	391 679	7 953	62 500	950 000	205 522	3 384 000
1940	154 402	64 780	852 903	401 866	8 113	60 000	1 245 000	218 659	3 424 000
1941	142 317	55 828	917 001	466 249	4 503	56 400	185 000	203 011	2 935 000
1942	51 129	41 200	841 301	547 051	3 721	35 200	181 000	133 854	1 582 000
1943	25 573	45 240	741 816	1 030 601	2 259	36 100	70 000	57 588	808 000
1944	16 047	2 360	262 372	2 198 790	1 338	60 000	65 000	29 548	413 000
1945	2 150	1 240	87 529	632 005	686	14 400	20 000	13 082	98 000
1946	36 912	66 282	672 676	143 860	3 647	37 836	—	24 145	714 000
1947	133 949	74 329	772 428	83 565	7 432	31 158	—	51 772	1 599 000
1948	165 726	72 167	769 730	162 898	16 852	47 623	337 000	53 016	2 404 000
1949	274 468	95 703	702 327	163 980	26 727	97 356	552 000	83 243	3 051 000
1950	493 038	118 804	281 602	229 761	35 503	115 970	981 000	117 481	2 331 000
1951	1 030 289	173 903	399 943	454 149	43 717	176 180	987 000	213 840	3 050 000
1952	1 260 293	290 879	929 126	627 064	62 262	179 510	1 019 000	357 918	3 803 000
1953	1 318 059	434 585	1 391 031	521 759	98 405	212 704	1 184 000	663 484	4 673 000

Source: Tsusho Sangyo-sho (Ministry of International Trade and Industry), *Kokogyo Seisan Shisu* (Production Indexes of Mining and Manufacturing Industries), 1955.

competitive state was the result of the basic situation of these industries, with large numbers of firms and low barriers to new entry. We cannot find any direct links between the Deconcentration Policies and an environment favoring competition in these industries, with rare exceptions. We therefore must search for other factors if we wish to explain Japan's industrial success.

6.4 A BRIEF HISTORY OF DECONCENTRATION POLICIES

Here I provide a brief overview of the various Deconcentration Policies. I will not detail the history of the specific kind of measures adopted, the time schedule of their execution, the conflicts of interests and controversies that arose in the process, or how and why policy changed to begin with. Other studies[9] do this well, while space here is limited. I thus limit myself to providing a brief chronology of the Deconcentration Policies, to giving selected data that show or suggest the magnitude of the policy effects, and to offering interpretations only as necessary for subsequent sections.

Midway through the Occupation period, there was a fundamental and complete change in the objectives of Occupation policy, reflecting the beginning of the Cold War.

15 August 1945	End of the war
March 1947	Truman Doctrine proclaimed
July 1947	Beginning of Marshall Plan
28 April 1952	End of the Occupation

The influence of changes in US foreign policy were clearly reflected in Occupation policies by the end of 1947. The basic objectives of the Occupation policies before this so-called 'reverse course' is set forth in the 'Basic Directives for Post-Surrender Military Government in Japan Proper' dated 3 November 1945. The section entitled 'Democratization of Japanese Economic Institutions' decrees that the Occupation under General MacArthur will 'require the Japanese to establish a public agency responsible for reorganizing Japanese business. . . . You will require this agency to submit, for approval by you, plans for dissolving large Japanese industrial and banking combines or other concentrations of private business control.'

The change in the policy objectives is clearly reflected in shifts in reparation policies, which aimed initially at the permanent elimination of Japanese production capacity along with reparations to the Philippines and elsewhere.

Reparation Policies

6 December 1945	Interim Reparation Policy – Pauley Report (Report of the United States Reparation Mission), which suggests the Immediate [Reparation] Programme.
18 February 1947	Report on Japanese Reparations (First Strike Report[10]), whose first point is that 'the Committee recommends that the present reparation program in respect to plant removals be abandoned'.
4 April 1947	Interim Directive Regarding Advance Transfers of Japanese Reparations.
26 February 1948	Second Strike Report.
26 April 1948	Report on the Economic Prospects of Japan and Korea: Measures Required to Improve Them – Johnston Report (this committee is sometimes referred to as the 'Draper Mission'). It states that 'the United States should now assist the recovery of Japan. . . . In our opinion, the capacity that can be spared without affecting Japan's useful peacetime productivity is not great. It is most important that the present uncertainty be removed and the reparation issue finally settled.'
6 May 1949	National Security Council Recommendations with Respect to US Policy toward Japan, which states, 'it should be the policy of the United States Government that current transfer of reparations under unilateral US directives should be terminated'.

Thus, the US's changing foreign policy was reflected only gradually in its Occupation policy, amidst profound conflicts of opinion between Washington and Tokyo.

Let us now turn to Deconcentration Policies.

Zaibatsu Dissolution and the Excessive Concentration Law

6 November 1945	Following the 'Basic Directives', the establishment of the public agency responsible for reorganizing Japanese business is ordered.
March 1946	Edwards Report (on policy towards the Zaibatsu) issued, which proposes that 'the larger Japanese business enterprises be systematically surveyed in order to make sure that all the zaibatsu have been identified and subjected to the programme for ending zaibatsu power'.[11]
12 May 1946	'Policy on Excessive Concentrations of Economic Power in Japan', known as FEC-230 (Far Eastern Commission 230), which declares that 'the over-all objective of occupation policy in dealing with excessive concentration of economic power in Japan should be to destroy such concentrations as may now exist, and to prevent the future creation of new concentrations. Especial care should be taken to avoid the futile gesture of destroying one Zaibatsu class only to create another; a drastic change in the nature as well as the identity of the groups controlling Japanese industry and finance should therefore be effected.'
August 1946	The Holding Company Liquidation Commission was established and began its work. From the first the 'Big Four' Zaibatsu and Fuji Industries (Fuji Sangyo) were designated; the number of the companies on the target list amounted to 83 by July 1947.
July 1947	The Dissolution of Trading Companies – Mitsui Trading Co. and Mitsubishi Trading Co.
6 September 1947	'Kauffman Report' (Report on Conditions in Japan as of 6 September 1947), which introduces the contents of the then-confidential FEC-230. The essence of this report was published in *Newsweek* that December.
December 1947	Law for the Elimination of Excessive Concentration of Economic Power enacted. The

	number of companies on the Designation List was 325 by February 1948.
6 January 1948	Royall, the Secretary of the US Army, makes a speech 'On American Policy Towards Japan', which symbolically reveals the reverse-course policy change. This is reflected in the McCoy Statement at the Far Eastern Commission meeting on 21 January.[12]
1 May 1948	Beginning of the removal of companies from the 'Designation List'.
4 May 1948	The Deconcentration Review Board headed by Roy S. Campbell comes to Japan. Its Initial Report was submitted to the Department of the Army on November 3.
December 1948–January 1950	Of the 18 companies still remaining on the List, 11 are ordered to reorganize.

Anti-Monopoly Law and Enterprise Reconstruction and Reorganization Law

19 October 1946	The Japanese Diet passes the 'Law on Special Measures for Wartime Compensation' (Senji Hosho Tokubetsu Sochi-ho), which in effect cancels war-related debts owned by the government and puts almost all major corporations in Japan into a state of insolvency or near-insolvency. To prevent bankruptcies, at the same time the Enterprise Reconstruction and Reorganization Law and the Financial Institutions Reconstruction and Reorganization Law are enacted.
July 1947	Anti-Monopoly Law introduced.

Although these laws were not part of the Deconcentration Policies, the Supreme Commander for the Allied Powers (SCAP) began to use them and in 19 May 1947 listed 'the Standards of Economic Reorganization'. The Excessive Concentration Law was planned as a continuation and there is the view that, after removing firms from its Designation List, some SCAP members still tried to force through additional reorganizations by using the Enterprise Reconstruction and Reorganization Law.[13] They were unsuccessful.

To answer fully the question of the economic consequences of the

Table 6.2 Summary of the deconcentration policy actions

Desposition of Holding Companies		
Outright dissolution	16	
Dissolution with reorganization	26	
Reorganization without dissolution	11	
Untouched	30	
Stock Dispersal Programme – Antitrust and other Programmes		
Antitrust:		
Holding Company Liquidation Commission (proceeds from sale)	¥8.3 billion	
Fair Trade Commission (paid up value)	¥1.3 billion	
Other Programmes:		
Finance Ministry (Capital Levy Tax, proceeds from sale)	¥1.7 billion	
Closed Institutions Liquidation Commission (proceeds from asset sales)	¥3.1 billion	
Personnel Programmes		
Economic purge	1535	executives
Zaibatsu appointees	40	
Total	1575	
Break-up of 'Excessive Concentration'		
Companies split	11	
Companies where only individual plants or shareholding in other companies was affected	7(*)	
Total	18(*)	

Source: Hadley, Eleanor M.; *Antitrust in Japan* Copyright © 1970 by Princeton University Press. Reprinted / reproduced by permission of Princeton University Press.

* Hadley (1970) has 8 and 19, but 7 and 18 is correct. See Ministry of Finance (1981, pp. 554-61).

Deconcentration Policies is almost impossible. Here we simply quote the table of Hadley (1970, p. 443), which summarizes the policy actions. As should be obvious, the final results are very modest compared with the initial targets, or relative to the size of the economy.

6.5 EVALUATION OF THE ECONOMIC EFFECTS

It is not easy to find cases where the Deconcentration Policies outlined above had a direct and clearly identifiable impact on the machinery industries. In principle, for these policies to have had a significant positive impact, we would need to find changes in one or more of the following:

(a) Did the policies increase the number of firms in each industry? If yes, did this increase serve to strengthen competition?
(b) Did the policies lower the barriers to new entry? If yes, did this effect work as a stimulus to fierce competition?
(c) Did the policies have any other noticeable effects favorable for competition, for example, in the speed of diffusion of technology or in the availability of financing?
(d) In addition to a direct impact on market structure, did these policies change the basic conditions that underlay the market structure, for example, by increasing demand or changing the cost of inputs? Alternatively, did they affect the behaviour of firms in these industries?

A quick examination of the individual policies suggests there was no significant positive impact.

Zaibatsu Dissolution The measures adopted in the name of Zaibatsu Dissolution have as their common character a focus on interindustry relations, not on intraindustry ones. For example, the dissolution of 'Zaibatsu' holding companies, the consequent changes in the stock ownership structures, changes in the way of selecting top management, and the elimination of interlocking directorships in fact all had this character. Therefore, Zaibatsu Dissolution did not greatly contribute to the formation of competitive markets in these industries. The only possible exception, if any, is the prohibition of using the three Zaibatsu names (Mitsui, Mitsubishi, Sumitomo) for a short period, which might have lessened the reputational advantages of established firms.[14]

The Law for the Elimination of Excessive Concentration of Economic Power This had a strong impact in several industries, such as steel, pulp and paper, general trading companies (*sogo shosha*) and beer brewing. However, in machinery industries, shipbuilding is the only possible exception, as the largest firm, Mitsubishi Heavy Industries Ltd (Mitsubishi Jukogyo), was split into three firms. Therefore, the Excessive Concentration Law did not serve greatly to aid the formation of competitive markets in machinery, with the possible exception of shipbuilding. (I will return to that case below.)

The Enterprise Reconstruction and Reorganization Law The execution of this law as a part of the Deconcentration Policies had limited impact, as noted above, and the overall impact was similar to that of the Excessive Concentration Law.

The Economic Purge It is not easy to identify and evaluate the impact of the changes of top management caused by the Economic Purge. It is widely held that the Purge lowered the age of managing officers and rejuvenated the management of firms, contributing greatly to the formation of competitive markets. But to make this argument persuasive, we must clear many hurdles, such as whether the number of purged officials was large enough to cause the alleged effects, and whether lowering the average age of top management makes firms more aggressive. My tentative judgement here is also negative, since the number of purged officers was quite small (Table 6.2).

As Sakisaka (1960, p. 82) and other studies point out, consumer machinery industries such as sewing machines, cameras and bicycles were from the start characterized by many firms and fierce competition. For example, there were 50 watch and clock suppliers in April 1949, 63 bicycle suppliers in August 1950,[15] and 76 firms manufacturing sewing machine heads in 1955.[16] Similarly, there were 34 firms supplying radio receivers in 1946 and 71 in 1948, though this declined to 26 by 1954. Even then, the top firm in 1954 held only 31.6 per cent of the market and the top 3 held 53.0 per cent, while even the top 10 held only 84.8 per cent. Likewise, there were 30 manufacturers of black-and-white TVs in 1954, and the market share of the top 10 was 89.1 per cent.[17]

The case of shipbuilding is somewhat different. The main restriction for shipbuilding firms in the late 1940s was that, under the reparations policy, most of their production capacity was slated for removal to outside Japan and in the interim they were prohibited from using these facilities.[18] Also the materials bottleneck, especially of steel, was quite severe. Ultimately their facilities were not used for reparations in kind, and when steel availability improved in the 1950s, exports increased explosively. In 1958, on a completion ton base, the market share of the top firm was 15.5 per cent, the top 3 was 31.8 per cent, the top 5 was 45.1 per cent, the top 10 was 66.7 per cent and the top 21 was 81.5 per cent. The top share was for 1 of the 3 firms split off from Mitsubishi Heavy Industries, while the other two parts were ranked 5 and 7. But even if the separate 'Mitsubishi' shares were combined, they come up to 26.6 per cent. The top 3 and 5 firms would then account for 42.9 and 56.2 per cent respectively, which still cannot be classified as a highly concentrated industry.[19] Since 1956, Japanese shipbuilders have held the largest share in the world market,[20] and in 1956 more than 70 per cent completed tonnage exported. Shipbuilding, however, is the only exception where policy effects could be profound.

As for the striking development of passenger cars, tremendous advances began in the mid-1950s, and we can see the history of dynamic competition in this market during which some old firms sank and new entrants, such as Honda, Mazda and Mitsubishi, gained large markets. The Deconcentration Policies, however, had no impact whatever on the auto industry (see Table 6.3).

6.6 THE ANTI-MONOPOLY LAW

In Japan, an Anti-Monopoly Law was introduced in 1947. There are a wide array of opinions about the role played by this law.[21] For the purpose of this paper it is enough to mention the following two points. First, as mentioned above, this new law was expected to supplement the Deconcentration Policies and to maintain their achievements. For example, article 9 prohibits the establishment of holding companies and article 11 places constraints on stockholdings by financial institutions. However, this aspect of the Law has not had an important effect, in terms of my criteria, for the same reasons as in the previous section: at most they restrained corporate concentration, and did not increase competition.

Second, the implementation of the Anti-Monopoly Law, or more precisely application of each article, is intended to stimulate competition within individual industries. The symbolic portion here is the latter half of article 3, which prohibits cartels. However, the introduction and enforcement of this law by itself did not greatly stimulate competition and hence raise the performance of industry, at least for the first 20 or 30 years.

It took a long time for this law to be recognized by most Japanese people as reflecting a basic prerequisite of a market economy, and thus to acquire a place among the core tools of economic policy in Japan. Even for those who believe this law had a great impact, the first occasion when it appeared to actually be used as an important policy instrument was in the first half of the 1960s in combating 'Administered Prices' associated with creeping inflation. Indeed, the previous era for the law is sometimes called its 'winter time' (*fuyuno*

Table 6.3 Japanese passenger car production and exports

Year	Production	% Exported
1945		
1946		
1947	110	0.0
1948	381	0.0
1949	1 070	0.0
1950	1 594	0.0
1951	3 611	0.0
1952	4 837	0.0
1953	8 789	0.0
1954	14 472	0.0
1955	20 268	0.0
1956	32 056	0.1
1957	47 121	0.9
1958	50 643	4.7
1959	78 598	6.2
1960	165 094	4.2
1961	249 508	4.6
1962	268 784	6.0
1963	407 830	7.7
1964	579 660	11.6
1965	696 176	14.5
1966	877 656	17.4
1967	1 375 755	16.2
1968	2 055 821	19.8
1969	2 611 499	21.5
1970	3 178 708	22.8
1971	3 717 858	34.9
1972	4 022 289	35.0
1973	4 470 550	32.5
1974	3 931 842	43.9
1975	4 567 854	40.0
1980	7 038 108	56.1
1985	7 646 816	57.9

Source: Nihon Jidosha Kogyokai (Japan Automobile Manufacturers' Association), *Jidosha Tokei Nenpo, Jidosha Tokei Nenpyo*.

jidai),[22] reflecting its weak enforcement. It was after and through the experiences of the flood of cartels during the period of First Oil Shock and its accompanying inflation in 1973–4 that Japan really recognized the importance of this law and began to support it. These experiences led the government to revise the law in 1977. An administrative fine on cartel participants was introduced, which was intended to overcome the situation where cartels faced no substantive penalty.

With the introduction of the law, there were changes on the surface. But in my view they were slight and applied only in rare cases to alter the behaviour of firms, the forms of government intervention into industry, and the co-operation and relations between government and industry. These changes do not suggest profound effects. In some cases, attempts to restrain cartels or cartel-like behaviour, often supported by the government, were neutralized by the action of other parts of the government. The symbolic case of this type was in 1947, when the cartel of banks that set the interest rates for loans and deposits was accused of violating article 3 in the first test case of the application of this law. The quick response of the government was to enact a new law to temporarily exempt the application to this article to the financial sector.[23]

What should be pointed out is that competition in the industries in question was so severe in those days that the government tried, sometimes in response to the requests of the majority of firms in those industries, to intervene in order to restrict market competition. This so-called 'excessive competition' (*kato kyoso*) was certainly not the product of Anti-Monopoly regulation.[24] Thus, the introduction and enforcement of the Anti-Monopoly Law did not have a great effect in strengthening competition in the machinery industry, and therefore, could not have been notably effective in improving the performance of these industries.[25]

6.7 REMAINING POINTS

Is it possible, however, to generalize on the case of the machinery industry? I believe the answer is 'yes'. For the effects of Zaibatsu Dissolution type policies, the same reasoning can be applied to other industries. As with machinery, the dissolution of Zaibatsu holding companies, changes in stock ownership, the breaking of interlocking directorships, and changes in the selection and role of top management had little or no effect. In short, not only for machinery but also for the whole economy, Zaibatsu Dissolution and related policies were not critical in stimulating competition and improving the industrial performance.[26]

However, in a few industries such as steel, paper and pulp, and export–import trading, the top firms (for example, Japan Steel Corporation, Oji Paper Company, and Mitsui Trading Company and Mitusbishi Trading Company) were dissolved under the Deconcentration Policies. It is widely accepted that the dissolutions directly and tremendously strengthened competition in these industries. It is claimed, too, that this strengthened competition diffused to other industries and made the Japanese economy as a whole much more competitive. Even in these specific industries, it is not easy to substantiate this claim, and at least in the case of steel, the evidence again suggests a minimal impact.[27] In any event, it is really the persuasiveness of the second half of the claim that is crucial for our purpose here. There is no evidence to support the view that Deconcentration Policies had a macro impact, nor can we find any direct link which might have helped the diffusion from one to another industry. Given that the number of industries directly influenced by Deconcentration Policies was small at best (and nil for the important machinery industries), it is hard to believe that they were one of the main factors stimulating competition.

A second purported impact of Deconcentration Policies was on the separation of ownership and management in Japanese firms. Some claim that these policies accelerated the tendency towards the separation of management from ownership in Japanese firms. This is one of the peculiarities of Japanese firms at present, making them aggressively competitive and allowing them to pursue long-run objectives.[28] Again, it is not necessary for us to discuss the persuasiveness of this view here.[29] We only need pay attention to the following facts. First, most big firms today, especially in the field of machinery, did not have their ownership structure or interlocking directorships influenced by Zaibatsu Dissolution. Second, we do not find evidence that the management in non-Zaibatsu big firms was any less separated from ownership than in the ex-Zaibatsu firms. Therefore, we can presume that, even without the Zaibatsu Dissolution, the stockholding structure and the degree of the separation of ownership and management would not differ greatly from the present situation.

6.8 CONCLUDING REMARKS

I will not repeat here the conclusions reached above. While, the formation of a competitive industrial environment was one of the main engines of Japan's rapid economic growth, I argued that the Deconcentration Policies played no substantial role in strengthening competition. However, this conclusion does not mean that those policies were failures and the energies devoted to them were a waste. It is incorrect to answer that these policies had no effect. My conclusion, however, is more a complement to previous studies than a contradiction of them.

The main reason for my revisionist conclusion is because most previous research did not seek to identify and evaluate the policy effects in isolation. There has been a strong tendency to assert, quite often without any empirical evaluation, that in total the postwar Reforms had a revolutionary impact. But this effectively lumps together not only the Economic Reforms such as the Deconcentration Policies, Land Reform and Labour Reform, but also changes in the fields of politics, culture, education and macroeconomic and trade policy. And while some of previous research does try to find and detail the actual effects of these policies, quite often this is done without any evaluation of their relative importance.[30] Deconcentration Policies were at best a supporting cast to the stars or an appreciative audience that served to encourage the main players.

Notes

1. The same kind of uncritical evaluations and misunderstandings can be found in research of industrial policy. See Miwa (1990b) ch. 11.
2. Of course, this limitation affects any economic study, so the problem here is a matter of degree rather than kind.
3. From the 'Basic Directives' dated 3 November 1945. We will return to this statement in Section 6.4
4. Testimony at the Hearings on Economic Concentration, US Senate, 1964, cited in Hadley (1970, p. 108).
5. Although the growth rate of the Japanese economy had been quite high even before the High Growth Era (Kodo Seicho-ki), most people considered it as a temporary effect of the recovery and catch-up process. Only after 1965 did the view that this rapid growth was lasting become dominant. Analysis of the causes and of growth increased thereafter, with attention paid to the cause and implications of the high savings rate, the role of industrial policy, and the sources of technical progress, but not to the role of the postwar Reforms.
6. This limitation is only for convenience. The same kind of test can be made in other industries. With a few exceptions, I believe the results would prove almost the same as in machinery.
7. The amount of foreign currency reserves in 1968 was only around U$ 2 billion, which is equivalent to the amount of the value of imports in 2 or 3 months at that time.

8. Of course we can find exceptions, such as cotton textiles in the early stage, and steel products in the 1960s.
9. See, for example, Okura-sho (Ministry of Finance) (1981).
10. Special Committee on Japanese Reparations, War Department (in Tokyo).
11. It also states that, 'in this survey, the term zaibatsu should be interpreted to include any private enterprise conducted for profit, or combination of such enterprises, which, by reason of relative size in any line or the cumulative power of its position in many lines, restricts competition or impairs the opportunity for others to engage in business independently, in any important segment of business; and any individual, family, allied group, or judicial person owing or controlling such an enterprise or combination.'
12. Chairman of the Far Eastern Commission and US representative.
13. Uekusa (1979) claims tremendous importance for the additional reorganizations. However, Miyazaki *et al.* (1982) argues against this. See also Okura-sho (Ministry of Finance) (1981) pp. 560–7.
14. Of course, this would be only a minor benefit.
15. See *Showa Sangyo-shi* (History of Industries in the Showa Era) (Tokyo: Toyo Keizai Shinpo-sha, 1950) vol. 1, pp. 443 and 456 respectively.
16. More than 90 per cent of the sewing machines produced in 1955 were exported. Likewise, more than 90 per cent of binoculars were exported, mostly to the US. For a detailed analysis of the binocular industry during 1955–64, see Tsuruta (1978).
17. Report of the Study of the Production Structure of Radio and Communication Apparatus Industry (mimeo, in Japanese), by Federation of the Associations of Machinery Industry (Nihon Kikai Kogyo Rengo-kai) 1956, pp. 15 and 24 respectively.
18. See, for example, Sakisaka (1960), pp. 136f. This industry was completely freed from being designated for reparation in 1952.
19. See the figures and tables on p. 198 and 202 of Sakisaka (1960).
20. For example, Japanese shipbuilders supplied 26.2 per cent of world demand in 1956 and 28.6 per cent in 1957. See Tsusho Sangyo-sho (1958), pp. 86–89.
21. For example, in emphasizing the importance of the conflicts between the Anti-Monopoly Law and industrial policy, Iyori (1986), a former high official of the Fair Trade Commission of Japan, states that 'whether Japan's remarkably high rate of economic growth . . . can be attributed to the maintenance of competition by means of antimonopoly policy or to skilful control and guidance through the use of industrial policy is subject to unending debate'. (p. 71) This picture has been widely accepted as persuasive. However, as I wrote in a book review (Miwa, 1990a), 'he overestimates the importance of the role of the government. Today many Japanese economists think that the contribution, if any, of the Government in attaining economic growth is indirect and rather minor' (p. 95).
22. In my review of the debate in the first half of the 1960s over the proposed Bill on Temporary Measures for the Promotion of Designated Industries (Tokutei Sangyo Shinko Rinji Sochi-hoan), which ultimately failed to

pass the Diet, and the merger case of Nippon Steel Corporation (Shin Nippon Seitetsu) in the second half of the 1960s, it is obvious that the Anti-Monopoly Law was still very weak even at the end of the 1960s.

23. In fact, this 'temporary' law is still in effect now, 35 years later.
24. Even in the decade beginning in the second half of the 1950s, cartel-like behaviour, while in substance exempt from the application of the Anti-Monopoly Law, could not maintain its stability for long. For a short history of this in the steel and oil refining industries, see Miwa (1988).
25. There is a widely held view that the original Anti-Monopoly Law was weakened through revisions on several occasions, especially in 1953, and this is why it has not been so influential. Even if this is the case, our conclusion need not be changed, as the factual judgement about their effects are the same. However, I believe it is not true that the law had been gutted in the 1953 revision. The changes stand out primarily because the original law was in some respects quite extreme in character.
26. This view is closely related to the evaluation of the role and importance of industrial groups (*kigyo shudan*). The still dominant view is that the industrial groups, formed mainly in the 1960s, were in large measure revivals of the ex-Zaibatsu, and that they greatly influenced corporate behaviour and changed the industrial organization (See Miyazaki, 1976). However, careful and detailed study leads me to conclude that this view is not persuasive or even false. For a detailed criticism, see chapter 7 of Miwa (1990b). More briefly, see Miwa (1991).

    In addition, it should be noticed also that the basic view underlying the 'one set' hypothesis of Japanese corporate groups is that firms with access to capital funds can enter into any of new markets. That this view was accepted quickly and now occupies a dominant position suggests that many people, especially the majority of top executives and industrial journalists, actually judged that entry barriers are not very high. If that is true, this leads to the conclusion that even if the Zaibatsu had not been dissolved, competition in each individual market would still have been very fierce.
27. Kosai (1989) supports this view. My judgement is drawn from a study of competition in new plant investment by steel firms in the 1950s and 60s. See chapter 9 of Miwa (1990b).
28. For example, Tamaki (1976) states that 'I think that Zaibatsu Dissolution played a kind of revolutionary role. Of course, it was neither political nor social revolution. It had functioned objectively as a "managerial revolution". . .' (p. 48) However, there are conflicting views about this. Okazaki (1991) asserts that, in comparison with non-Zaibatsu firms in the 1930s, management in Zaibatsu firms was already separated from ownership.
29. I do not find this view persuasive. We should investigate beforehand at least the following: Why has such separation occurred? Are they in fact separated? Why should separation increase competition? Why should separation make managers pursue long-run objectives?
30. See, for example, Kosai (1989).

References

Hadley, Eleanor M. (1970) *Antitrust in Japan* (Princeton: Princeton University Press).

Iyori, Hiroshi (1986) 'Antitrust and Industrial Policy in Japan: Competition and Cooperation', in *Law and Trade Issues of the Japanese Economy: American and Japanese Perspectives*, ed. by Gary Saxonhouse and Kozo Yamamura (Washington: University of Washington Press).

Kosai, Yutaka (1989) 'Kodo-Seicho heno Shuppatsu' (Take-off to the Era of High Economic Growth), in *Nihon Keizai-shi* (Japanese Economic History), ed. by Takafusa Nakamura (Tokyo: Iwanami Shoten).

Masamura, Kimihiro (1985) *Sengo-shi I* (History of Postwar Japan, I) (Tokyo: Chikuma Shobo).

Miyazaki, Yoshikazu (1976) *Sengo Nihon no Kigyo Shudan* (Industrial Groups in Postwar Japan) (Tokyo: Nihon Keizai Shinbun-sha).

Miyazaki, Masayasu, Norio Tominaga, Osamu Itoh, Isao Arai and Hideaki Miyajima (1982) 'Senryo-ki no Kigyo Saihensei' (Reorganization of Firms During the Occupation), in *Taiheiyo Senso* (The Pacific War), ed. by Kindai Nihon Kenkyu-kai (Tokyo: Yamakawa Shuppan-sha).

Miwa, Yoshiro (1988) 'Coordination Within Industry: Output, Price, and Investment', in *Industrial Policy of Japan*, ed. by Ryutaro Komiya et al. (Tokyo: Academic Press).

Miwa, Yoshiro (1990a) 'Book Review of Saxonhouse and Yamamura, eds, *Law and Trade Issues of the Japanese Economy*', *Journal of the Japanese and International Economies*, 4, pp. 93–5.

Miwa, Yoshiro (1990b) *Nihon no Kigyo to Šangyo Soshiki* (Firms and Industrial Organization in Japan) (Tokyo: University of Tokyo Press).

Miwa, Yoshiro (1991) 'Keiretsu Trades and Product Imports', mimeo, Paper presented at the 8th International Symposium held by Economic Research Institute of Economic Planning Agency of Japan on Trade Imbalance, Intra-Industry Trade, and Keiretsu, on 22–23 January in Tokyo. (Also available as a discussion paper of the University of Tokyo, no. 91-F-2.)

Okazaki, Tetsuji (1991) 'Senji Keikaku Keizai to Kigyo' (Firms in the War-Time Planned Economy), in *Gendai Nihon Shakai, vol. 4 Rekishiteki Zentei* (Modern Japanese Society: Historical Antecedents) ed. by Institutes of Social Sciences of the University of Tokyo (Tokyo: University of Tokyo Press).

Okura-sho (Ministry of Finance) (ed.) (1981) *Showa Zaisei-shi* (The Fiscal History of the Showa Era), vol. 2 (Tokyo: Toyo Keizai Shinpo-sha).

Sakisaka, Masao ed. (1960) *Gendai Nihon Sangyo Koza, V* (Studies of Industries in Modern Japan, vol. 5) (Tokyo: Iwanami Shoten).

Tamaki, Akira (1976) 'Sengo Kaikaku' (Postwar Reforms) in *Gendai Nihon Keizai-shi* I, ed. by Tsuneo Iida *et al.* (Tokyo: Chikuma Shobo).

Tsuruta, Toshimasa (1978) 'Chusho-Kigyo Karuteruni Kansuru Jisshoteki Kenkyu' (An Empirical Study of Cartels among Small Firms), *Kokumin-Keizai*, nos. 139 and 140.

Tsusho Sangyo-sho (Ministry of International Trade and Industry) (1958) *Tsusho Hakusho* (White Paper of MITI).

Uekusa, Masu (1979) 'Senryo-ka no Kigyo Bunkatsu' (Corporate Dissolutions in the Occupation Era), in *Senryo-ki Nihon no Keizai to Seiji* (Economy and Politics in the Occupation Era), ed. by Takafusa Nakamura (Tokyo: University of Tokyo Press).

7 Financial Sector Reform after the War

Juro Teranishi*

7.1 INTRODUCTION

The transition of the Japanese financial system to a truly market-based system was a protracted affair. It is true that the wartime system was highly regulated. But the financial system in the high growth era (HGE), that emerged gradually in the turmoil of the war devastation and became firmly established during the 1950–5 period, was also under strict government control. It was only after the 1970s that the transformation into a truly market-oriented system occurred (Teranishi, 1993).

The wartime and the HGE financial systems were remarkably similar. First. the flow of funds from deficit to surplus units mainly took the form of indirect financing. In other words, financial intermediation through bank deposits and lending was the linchpin of financing in both periods. Second, the allocation of funds among various sectors was more or less regulated. The government intervened in the allocation of bank lending and the intervention was strongest in the market for corporate bond issues. Third, the main bank system, sometimes thought to be a major structural characteristic of the Japanese financial system, also originated during the war. The Designated Bank System, invented by the government in 1944, had its origin in the loan consortium that emerged around 1936 and has much in common with the main bank system of today.

These similarities notwithstanding, the two systems differ in important and significant respects. First, though allocation of bank lending was under government control in both periods, the method of control differed. The wartime system relied on direct controls while the HGE system resorted to indirect controls such as restricting the activities of each financial institution to certain specified areas, favourable treatment by the Bank of Japan (BOJ) or signalling by public sector financial institutions. That is to say, in contrast to the centralized system of credit allocation during wartime, the HGE system was characterized by decentralized decision-making by individual financial institutions within a framework determined by the government and following an official incentive and signalling system. A second important difference between the two systems was in terms of the degree to which each used the price mechanism. In the wartime system, while credit allocation to individual sectors or firms was strictly controlled, interest rates (price of credit) were basically determined in markets without government intervention. However, in the HGE system, the government tried to control the price, that is, interest rates. Not only were the interest rates on deposits and lending regulated but the issue rate of bonds was also strictly controlled. More important, in the HGE system, controls on the behaviour of individual financial institutions were significantly strengthened. Besides the usual balance-sheet, branching and entry regulations, bureaucratic intervention was extended to the income and expenditure structure of individual institutions. For example, banks were asked to report bank employees' wages to the authorities and bureaucratic guidance was brought to bear on determination of the dividend rate for each bank.

What factors lie behind these similarities and differences? Why did the termination of the war not bring about a complete deregulation of the financial system? It is sometimes argued that the regulated nature of the HGE system derives from bureaucratic continuity; the wartime bureaucrats continued in office with their regulatory techniques intact. This continuity, along with the economic thinking regarding the role of government intervention, is no doubt an important factor and we will touch on this aspect later in this chapter. However, a proper understanding of the overall similarities in the two systems requires a closer look at the basic characteristics of the real side of the economy. We suggest, here, that the government continued to regulate the HGE financial system much as it had during the war, because the Japanese economy was essentially in the same development phase; accelerated industrialization based on heavy and chemical industries or secondary import/export substitution. We argue that excess demand for long-term funds and a relative scarcity of information on new firms, that characterizes this phase of development, necessitated significant government involvement in the financial system. Why, then, was the method of control different in the two periods? Democratization and the diversification of economic goals may be sufficient to explain the shift to indirect controls in the HGE system. The shift in the objective of economic control, from the sole objective of military procurement to multiple objectives of stabilization and structural change for development, seems to have necessitated the shift in method of credit allocation from totalitarian coercion to more democratic methods based on private initiative. The explanation for the need to suppress the price mechanism or imposition of stricter controls over the behaviour of individual financial institutions needs to be sought in the shock of the war defeat. Huge losses arising from suspension of wartime compensations and concomitant restructuring of financial institutions weakened the control of the banks' shareholders. The experience of bureaucratic control inherited from the wartime and the strong anti-big business sentiments held by SCAP (Supreme Commander for the Allied Powers) and generally prevalent in the society worked to strengthen the tendency to partially replace control by shareholders with bureaucratic control over the financial institutions.

Section 7.2 below traces the effects of postwar reforms by comparing the HGE and wartime financial systems. Section 7.3 discusses the relation between the characteristics of the financial system and the development phase and shows that the similarities between the HGE and wartime financial systems derive from this relationship. Section 7.4 examines the impact of war devastation, especially the resultant restructuring of financial institutions, on the formation of the HGE financial system. A chronology of the evolution of financial institutions in the immediate postwar period is provided in the Appendix.

7.2 WARTIME AND HGE FINANCIAL SYSTEMS: A COMPARISON

7.2.1 The Wartime Financial System

The main characteristics of the wartime financial system can be summarized as follows:

(a) Indirect Financing

The flow of funds through the banking sector increased gradually. Table 7.1 indicates that while the percentage share of borrowing from private financial institutions rose during the 1931–45 period, the share of equity financing and retained earnings declined gradually. The movements in the stock variable also confirm this tendency. The second column of Table 7.2 shows that the net worth ratio of large

Table 7.1 Distribution of sources of funds raised by private industries (annual flow, in percent)

	Equity	*Bond*	*Borrowing from private financial institutions*	*Borrowing from government financial system*	*Bank of Japan foreign exchange loans*	*Retained earnings*
1931	34.0	11.7	–3.2	11.3	0.0	46.2
1932	22.0	16.7	–54.3	–3.9	0.0	119.7
1933	31.1	–4.0	–40.4	8.0	0.0	105.2
1934	55.4	2.9	–11.4	–1.6	0.0	54.8
1935	32.9	1.1	14.9	–0.5	0.0	51.6
1936	33.5	–2.3	18.3	3.1	0.0	47.4
1937	35.5	–0.1	31.9	–0.5	0.0	33.3
1938	34.6	5.4	29.9	–0.3	0.0	30.5
1939	24.5	7.9	38.4	2.1	0.0	27.2
1940	26.7	5.5	38.3	1.0	0.0	30.4
1941	29.1	10.1	28.1	–0.9	0.0	33.6
1942	25.7	8.9	32.9	1.4	0.0	31.2
1943	22.6	7.8	35.8	3.4	0.0	30.3
1944	9.1	8.3	57.8	0.7	0.0	24.2
1945	6.1	0.7	90.9	2.3	0.0	0.0
1946	5.8	–1.6	71.9	–0.3	0.0	24.2
1947	5.1	0.0	45.4	25.0	0.0	24.4
1948	11.3	0.0	59.2	12.5	0.0	17.0
1949	16.6	2.3	55.4	1.1	0.0	24.6
1950	3.7	5.1	43.4	1.6	6.1	40.2
1951	5.1	2.3	47.2	5.3	3.1	36.6
1952	8.3	2.5	54.2	6.6	–2.1	30.4
1953	9.7	2.4	43.1	5.5	1.7	37.6
1954	11.6	1.5	31.3	9.6	–5.7	51.8
1955	14.2	3.9	68.9	14.3	–1.3	0.0

Source: Bank of Japan, *Keizai Tokei Nenpo* (Economic Statistics Annual).

business firms declined after 1937 (the beginning of the Sino-Japanese War). The role of external borrowing was known to be on the rise especially for Zaibatsu firms. The net worth ratio for the Mitsubishi Zaibatsu was 50.4 per cent in 1937 but declined to 28.3 per cent in 1945. The share of within-group equity financing to the total equity financing of the Zaibatsu groups also declined from 49.3 per cent (1917–26) to 31.1 per cent (1942–5).[1] A similar phenomenon has also been reported for the Sumitomo and Mitsui Zaibatsu.[2]

Table 7.2 Indexes of asset holdings and savings mobilization

	Percentage composition of time deposits in total deposits *(1)*	*Ratio of net worth to total assets of large business firms* (2)	*Ratio of total deposits to GNP* *(3)*	*GNP deflator (average of 1934–6 = 1)* *(4)*
1930	49.1	0.55	0.81	1.027
1931	49.6	0.56	0.86	0.902
1932	47.9	0.64	0.85	0.927
1933	48.2	0.63	1.16	0.978
1934	49.5	0.59	0.78	0.965
1935	50.6	0.61	0.78	1.007
1936	49.8	0.61	0.79	1.038
1937	47.7	0.54	0.68	1.099
1938	46.2	0.59	0.74	1.220
1939	42.5	0.57	0.79	1.497
1940	41.7	0.55	0.83	1.910
1941	40.7	0.52	0.88	2.417
1942	37.8	0.49	0.92	2.612
1943	37.3	0.45	0.88	3.027
1944	49.5	–	1.05	3.704
1945	29.3	0.28	–	–
1946	20.2	0.27	0.31	43.6
1947	14.5	–	0.18	109.4
1948	15.9	–	0.19	191.4
1949	26.0	–	0.23	233.3
1950	30.7	0.23	0.27	243.0
1951	35.4	0.27	0.28	288.3
1952	38.5	0.36	0.36	299.7
1953	41.7	0.35	0.38	317.5
1954	42.3	0.39	0.39	332.7
1955	45.3	0.39	0.43	336.7
1965	50.3	0.24	0.65	516.2
1975	53.8	0.19	0.58	1092.4

Notes and Sources: Time and total deposits are for all banks (*Zenkoku ginko*) obtained from the Bank of Japan, *Keizai Tokei Nenpo* (Economic Statistics Annual). Net worth and total assets of large business firms are obtained from Mitsubishi Keizai Kenkyujo's *Shuyo Kigyo Jigyo Seiseki Bunseki* except for 1945 and 1946, 1965 and 1975. Data for 1945 and 1946 are from Okura-sho (Ministry of Finance) *Showa Zaisei-shi (The Fiscal History of the Showa Era)*, vol. 13, pp. 754–5, and data for 1965 and 1975 are from the Bank of Japan, *Shuyo Kigyo Keiei Bunseki*. GNP is from Kazushi Ohkawa and Miyohei Shinohara (eds) (1979) *Patterns of Japanese Economic Development* (New Haven: Yale University Press) and GNP deflator from the Bank of Japan's *One Hundred-year History (Statistics)*. Figures are end of year or annual average except for the second column, where they refer to the end of first half of the fiscal year.

(b) Direct Regulation of Credit Allocation

Credit allocation by private financial institutions was directly controlled by legislation. The Temporary Fund Adjustment Law (Rinji Shikin Chosei-ho) of 1937 forbade the lending of investment funds to and the issuance of corporate securities by firms not related to military production. In 1940, this legislation was extended to include lending for operating funds. Moreover, a system of compulsory loans (*meirei yushi*) to designated firms was introduced. First, it was implemented through the Industrial Bank of Japan (Hihon Kogyo Ginko: IBJ) – a semi-government institution at that time – but, shortly afterwards (in 1940), was extended to all banks.

Incidentally, at the end of 1945, of the total lending by all ordinary and savings banks and IBJ amounting to 112.2 billion yen, 23.9 per cent or 26.8 billion yen is estimated to have been for military purposes. The share of war-related bank lending, including war insurance etc., is much larger and is estimated to be 83.5 billion yen, or 75.2 per cent of the combined loans by all banks (*zenkoku ginko*) of 111 billion yen (end of March 1946).

(c) Homogenization of Financial Institutions

Since most firms engaged in military production were the clients of either large Zaibatsu banks or the IBJ, other banks functioned simply as deposit-takers. For this purpose, various types of financial institutions were virtually converted into deposit-taking ordinary banks and bank mergers were encouraged with a view to reducing intermediation costs. The number of ordinary banks decreased from 286 in 1940 to 61 at the end of 1945. In the wake of the 1943 legislation allowing ordinary banks to function as savings banks as well as trust banks, the number of savings banks decreased from 67 in 1943 to 5 in 1945 and that of trust banks from 21 to 7 over the same period. Even the public sector financial institutions were geared to function as deposit-taking institutions; the ceiling on deposit/net-worth ratio placed on the Hypothec Bank of Japan (Nihon Kangyo Ginko) was removed in February 1945. A new financial institution – Wartime Finance Corporation (Senji Kin'yu Kinko) – was created in 1942 for the sole purpose of financing military production.

The flow of funds within the financial sector changed drastically. Before the war, local banks, typically weak and small, were a deficit (lendings greater than deposits) sector reflecting their low deposit mobilizing capabilities. The big city banks, on the other hand, were a surplus (deposits greater than lendings) sector due to the perceived

Table 7.3 Inter-bank flow of funds (percentages)

	City banks		Local banks		Sogo banks	
	Ratio of net interbank loans to deposits	*Ratio of lending to deposits*	*Ratio of net interbank loans to deposits*	*Ratio of lending to deposits*	*Ratio of net interbank loans to deposits*	*Ratio of lending to deposits*
1930	3.3	63.0	–10.3	74.2	–2.6	46.8
1931	2.6	65.1	–11.1	74.2	–3.7	51.9
1932	6.2	60.4	–9.2	70.2	–3.3	45.6
1933	7.4	54.9	–10.1	65.0	–3.2	46.8
1934	5.8	50.8	–8.1	59.1	–2.8	48.1
1935	5.7	52.2	–7.1	56.1	–1.8	53.5
1936	4.0	56.4	–6.2	52.9	–0.8	56.2
1937	5.2	60.7	3.0	50.9	–0.6	60.8
1938	3.3	57.0	–1.8	46.4	–0.5	62.5
1939	3.2	57.5	–2.0	43.5	–0.6	33.4
1940	3.3	60.9	–0.3	38.8	–0.4	37.4
1941	1.7	59.1	–0.4	33.7	–0.3	39.4
1942	–0.3	56.6	–1.4	31.3	–0.4	41.6
1943	–6.1	63.5	–0.5	27.8	–0.9	42.9
1944	–20.6	82.6	–0.1	27.9	–1.3	39.0
1945	–36.9	93.3	–8.7	28.4	–1.5	36.0
1946	–34.7	119.4	–0.8	36.6	–4.3	31.0
1947	–15.2	75.4	–1.4	44.9	–3.7	33.3
1948	–13.8	74.7	–1.6	66.3	–1.5	37.3
1949	–13.7	83.2	–4.4	78.1	–0.4	45.7
1950	–16.9	90.1	–8.0	86.3	–0.5	51.9
1951	–22.4	100.0	–0.6	82.4	–	–
1952	–17.2	92.8	–0.3	81.7	0.4	45.2
1953	–18.7	96.4	0.4	82.8	0	50.2
1954	–15.2	91.6	2.2	81.2	1.3	53.7
1955	–6.2	77.3	3.0	78.8	0.9	52.0

Notes: Local banks are ordinary banks other than city banks, and saving banks. Coverage of city banks differs depending on the year. Net inter-bank loans are call loans + bills bought + lending to financial institutions – call money – borrowings – bills sold. End of year figures. Sogo banks before 1951 refer to *Mujin Gaisha*.

Sources: Bank of Japan, *Keizai Tokei Nenpo* (Economic Statistics Annual) and company histories of individual city banks.

safety of their deposits (Teranishi, 1990). However, this structure was completely reversed during the war with city banks becoming the deficit and the local banks becoming the surplus sector as revealed in Table 7.3.

(d) Regulation of the Bond Market

New issues of corporate bonds were regulated in 1940 by the Bond Issues Planning Committee (Kisai Keikaku Kyogikai) in order to raise long-term funds for military firms. Such bonds were preferentially allotted to large firms in the heavy and chemical industries and war-related 'national policy firms' (*kokusaku-gaisha*) based on the Temporary Fund Adjustment Law. Bond prices, however, were unregulated throughout the period and were determined by negotiations between the issuing firm and the underwriting institutions.

(e) Interest Rates

Not only bond issue rates but other interest rates were also free of direct controls. Though the BOJ bought between 60 and 80 per cent of the government bonds to begin with, 80 per cent of these were sold to the public at market price. Various devices, such as the issuance of low denomination and discounted bonds and increasing the frequency of interest payments and the like, were used to induce the public to hold these bonds. This phenomenon resembles closely various sales efforts of the government after 1975 when a large number of government bonds were issued again. The government put a strong downward pressure on deposit rates by enforcing cartel agreements but individual banks were still able to set their own rates. As of the end of March 1941, dispersion in interest rates was still quite significant, ranging from over 4.0 per cent to less than 3.3 per cent.[3] Moreover, there was no attempt at regulating lending rates. Even the lending for military production was at market rates. Only towards the end of the war (July 1944), did the National Committee on Financial Regulation (Zenkoku Kin'yu Toseikai) specify a cartel rate. But even this was confined to the loans related to the Designated Bank System (see below).

(f) Loan Syndication

As the banks were forced to lend to newly established 'national policy firms' on which they had scant information, and as dependence of these firms on external borrowing increased generally, the perceived risk to the banks tended to rise. The banks thus tried to protect themselves by means of loan syndication and stricter monitoring. Loan syndicates, known as *kyodo yushidan*, emerged spontaneously among the private banks in 1936. As of the end of 1941, the number of such syndicates had risen to 121; 82 led by IBJ, 17 by other banks and 22 by trust companies. In 1944, this system was formalized by introducing the Designated Bank System for financing military production. Five specialized banks, including IBJ, nine city banks and four local banks were designated to become leading banks in syndicated lending.[4]

7.2.2 The Financial System of the High Growth Era

The main characteristics of the HGE financial system can be summarized as follows:

(a) Indirect Financing

Corporate financing continued to lean heavily on bank lending throughout the HGE. To date a major proportion of corporate funds is raised via indirect financing though there has been a remarkable increase in equity financing during the 1987–90 period (Teranishi, 1993).

(b) Indirect Controls over Credit Allocation by Financial Institutions

Except in the immediate postwar period (1945–9), when direct credit controls were resorted to, the allocation of funds was more or less left at the discretion of private financial institutions. This was particularly true for the city banks. Despite the strict regulations imposed on liabilities, such as BOJ lending and deposit rates, the allocation of funds by the city banks was completely free of regulations (except for compulsory bond holdings) and funds raised by the banks through their deposit instruments and in the interbank call market were allocated to the growing heavy and chemical industries. However, it is important to note that three types of indirect credit control measures were in force.

First, BOJ credit was used as an incentive for allocating funds to particular sectors. Though this measure was used extensively only until 1955, special rates applied to the discounting of export and import bills continued to exist till 1971 (BOJ, *One Hundred-year History*, vol. 5). Second, the areas of lending by non-city banks were specialized and this had an important influence on directing funds into particular channels and was especially important in the financing of small- and medium-scale enterprises. Third, the role of public sector finances in the private sector gained importance after the war. The balanced-budget policy adopted after 1949 freed public sector funds (since these were not needed to finance budgetary deficits) raised mainly through the postal savings system, which were utilized to complement private flows. Table 7.1 clearly shows an increase in the proportion of public sector in total private sector financing after the war.

(c) Specialized Financial Institutions

In marked contrast to the homogenization of the financial system during the war, the HGE financial system was organized according to the principle of a 'division of labour' among institutions. In view of the serious problem of under-employment and the plight of small- and medium-scale firms, financial institutions like Sogo banks and Shinkin banks, specializing in the financing of small- and medium-scale businesses, were established and promoted from 1951 onwards. Agricultural financing institutions were also reorganized and an hierarchical system, with the Norinchukin Bank (Norin Chuo Kinko) at the top, was strengthened. Trust companies were converted into trust banks and two long-term credit banks (one resulted from the conversion of the IBJ) were established in 1952 for the special purpose of supplying long-term funds to industries.

Fund flows in the financial sector retained their wartime characteristics. As indicated by the figures in Table 7.3, city banks continued to be deficit and the local and Sogo banks the surplus sector though the reasons behind such a structure were quite different from those operating in the wartime system, as will be explained in the next section.

It is also worth noting that the same principle of 'division of labour' was also applied to the public sector financial institutions. The People's Finance Corporation (Kokumin Kin'yu Koko, est. 1949) and the Small Business Finance Corporation (Chushokigyo Kin'yu Koko, est. 1953) were set up to provide financing for small- and medium-scale firms. The Export-Import Bank (Nihon Yushutsunyu Ginko, est. 1951) and the Housing Finance Corporation (Jutaku Kin'yu Koko, est. 1950) were also created to meet specific financing needs. It is also worth emphasizing that these public sector financial institutions were more or less complementary to the private financial institutions. Thus, while the growing heavy and chemical industry was financed mainly by private financial institutions, the public sector financial institutions provided finances to infrastructure and declining industries after the end of the reconstruction period around 1955.

(d) Regulation of the Bond Market

Bond market regulations were not only continued but strengthened. Regulations on eligibility conditions for the issue of new corporate bonds were resumed in 1947 and continued throughout the HGE. The price of new issues was also controlled and the city banks were obligated to purchase bonds at higher than market price. Since these bonds, issued mainly by steel and electricity-generating companies, were eligible as collateral for BOJ credit, the city banks were able to compensate for the loss incurred on the purchase of high-priced bonds against the implicit subsidy arising out of low-interest credit from the BOJ (Teranishi, 1993).

(e) Interest Rate and Other Regulations

In addition to the bond issue rate, deposit and lending rates were also controlled during the HGE. The effectiveness of lending rate controls is doubtful due to the use of practices such as compensating balances to circumvent these regulations. Controls on deposit rates, however, are considered to have been quite effective.[5] More important, the banks in the HGE were subject to administrative controls not only via interest rate regulations but also by conditions placed on their income and profits in general. The banks were asked to report bankers' wages as well as their real estate transactions. The dividend rates of the eleven city banks were exactly the same at least since the later half of fiscal 1949. Though dividend rates in the local banks varied widely to begin with, these tended to converge due to strong guidance by the Ministry of Finance (Okura-sho: MOF).

(f) Main Banks

It is generally believed that during the HGE, almost every business firm in Japan, including medium-sized firms, had a main bank. Among the several banks from which a business firm borrows, a bank that (i) is the largest lender to the firm; (ii) has a long-term commitment to the firm; (iii) holds equity in the firm; (iv) delegates directors to the firm; and, (v) is involved in comprehensive transactions, such as annuity investments and accounting services, with the firm, is considered to be the main bank for that firm. The main bank has two roles. The first of these emphasizes properties mentioned under (i), (ii) and probably (v) above and concerns the role of the *main bank as a commercial bank*. The role of the main bank in this connection is to produce information on the borrower. It has been argued that the main bank, as a delegated monitor, saves on the costs of information production and also helps in preventing the problem of moral hazard, thereby reducing the agency costs of debt financing. In the absence of adequate monitoring by the main bank, shareholders may have an incentive to undertake riskier projects to the disadvantage of lenders. With information asymmetry, the probability of moral hazard raises the lending rate even for the firm with no possibility of moral hazard. The resulting distortion in the allocation of resources comprises the agency cost for the economy.

The second role played by the main bank focuses on characteristics (iii) and (iv) and relates to the role of the *main bank as a shareholder* or *as a member of a keiretsu*. The importance of the main bank in this regard lies in its cooperative behaviour with the firm. It is said that the main bank acts as a substitute for corporate take-overs with positive welfare implications since the take-over is not an efficient device of corporate control in the presence of informational asymmetry (Stiglitz, 1985). Management of a firm with poor performance is effectively replaced by new management chosen by the main bank. It is also believed that the main bank provides a risk-sharing or insurance mechanism for the firm. Interest rates on debt are flexibly adjusted according to the profit–loss position of the firm.[6]

With this backdrop, we are now in a position to compare the financial system in the two periods and focus on the continuities and changes in the financial system brought about by postwar financial reforms. First, let us note some of the similarities in the two systems, i.e., the characteristics of the wartime system that were kept intact by the postwar financial reform: (i) The flow of funds continued to be dominated by indirect financing. Bank deposits and lending remained key instruments for channelling investible funds from surplus to deficit sectors of the economy. Moreover, the structure of fund flows within the financial sector did not change; the city banks being the deficit and local banks the surplus sector. (ii) Government intervention in credit allocation continued to play an important role though the extent of intervention was significantly reduced. (iii) Special bank–firm relations that emerged during wartime as loan syndicates continued to exist in the form of the main bank system.

While there were similarities, it is important to note that there were significant differences as well: (i) The method of government intervention in credit allocation changed considerably. Direct and centralized controls during wartime were replaced by indirect and decentralized means during the HGE. (ii) While prices were still flexible in the wartime system, they were substantially suppressed in the postwar period. Not only were interest rates controlled, the income and expenditure of the banks were also brought under strict control.

Incidentally, the division of labour among the financial institutions, discussed earlier, is believed to be a 'principle' first advocated by Masayoshi Matsukata (Minister of Finance for almost ten years during 1885 to 1900) and established during the Taisho era (1912–26). Also, it appears that this principle, by implication, was based on the concept of economies of scale (or benefits of specialization) as opposed to economies of scope. In the controversy over the postwar financial reform, this was frequently referred to as the basic principle of the Japanese financial system. However, judging by the lack of any documents devoted to investigating into and justifying the use of this principle, it seems that the principle was taken as a truism by everyone at that time.

7.3 DEVELOPMENTAL PHASE AND CHARACTERISTICS OF THE FINANCIAL SYSTEM

The financial system of an economy is usually tailored to meet the needs specific to the real economy of that time. In order to understand the changes in the financial system after the war, therefore, it is necessary to grasp the changes that occurred in the real economy of Japan.

The trade-based phasing of Japanese economic development designates the period from the Second World War to the end of the HGE as the period of secondary import and export substitution. The heavy and chemical industry, introduced during the First World War, was the engine of growth during this period, though the economy was still heavily dependent on agriculture in terms of employment, and on the silk and cotton spinning industries in terms of export earnings. It is important to note that the process of heavy and chemical industrialization accelerated during this period. During the war, enhanced military power was synonymous with the expansion of production in the heavy and chemical industries. In the HGE, the huge technological gap with Western countries, emerging as a result of the isolation of Japan from developments in the West, became the main driving force.

Industrialization based on the heavy and chemical industries strains the financial system in two ways. First, it results in a gap in the demand and supply of long-term funds. The introduction of heavy and chemical industries requires large amounts of fixed long-term capital investment. The supply of funds by surplus units (asset holders), on the other hand, consists of short-term assets due to low levels of asset accumulation and limited access to formal lending facilities. This makes the problem of maturity transformation – conversion of short-term funds into long-term funds – all the more important and increases the strain on the financial system. It is worth noting here that during the period under consideration, the maturity of funds supplied by the surplus units actually shortened. Column 1 of Table 7.2 shows a decrease in time deposits as a percentage of total deposits from 1935 to 1955 (excluding 1944). Needless to say, this reflects inflationary pressure during this period as indicated in column 4. Second, a gap usually develops in the supply of and demand for information. Heavy and chemical industrialization entails a high degree of vertical division of labour in the production system resulting in a drastic increase in the number of intermediate products and producers. At the same time, the supply of information on these new products and producers is limited due to aversion to information disclosure by the more or less family-owned producers as well as the time required for the accumulation of information processing capabilities within the financial sector. Information held by the financial sector on a large number of 'national policy firms' set up in the occupied territories during the war was at best insufficient. During the HGE, rapid growth of the heavy and chemical industries gave rise to numerous new firms.

It was natural, under these conditions, for the flow of funds to rely heavily on indirect financing during the war as well as in the HGE. First, self-financing, though desirable due to low agency costs involved, is innately limited in its potential for mobilizing large savings. This was absolutely clear even to Zaibatsu firms during the war. The situation worsened during the HGE as the financial assets accumulated in the prewar period were wiped out due to hyper-inflation in the immediate postwar period. Second, the development of the corporate bond market during the war was limited due to the lack of information. Bonds, in this period, were predominantly floated by the 'national policy firms' due to the controls exercised by the Bond Issues Planning Committee. Though most of these bonds were issued with a government guarantee, the public was reluctant to hold these in their portfolio due to the paucity of information, apparent riskiness and because these were without collateral. (The fact that the government failed to fulfil its loan guarantees after the defeat in the war, shows that the public's expectations were probably 'rational'.) The Committee's intention to sell one-third of the new issues to the public, therefore, was difficult to realize.[7] During the HGE, since the government regulated the issue price of corporate bonds and kept them above the market price, the city banks did not try to sell these on the market, with the result that the secondary market was virtually non-existent. Third, in view of the serious information asymmetry during the two periods, the superiority of the banks, in terms of information production, over institutions such as rating companies, may have been an important factor in the relatively greater expansion of their activities. It is well known that financial intermediation by the banking system is advantageous to information production due to (a) the existence of efficient information channels in the form of lender-customer relations; (b) the non-existence of free-rider problems, as the information is used internally; and, (c) the ability to produce information on multiple borrowers, since banks can collect monitoring fees from ultimate borrowers, in contrast to rating companies which target only the borrowers that are willing to pay such fees.

It is not difficult to see why the controls on credit allocation shifted from direct to indirect measures after the war. The wartime economy was driven by the single-minded pursuit of production for military build-up with all other issues sidelined. Light industries, not directly linked to military demand, were simply 'sacrificed' and factors of production were shifted to military-related industries. Besides, there was more-than-full-employment in the labour market during this period due to military mobilization. In the postwar period, on the other hand, the economy faced multiple objectives. Not only was there a necessity to promote heavy and chemical industries but the employment situation was also quite serious. Excess supply of labour in the Lewisian sense, vanishing temporarily during the war, resurfaced and manifested itself in low-wage employment in the small- and medium-scale firms and excess labour in agriculture and services sectors. Moreover, with the development of heavy and chemical industries, industrial adjustment of declining industries such as coal mining, marine transport and textiles, emerged as a serious problem. To cope with these problems, specialization of the financial system and division of labour among institutions was considered an effective means probably because it was expected to promote scale economies. More important, the implicit understanding at the time seems to have been that utilization of private sector creativity was the best strategy for this situation. Towards this end, controls were kept to a minimum, confined to offering a broad framework for private sector activities.

The prevalence of the main bank system after the war and the emergence of its predecessor during the war, in part, is related to the prevalence of indirect financing itself. The possibility of moral hazard on the part of existing shareholders at the cost of banks as lenders was a sufficient reason for lenders to call for close monitoring by designating one of them as a main bank. In addition, the high risk factor of 'national policy firms' during the war and firms born during the HGE, coupled with the rapid increase in the number of such firms, necessitated such measures as delegating the monitoring role to a main bank in order to save on information production costs.

Finally, let us look at the characteristics of inter-bank flows of funds. It is not difficult to visualize why city banks became deficit and the other banks surplus units during the war when the sole objective of the economy lay in the mobilization of funds for military production. To understand why such a fund-flow pattern continued after the war, one needs to examine the effect of branching. In view of the difficulties faced by the small- and medium-scale firms after the war, especially after the Dodge deflation, authorities came to pay special attention to their financing. In addition to the reorganization of the financial system for this sector, special attention was given to the policy governing branching of the financial institutions. While the number of city banks' branches was kept almost constant, local and Sogo banks (private banks specializing in small- and medium-sized firm financing) were allowed to expand generously. For example, while the total number of offices related to the eleven city banks rose from 1523 in 1948 to 1572 in 1952, that of local banks rose from 2404 to 3507 and of Sogo banks from 397 to 1443. Moreover, while the number of regular offices of city banks was kept constant, they were encouraged to expand branch offices specializing in lending to small-

and medium-scale firms after 1950.[8] At the end of March 1954, the number of such offices stood at 76.

Even though an increase in the number of branch offices is effective for increasing deposits, expansion of lending is not easy, due to the time and resources required for accumulating information on customers. Much to the disappointment of the Ministry of Finance, the lending–deposit ratio of many special branch-offices of the city banks stayed very low (MOF, *Ginko-kyoku Nenpo*, 1952) and a similar situation prevailed in the local and Sogo banks as well. On the other hand, the lending–deposit ratio of the city banks rose sharply (Table 7.3), as demand for funds by clients in the growing heavy and chemical industries soared while their deposit mobilization capacity was limited on account of the insufficiency in the number of branch offices. This seems to have been the basic reason behind the pattern of inter-bank flow of funds during the HGE.

7.4 WAR DEVASTATION AND FINANCIAL SECTOR REFORMS

One important characteristic of financial reform after the war was the suppression of the price mechanism and stricter control over the behaviour of financial institutions. No doubt a socialist orientation in economic thinking in the wake of the 'success' of the Soviet economy, a general atmosphere of disbelief in the efficiency and stability of market-based economies, and the influence of Keynesian economics, provided the backdrop for the suppression of the price mechanism. However, another reason for following such a course lay in the process of economic reconstruction and restructuring in the immediate postwar period. It appears that during this process the autonomy of financial institutions, especially control by the banks' shareholders, weakened while the powers of the Bank of Japan and the bureaucrats over economic matters increased considerably. It is suggested that such a change in the power structure within financial circles is highly likely to give rise to the pattern of intervention that emerged during the HGE. We discuss these three points below.

First, in the process of financing the reconstruction of the Japanese economy after the war, the control of BOJ over financial institutions increased in the following ways:

(a) Allocation of credit was controlled directly as well as indirectly. For direct control, new legislation, the Rules Governing Supply of

Funds by Financial Institutions (Kin'yu Kikan Shikin Yuzu-junsoku), was enacted in 1947 which bore close resemblance to the wartime Temporary Fund Adjustment Law. This time, however, the financial institutions were requested to provide investment and operating funds in strategic industries such as coal mining, iron and steel and fertilizers as well as in government bonds. The actual implementation and monitoring of this rule, as during wartime, was assigned to the BOJ. Indirect methods of control included making the bills, issued by industries like coal mining, fertilizers, textiles or other local strategic industries along with the export and import bills, eligible for BOJ collateral and applying favourable lending rates.

(b) The financing of industry became heavily dependent on BOJ loans. The Reconstruction Finance Bank (Fukko Kin'yu Kinko), established in 1947, played a central role in reconstruction financing and was mainly financed by BOJ credits. Of the total amount of debentures issued by this institution, 167 billion yen during fiscal years 1946–8, 118 billion yen worth (71 per cent), were bought by the BOJ. Moreover, private financial institutions, especially the city banks, became heavily dependent on borrowing from the BOJ. The average share of BOJ credit to total financing during the 1945–9 and 1950–4 periods was 19 per cent for the city banks and 14 per cent and 13 per cent for the Zenkoku banks (BOJ, *One Hundred-year History*, vol. 5).

(c) Loan syndication, analogous to that by the main banks during the HGE or the *kyodo yushidan* of the wartime, was used during this period too but this time it was under the leadership of the BOJ. During the period from January 1947 to April 1950, as many as 5964 syndicated loans amounting to 315 billion yen were organized by the BOJ (*One Hundred-year History*, vol. 5, p. 352). While there is no doubt that the high degree of risk faced by the private sector banks at this time necessitated such loan syndication, it is also true that, in the process, the position of the BOJ became extremely strong. Incidentally, at this time, a large number of businesses were in the red due to high wage costs, low capacity utilization resulting from shortages of imported raw materials and the shortage of electricity. For example, during the first half of fiscal 1946, the total net deficit of 201 large firms amounted to 1.8 billion yen; equivalent to 9.6 per cent of the total net worth of 18.7 billion yen or 2.7 per cent of the total assets of 67.2 billion yen (Okura-sho, 1983 p. 756).

Second, the suspension of wartime compensation and the ensuing restructuring of the financial system had a profound effect on the power structure within the financial industry. In October 1946, under strong pressure from SCAP, the Law on Special Measures for Wartime Compensation (Senji Hosho Tokubetsu Sochi-ho) was promulgated stipulating (i) suspension of wartime compensation estimated at 67 billion yen; (ii) suspension of compensation for the losses arising out of compulsory loans (*meirei yushi*); and, (iii) invalidation of government guarantees on the liabilities of various institutions. Since this legislation was expected to have serious adverse effects on heavily debt-ridden business firms and, eventually, on financial institutions, the following measures were taken to mitigate its effects.[9] (i) Balance-sheet items were divided into two categories, old and new. As shown schematically in Table 7.4, old accounts consisted of wartime impaired lending and deposits and net worth including retained earnings considered to have benefited from wartime business. (ii) Financial institutions were allowed to operate only on new accounts. (iii) Old accounts were re-evaluated at the end of March 1948 and the identified losses were made to bear on the following items in order of priority:

Table 7.4 Division of the balance sheet of financial institutions

	Assets	*Liabilities*
Old accounts	Lending, corporate bonds, equities and other assets	Second-line frozen deposits, capital, retained earnings, and other liabilities
New accounts	Cash, government bonds, claims on financial institutions	Free deposits, first-line frozen deposits, liabilities to financial institutions, deposits of tax revenue

Note: In order to contain the hyper-inflation, all the cash was ordered to be deposited on 17 February 1946 and people were allowed to withdraw amounts necessary to cover living expenses. On 5 August 1946, these frozen deposits were classified into two categories: deposits less than 3 thousand yen for households, and less than 15 thousand yen for corporations, were classified as first-line frozen deposits and the remaining deposits as second-line frozen deposits. Deposits accepted after 17 Feb. 1946 were called free deposits.

Source: Okura-sho (Ministry of Finance), *Showa Zaisei-shi* (The Fiscal History of the Showa Era), vol. 13, pp. 225–7.

(1) capital gains on assets;
(2) retained earnings;
(3) 90 per cent of the bank capital;
(4) second-line frozen deposits.

The final result of re-evaluation for all financial institutions was as follows (figures in parentheses pertain to the banking sector alone).[10]

Total losses of 447(275) billion yen
= reduction in capital gains 80(62) billion yen
+ reduction in retained earnings 19(13) billion yen
+ reduction in bank capital 20(16) billion yen
+ reduction in second-line frozen deposits 209(180) billion yen
+ government subsidies 122(4) billion yen

The pattern of final settlement differed among individual banks.[11] However, since all the banks were obliged to cut 90 per cent of their capital, the loss borne by the banks' stockholders was enormous. Those who could not afford to purchase the new issue of stocks after restructuring were forced to drop out of a controlling position. Moreover, purchase of new stock issues by old stockholders (except for financial institutions) was strictly forbidden till the September 1951 ratification of the Japan–US Peace Treaty (Miyajima, 1991).

Third, it must be pointed out that the process of demilitarization and democratization of Japan, carried out by SCAP, also strengthened bureaucrats power *vis-à-vis* business leaders. Zaibatsu dissolution was the final blow to the already weakening control of the Zaibatsu families and the holding companies. The purge of personnel was largely confined to business leaders while the bureaucracy, inherited from the wartime, was virtually untouched.[12] It is also worth emphasizing that the so-called new-dealers who led SCAP were strongly bureaucratic-control oriented. Though aborted in the face of opposition from Washington, their efforts to establish a central bureau ('banking board') controlling all financial institutions is well documented.[13] Besides, their strong anti-big-business sentiments also worked in favour of the declining control of business leaders.[14]

All these factors seem to have worked to weaken the autonomy of the financial institutions and strengthen bureaucratic control. Bureaucratic control came to bear directly on the profit-and-loss conditions of the financial institutions. Throughout the early postwar period, the ratio of expenditure to revenue of each institution came to be used as the most potent measure for banking policy. Not only were branching, new equity issues and entry decisions controlled by the Ministry, bank employees' wages, real estate transactions as well as dividend rates were also brought under its surveillance. Thus, during the HGE, the balance-sheet-related behaviour and interest-rate setting by each bank came to be strictly monitored and controlled by the BOJ.

7.5 CONCLUDING REMARKS

Financial reform after the war was carried out under the strong influence of the economic thinking of the time and the power structure of the society. Since the real economy was in the middle of a 'catching-up' process based on heavy and chemical industrialization, the new financial system was required to respond to the necessity of providing long-term funds given the informational problems that are usually acute in this phase of development. It was only after the completion of the 'catch-up' process and internationalization of the economy that the transition to a truly market-based system was brought about.

How the HGE financial system, thus established, worked, was an important and intriguing question that needs to be explored. Let us conclude this chapter by briefly discussing this point. Though the banking sector within this system was highly regulated, this does not imply a lack of competition. Instead, keen competition, based on the pursuit of maximum deposits, emerged among the banks, especially the city banks. One reason for this can be found in the fact that government regulation, including some forms of preferential treatment, was based on deposit volume. Moreover, given a constant deposit rate, the maximization of deposits was more or less synonymous with profit maximization for the city banks (assuming economies of scale) since they were faced with an unrestricted and rapidly expanding loan market and were not required to specialize in their loaning activities.

This competition, however, was insufficient to wipe out all the inefficiencies in the system. Though financial intermediaries, such as the banks catering to the small- and medium-sized firms and agriculture, did a good job in terms of producing information on the unknown but promising firms which proved to be the basic driving force behind the rapid growth, they are believed to have suffered from significant internal inefficiencies. This was due to the fact that while they were protected by low deposit rates, they were also segregated from competition through regulations on their lending activities.

The most significant cost of regulation on the financial system was its effect on income distribution. Depositors, among others, suffered due to low asset income. Investors in securities also suffered from constantly high brokers' fees. Moreover, borrowers, unable to get hold of rationed subsidized credit, suffered from unfair competitive conditions, possibly resulting in distortions in resource allocation.

The 'division of labour' among different categories of private financial intermediaries and between governmental and private financial systems seems to have worked fairly well, giving rise to merits of specialization. However, toward the end of HGE, the system revealed serious drawbacks due to rigidity arising out of the regulations. For example, some government financial institutions had significant amounts of unused funds.

Finally, though indirect financing is considered desirable especially in terms of the *production* of information on borrowers, regulations on the securities markets, especially bond markets, seem to have been responsible for the underdevelopment of the corporate bond market in Japan. The relative underdevelopment of the short-term money market until recently can also be attributed, at least partly, to government regulations.

These points are discussed extensively in Teranishi (1990; 1993).

APPENDIX: INSTITUTIONAL CHANGES IN THE FINANCIAL SECTOR IMMEDIATELY AFTER THE WAR

This appendix summarizes institutional changes in the financial sector immediately after the war. For more details refer to the Bank of Japan, 'Postwar Reorganization of the Financial System' (From August 1945 to 1952) (*Sengowagakuni Kin'yuseido no Saihensei, Nihon Kin'yu-shi Shiryo, Showa Zokuhen*, vol. 10), and Ministry of Finance, *Showa Zaisei-shi*, vol. 13.

(1) *Dissolution of Wartime Financial Institutions*

October 1945	Closure of Wartime financial institutions such as Wartime Finance Corporation (Senji Kin'yu Kinko) and colonial financial institutions.
June 1947	Dissolution of Yokohama Specie Bank (Yokohama Shokin Ginko) (the Bank of Tokyo (Tokyo Ginko) was established in December 1946, inheriting the domestic business of the Yokohama Specie Bank).

(2) *Establishment of Private Long-Term Credit Institutions*

August 1948	Conversion of the Hokkaido Colonial Bank (Hokkaido Takushoku Bank) into an ordinary bank.
September 1948	Conversion of Hypothec Bank of Japan (Nihon Kangyo Ginko) into an ordinary bank.
March 1950	The Industrial Bank of Japan (IBJ) converted into an ordinary bank but allowed to issue financial bonds.
June 1952	Enactment of Loan Trust Law (Kashitsuke Shintaku-ho).
December 1952	Enactment of Long-Term Credit Bank Law (IBJ converted into long-term credit bank, and the Long-Term Credit Bank of Japan (Nihon Choki Shin'yo Ginko) established).
April 1957	Nippon Fudosan Bank established (later name changed to the Nippon Credit Bank (Nippon Saiken Shin'yo Ginko)).

(3) *Establishment of Private Financial Institutions for Small- and Medium-sized Firms, and Agriculture*

December 1947	Enactment of Agricultural Credit Co-operative Law (Nogyo Kyodokumiai-ho).
December 1950	Enactment of Law on Loan Insurance for Small- and Medium-sized Firms (Chushokigyo Shin'yo Hoken-ho).
June 1950	Enactment of Sogo Bank Law (Sogo Ginko-ho) and Shinkin Bank Law (Shin'yo Kinko-ho).

(4) *Reform of Capital Markets*

March 1947	Promulgation of Securities and Exchanges Law (Shoken Torihiki-ho).
June 1947	Establishment of Bond Issues Adjustment Committee (Kisaichosei Kyogikai).
March 1948	Promulgation of Revised Securities and Exchanges Law.
May 1949	Resumption of the activity of Securities Exchanges.
December 1949	Establishment of Japan Security Finance Corporation (Nihon Shoken Kin'yu Kaisha).
June 1951	Enactment of Law on Mutual Trust Funds (Shoken Toshi Shintaku-ho).

(5) *Development of Government Financial Institutions*

May 1950	Enactment of Housing Finance Corporation Law (Jutaku Kin'yu Koko-ho).
December 1950	Enactment of the Export Bank of Japan Law (later changed to the Export-Import Bank of Japan Law,

	Nihon Yushutsunyu Ginko-ho).
March 1951	Enactment of Japan Development Bank Law (Nihon Kaihatsu Ginko-ho).
April 1951	Enactment of Shikin Un'yobu-ho (Deposit Bureau of the Ministry of Finance converted into Trust Fund Bureau, and Fiscal Investment and Loan Programme initiated from fiscal year 1953).

Notes

*The author is greatly indebted to Hugh Patrick, Yutaka Kosai, Hideaki Miyajima, Anil Khosla and Ulrike Shaede for helpful comments.

1. Asajima (1986) pp. 178–81 and 335–6. The net worth ratio refers only to firms engaged in non-financial business.
2. See Asajima (1983) and Shibagaki (1968).
3. Bank of Japan, *Senji Kin'yu Tosei no Tenkai* (Wartime Regulation of the Financial System) 1943 (reprinted in *Nihon Kin'yu-shi Shiryo – Showahen*, vol. 27).
4. In March 1945, this system was extended to cover all major firms including those not directly related to military production (Gunji Kin'yu Tokubetsu Sochi-ho). But under this new system, each firm was related to one bank and not to a syndicate. In this sense, this system was qualitatively different from the previous one.
5. The relatively low figures for deposits-to-GNP ratio in Table 7.2, however, suggest the possibility of financial disintermediation by large asset holders like the corporate sector by way of investments in real estate and the like. This raises the possibility of under-the-table payments on deposits by large depositors. Even the Ministry of Finance (MOF) issued a circular in 1954 warning banks about payments of illegally high rates of interests on deposits (*Ginkokyoku Nenpo*, 1954).
6. The first aspect is stressed in Horiuchi, Packer and Fukuda (1988) and the second in Nakatani (1984) and Sheard (1989).
7. The government finance system planned to hold one-third with the remaining third to be held by the syndicated financial institutions.
8. The branch offices were allowed to lend to firms with capital or total assets less than three million yen (five million yen after 1951).
9. Similar measures were taken for business firms as well. However, the restructuring of businesses was delayed considerably due to the confusion following the implementation of the Law for the Elimination of Excessive Concentration of Economic Power (Kado Keizairyoku Shuchu Haijo-ho) and was completed only in 1951.
10. Okura-sho, *Ginko-kyoku Nenpo*, 1953, p. 216.
11. The final loss and the loss borne by stockholders was a bit lighter since some of the loans that were initially identified as bad loans turned out be sound at later stages. The final settlement of balance-sheets was carried out at the end of March 1957. Cf. Okura-sho (1983), p. 325.

12. Johnson (1982), Hadley (1970), Miyajima (1991).
13. BOJ, 'Sengo Wagakuni Kin'yu Seido no Saihensei (August 1945–52)', 1942 (reprinted in *Nihon Kin'yu-shi Shiryo (Showa Zokuhen)*, vol. 10.
14. For the political and philosophical implications of SCAP, cf. Nakamura (1979).

References

Asajima, Shoichi (1983) *Senkanki Sumitomo Zaibatsu Keiei-shi* (History of Sumitomo Zaibatsu during Interwar Period), (Tokyo: University of Tokyo Press).

Asajima, Shoichi (1986) *Mitsubishi Zaibatsu no Kin'yu Kozo* (Financial Structure of Mitsubishi Zaibatsu), (Tokyo: Ochanomizu shobo).

Hadley, Eleanor M. (1970) *Antitrust in Japan* (Princeton: Princeton University Press).

Horiuchi, Akiyoshi, Frank Packer and Shinichi Fukuda (1988) 'What Role Has the "Main Bank" Played in Japan?', *Journal of Japanese and International Economies*, vol. 2, no. 2.

Johnson, Chalmers (1982) *MITI and the Japanese Miracle* (Stanford: Stanford University Press).

Miyajima, Hideaki (1991) 'Zaibatsukaitai' (Dissolution of Zaibatsu), mimeograph.

Nakamura, Takafusa (1979) 'SCAP to Nihon' (SCAP and Japan), in *Senryoki Nihon no Keizai to Seiji*, ed. by Takafusa Nakamura (Tokyo: University of Tokyo Press).

Nakatani, Iwao (1984) 'The Economic Role of Financial Corporate Grouping', in *The Economic Analysis of the Japanese Firm*, ed. by Masahiko Aoki (Amsterdam: North-Holland).

Okura-sho (Ministry of Finance) (1983) *Showa Zaisei-shi* (The Fiscal History of the Showa Era), vol. 13 (Tokyo: Toyo Keizai Shinpo-sha).

Sheard, Paul (1989) 'The Main Bank System and Corporate Monitoring and Control in Japan', *Journal of Economic Behavior and Organization*, 11(3), pp. 399–422.

Shibagaki, Kazuo (1968) *Mitsui, Mitsubishi no Hyakunen* (A Hundred-year History of Mitsui and Mitsubishi) (Chuko Shinsho no. 172), (Tokyo: Chuokoron-sha).

Stiglitz, Joseph J. (1985) 'Credit Markets and the Control of Capital', *Journal of Money, Credit, and Banking*, 17(2), pp. 133–52.

Teranishi, Juro (1990) 'Financial System and the Industrialization of Japan: 1900–1970', *Banca Nazionale del Lavoro Quarterly Review*, no. 174, September, pp. 309–41.

Teranishi, Juro (1993) 'Japan, Finance and Economic Development', in *Financial Development of Japan, Korea and Taiwan*, ed. by Yung Chul Park and Hugh T. Patrick (forthcoming).

8 Land Reform in Postwar Japan

Toshihiko Kawagoe*

8.1 INTRODUCTION[1]

In prewar Japan, where agriculture occupied a dominant share in the economy, farmland was the most important resource and those who controlled it dominated society. 'Landlords (*Jinushi*)', owned nearly half of the farmland and had overwhelming power in rural communities. The House of Peers included many landlords and any attempts to improve the tenantry status, to their disadvantage were blocked. On the other hand, the farmland was cultivated by 5.5 million peasantry households, one-third of which were comprised of tenant cultivators (*kosaku*), who did not own their own land but rented small plots from their landlords. These cultivators had to pay nearly half their product to their landlords as land rent and struggled in a poverty, that became the root cause of social unrest in prewar Japan. Such practices were to continue until the drastic land reform executed just after the Second World War. This reform accomplished its objective to give land to the tillers and abolish landlordism. Land reform in Japan, thus, has been considered an example of a monumental success in the history of agricultural reform. In fact, Japan's experience has been a rare exception, since most attempts at land reform in the Third World have utterly failed.

Several questions will now arise. How was it possible for land reform in Japan to be accomplished so drastically and completely? How did the reform contribute to agricultural production? What kind of lessons can be drawn from this experience? The purpose of this chapter is to answer these questions. The process and economic implications of reform are also investigated. After a brief introductory discussion on the land tenure system in the prewar period in section 8.2, section 8.3 reviews various regulations pertaining to agriculture that were introduced during the war. Section 8.4 describes the process of land reform and its results. Possible economic implications of reform are discussed in section 8.5 as concluding remarks.

8.2 LAND TENANCY SYSTEM IN PREWAR JAPAN[2]

Throughout the prewar period, Japanese agriculture was dominated by landlordism while small tenant farmers struggled in poverty. This section provides an overview of the land tenure system in the prewar period and the related social unrest occurring in rural areas in the 1920s and 1930s. Major land policies are summarized chronologically in Table 8.1.

Table 8.1 Chronological summary of Japanese agricultural land policies

Year	*Major land policies*	*Related issues and comments*
1868	Meiji Restoration	
1873–81	Land Tax Revision	Change from feudal tax into modern land tax system
1920	Tenancy System Research Committee	(Land tenancy disputes occur frequently through the 1920s to 1930s)
1924	Land Tenancy Conciliation Law	
1926	Owner-Farmer Establishment rule	(Agricultural crisis)
1938	National Mobilization Law; Agricultural Land Adjustment Law	(Regulation during the war) Strengthen tenantry rights
1939	Land Rent Control Order	Control of land rent
1941	Land Price Control Order; Land Control Order	Control of land prices Control of changes of rights on land
1942	Food Control Law	Subsidy for rice producers
1945		
December	First Land Reform Law	The government prepared the first land reform plan
1946		
October	Second Land Reform: Agricultural Land Adjustment Law (amendment);	Legislation of the drastic land reform plan under the guidance of SCAP

continued on p. 180

Table 8.1 Continued

Year	*Major land policies*	*Related issues and comments*
	Owner-Farmer Establishment Special Measures Law	
December	Election of Village Land Committees	(Execution of the reform)
1947		
February	Election of Prefectural Land Committees	
March	First compulsory purchase	(Purchases were carried out successively 16 times until 1950)
1952	Agricultural Land Law	Strict protection of cultivators

Source: *NKTG*, pp. 1352–7.

8.2.1 Landlordism and the Peasantry

Japanese agriculture was traditionally shouldered by the peasantry, comprised of a large number of small family farms distributed unimodally. This characteristic, inherited from the feudal Tokugawa era (the seventeenth century to the mid nineteenth century), has been strengthened over the period of modern economic growth since the Meiji Restoration of 1868.[3] During the Meiji era, the Japanese government attempted to catch up with the Western nations through the development of industries under capitalism. As agriculture was the most important source for national revenues a Land Tax Revision (Chiso Kaisei) was implemented in 1873.[4] Feudal land taxes had been assessed annually on the basis of crop yields and were paid in kind. Through the revision this kind of tax was replaced by a modern land tax, based on land value. The annual tax rate was fixed at 3 per cent of the land value, which was calculated from the discounted annual net income of the land. The revision required a nationwide survey to ascertain land area (including forests), price and landownership. Based on this survey, which took nine years to complete and cost the government almost a full year's revenue (Hayami *et al.*, 1991, p. 64), landowners were issued certificates of title to their land. While formal landownership rights were given to the *de facto* landowners, who had paid the feudal land tax, traditional tenantry rights were neglected. In

Table 8.2 Number of farm households and cultivated land area by land tenure status in prewar Japan

Year	*Owner-farmer*	*Owner-cum-tenant*	*Tenant farmer*	*Total*
		Number of farms[a] *(thousand):*		
1910	1777	2139	1501	5417
1920	1683	2244	1558	5485
1930	1684	2350	1478	5512
1938 (1)	1626	2408	1407	5441
		Cultivated land area (thousand ha):		
1938 (2)	1577	2762	1108	5447
		Average farm size (ha/farm):		
1938 (2)/(1)	0.97	1.15	0.79	1.00

[a] Figures include farming landlords.

Sources: Kayo (1977) table C-a-2; Kurihara (1947) table 29 for 1938.

short, as a result of this law the landlords' position was strengthened and the basis of landlordism in the Meiji era was established.

Throughout the prewar period, the number of farms in Japan remained roughly constant at a level of 5.5 million. These farms were basically operated as family farms, mainly relying on their family labour. About 30 per cent of the farmers were tenant farmers, 30 per cent were owner cultivators, while the remaining 40 per cent were owner-cum-tenant farmers, who cultivated both their own and tenanted land (Table 8.2). Note that average operational farm size per household was larger for owner-cum-tenants than for owner farmers and tenant farmers. This fact suggests that owner farmers expanded their operations, if they had a sufficient labour force or entrepreneurial ability to manage a larger area. On the other hand, most of the tenant farmers cultivated very small areas, with one-third of them cultivating less than 0.3 hectares. In addition, these tenant farmers had to pay nearly half of their farm produce as land rent to landlords. With respect to paddy land, land rent was generally fixed according to the size of the harvest, and was paid in kind with the possibility for year-by-year reductions depending on the harvest. For example, when 3.5 tons of brown rice was produced per hectare of paddy land in the mid-1930s, about 1.7 tons of it was paid to landlords as land rent.[5] Very small farm size and the heavy burden imposed by

Table 8.3 Distribution of farmland owned by farmer and landlord, 1872–1947

Year	*Farmland area owned by*			*Total farmland area*	*Share of tenant cultivated area*
	Farmer		*Non-farming landlord*		
	Own cultivation	*Leased out* *(1)*	*(2)*	*(3)*	*(1) + (2)* / *(3)*
	(thousand ha)				(%)
1872				4556[a]	(29)
1883				4713	(36)
1903	2899	2324		5223	(44)
1915	3151	2660		5811	(46)
1930	3016	2792		5808	(48)
1947	3006	1143	821	4970	(40)

[a] Figure in 1874.

Sources: 1872 and 1883: Farmland: Umemura *et al.* (1966) table 32; Share of tenant cultivated area: Tohata and Uno (1959) p. 192, table 4.1; 1903–15: Kayo (1977) table B-b-1; 1947: *NKTG*, p. 598, table 12.

the land rent were the major sources of the poverty experienced by tenant farmers in prewar Japan.

The arable land was owned by 5 million landowners, including owner farmers. Just after the Meiji Restoration, the share of tenanted land was 30 per cent of the total arable land. This was gradually increased to around 45 per cent at the beginning of this century and further increased to nearly 50 per cent in the 1930s (Table 8.3). Due to the heavy burden of a land tax fixed in cash, coupled with the small size of land holdings, farmers were often unable to pay the tax, particularly in years of poor harvests or low farm prices. They were thus obliged to borrow money from landlords and often lost their land through foreclosure. This tendency accelerated during the Matsukata deflation in the 1880s, which brought a drastic decline in farm prices (Hayami *et al.*, 1991, p. 65). Since half of the owner farmers owned less than 0.5 hectares economically and socially there was little that differentiated them from the tenant farmers (Table 8.4).

Table 8.4 Size distribution of land holdings by landowners in prewar Japan, 1938

Size of land holdings (ha)	*Below 0.5*	*0.5 to 1.0*	*1.0 to 3.0*	*3.0 to 5.0*	*5.0 to 10*	*10 to 50*	*Above 50*	*Total*
	— (Number of thousand households[a])(%) —							
Landowner:								
Farmer	1978	1263	701	66	26[b]	–	–	4033
Non-farming landlord	453	21	215	154	83	44	3	973
Total	2430	1284	916	220	109	44	3	5006
	(49)	(26)	(18)	(4)	(2)	(1)	(–)	(100)

[a] Percentage distribution of landholdings by landowners is shown in parentheses.
[b] Includes farmers who owned more than 10 hectares.

Sources: Kayo (1977) table B-b-3; Kurihara (1947) p. 135.

8.2.2 Japanese Landlords

In order to facilitate the discussion here, we shall try to classify landlords into a few distinct categories. Owners of agricultural land can be divided into farmers and non-farmers. Farmers, who lease out some of their land while cultivating the rest of it, may be called farming landlords. According to the Special Agricultural Census (*Rinji Nogyo Sensasu*) taken in 1947, about 1.3 million farms, or one-fifth of total farm households, were farming landlords.[6] Although they leased out 1.14 million hectares of land in total (Table 8.3), average leased-out land area per farm was only 0.87 hectares, less than the size of an average farm, and 62 per cent of them leased out less than 0.5 hectares. Most of these farmers owned relatively large farms and supplemented their income by leasing a small plot of additional land. The land holdings of the Japanese peasantry were divided into many parcels of about 0.06 hectares on average.[7] After centuries of land exchange, trade, and inheritance, peasantry landholding was scattered widely over an area. Hence, for the sheer convenience of cultivation, farmers often leased out some of their land in more distant areas and leased more conveniently located land from other farmers for their own cultivation. Many farmers were, thus, both landlords and tenants.

Landowners who do not engage in farming themselves may be called non-farming landlords. Unfortunately, national level statistics do not tell us much about landlords, since no survey was done on them in the prewar period, except a survey in 1924 on landlords holding more than 50 hectares. Therefore, it is uncertain how many non-farming landlords there were during the prewar period. However, if we subtract the number of landowning farmers from the total number of landowners, we can roughly estimate that there were nearly 1 million non-farming landlords at that time.[8] These non-farming landlords are further divided into absentee landlords and village landlords. Absentee landlords are landowners who do not reside in or near the village where their land is located,[9] such as farmers' sons who had left for non-farm jobs but retained the family land by inheritance, or merchants and money-lenders from nearby towns, who acquired land through foreclosure or seizure. Village landlords are non-farming landlords residing in the village. Some of them were landowners, who owned large parcels of land and could draw sufficient income from land rent to allow them to devote themselves to politics, money-lending activities or hobbies. There were also small village landlords who had other primary sources of income, such as village officials, shopkeepers, doctors, or priests (Dore, 1959, pp. 23–5).

During the early Meiji era, large farming landlords, including wealthy farmers called *gono*, played an important role in agricultural development. They introduced new technology and invested in infrastructure, such as drainage and irrigation schemes. They also took the initiative in organizing agricultural discussion societies (*nodankai*), in which information on new technology and new plant varieties were exchanged. They were proud of acting as village leaders and of patronizing peasants. However, by the beginning of this century, these progressive and paternalistic landlords disappeared and were replaced by more parasitic landlords who acted as sheer rentier (Tohata, 1947, pp. 68–70).

The number of non-farming landlords in 1938 by size of land holdings is estimated in Table 8.4. A striking feature of Japanese landlordism is the existence of a large number of landowners with small holdings. Of these non-farming landlords, half owned less than 0.5 hectares and only 13 per cent owned more than 5 hectares (Table 8.4). Note that, by 1936 in order to secure an income equivalent to the salary of an urban civil servant or teacher, it was necessary to rent 6.5 hectares of paddy field of medium quality (Dore, 1959, p. 29).

Landlords owning more than 50 hectares comprised only 2400 households, and these households owned about 250 000 hectares of land (Tohata, 1947, pp. 38–45).[10] Thus the real landlord, who held a social and political position of the kind implied by the word *landlord* in English, was a rare exception in Japan, and most Japanese landlords were small landowners, who had other primary sources of income and land rent only complemented their household income.

8.3 TRANSITION OF LANDLORDISM

The agricultural crisis caused by a rapid decline of farm prices in the interwar period affected the peasantry, especially poor tenant farmers, resulting in social unrest and conflicts. Land tenancy disputes were a common phenomenon from the 1920s on. As the war in China progressed, various regulations were gradually strengthened under growing totalitarianism, and the firm basis of landlordism was undermined.

8.3.1 Land Tenancy Disputes in the Interwar Period

During the 1920s, farm prices were depressed, due to the postwar recession, coupled with the deflationary policies of the government. The situation was aggravated by the competition with rice imported from Korea and Taiwan. While wage rates of the non-farm sectors, as well as the farm wage rate, began to rise from the 1920s, the tenants' labour income did not improve. The frequency of tenancy disputes, resulting from demands for rent reduction, especially in years of bad harvest, increased rapidly (Figure 8.1). Local tenants' unions were organized and collective actions were taken by 70 to 80 tenant farmers at a time against landlords. These disputes, in which the primary target was rent reduction, were concentrated in relatively industrialized areas in central Japan, where parasitic landlords were prevalent.

Just after the return to the gold standard in 1930 at prewar parity, the Japanese economy, including farm prices and farm income, became severely depressed, resulting in a serious agricultural crisis. Although farm prices had already declined more than 20 per cent from 1925 to 1929, they further dropped by 30 per cent during the successive two years. The decline in farm prices was steeper than the fall in consumer prices (Figure 8.2). Unemployment in industrial sectors further aggravated the income levels of part-time farmers.

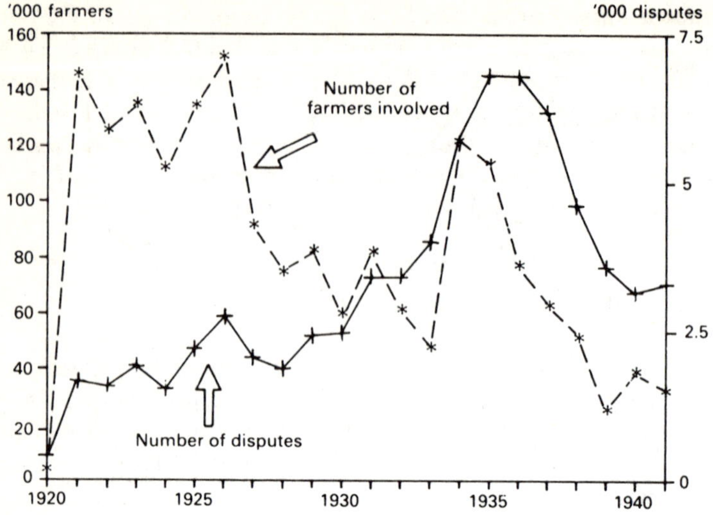

Figure 8.1 Number of tenancy disputes and farmers involved, 1920–41

Source: Kayo (1977) table B-b-4.

Farm income, especially of tenants, decreased sharply from 1413 yen per household in 1925 to 994 yen in 1929 and further dropped to 442 yen in 1931 (Figure 8.2). This resulted in a further increase in the number of land tenancy disputes, which were mainly caused by landlords' attempts to evict tenants from the land. The depression and increases in unemployment compelled small non-farming landlords to take back land for their own cultivation. Such disputes were particularly widespread in northern Japan, where more paternalistic landlords resided. In contrast to the organized actions in the 1920s, the disputes arising in the 1930s were more often individual actions between small landowners and tenant farmers. This was due in part to the suppression of left-wing activities and partly to the tightened social structure under the slogans of national emergency, as the war on the Asian continent continued.

As such social unrest continued to grow in the rural society, a reformist group in the Ministry of Agriculture and Commerce (Noshomu-sho:MAC)[11] began to argue that tenants' rights had to be more secure. Since the 1920s this group attempted to solve tenancy problems in order to remove the root cause of the disputes. A consultative body under MAC, the Tenancy System Research Com-

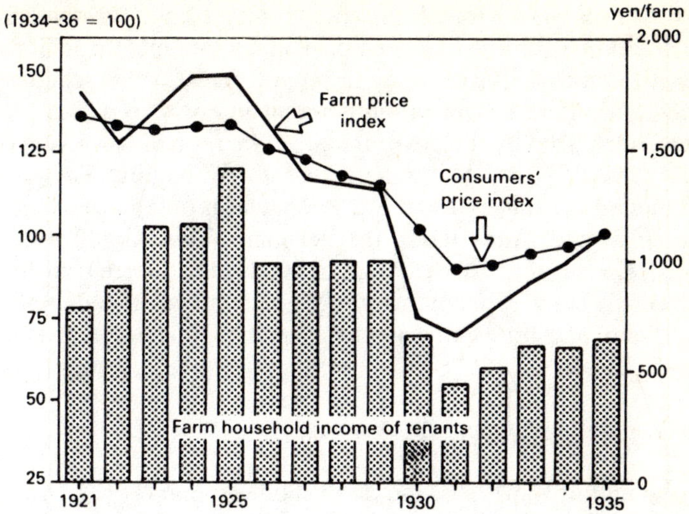

Figure 8.2 Changes in farm and consumer prices and tenant farm household income during the depression 1920–35
Note: Consumers' price index of all items for farm households, 1934–6 = 100; price index of agricultural products for all commodities, 1934–6 =100; average household income of tenant farmers, yen per household, excluding Hokkaido.

Sources: Ohkawa *et al.* (1967) tables 2 and 11; Kayo (1977) table M-a-2.

mittee (Kosaku Seido Chosa-iinkai), was set up in 1920. The Committee prepared a report recommending the drafting of a tenancy law, which, by the standard of the times, was extremely favourable to tenants. But it was difficult to implement their proposal because of the opposition of the conservatives, plus landlord interests in preventing any radical reforms (Dore, 1959, pp. 80–5, 106–12).

Instead, two indirect and modest measures were taken to tackle the issue. The first measure was the enactment of the Land Tenancy Conciliation Law (Kosaku Chotei-ho) of 1924, which was designed to mediate voluntary submitted tenancy disputes by local courts and Conciliation Committees. Tenancy officers were also appointed in each prefecture to advise and assist the committee. Although it did not much improve the situation, tenants' interests were, to some extent, protected under this law (Saito, 1989, pp. 312–13). The second measure was the enhancement of the Owner-Farmer Establishment Rule (Jisakuno Sosetsu Iji-kisoku) of 1926, which was intended as a means to transform tenants into owner farmers. Since 1920 a credit programme had been provided to tenants through credit cooperatives for the purchase of farmland. In 1926 this scheme was enlarged and offered loans at 4.8 per cent interest, in which 1.3 per cent was subsidized by the government, to be repaid over twenty-five years, if tenants wished to purchase land for cultivation. The government planned to transfer about 112 000 hectares of tenanted land into owner cultivated land under this scheme. This target was well achieved, since from 1926 to 1937, 114 000 hectares were transferred. However, the converted land was only 4 per cent of the tenanted land in 1926, and had little impact on the land tenancy system (Ouchi, 1960, pp. 234–5).

8.3.2 Regulation During the War

Since the end of the 1930s, the domestic food market was gradually tightened. The decline in both food imports and domestic production caused by the shortage of raw materials and labour force for agricultural production, aggravated the situation as the war progressed. Although the country continuously imported rice from Korea and Taiwan, the severe drought that hit Korea and west Japan in 1939, served as the beginning of a serious food shortage lasting a decade. Since then the primary target of agricultural policy was to promote agricultural production so as to secure food self-sufficiency. In order to encourage production, especially of rice, the government successively adopted various regulations on agriculture under increasing totalitarian control of domestic affairs. The National Mobilization Law (Kokka Sodoin-ho) enacted in 1938 enabled the government to mobilize physical and human resources for war. The land tenancy system was not an exception to such regulations. It was a good chance for the reformist group in the MAC to seek agrarian reform under the slogan of enhanced food production.

As a first step in reform, the Agricultural Land Adjustment Law (Nochi Chosei-ho) was enacted in 1938. This law allowed the prefectural governments and village authorities to take the initiative in establishing owner farmers by suggesting to landlords that they should sell their land. Compulsory purchase was also allowed by the local authorities in the case of uncultivated land. The tenancy title was recognized as a property right, which was to remain intact even after a change in ownership of the land. The landlords' rights to evict tenants or to terminate the tenancy contract were slightly restricted. A provision of the Land Tenancy Conciliation Law of 1924 was also enhanced such that the tenancy officers were allowed to submit disputes to the court for compulsory mediation. A Farmland Committee (Nochi-iinkai) was set up in each village and prefecture as a body coordinating various land-related issues (Ouchi, 1960, p. 270; *NKTG*, pp. 92–3; Dore, 1959, pp. 109–10). Although this law was far from sufficient for securing the tenants' interests, it was a slight advance in the coming land reform.

In 1939 the Land Rent Control Order (Kosaku-ryo Tosei-rei) was issued under the National Mobilization Law. This order was one of several anti-inflationary measures taken in, which covered a wide range of prices. The Land Rent Control Order imposed a freeze on rents at their 1939 level. The order also allowed prefectural governments to order rent reduction when necessary. In fact, until 1943, rental rates of about 330 000 hectares of land were reduced by orders of the local authorities under this ordinance (Ouchi, 1960, p. 271). As a second step, land prices were also frozen by the Land Price Control Order (Rinji Nochi Kakaku Tosei-rei) issued in 1941. The order imposed fixed prices on farmland at the 1939 level, calculated based on the rent value (the basis of land tax assessment) multiplied by a locally determined fixed rate. The land price under control was 6329 yen per hectare for paddy land and 3763 yen/ha for upland on average.[12] Land ownership was further restricted by successive regulations. The Land Control Order (Rinji Nochi-to Kanri-rei) issued in 1941 stipulated that the conversion or trade of farmland for non-agricultural purposes was to be subject to the approval of local authorities. The government or local authorities were allowed to order which crop should be planted in order to secure maximum production of the most important crops. Although these regulations were imposed to sustain farm production, they functioned as a *de facto* tenancy law, strengthening the tenants' status, while restricting the landlords' interests.

Another blow to the landlords came from food price policies. During the war, food shortage in the country had worsened. In 1942 the Food Control Law (Shokuryo Kanri-ho) was enacted and the whole marketing process, including the pricing of staple foods, was directly controlled by the government. The number of commodities under rationing was quickly increased. The most important crop was rice, which has always been the staple food for the Japanese diet. The government had to procure sufficient rice for maintaining the rationing programme. Farm producers were ordered to sell all produce to the government, except an amount reserved for their own consumption, which was restricted to 4 *gou* (= 574 grams) of rice per day per adult. The same rule was applied to the landlords. Although land rent was usually paid in kind to landlords in the prewar period,[13] under this law the rent in kind was, except for the portion for landlords' own consumption, ordered to be delivered directly to the government by tenants. After the government purchased rice, tenants paid land rent by cash.

During the 1940s it became increasingly more difficult to secure the maximum deliveries of rice. Prices needed to be raised in order to give incentives to producers to maintain production. However, price increase were incompatible with anti-inflationary policies. Thus the Ministry of Agriculture adopted an intricate measure, which gave subsidies to farm producers, while the rice price itself remained unchanged. Farm producers could receive subsidies for the amounts delivered to the government. In addition, subsidies were also given for a portion of the land rent, if it was delivered by tenant farmers to the government. The tenants were then allowed to pay the land rent in cash on the basis of the rice price, excluding the subsidy. When this scheme was first introduced in 1941, the subsidy was 5 yen per *koku* (= 150 kilograms of brown rice) and the rice price was 44 yen/*koku*. Thus the producers' price was 49 yen, while the landlords' price was 44 yen. The subsidiary level was gradually raised and thus the producers' price was increased to 62.5 yen in 1943, 300 yen in 1945, and 550 yen when the war ended. On the other hand, the rice price, i.e. landlords' received price, was raised only slightly during this period (Table 8.5). The gap between the price received by landlords and tenants widened. Despite the government's efforts, an inflationary tendency was prevailing during the war. Compared with the wholesale price index for all commodities, the producers' price for rice was maintained at the same pace, while the landlords' price was drastically suppressed in real terms (Table 8.5).

Through these regulations on the land market coupled with food price policies, the economic power of the landlords was undermined. By the end of the war in 1945, land was no longer an attractive source of income for landlords.

8.4 LAND REFORM

There is no general agreement on the definition of land reform. However, if we narrowly define it as the redistribution of land ownership rights from landlords to tillers, the land reform in Japan was a

Table 8.5 Changes in the government's procurement price of rice, 1940–6

Year	*Rice price* (1)	*Subsidy paid to producers (yen/koku*[a]*)* (2)	*Producers' price* (1)+(2)	*Wholesale price index (All commodities) (1940=43)*[b]
1940	43	–	43	43
1941	44	5	49	48
1942	44	5	49	50
1943	47	15.5	62.5	56
1944	47	15.5	62.5	64
1945	55	245	300	106
1946	75	475	550	566

[a] 150 kg of brown rice.
[b] Index based on 1933 weights is set equal to 43 in 1940 for a comparison with producer price. The index shows in November for each year.

Sources: *NKTG*, pp. 495–6; Bank of Japan (1948 and 1949).

programme conforming to this context and, according to Hayami's definition, can be categorized as a non-communist Asian model.[14]

8.4.1 Legislation of the Reform

After the devastation caused by the war, the country faced starvation. Imports had been stopped and domestic agriculture was critically exhausted. The government had to overcome severe food shortages in the country. Under this situation, a drastic land reform was carried out from 1946 to 1950 under strong guidance from the Supreme Commander for the Allied Powers of the occupation forces (SCAP).

Just after the war, the Japanese Ministry of Agriculture independently drafted an outline for reform, when SCAP had not yet shown any clear stance against reform. This outline was approved by the Cabinet (22 November 1945), and the first Land Reform Bill (Nochi Kaikaku-hoan) was prepared as a revision of the Agricultural Land Adjustment Law of 1938. The bill contained three main provisions: first, compulsory transfer of all land owned by absentee landlords and all tenanted land of other landowners whose individual holding exceeded five hectares; second, replacement of traditional land rent in kind by an equivalent cash rent, calculated on the basis of landlords' rice price – this implied a substantial reduction of the rent level, since the landlords' price was considerably lower than the producers' price; third, reorganization of the Farmland Committees.

This bill was proposed to the Diet on 4 December 1945 though it almost talked out due to the obstinate resistance of conservatives. However, on 9 December 1945, SCAP issued a memorandum ordering the Japanese government to draw up plans for an agrarian reform, stating as its objective,

> . . . [to] remove economic obstacles to the revival and strengthening of democratic tendencies, establish respect for the dignity of men, and destroy the economic bondage which has enslaved the Japanese farmer to centuries of feudal oppression.[15]

It pointed out a number of pernicious ills that blighted the agrarian structure, such as intense overcrowding of land and widespread tenancy under conditions highly unfavourable to tenants. The Japanese government was ordered to submit a programme of rural land reform, which contained measures to insure a more equitable transfer of farmland from non-operators to cultivators, and to protect new landowners against reversion to tenantry (SCAP/SCAPIN-411; Hewes, 1950, pp. 741–3). It was not clear whether the purpose of the memorandum was to help the Japanese government get the bill passed in the Diet. However, whatever its intentions, the Diet was frightened and resigned itself to passing the bill into law (Dore, 1959, pp. 133–5).

SCAP, however, felt that the land reform programme was deficient in many respects, and did not give the government approval for their plan. To begin with, only 100 000 landlords' or 900 000 hectares of tenanted land were subject to compulsory transfer, since few village landlords had holdings larger than five hectares per person. Moreover, the definition of absentee landlord was not clear, and thus many such landlords might have been able to avoid compulsory transfer. Discussions continued between SCAP and the Ministry of Agriculture until the first plan was gradually elaborated[16] and a drastic land reform plan drawn up, which comprised an amendment of the Agricultural Land Adjustment Law of 1938 and enactment of the Owner-Farmer Establishment Special Measures Law (Jisakuno Sosetsu Tokubetsu Sochi-ho). These bills were passed during the first Diet session held on 11 October 1946 without modification. On the same day, General MacArthur issued a short statement, commenting on the bill, closing with the following passage;

> There can be no firmer foundation for a sound and moderate democracy and no firmer bulwark against the pressure of an extreme philosophy. (*NKSS* 14, p. 445)

Drastic land reform measures were embodied in these laws. The main provisions were (*NKTG*, pp. 128–30; Dore, 1959, ch. 6; Hewes, 1950, pp. 761–75):

(a) All farmland owned by absentee landlords was to be subject to compulsory purchase. The term 'absentee landlord' was rigorously defined as any landowner who did not reside in the same village of the leased-out land. Therefore, farming landlords' leased-out land extending into neighbouring villages, was regarded as 'absentee'-owned land. All tenanted land of village landlords in excess of 1 hectare (4 hectares in Hokkaido) was also to be compulsorily purchased.[17] Owner cultivated land in excess of 3 hectares (12 hectares in Hokkaido) was to be purchased, if its cultivation was judged to be inefficient in terms of land productivity. These limits were to be applied on a per household basis.

(b) Land Committees were set up at three levels, village (or town), prefectural and central. The ten members of the Village Land Committees were elected separately by three different groups, 5 by tenants, 3 by landlords and 2 by owner farmers. Purchase plans were to be drawn up by Village Land Committees with the approval of the Prefectural Land Committee and purchased directly by the government. The status quo as of 23 November 1945 was taken as the basis of the purchase plan, when the first land reform plan was released to the press. All subsequent changes of cultivating or ownership rights were declared void.

(c) The purchase price was the same as that in the first Land Reform Law (Nochi Kaikaku-ho), and was calculated by multiplying the rental value by a fixed factor. The rental value was an officially determined figure used for taxation purposes and set in 1938, or about 20 yen/*tan* (= 0.099 hectares) for paddy land and 10 yen/*tan* for upland. The fixed factor was calculated as the ratio of the land value to a capitalized land rent, imputed from typical owner farmers' operation at 1945 price levels.[18] Thus the factor was determined to be 40 for paddy land and 48 for upland. And the purchase price was to be about 760 yen/*tan* and 450 yen/*tan*, respectively in paddy land and upland. An additional bonus payment of 220 yen/*tan* (paddy land) and 130 yen/*tan* (upland) was made to landowners for the first 3 hectares (12 hectares in Hokkaido).

(d) The payment to landlords was to be made in National Bonds bearing an interest of 3.6 per cent and redeemable within 30 years. The purchase price for tenants was the same as the landlords' selling price. Payments could be made in cash or in annual instalments over a period of 30 years at a 3.2 per cent interest rate.

(e) In addition to the provisions outlined above, various regulations were introduced to control tenancy relations. All rents were to be paid in cash and the level was frozen. Tenancy contracts could not be terminated nor refused for renewal without the permission of the Land Committee. Thus tenants' rights were extremely enhanced.

8.4.2 Execution and the Results

The Land Reform Law was hard to execute, since it involved changes in the property rights of some 6 million families, 2 million of which had every reason to try to obstruct its purposes (Dore, 1959, p. 149). More than 400 000 persons were engaged in the execution of the programme, and just after the enactment of the law, 16 781 personnel were involved in it (Hewes, 1950, pp. 792–6). The programme, however, required the employment of a considerable number of personnel at both the national and prefectural level. Fortunately, there were fairly well-trained individuals in the Ministry of Agriculture and at the prefectural level, such as the Tenancy Officers, who were specialists in the tenancy problem, appointed under the tenancy programme based on the Land Tenancy Conciliation Law of 1924 (Tohata, 1966, pp. 309–11). By the beginning of 1947, 415 000 persons were mobilized, including 32 000 Committee secretaries and 116 000 committee members. The figure also included about 260 000 Committee assistants, who worked for the programme without pay (*NKTG*, pp. 156–7). The total costs of the programme reached more than seven billion yen during the first three years from 1946 to 1948, of which about 80 per cent was used for operations, while the rest represented institutional costs.[19]

As a first step in the execution of the programme, members of the Village Land Committees were elected in December 1946 and those at the prefectural level in February 1947. As SCAP had ordered that the reform had to be accomplished within two years, the first compulsory purchase was carried out in March 1947, just after the election of the committees. Such purchases were successively executed more than ten times and 1 630 000 hectares of farmland were acquired by the government by the end of 1948.[20] This land was sold to cultivators soon after. During this period, the land price paid to landlords, fixed at the 1945 price level, was reduced to a negligible level as a result of rapid inflation. In fact, the prices for consumer goods on the black market in Tokyo increased about eight times from October 1945 to the middle of 1949 (Bank of Japan, 1949, p. 178). In 1939 the price of 1 *tan* (= 0.099 hectares) of good paddy land was equivalent to over 3000 packs of cigarettes or 31 tons of coal. In 1948, however, it was equivalent to only 13 packs of cigarettes or 0.24 tons of coal.[21] On the other hand, the inflation enabled tenants to pay any remaining balance within a year or two of their purchase.

During the five years that this drastic reform was carried out, most of the farmland under tenancy came into cultivators' hands. Before the reform in 1941, nearly half of the farmland was cultivated by tenant farmers (Table 8.6). Ownership of these lands was transferred to the former cultivators of the land. By 1949 when the land reform was almost complete, 13 per cent of the farmland remained as tenanted land; by 1955 it had further declined to only 9 per cent. Accordingly, the number of owner cultivators increased from 31 per cent of farm households in 1941 to 70 per cent in 1955, and the percentage of tenant farmers who did not own any farmland decreased drastically during this period from 28 per cent to only 4 per cent (Table 8.6). The number of tenant-cum-owner farmers whose landownership was less than half their total cultivating area also decreased from 21 per cent to 5 per cent. On the other hand, absentee landlords disappeared, since 80 to 90 per cent of their land, estimated at about 560 000 hectares, was transferred to tenants (*NKTG*, p. 783). About 70 to 80 per cent, or over 1 million hectares, of the leased-out or own-cultivated land held by village landlords was also transferred. Thus landlordism in Japanese agriculture was abolished.[22]

Table 8.6 Changes in distribution of cultivated land area and number of farms by tenure status, 1941–55

	1941	*1949*	*1955*
Farmland area (thousand hectare)[b]:			
Owner cultivated	3099 (54)	4274 (87)	4678 (91)
Tenant cultivated	2660 (46)	643 (13)	462 (9)
Total	5759 (100)	4917 (100)	5140 (100)
Number of farm households (thousand)[b]:			
Owner[a]	1656 (31)	3564 (57)	4200 (70)
Owner-cum-tenant[a]	1123 (21)	1735 (28)	1308 (22)
Tenant-cum-owner[a]	1093 (20)	458 (7)	285 (5)
Tenant[a]	1516 (28)	489 (8)	239 (4)
Total	5412 (100)	6247 (100)	6043 (100)

[a] Owner: farmers who own more than 90 per cent of their cultivating land. Owner-cum-tenant and tenant-cum-owner: farmers who own 50 to 90 per cent and 10 to 50 per cent of their cultivating land, respectively. Tenant: farmers who own less than 10 per cent of their cultivating land.

[b] Percentage distribution of farmland area and farm households is shown in parentheses.

Sources: Kayo (1977) tables B-b-1 and C-a-2; *NKTG*, pp. 646–7, table 26.

From late 1948 there was talk among Japanese policy-makers of terminating the reform, since the transfer of farmland had been mostly completed. SCAP, however, expressed concern about this tendency (*NKSS* 14, pp. 687–9). On 21 October 1949, General MacArthur sent a letter to the Prime Minister of Japan, stating:

> the most successful land reform program in history. . . . The benefits of the reform must become a permanent part of the texture of Japanese rural society. Any possibility of a gradual reversion in the land tenure system as it existed before the reform must be forestalled. (*NKSS* 14, pp. 689–91)[23]

In order to maintain the results of the reform, the Japanese government proposed the amendment of the Owner-Farmer Establishment Special Measures Law of 1946. However, this amendment did not pass the Diet. The government then issued Order No. 307 (the order on the sale of farmland, to which the Owner-Farmer Establishment Special Measures Law and the Agricultural Land Adjustment Law should be applied) in 1950 as a temporary measure until the Agricultural Land Law (Nochi-ho) would be enacted.

8.4.3 Agricultural Land Law

In order to secure the results of the land reform and prevent the revival of landlordism, the Agricultural Land Law was enacted in 1952. In this context, the law was of an inherently defensive and negative nature, characterized by its strong owner-farmer orientation, which envisaged that farmland should be owned by its cultivators (Kato, 1967). The law was not a new one, rather, it brought together the provisions of the Owner-Farmer Establishment Special Measures Law, the Agricultural Land Adjustment Law and Order No. 307 of 1950.

The law strictly controlled the markets on farmland. Transactions of farmland were subject to the approval of the local authorities. Landlords were not allowed to sell their land to anyone other than their tenants, which meant that if the land was under tenancy the only possible buyer was the cultivator. The legal maximum on farmland holdings was set at 3 hectares (12 hectares in Hokkaido). Land could be traded at market prices, unless the purchaser's land holdings exceeded the limits. However, only farmers who were cultivating more than 0.3 hectares of farmland (2 hectares in Hokkaido) were allowed to purchase. Land rent was also strictly controlled and set at a very low level. Tenantry rights were so heavily protected that it was almost impossible for landlords to evict tenants from land that they were cultivating. Absentee ownership was not allowed, though village landlords could hold up to one hectare of tenanted land. Land ownership and use, thus, has been frozen in the state in which it emerged after the land reform (Dore, 1959, p. 198).

8.4.4 Background to the Completion

Why might the land reform in Japan be 'the most successful land reform programme in history' as stated by General MacArthur? Note that the term 'successful' was used in terms of the reform's political objective, that of providing 'land to tillers', the well-publicized slogan of the land reform programme. An important factor in this success was the existence of the overwhelming power of SCAP, which resolved to reform the agrarian structure (Walinsky, 1977, p. 94; Tuma, 1965, p. 136). However, this would not have been a sufficient condition. There were several pre-conditions which enabled the country to achieve the goals of reform. First, with the implementation of the Land Tax Revision (1873–81), an accurate record on landownership had been obtained for the purpose of taxation. Tenantry conditions had been closely surveyed while the close-knit social structure of the Japanese village enabled identification of tenancy relations. Second, there was a tradition of reformist groups in the Ministry of Agriculture who worked to tackle land problems. Many specialists such as Tenancy Officers were thus available at prefectural level (Tohata, 1966, pp. 303–5). There were also a large number of well-educated people who could engage in numerous operational tasks, when other job opportunities were rather limited owing to the devastation caused by the war. Third, the landlords' power had already been undermined due to various regulations during the war. The political situation was also favourable, because the power and confidence of ruling conservative elites were diminished through defeat and occupation by foreign forces (Hayami *et al.*, 1990, p. 167). Thus these preconditions played an important role in Japan's successful attempt at agricultural land reform.

8.5 SUMMARY AND ECONOMIC IMPLICATIONS

The land reform brought about a more equal distribution of assets and income among the members of rural society, and this ultimately contributed to the democratization and social and political stability of postwar Japan. The reform broke with old customs and traditions, and many of the beneficial effects of the reform on farm production have come about not simply through the direct impact of the reform, but through its indirect effects in changing the whole tenor of village life (Dore, 1959, p. 218). Given these social and political benefits, what kind of economic implications can be drawn from the drastic land reform in Japan?

First, what was the impact on the production structure of agriculture? The land reform programme in Japan itself contained little future perspective with regard to production structure. The immediate objective was political: to achieve equity by transferring landownership from landlords to the tillers of the soil. Thus small tenant farmers became small owner cultivators, without any apparent change in farm size. The production structure of traditional agriculture since the prewar period remained intact. After the reform, operational farm size even declined on average, from 1.09 hectares in 1941 to 0.94 hectares in 1955 (see Table 14.3 in Chapter 14).

Since no strong economies of scale were revealed at that time, the small size of farm units was not so disadvantageous in terms of productivity (Hayami and Kawagoe, 1989). In fact, farm production itself increased at a relatively high rate during the postwar period (Hayami *et al.*, 1991, p. 87). The next question, then, is whether this rapid growth can be attributed to the land reform. The positive impacts of the reform on growth have often been stressed in the literature, such as inducements to farm investment and more intensive operations through new incentives given to former tenants who acquired their own land (Raper, 1951, p. 181; Dore, 1959, p. 216; Raup, 1967, p. 278; Ogura, 1967, p. 37). If we assume that such incentives could have promoted growth, it means that tenant farmers' farm operation before the reform had been inefficient and productivity differences should have been observed between owner and tenant farmers. However, in the 1930s no significant difference was found in terms of yield per hectare, labour productivity, and average cost of rice production (Table 8.7). The reform may have contributed to an increase in the standard level of living for rural people through the redistribution of wealth and thereby income (Kawano, 1969, p. 385). However, it is not clear whether the reform contributed to capital formation in the agricultural sector. A quantitative analysis finds no significant effects in this respect (Kawano, 1969). Hayami *et al.* (1991, p. 87) point out that the major factor underlying rapid agricultural growth in the postwar period may be identified as the technological potential accumulated since the 1930s. Although this potential had been limited by the critical shortage of fertilizers and other factors

Table 8.7 Comparison of the productivity of owner and tenant farmers, 1939–41 averages

	Owner farmer	*Tenant farmer*
(1) Yield (kg/ha)	3780	3687
(2) Total cost (yen/ha)	960	922
(3) Labour input (days/ha)	189	188
Labour productivity (1)/(3) (kg/day)	20	19.6
Average cost (2)/(1) (yen/kg)	0.25	0.25

Source: Kayo (1977) table L-a-2 (rice production costs estimated by Ministry of Agriculture).

during the war, it was quickly realized once the supply of these inputs was made possible after the war.

Finally, we need to consider what kind of lessons can be drawn from the experience of Japanese land reform. In terms of equity, Japanese land reform was successful because it was carried out under favourable political and social conditions. The traditional land reform design, exemplified by the Japanese case, where the aim is limited to the attainment of a more equitable distribution of landownership through the compulsory transference of farmland, would be likely to fail, if attempted in countries where favourable conditions do not exist. Hayami suggests a need to abandon the traditional design and shift to a new land reform paradigm, which would include institutional and organizational changes, for the countries in the Third World (Hayami *et al.*, 1990, pp. 166–7).

Moreover, we should note that when the Japanese land reform programme was designed, there had already been a strong preconception among the policy-makers of the Japanese government, as well as those of SCAP, that landlordism was the source of many evils, which could only be corrected by establishing owner farmers. Thus the strict controls on the farmland market imposed under the Agricultural Land Law later became a major impediment for the structural adjustment of agriculture, as discussed in Chapter 14. The Japanese experience suggests that a land reform programme should include a broad conception of the future production structure of agriculture, and should not limit its objective to the distribution of rights in land. Shortsighted programmes based on ideological preconceptions will hamper flexible resource allocations and may become stubborn obstacles to the wholesome growth of agriculture.

Notes

* I am grateful for helpful comments and suggestions from Kunio Ohkama, Masao Kikuchi, Juro Teranishi, Yutaka Kosai, and the members of the study project at the Japan Center for Economic Research.

1. The following abbreviations are used in this chapter. *NKTG*: *Nochi Kaikaku Tenmatsu Gaiyo* by Nochi Kaikaku Kiroku-iinkai; *NKSS*: *Nochi Kaikaku Shiryo Shusei* by Nochi Kaikaku Shiryo Hensan-iinkai.
2. This section draws on Dore (1959, part I), and Hayami *et al.* (1991, ch. 2).
3. See Smith (1959) on Japanese agriculture during the Tokugawa feudal era.

4. Just after the Revision in the early 1880s the land tax comprised nearly 70 per cent of the government's tax revenue (Tohata and Ohkawa, 1956, p. 421).
5. Five-year average of 1933 to 1937 for tenant farmers, surveyed by Ministry of Agriculture (Kayo, 1977, table L-a-2).
6. There were 1.317 million farm households, who leased out 1.143 million hectares of farmland in 1947 (*NKTG*, p. 605, table 21). The figure in this census should be interpreted with caution, since the land reform was already ongoing when the survey was conducted.
7. Excessive parcelling is a common phenomenon in peasantry societies, and has been widely observed in Asia, as well as in the Middle Ages in Europe (Blum, 1978, pp. 119–20).
8. Note that this figure is to some extent overestimated, because an owner with land in two different administrative areas appears as two owners in statistics.
9. A more rigorous definition was used in the land reform legislation: absentee landlords meant any landowners who did not reside in the same village of their leased-out land. Therefore, farming landlords' leased-out land, extended into neighbouring villages, was also regarded as 'absentee'.
10. Excluding about 800 landlords in Hokkaido, where extensive agriculture was practised and the whole scale of operation is larger than that in the rest of Japan. The land ownership of 50 hectares in Hokkaido cannot be comparable with other regions as a source of income.
11. In 1925 the Ministry of Agriculture and Commerce became two separate ministries: the Ministry of Agriculture and the Ministry of Commerce and Industry.
12. Ogura (1951, pp. 744–5). The fixed rates were estimated to be 33 for paddy land and 40 for upland, on average.
13. For most farmland under tenancy, (91.7 per cent of paddy land and 47.3 per cent of upland) the rent was paid in kind (*NKTG*, p. 95).
14. Hayami *et al.* (1990, p. 5) defined the non-communist model as one in which the redistribution of all or a part of land property rights is carried out, while in the communist model land property rights are abolished, and lands confiscated from landlords and owner farmers are consolidated into collective or state farms. Under the non-communist model, the Asian model limits the reform to a redistribution of land rights from landlords to tenants, while in the Latin American model semi-feudal estates based on bonded labour are transformed into landowning family farms.
15. GHQ/SCAP SCAPIN-411 (Rural Land Reform), memorandum for the Imperial Japanese Government on 9 December 1945, reprinted in *NKSS*, vol. 14, pp. 114–16.
16. For details of this process, see Hewes (1950).
17. Note that the limit showed is an average. In fact, it varied between prefectures from 1.5 hectares in northern Japan to 0.6 hectares in western Japan, according to the local average farm size (*NKTG*, pp. 228–31).
18. The interest rate for National Bonds, 3.68 per cent, was used for capitalization (*NKTG*, p. 142).

19. Hewes (1950, pp. 803–7). See also *NKTG*, pp. 1163–211 for further details.
20. *NKTG*, p. 249. Compulsory purchases continued with an additional 139 000 hectares purchased from 1949 to 1951.
21. A. J. Grad *Land and Peasant in Japan* (New York, 1952), p. 219. Quoted in Dore (1959, p. 139).
22. In addition to land purchased from the landlords, uncultivated land, pastures and forests were also acquired by the government for the development programme. SCAP reported on 31 March 1949, that 3 044 310 hectares of the land, including pasture and other land for development, was purchased or acquired, and sold or awaiting disposal (Hewes, 1950, p. 841, table J).
23. The United States had the liberal Jeffersonian tradition of agrarian reform, which regarded the family farm, owned and operated by cultivators, as the only sound foundation of social equality and political stability (Ruttan, 1964).

References

Bank of Japan (1948, 1949) *Honpo Keizai Tokei* (Economic Statistics of Japan), (Tokyo: Bank of Japan).

Blum, Jerome (1978) *The End of the Old Order in Rural Europe* (Princeton, New Jersey: Princeton University Press).

Dore, R. P. (1959) *Land Reform in Japan* (London: Oxford University Press).

Hayami, Yujiro and Toshihiko Kawagoe (1989) 'Farm Mechanization, Scale Economies and Polarization', *Journal of Development Economics*, 31, pp. 221–39.

Hayami, Yujiro, Ma. Agnes R. Quisumbing and Loudes S. Adriano (1990) *Toward an Alternative Land Reform Paradigm: A Philippines Perspective* (Manila: Ateneo de Manila University Press).

Hayami, Yujiro, Saburo Yamada, with Masakatsu Akino, Lee Thanh Ngiep, Toshihiko Kawagoe and Masayoshi Honma (1991) *The Agricultural Development of Japan: A Century's Perspective* (Tokyo: University of Tokyo Press).

Hewes, Laurence I. Jr (1950) *Japanese Land Reform Program*, Natural Resource Section Report No. 127, NRS, General Headquarters Supreme Commander for the Allied Powers, reprint in *NKSS*, vol. 14, pp. 708–910 (page references are to reprint edition).

Kato, Ichiro (1967) 'Nochi-ho no Rippo Ronri' (Legislative Logic of the Agricultural Land Law), in *Nihon Nosei no Tenkai Katei*, ed. by Ichiro Kato and Kusuhiko Sakamoto (Tokyo: University of Tokyo Press).

Kawano, Shigeto (1969) 'Effects of Land Reform on Consumption and Investment of Farmers', in *Agricultural Economic Growth: Japan's Experience*, ed. by Kazushi Ohkawa, B. F. Johnston and Hiromitsu Kaneda (Tokyo: University of Tokyo Press).

Kayo, Nobufumi (ed.) (1977) *Kaitei Nihon Nogyo Kiso Tokei* (Basic Statistics on Japanese Agriculture, revised version), (Tokyo: Norin Tokei Kyokai).

Kurihara, Hakujyu (1947) *Nihon Nogyo no Kiso Kozo* (Fundamental Structure of Japanese Agriculture), (Tokyo: Chuo Koron-sha) (reprint in *Showa Zenki Nosei Keizai Meicho-shu*, ed. by Yasuo Kondo, no. 7, Tokyo: Nosangyoson Bunka Kyokai, 1979) (page references are to reprint edition).

Nochi Kaikaku Kiroku-iinkai (ed.) (1951) [*NKTG*] *Nochi Kaikaku Tenmatsu Gaiyo* (Summary Accounts of the Land Reform), (Tokyo: Nosei Chosa Kai) (reprint, Tokyo: Ochanomizu Shobo, 1977).

Nochi Kaikaku Shiryo Hensan-iinkai (ed.) (1982) [*NKSS*] *Nochi Kaikaku Shiryo Shusei* (Collected Documents on Land Reform, vol. 14 GHQ/SCAP documents), (Tokyo: Nosei Chosakai, Ochanomizu Shobo).

Ogura, Takekazu (1951) *Tochi Rippo no Shiteki Kosatsu* (Agrarian Problems and Agricultural Policy in Japan: A Historical Sketch), Research monograph No. 17 (Tokyo: Nogyo Sogo Kenkyusho) (reprint, Tokyo: Chugai Shobo, 1975).

Ogura, Takekazu (1967) *Agrarian Problems and Agricultural Policy in Japan*, I.A.E.A. Occasional Papers Series no. 1 (Tokyo: Institute of Asian Economic Affairs).

Ohkawa, Kazushi, Tsutomu Noda, Nobukiyo Takamatsu, Saburo Yamada, Minoru Kumazaki, Yuichi Shionoya and Ryoshin Minami (1967) *Bukka* (Prices), Estimates of Long-term Economic Statistics of Japan since 1868, vol. 8 ed. by Kazushi Ohkawa, Miyohei Shinohara and Mataji Umemura (Tokyo: Toyo Keizai Shinpo-sha).

Ouchi, Tsutomu (1960) *Nogyo-shi* (History of Agriculture), (Tokyo: Toyo Keizai Shinpo-sha).

Raper, Arthur F. (1951) 'Some Effects of Land Reform in Thirteen Japanese Villages', *Journal of Farm Economics*, 33, pp. 177–82.

Raup, Philip M. (1967) 'Land Reform and Agricultural Development', in *Agricultural Development and Economic Growth*, ed. by Herman M. Southworth and Bruce F. Johnston (Ithaca and London: Cornell University Press).

Ruttan, Vernon W. (1964) 'Equality and Productivity Objectives in Agrarian Reform Legislation: Perspectives on the New Philippine Land Reform Code', *Indian Journal of Agricultural Economics*, 19, pp. 114–30.

Saito, Hitoshi (1989) *Nogyo Mondai no Tenkai to Jichi Sonraku* (Evolution of Agricultural Problems and Self-Governing Rural Communities), (Tokyo: Nihon Keizai Hyoron-sha).

Smith, Thomas C. (1959) *The Agrarian Origins of Modern Japan* (Stanford: Stanford University Press).

Tohata, Seiichi (1947) *Nochi o Meguru Jinushi to Nomin* (Landlords and Peasants on Farmland), (Tokyo: Kantosha).

Tohata, Seiichi and Kazushi Ohkawa (eds) (1956) *Nihon no Keizai to Nogyo* (The Economy and Agriculture in Japan), (Tokyo: Iwanami Shoten).

Tohata, Seiichi and Kozo Uno (eds) (1959) *Nihon Shihon Shugi to Nogyo* (Capitalism and Agriculture in Japan), (Tokyo: Iwanami Shoten).

Tohata, Shiro (1966) 'Nochi Kaikaku no Sai-hyoka ni yosete' (Land Reform Revisited), reprint in *Nochi Kaikaku-ron I*, ed. by Shuzo Teraoka (Tokyo:

Nosangyoson Bunka Kyokai, 1985) (page references are to reprint edition).
Tuma, Elias H. (1965) *Twenty-Six Centuries of Agrarian Reform: A Comparative Analysis* (Berkeley: University of California Press).
Umemura, Mataji, Saburo Yamada, Yujiro Hayami, Nobukiyo Takamatsu and Minoru Kumazaki (1966) *Choki Keizai Tokei 9: Noringyo* (Estimates of Long-term Economic Statistics of Japan since 1868, vol. 9, Agriculture and Forestry) ed. by Kazushi Ohkawa, Miyohei Shinohara and Mataji Umemura (Tokyo: Toyo Keizai Shinpo-sha).
Walinsky, Louis J. (ed.) (1977) *Agrarian Reform as Unfinished Business: The Selected Papers of Wolf Ladejinsky* (Oxford: Oxford University Press).

9 Postwar Reform in Management and Labour: The Case of the Steel Industry

Seiichiro Yonekura*

9.1 INTRODUCTION

It is impossible to understand Japan's amazing economic expansion in the post Second World War period without considering its innovative management and cooperative labour relations. However, these two important factors were not given conditions immediately after the war. Rather, they evolved as a result of drastic reforms and labour struggles during the postwar period. The postwar reforms in management and labour were thus crucially important to the creation of competitive industries. However, it should not be assumed that the reforms automatically created competitive industries in Japan. The external reforms worked only when the internal reformees were ready to accept them and exploit them.

This chapter will investigate how competitive industries and their management and labour union systems developed in Japan and postulate relationships between the postwar economic reforms and postwar Japanese management and industrial relations. To understand this process is to know how Japanese industries transformed from a prewar monopolistic structure to a democratic but competitive one and how they changed traditional industrial relations into modern but cooperative ones. In order to study this theme effectively, this chapter examines the steel industry as a case study. The main reason for choosing the steel industry is that it was one of the largest controlled industries in the wartime economy and one of the most successful and competitive industries in the postwar period.

9.2 POSTWAR ECONOMIC REFORMS IN THE STEEL INDUSTRY

On 15 August 1945, Japan surrendered to the Allied Powers and Japan's reckless war venture ended. The Supreme Commander for the Allied Powers (SCAP), mainly consisting of American military forces, occupied Japan and initiated democratic reforms in politics, economics, and education. In order to prevent Japan from becoming a hostile nation again, SCAP tried to transform it into a democratic country. In the economic field, SCAP tried to introduce free market principles and a competitive environment. Substantially, SCAP carried out three major programmes for economic reform: (i) the dissolution of big business including the Zaibatsu and large corporations and the introduction of the concept of anti-trust; (ii) severing personnel ties through the economic purge, and (iii) the introduction of a democratic labour movement. We will examine these three reforms in the steel industry.

9.2.1 Dissolution of Big Business: The Breakup of Japan Steel

The dissolution of big business and the establishment of the Anti-Monopoly Law were the major planks of SCAP's economic democratization programme. In order to democratize the Japanese economy, it was necessary for SCAP to deconcentrate Japanese industries and to promote a competitive environment. To pursue this goal, SCAP ordered the dissolution of big business, the Zaibatsu and munition companies in particular. SCAP also introduced the Anti-Monopoly Law and the Law for the Elimination of Excessive Concentration of Economic Power (Kado Keizairyoku Shuchu Haijo-ho: EECEP) in December 1947. Under these laws, SCAP designated 325 firms as having excessive economic power and ordered them to be split.[1] In the steel industry, thirteen firms including the largest five companies – the Japan Steel Corporation (Nippon Seitetsu: hereafter Japan Steel), Japan Steel Tube Corporation (Nihon Kokan: hereafter NKK), Kawasaki Heavy Industries (Kawasaki Jukogyo: hereafter KHI), Sumitomo Metal Industries (Sumitomo Kinzoku Kogyo: hereafter Sumitomo), and Kobe Steel (Kobe Seikosho: hereafter Kobe), were selected for dissolution. When we consider the size of Japanese steel demand, SCAP's estimation that thirteen steel companies had excessive market power theoretically did not make any sense. In 1943, at its prewar peak, the Japanese steel industry produced about 7 million tons of crude steel, while its American counterpart produced about 80 million tons. Using SCAP's estimation, in order for the American steel industry to have abided by the Anti-Monopoly Law introduced in Japan, there would have had to have been more than 130 steel firms in the United States. If this had been the case, it would have been impossible to achieve economies of scale. SCAP's order was therefore based on the intention to punish, and not on economic rationality.

With the outbreak of the Cold War, particularly after the Greek Rebellion of 1947, the government of the United States began to change its occupation policy from one which emphasized punishment to one which aimed at supporting Japan's economic recovery. The US government decided to aid Japan's economic development in order to prevent the spread of communism in the Far East. As a result of this change the Anti-Monopoly Law and the EECEP were applied less strictly. Only 18 out of 325 designated companies were actually split under the law. However, we should not underestimate the impact of dissolution. The number of dissolved companies is not as important as the qualitative change produced by dissolution.[2]

The steel industry was no exception. SCAP subsequently released the designated large steel firms from the breakup order, except for one company – Japan Steel. SCAP insisted that it be divided into two private companies because it regarded Japan Steel one of the largest munitions companies during the war, as having too much economic power. In 1943 for example, it dominated the industry with market shares of 78.2 per cent (3.56 million tons) in pig iron and 48.2 per cent (3.75 million tons) in crude steel. Japan Steel had been incorporated by merging the Yawata State-owned Works, the largest integrated iron and steelworks in Japan, with several private iron and steel firms in 1934. Therefore, the government controlled more than 50 per cent of its stockholdings. Even after the easing of the Anti-Monopoly Law, it seemed to SCAP that Japan Steel had excessive economic power and should be split. In 1950, despite opposition from the Japanese government and the industry, Japan Steel was split into two private companies: Yawata Steel (Yawata Seitetsu) and the Fuji Steel Corporation (Fuji Seitetsu). The split drastically changed the market structure of the industry.

As Table 9.1 and Figure 9.1 show, after the breakup the Japanese steel industry developed an oligopolistic structure with six large, integrated firms: Yawata, Fuji, NKK, Kawasaki, Sumitomo, and Kobe. This oligopolistic market structure was very different from the

Table 9.1 The distribution of production shares (thousand tons and per cent in parentheses)

	1940	*1945*	*1950*	*1955*	*1960*	*1965*	*1970*
Pig iron							
Japan { Yawata	2 582 (73.5)	837 (85.7)	787 (35.2)	1 659 (31.8)	3 732 (31.0)	6 758 (24.2)	30 369 (44.0)
Japan { Fuji			900 (40.3)	1 785 (34.6)	3 306 (27.4)	6 851 (24.5)	
Nihon Kokan (NKK)	583 (16.6)	72 (7.3)	453 (20.3)	953 (18.1)	1 722 (14.3)	3 750 (13.4)	11 032 (16.0)
Kawasaki	–	–	–	331 (6.3)	1 065 (8.9)	3 788 (13.6)	9 901 (14.3)
Sumitomo	–	–	–	145 (2.8)	605 (5.0)	3 471 (12.4)	9 215 (13.4)
Kobe	–	–	–	163 (3.1)	993 (8.2)	1 756 (6.3)	5 035 (7.3)
Others	347 (9.9)	68 (7.0)	93 (4.2)	222 (4.2)	629 (5.2)	1 557 (5.6)	3 476 (5.0)
Total	3 512 (100.0)	977 (100.0)	2 233 (100.0)	5 257 (100.0)	12 052 (100.0)	27 930 (100.0)	69 023 (100.0)
Crude steel							
Japan { Yawata	3 010 (43.9)	1 021 (52.0)	1 466 (30.0)	2 361 (24.1)	5 206 (22.5)	7 748 (18.8)	32 982 (35.9)
Japan { Fuji			868 (17.9)	1 886 (19.3)	3 683 (15.9)	7 169 (17.4)	
Nihon Kokan (NKK)	953 (13.9)	91 (4.6)	658 (13.6)	1 201 (12.3)	2 346 (10.1)	4 265 (10.3)	12 698 (13.7)
Kawasaki	373 (5.4)	74 (3.8)	437 (9.0)	805 (8.2)	2 070 (8.9)	4 348 (10.5)	10 948 (11.8)
Sumitomo	198 (2.9)	41 (2.1)	209 (4.3)	623 (6.4)	1 349 (5.8)	4 184 (10.1)	11 073 (12.0)
Kobe	261 (3.8)	23 (1.2)	276 (5.7)	514 (5.2)	1 482 (6.4)	2 436 (5.9)	5 051 (5.5)
Others	2 060 (30.0)	713 (36.3)	925 (19.1)	2 401 (24.5)	7 025 (30.4)	11 146 (27.1)	19 654 (21.3)
Total	6 858 (100.0)	1 962 (100.0)	4 839 (100.0)	9 791 (100.0)	23 161 (100.0)	41 296 (100.0)	92 406 (100.0)
Sheet steel							
Japan { Yawata	2 086 (46.1)	599 (66.7)		1 584 (22.1)	3 778 (22.5)	6 194 (19.9)	24 380 (36.2)
Japan { Fuji				1 156 (16.1)	2 789 (16.6)	5 374 (17.2)	
Nihon Kokan (NKK)	684 (15.4)	85 (9.5)		799 (11.1)	1 645 (9.8)	3 015 (9.6)	9 467 (14.4)
Kawasaki	232 (5.1)	24 (2.7)	n.a.	590 (8.2)	1 469 (8.7)	3 470 (11.1)	8 462 (12.6)
Sumitomo	74 (1.6)	26 (2.9)		413 (5.8)	923 (5.5)	2 895 (9.3)	7 336 (10.8)
Kobe	182 (4.0)	9 (1.0)		337 (4.7)	845 (5.0)	1 479 (4.7)	2 517 (3.8)
Others	1 264 (30.0)	155 (17.3)		2 299 (32.1)	5 428 (32.3)	9 077 (29.1)	15 107 (22.4)
Total	4 522 (100.0)	898 (100.0)		7 174 (100.0)	16 817 (100.0)	31 261 (100.0)	67 269 (100.0)

Source: Shoko-sho (Ministry of Commerce and Industry) and Tsusho Sangyo-sho (Ministry of International Trade and Industry), *Seitetsu Sanko Shiryo*, Annual Reports.

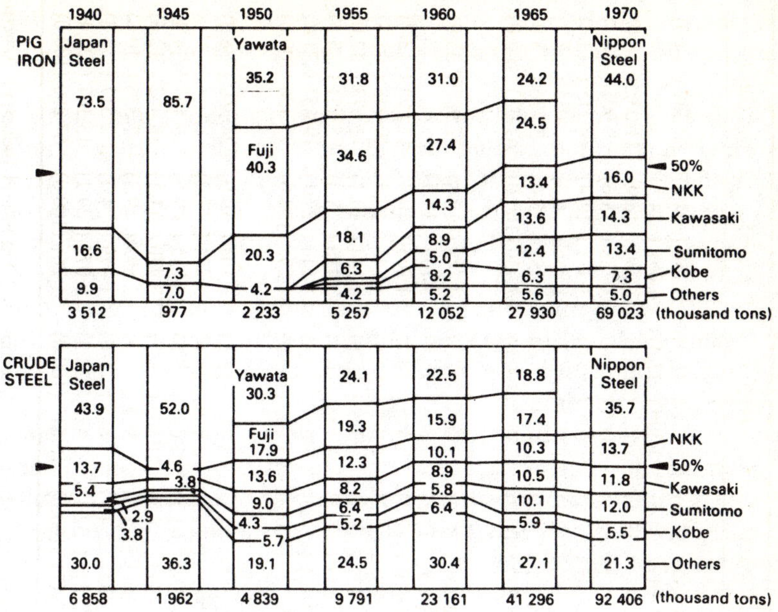

Figure 9.1 Distribution of production shares

Source: See Table 9.1

prewar monopolistic structure. The two halves of Japan Steel, Yawata Steel and the Fuji Steel Corporation, began to compete with each other as rivals. It is too simple, however, to argue that the breakup of Japan Steel automatically resulted competitive oligopolistic structure in the industry. To understand the essence of the breakup, a closer examination is necessary.

First of all, it must be noted that Japan Steel was not a totally state-owned enterprise unlike state-owned steel companies in socialist countries. Also, the breakup was not the first attempt to privatize the company. As mentioned above, Japan Steel was established by merging the Yawata State-owned Works with several private firms in 1934. At that time the Yawata Works, the largest steelworks in Japan, had a dominant position with around a 65 per cent share in both pig iron and crude steel demand. However, the Yawata Works had been criticized for inefficiency and slow decision-making by both insiders and outsiders.[3] The Japanese government, therefore, decided to privatize the Yawata Works by merging it with several private companies in the early 1930s. A speech made by Nakajima

Kumakichi, Minister of Commerce and Industry, in the Diet in 1934 indicates the government's view with respect to the privatization:[4]

> The state-owned steelworks has many limitations and obstacles which hinder the further development of the industry. Timely capital procurement, in particular, is very difficult for a state-owned enterprise because it depends on the political and economic situation of the time. In order to catch up with the rapid progress of technology in the West, it is necessary for the steelworks to have a flexible decision-making process and timely capital procurement. Compared to a state-owned enterprises, there is no doubt that private companies are more flexible in their procurement and investment decisions.
>
> Recently, we often hear scholars and businessmen advocate a planned or controlled economy. However, the Soviet Union, under totalitarian principles, for example, practises its controlled economy so thoroughly that it ignores the political and economic freedom of the people.
>
> It is also true that in the contemporary capitalist world, the market mechanism does not work as well as it used to do. Therefore, a shift from laissez-faire principles to some kind of state control is inevitable. However, it is still unclear whether a state-controlled economy is more efficient than a free economy. A controlled economy deprives people of their political freedom and individual creativity, and this is the worst part of the system. In order to compensate for this flaw in the controlled economy, I believe the proposed consolidation in the form of the Japan Steel Corporation will be able to retain individual creativity within the framework of a state-controlled economy.

As early as 1934, the Japanese government recognized the limitations of state-owned enterprises and socialist economies. Thus, Japan Steel was privatized in 1934, although the government continued to control 50 per cent of its stock. After the merger, Japan Steel established an independent management system and a self-paying accounting basis, and its top managers had to pay great attention to managerial efficiency.[5]

In addition, Japan Steel was managed by private, professional managers as well as bureaucrats from the Ministry of Commerce and Industry (Shoko-sho: MCI). Through the merger of 1934, Japan Steel acquired not only private facilities but also able and entrepreneurial managers from the merged firms, such as Miki Takashi from Mitsui's

Kamaishi steelworks and Nagano Shigeo from Fuji Seikosho. These men became the first presidents of the two separated companies as we will see later. Moreover, the managers from the merged companies had engaged in the steel business during the difficult years of the late 1920s and the early 1930s.

Second, we need to examine the internal structure of the oligopoly because more fundamental changes occurred than just the increase in the number of companies. After the breakup of Japan Steel, the six largest companies, Yawata, Fuji, NKK, Kawasaki, Sumitomo, and Kobe began to compete with each other in both steelmaking and ironmaking, as Figure 9.1 indicates. This means that Kawasaki, Sumitomo, and Kobe entered iron production as well as steel production. In other words, these six large companies were all 'integrated' firms. 'Integrated' means a producer who makes both iron and steel within an integrated system. In the prewar period, there was a clear distinction between iron and steel producers in the industry. While non-integrated producers occupied around 50 per cent of crude steel production, the only integrated producers were Japan Steel and NKK. Also, while the steel market was self-sufficient with 7 million tons, the pig iron market was unstable and not self-sufficient with 3.5 million tons in 1940. That prewar demand structure meant that the non-integrated producers depended on imported pig iron or imported scrap for their raw materials. The unbalanced development between iron and steel producers and the consequent large imports of pig iron and scrap had been a major problem for both the government and industry since before the war.[6]

On the one hand, in order to produce competitive steel, the steel producers needed inexpensive imported pig iron or scrap. However, in order to be self-sufficient, the pig iron producers had to compete with this imported iron and scrap, and therefore had to ask for government protection such as tariffs and subsidies. The interests of the steel and iron producers thus contradicted one another. In addition, the technological flexibility of steel production made the conflict worse. By using the open hearth furnace, steel producers were able to choose pig iron or scrap as their raw material in accordance with the price at the time. This bargaining advantage of steel producers made the pig iron market more unstable.

After the breakout of the war in China, in order for the Japanese government to increase steel production, it kept tariffs on imported iron and scrap low and subsidized iron producers. In addition, the government directed Japan Steel to supply inexpensive iron to non-integrated steel producers. During the Second World War, therefore, Japan Steel was no longer in serious competition with the non-integrated producers as the iron and steel industry had become a static state-controlled industry.

After the breakup of Japan Steel in 1950, however, this situation radically changed. The newly established Yawata and Fuji Steel corporations became uncontrolled private companies and the iron and steel market became more competitive, led by these two integrated companies and NKK. Furthermore, Kawasaki Steel announced their entry into integrated production in 1950 and Sumitomo and Kobe followed soon thereafter. Thus the Japanese iron and steel industry suddenly became oligopolistic and fierce competition ensued. For the creation of competitive patterns as well as a competitive industry, Kawasaki's decision and implementation of integration were critically important and innovative.[7] There were two main reasons why Kawasaki Steel decided to enter iron production. One was the breakup of Japan Steel and the other was the strong leadership of Nishiyama Yataro who became the company's new president after the economic purge.

During the Second World War, the main task assigned to Japan Steel was to provide non-integrated producers with cheaper and better iron and semi-finished steel under the supervision of the government and the control association. In this sense, Japan Steel had not really competed with the private non-integrated steel firms, such as Kawasaki, Sumitomo, and Kobe during the war. Rather, it played the role of a stable supplier. After the war, SCAP decided to dissolve Japan Steel to bring healthy and free competition into the industry. The breakup meant that Yawata and Fuji became not only the strong competitors of the non-integrated producers, but also tough negotiators when the non-integrated producers wanted to purchase pig iron. Having experienced a serious pig iron shortage during the war, Nishiyama Yataro, president of Kawasaki Steel, saw the breakup as a great threat and viewed entering the field of pig iron production as a measure of self-defence.

In 1950, soon after Nishiyama spun-off KHI's steel division as the independent Kawasaki Steel, he announced the new company's entry into integrated production. Once Kawasaki decided to integrate, the other non-integrated producers like Sumitomo and Kobe, which were in the same situation as Kawasaki, had to follow suit. By 1955, therefore, the Japanese iron and steel industry suddenly became more oligopolistic than SCAP had anticipated. SCAP had thought that the breakup of Japan Steel and consequent integration of the three major firms was enough to make Japan's steel industry competitive. Nishiyama's bold decision, however, exceeded SCAP'S original intention and created an oligopolistic industry with six large integrated firms. The fierce competition and strong rivalry among the six largest integrated companies would drive the Japanese steel industry from the 1950s to the 1980s.

There is no doubt that the breakup of Japan Steel was one of the most important reforms in the steel industry. However, the breakup did not automatically result in the oligopolistic structure of six firms which would enable the industry to become bigger and stronger. This competitive structure arose only after the non-integrated steel producers led by Kawasaki aggressively responded to the breakup. Without considering the dynamic reactions of the other private firms, we might overestimate the impact that the breakup of Japan Steel had on the industry as a whole.

When we consider why Kawasaki Steel chose to act as it did, we can not ignore the strong leadership of the newly-promoted young executive Nishiyama Yataro. Another postwar reform, the so-called 'economic purge', played a significant role in his promotion. In the following section we examine this purge.

9.2.2 The Economic Purge

In order to promote a democratic economy, SCAP dissolved the Zaibatsu and other big businesses. Along with these dissolutions, SCAP decided to sever the personnel ties among the business world and get rid of inappropriate personnel. In dissolving the ten Zaibatsu families, SCAP designated 56 Zaibatsu family members to be removed from all executive positions. In addition, SCAP expanded the range of its political purge to the economic areas. The economic purge of January 1947 grew out of the political purge carried out a year earlier. In the economic purge, the concept of 'public service' was expanded to include top positions in major companies in the private sector. The major part of the economic purge related to persons holding key positions in 245 major companies between the outbreak of the war in China and the end of the Second World War. The 245 companies from which the removal of top officers was mandatory were compiled from criteria which employed the phrase 'conspicuously monopolistic', though there was no concrete definition of this phrase. As Eleanor Hadley explained in her detailed study, technically the purge came as a result of the expansion of the final paragraph of the 4 January 1946 directive, calling for the removal of 'militarists and ultranationalists'.[8] In the economic purge, 'public service' was divided into two categories, 'principal public office' and 'ordinary public office', as in the original political purge. 'Principal public offices' and 'ordinary public offices' were defined as follows:[9]

> *Principal public offices*: president, vice president, chairman, vice chairman, Managing director, standing director, standing auditor, active advisor, or councillor, principal stockholder who owned 10% or more of capital stocks or who exercised, directly or indirectly, controlling influence in the management of the company, and any other official, regardless of his title, including branch managers in any Japanese-occupied territory, Axis or Axis-occupied country, who in fact exercised authority or influence.
>
> *Ordinary public offices*: director, auditor, advisor, councillor, head of the business or accounting department and any other official with commensurate authority.

Persons holding 'principal public office' were automatically removed and those holding 'ordinary public office' could be removed 'upon evidence'. The number of executives directly removed from positions was 639, and the number of those who had resigned in anticipation of removal or had earlier retired was 896, thus making a total of 1535. Including persons dismissed by the political purge, a total of 2210 business executives of 632 corporations were purged.[10] Although *Newsweek* at that time reported that some 25 000 to 30 000 of Japan's businessmen, financiers, and industrialists faced removal from their jobs, the real figure was at most 2000.[11] The purge, however, stirred lively discussion among both the Japanese and the Occupation authorities. While some held that the purging of only 220 000 individuals (180 000 former military officers, 1500 business executives, and others) was insufficient others held that the number, including a large proportion of the most capable leaders of Japan, was enough to endanger the necessary task of reconstruction.[12] In fact, when we consider the case of Germany where 100 000 Nazi members were imprisoned and more than a million people had their properties confiscated by the Allied Powers, the case of Japan seemed moderate. However, with four or five top leaders in every important institution in both the public and private sectors being purged in the space of one or two years, we should not underestimate its impact. In any case, it is still unclear how the purge affected the Japanese economy. According to Hadley's calculation, 'on the average less than four officers per company were purged'. Consequently no doubt she was moderate in her assessment of the effectiveness of the economic purge.[13]

> How much change could be anticipated from removal of four officers from boards consisting of 12, 16, 20, or more officers? Clearly, it was scarcely a 'wholesale' amount, particularly when replacements were largely by promotion. Probably the most that can be said is that the removal of a few key officers dramatized the attempt to create more independent boards among companies, most of which had previously been instructed in minute detail on how to act. The hope was that the removal of certain key executives would inspire more independent behaviour on the part of other board members.

On the contrary, many historical studies of Japanese managerial development have been very positive regarding the economic purge. Noda Kazuo, for example, argues that '(t)he purge brought new and fresh opportunities for a young generation of corporate managers', and shows that 'the average age of those who were presidents at the time of surrender and of those who had become new presidents by early 1952 were 60.2 and 51.8 years old, respectively, as of 1948'.[14] Michael Yoshino writes, '(F)reed from the control of the holding company and from stringent government regulations that had constricted Japanese industry for almost a decade and a half, the long-pent-up energies of these young men found fresh outlet.'[15] He also pointed out that the postwar Japanese managerial elite had a very high level of educational achievement. Using Aonuma Yoshimatsu's date, Yoshino showed that nearly 90 per cent of the 1500 executives studied were graduates of institutions of higher learning, including government and private universities and college-level technical institutes.[16] However, these studies do not show how these young executives found their outlet nor how the youth and higher level of education related to Japan's managerial development. In that regard, Wakimura Yoshitaro suggests that these young executives were the first generation to have seriously studied economics and management in the 1920s, when the Japanese national universities began to open economics and management departments.[17] Although Wakimura does not give any concrete examples, his point is worth examining.

We will now focus on a case study of the economic purge and its aftermath.

In the steel industry, all chairmen, presidents, and managing directors during the war were exiled or forced to retire as a result of the economic purge. Table 9.2 presents a comparison of the presidents of the largest six steel firms in 1943, 1945, 1948, and 1950. There were four significant characteristics of the postwar presidents. First of all, these new presidents were all professional salaried managers who had accumulated operational experience in their companies. This was quite different from the prewar situation. Toyoda Teijiro, the prewar president of Japan Steel, was a military politician based in the navy, rather than a steel executive. He had been Vice Minister of the Navy and a Navy Admiral. In 1941 under the third Konoe Cabinet, he became Minister of Foreign Affairs. Toyoda's inauguration as the president of Japan Steel was a direct result of the war. In April 1945, he resigned his post because he was appointed to the post of Minister of Munitions. After Toyoda resigned Watanabe Gisuke took the chair as president. Watanabe was an experienced bureaucrat in the Ministry of Commerce and Industry and specialized in the steel industry. He joined Japan Steel in 1934 as a general manager of the Yawata Works and held important positions in the company. He became the chairman of the Iron and Steel Control Association (Tekko Toseikai) in 1943 and president in 1945.[18]

Asano Ryozo of NKK was a family member of the Asano Zaibatsu. He was the second son of Asano Soichiro who had established the Asano Zaibatsu based on the cement business. Soichiro was the father-in-law of Shiraishi Motojiro, one of the founders of NKK. Therefore, Ryozo had a strong ownership interest in the company. He graduated from Harvard University and took several executive positions in the Asano Zaibatsu. Anticipating the purge, Ryozo resigned his post in April 1946. Managing Director Watanabe Masato succeeded Asano, but was purged by SCAP in 1947.[19]

Itani Shosuke of Kawasaki Heavy Industries graduated from Shimonoseki Commerce High School and studied business and English in Shanghai. In 1904, he joined Yokohama Sekitan Shokai's shipping division, the antecedent of Yamashita Shipping Company, one of the five largest shipping companies in prewar Japan. In 1918 when Yokohama Sekitan Shokai changed its name to Yamashita Shipping Company, he was promoted to the post of managing director. In 1923, he became president of Hokkaido Kogyo, one of Yamashita's subsidiaries. In 1933 he went to Kawasaki Heavy Industries to help in its

Table 9.2 Presidents of the Japanese steel industry in the 1940s

Company		*1943*	*1945*	*1948*	*Company*	*1950*
Japan Steel	name	Toyoda Teijiro	Watanabe Gisuke (purged)	Miki Takashi	Yawata Steel	Miki Takashi
	age	59	58	56		58
	school	Naval Academy	Tokyo Univ (Law)	Tokyo Univ (Law)		Tokyo Univ (Law)
					Fuji Steel	Nagano Shigeo
						51
						Tokyo Univ (Law)
Nippon Kokan (NKK)	name	Asano Ryozo	Asano Ryozo (purged)	Kawada Shige	NKK	Kawada Shige
	age	55	57	62		64
	school	Harvard (Economics)	Harvard (Economics)	Tokyo Univ (Law)		Tokyo Univ (Law)
Kawasaki Heavy Industries	name	Itani Shosuke	No president with five directors	No president with five directors	Kawasaki Heavy Industries	Tezuka Toshio
	age	84				62
	school	Shimonoseki Commerce High School				Tokyo Univ (Law)
					Kawasaki Steel	Nishiyama Yataro
						58
						Tokyo Univ (Mining and Metallurgy)
Sumitomo Metal Industries	name	Kasuga Hiromu	Kasuga Hiromu (purged)	Hirota Hisakazu	Sumitomo Metal Industry	Hirota Hisakazu
	age	59	61	50		52
	school	Tokyo Univ (Law)	Tokyo Univ (Law)	Kyoto Univ (Engineering)		Kyoto Univ (Engineering)
Kobe Steel	name	Tamiya Kaemon	Asada Chohei (purged)	Machinaga Saburo	Kobe Steel	Machinaga Saburo
	age	69	59	54		56
	school	Primary school	Kyoto Univ (Mining and Metallurgy)	Osaka Higher Technical School		Osaka Higher Technical School

Sources: Asahi Shinbun-sha (ed.), *Gendai Nihon Asahi Jinbutsu Jiten* (Tokyo: Asahi Shinbun-sha, 1990); Okita Saburo *et al.* (eds), *Zaikai no Shidosha* (Tokyo: Kodan-sha, 1987).

reconstruction, becoming president in 1935. Itani was a famous self-made businessman in prewar Japan.[20]

Kasuga Hiromu graduated from the law department of Tokyo University in 1911 and joined the corporate office of the Sumitomo Zaibatsu. He was appointed general manager of Sumitomo Copper, an antecedent of Sumitomo Metal Industries. He and Asada Chohei were exceptional salaried professionals in the prewar steel industry.[21]

Tamiya Kaemon of Kobe Steel was also a self-made man. Although he had only a primary school education, he was promoted to general manager of Kobe Steel, a part of the Suzuki Zaibatsu in 1905. He studied the steel business by himself and introduced several new innovations to the industry from abroad with his junior engineer Asada Chohei. Anticipating the purge, Tamiya handed over the presidency to Asada in September 1945. Asada Chohei was a professional manager with a strong technological background. He graduated from the department of mining and metallurgy at Kyoto University in 1911 and joined Kobe as a steel engineer. He and Tamiya were responsible for technological innovation at Kobe Steel. He succeeded to the presidency in 1945 but was purged in 1947. He came back to the company in 1952 when the purge was retracted.[22]

In contrast to these prewar presidents, the postwar presidents were all salaried professionals. Miki Takashi, the first postwar president of Japan Steel, started his business career at Mitsui's Kamaishi Mining Company in 1918 and later joined Japan Steel when it merged with Kamaishi in 1934. In 1939, he became general manager of the Seitsu Works, a newly built steelworks in colonized Korea and was appointed board director in the following year. In December of 1945, right after the war, anticipating some kind of purge by SCAP, eleven out of the twenty executives of Japan Steel retired from the board. Miki, relatively new and young, stayed on the board and became the general manager of the Yawata Works. In March 1946, president Watanabe and vice president Kojima Arakazu were purged by SCAP. Miki, the number four executive on the board, was appointed president. Although he was general manager of the Yawata Works, his appointment, especially his newness, astonished the Japanese business world. Comparing Miki to a comet appearing out of nowhere, the Japanese press treated him as a symbol of the new postwar executive.[23]

Nagano Shigeo of Fuji Steel also joined Japan Steel from Fuji Seikosho, a small non-integrated steel producer, through the merger in 1934. He joined Asano Bussan, a general trading company of the

Asano Zaibatsu after graduation from Tokyo University in 1924. He was dispatched to a nearly bankrupted Fuji Seikosho to turn around the company in 1925. After ten years' struggle, he turned around the company in the most difficult times at the beginning of the 1930s. In 1934, the company was merged with Japan Steel and he joined it as a sales section chief. He was in charge of sales and purchases at Japan Steel and became the youngest department head in 1940. During the war, he also became director of the control association of the industry. In May 1946, Nagano was appointed as managing director, the second in command in Japan Steel after president Miki.[24] Nagano was not a new face in the industry but he would hardly have been in the mainstream vying for the presidency. Miki and Nagano became presidents only because the economic purge eliminated their senior executives.

At NKK, the story was similar. By 1947, as SCAP purged Asano Ryozo's successor Watanabe and all senior directors, Kawada Shige, the youngest director, was suddenly promoted to president. Kawada joined NKK in 1918 after working at Taiyo Life Insurance Company for two years. He was in charge of general affairs at NKK and became a department head of general affairs as well as a director in 1942. He recalled his sudden inauguration as president as follows:[25]

> [after the economic purge], finally I was to be president of NKK. However, the problem was that there was no one who could introduce me as the new president at the stockholders meeting, since all of the other directors had been already purged. There was no way but to introduce myself.

The other new presidents, Nishiyama Yataro of Kawasaki, Hirota Hisakazu of Sumitomo, and Machinaga Saburo of Kobe, were all operational engineers. Except for Nishiyama, they also became presidents suddenly after the purge. It is interesting to note that the three non-integrated firms which would later challenge the big three integrated firms, Yawata, Fuji, and NKK, were all led by experienced engineers.

A second characteristic of the postwar presidents was their very high level of education. Miki and Nagano graduated from Tokyo University in 1917 and 1924 respectively. Miki majored in German law and Nagano studied law. Kawada of NKK also studied at Tokyo University and completed a law major. Nishiyama graduated from the department of metallurgy at Tokyo University in 1919 and won the most prestigious prize for steel engineers in 1938. Hirota Hisakazu graduated from the department of engineering at Kyoto University in 1923 and Machinaga Saburo majored in machinery at Osaka Higher Technical School in 1913.

A third characteristic was that their average age was almost five years younger than that of prewar presidents. The average age in 1943 was 61.2, while that in 1950 was 56.7.

A fourth point is that only two presidents came back to their former positions after the lifting of the purge in 1952: Watanabe Gisuke of Japan Steel and Asada Chohei of Kobe Steel. Watanabe came back only because Miki was suddenly killed in a plane crash in 1952. In the case of Kobe, Asada had been chief engineer for a long time and was regarded within the company and in the industry as the true successor to Tamiya Kaemon. It was, therefore, quite natural that Asada came back to office.

Above all, the postwar presidents were all salaried professional managers with high educational backgrounds. Because there was a clear separation between ownership and management, none of them owned their companies. At this stage, we have to examine how these new and young professional managers changed the industry and how their educational levels and work experience affected their decisions.

As mentioned above, the most important decision made by the postwar steel industry was undoubtedly Kawasaki's decision to integrate production. President Nishiyama's decision to construct the Chiba Works was one of the boldest and most exciting business decisions in postwar business history. Let's examine the case of Nishiyama Yataro and Kawasaki Steel.

Nishiyama was a steel engineer in the steel division of Kawasaki Heavy Industries (KHI). Before the war, KHI's main business had been shipbuilding and its steel division had been regarded as a means toward backward integration. After the war, president Itani Shosuke and senior directors at KHI were purged by SCAP. Although Nishiyama had been promoted to director of the board in 1941, he was not purged because SCAP regarded him as a mere engineer. In the chaotic situation of postwar Japan, KHI adopted a consensus management system with five directors, and no president or chairman, and Nishiyama was included as one of them. Thus, the economic purge promoted him to the highest position in the company. Furthermore, the purge encouraged him to take an unprecedented step forward. In 1949, he insisted on separating his steel division from KHI. In contrast to Japan Steel, the order to split KHI was retracted in 1949 and there was no obligation for the company to spin off its steel division. However, Nishiyama Yataro wanted to set up his division as an independent corporation. While conventional managers in the shipbuilding division were discouraged and tried to downsize the company's activities during the desperate postwar years, Nishiyama saw an extraordinary business opportunity. Right after the war, Nishiyama made a speech to his staff and workers.[26]

> The Japanese iron and steel industry must cut costs and develop the ability to compete internationally by switching to the American mode of production and away from the European mode of small-lot production. It is necessary to construct an integrated works with a blast furnace.

Even in the midst of an atmosphere of desperation, Nishiyama sensed the coming of the mass production era. Soon after he had organized the steel division into Kawasaki Steel Corporation (Kawasaki Seitetsu), he decided to enter into integrated production in 1950. Nishiyama proudly announced that the newly born Kawasaki Steel would build a state-of-the-art integrated works with annual capacities of 350 000 tons of pig iron and 500 000 tons of crude steel. The proposed construction budget was 16.3 billion yen, though Kawasaki's paid-in capital was a mere 0.5 billion yen. To the government, the industry, and the Bank of Japan, Nishiyama's decision seemed ridiculous for two reasons. First, as the total output of crude steel in 1950 was only 2 500 000 tons, Kawasaki's anticipated annual capacity of 500 000 tons seemed excessive. Second, as only 12 out of 37 existing blast furnaces were in operation, Kawasaki's two new blast furnaces were regarded as an unnecessary investment that would result in excessive supply. However, Nishiyama decisively carried out his plan and stimulated not only the creation of a competitive Japanese steel industry but also the pattern of investment-driven growth.[27]

What made Nishiyama take up this bold agenda? No doubt it was the economic purge. As he was one of the best steel engineers at that time and had accumulated his knowledge and expertise through operational experience, he understood the importance of integrated production.[28] In Kawasaki Heavy Industries where the main business was shipbuilding and which maintained a rigid hierarchy on the board, it had been impossible for him to carry out such a large and bold investment. By chance, he was freed from the conventional hierarchy of the old management and gained the authority to implement his own ideas. Hence, the economic purge and the consequent promotion of Nishiyama made this bold achievement possible.

The other effect of the economic purge was that at Sumitomo and Kobe experienced steel engineers were also promoted to president. It was very important that they were operational engineers, because they understood what Nishiyama was attempting to do. Therefore, Sumitomo and Kobe followed suit. Asada Chohei of Kobe Steel later recalled.[29]

> Nishiyama made history in the Japanese steel industry when he decided to implement an integrated system. Because Kawasaki had entered, Sumitomo and Kobe had to follow, since all were in the same situation.

They knew why Nishiyama had decided to implement an integrated system and how important his decision was. In 1953, Sumitomo and Kobe merged Kokura Steel and Amagasaki Steel, small integrated firms, as their first step toward integrated production in 1953 and 1954 respectively. By the late 1950s both of them had constructed seacoast steel works that were as advanced as Kawasaki's Chiba steelworks. The competitive oligopolistic industry thus was created by the newly-promoted steel executives.

Even though the average number of purged executives was around four or five per company, as Hadley pointed out, the economic purge had a more serious impact on the business world than indicated by this number. First of all, it must have been incredibly chaotic for companies to suddenly lose their top four or five executives. In the steel industry, SCAP's order to break up Japan Steel, the leading company, and the successive purge of the top executives brought a kind of crisis in the industry. However, the crisis presented a great opportunity. Thanks to their operational experience, the newly promoted executives, Nishiyama Yataro in particular, found a new opportunity in the breakup of Japan Steel and made an innovative decision that the prewar executives could not have imagined being able to make. The new and young but experienced executives thus changed the market structure of the industry. Without the economic purge, the industry would not have experienced such a dynamic change and the competitive energy of these young executives would never have been released.

9.2.3 Labour Union Movement: Rise of The Enterprise Union

The enterprise union (a union organized at the company rather than the industry level) and its cooperative attitude towards management have been named as one of the most important reasons for Japanese competitiveness.[30] The cooperative enterprise union is regarded as the foundation of the permanent employment and seniority wage systems. These three labour practices, the enterprise union, permanent employment, and the seniority wage system, are called the 'three treasures' of Japanese management and are regarded as its most important characteristics.

An enterprise union offers a cooperative workforce to management in exchange for job security and stable wage increases that come with seniority. Because of this stable labour force, management is able to commit to long-term investment, the successive introduction of new innovations, and the retraining of its workers when necessary. In addition, the enterprise union system does not require the kind of rigid job classifications that the industrial union does, since the wage is determined not by job classification but by seniority, rank, and merit evaluations with some attention to the objective attributes of the individual such as age and family size. Therefore, the organized workforce in Japan is flexible and trained for multi-functional duties by the company. In General Motors, for example, there were over 100 job categories in the 1970s while there were only 3 in Toyota.[31] The multi-functional workforce has made the famous just-in-time production system possible.

Japanese labour relations practices have thus contributed to productivity and competitiveness. However, the enterprise union, permanent employment, and seniority wages were not given conditions in postwar Japanese business history. As Andrew Gordon explained in his detailed study, the Japanese industrial relations system was not the simple result of Japanese culture or cultural values.[32] Rather it was created through severe struggle and conflict in the postwar period. Tsuda Masumi, one of the leading scholars of Japanese industrial relations, also came to a similar conclusion.[33] The following pages will discuss how the enterprise union emerged and how the postwar reforms made its emergence possible.

When the Supreme Commander for the Allied Powers (SCAP) occupied Japan, it placed emphasis on creating a democratic labour union movement as well as other democratic reforms. In October 1945, President Truman ordered that 'encouragement shall be given and favour shown to the development of organizations in labour, industry, and agriculture, organized on a democratic basis'. In implementation of the labour policy, SCAP took two lines of action: clearing away restrictions and building an institutional framework for organized labour.[34] A major step toward the dismantling restrictions was SCAPIN-93, the famous civil liberties directive, issued on 4 October 1945. In accordance with SCAPIN-93, the Public Peace Maintenance Law (Chian Iji-ho), the Protection and Surveillance Law for Thought Offences (Shisohan Hogo Kansatsu-ho), and many similar laws were abrogated on 15 October. SCAPIN-93 ordered the elimination of restrictions on civil liberties, the release of all political prisoners, and the abolition of all organizations or agencies created to carry out the provisions of those laws.[35]

SCAPIN-93 encouraged Japanese workers to form labour unions, since the unionization movement had been repressed by those laws. To establish an institutional framework, Supreme Commander Douglas MacArthur told the Japanese government to enact labour legislation to protect the rights of labour. In late December 1945, the Diet approved the Labour Union Law (Rodo Kumiai-ho), which guaranteed workers the right to organize, to bargain collectively, and to strike. Encouraged by SCAP and the Labour Union Law Japanese workers took action to unionize far in advance of the pace of SCAP's labour reforms.

As Table 9.3 indicates, more than 10 000 unions had been formed by May 1946 and more than three million workers were organized. In August, two nation-wide labour organizations were established: Nihon Rodo Kumiai Sodomei, hereafter Sodomei (Japan Federation of Labour), and Zen Nihon Sangyobetsu Rodo Kumiai Kaigi, hereafter Sanbetsu (Japan Congress of Industrial Unions). Sodomei consisted of 1699 enterprise unions and their 850 000 workers (22 per cent of all organized workers) and Sanbetsu of 21 industrial unions and 1000 representatives supported by 1.67 million workers (43 per cent of all organized workers).[36] Sodomei was the most conservative of the union federations and was led by the old, moderate labour leaders affiliated with the Japan Socialist Party (Nihon Shakai-to: JSP). Sanbetsu was led by members of the Japan Communist Party (Nihon Kyosan-to: JCP) who had just been released by SCAPIN-93. The Japan Communist Party regarded the union movement as a means of revolution and initiated several radical struggles against capitalists.[37] In the early years, Sanbetsu was more active than Sodomei, and real power resided in the national

Table 9.3 Growth of unions and union membership throughout Japan, August 1945–February 1947 (cumulative end-of-month totals)

Year	*Month*	*Unions*	*Membership*
1945	Aug	0	0
	Sep	2	1 177
	Oct	9	5 072
	Nov	75	68 530
	Dec	509	380 677
1946	Jan	1 517	902 751
	Feb	3 243	1 537 606
	Mar	6 538	2 568 513
	Apr	8 531	3 023 979
	May	10 541	3 414 699
	Jun	12 007	3 681 017
	Jul	12 923	3 814 711
	Aug	13 341	3 875 272
	Sep	14 697	4 122 209
	Oct	15 172	4 168 305
	Nov	16 171	4 296 589
	Dec	17 265	4 849 329
1947	Jan	17 972	4 922 918
	Feb	18 929	5 030 574

Source: Joe Moore, *Japanese Workers and the Struggle for Power 1945–1947* (Madison: University of Wisconsin Press, 1983) table 2.2, p. 42.

industry-wide and inter-industry federations rather than in the enterprise unions. Sanbetsu was an effective organ of the labour movement because of its concrete vision and tactics. Its radicalism, however, led to increased conflicts with management, the Japanese government and SCAP as well as among workers, and it became clear that the Sanbetsu vision of a socialist economy led by autonomous unions was hardly progress in Japan. It would be a mistake, however, to regard the early radicalism as of no historical significance.

The most creative tactics of the early union movement was production-control (*seisan kanri*), in which unions took over the factory and ran it without managers. The employees of the Yomiuri Newspaper originated the production-control tactic, and it did not take long for the tactics to spread to other companies. Between January and June 1946, 255 incidents of production-control involving 157 000 workers took place all over Japan.[38] Along with the rapid progress of postwar inflation and serious food shortage, the labour movement grew more radical, and the communist-led Sanbetsu organized the successful October offensive of 1946 for 'living wages' and job security. In the beginning of 1947 when Sanbetsu and Sodomei together called for all unions to plan for a national general strike on 1 February, many union leaders and workers believed that a Communist revolution would come soon in Japan. Hosoya Matsuta, the vice-secretary of Sanbetsu at that time, recalled:[39]

> I believed that a revolutionary situation would have emerged if we had had a general strike on February 1, since almost all workers in Japan, whether they were in the private or public sector or wherever they were, were awaiting the next directive from Sanbetsu on the evening of January 31.

However, SCAP prohibited the planned general strike and promoted an anti-Communist movement in the major unions. After the Cold War broke out in 1947, SCAP proposed to the Japanese government that it revise the Labour Union Law to deny public-sector workers the right to strike and brought several legal changes designed to restrict the political activity of unions. The mid-course shift in Occupation policy helped management regain their authority. In 1948, fighting against a destabilizing postwar inflation, SCAP invited Joseph Dodge, the former president of the Detroit Bank, to supervise economic policy. Dodge promoted a hyper-balanced fiscal budget, deflationary in other words, and a total reduction of governmental financial aid and subsidies. Because of his deflationary policy, many firms had to trim their workforce and facilities. This stirred further labour confrontation and radicalism in the unionization movement.

In the chaotic struggle between management and labour, the Japanese government, with a little help from SCAP, promoted the creation of management discussion councils (*keiei kyogikai*), by which management and workers were to negotiate management decisions and their contracts. By encouraging the formation of management discussion councils, the government intended not only to democratize industrial relations but also to increase production power, which had deteriorated due to the confrontations. However, the radical unions, led mainly by Sanbetsu and sometimes by Sodomei, exploited management discussion councils as a major tool for their political power struggle. By demanding disclosure of a company's financial situation, personnel decisions, and confidential files, the radical unions intervened in the overall policies of the company.[40]

Until 1947, unions almost invariably won agreements quite close to their initial demands. In the case of NKK's Tsurumi steelworks, the Sanbetsu-led union won a clause that management would have to gain union consent for all job transfers and layoffs, and the union at NKK's Kawasaki works, belonging to the Sodomei camp won a contract stipulating that managers were bound to consult and gain approval from the union for all firings, hirings, transfers, punishments, rewards, and changes in the work rules.[41] By June 1948, 44 per cent (15 055 members) of all unions were participating in management discussion councils.

In fighting back the spreading power of the unions, Japanese managers, with support from SCAP, created the Japan Federation of Employers' Associations (Nihon Keieisha Dantai Renmei: Nikkeiren) in August 1948 as the coordinator of a management agenda for reform of labour relations. The unions and Nikkeiren debated and fought vigorously in the management discussion councils, and in some cases bitter strikes and conflicts followed the meetings. Following Dodge's deflationary policy, union radicalism became extreme, and Nikkeiren and the Japanese government criticized the excessive power granted to such councils. Unions naturally defended the privileges won through the councils and struggled to protect their vast interests. Finally the Red Purge carried out by SCAP and the Japanese government in 1950 replaced radical unions by cooperative 'second unions'.

These councils, and struggles, however, were significant in establishing the basis of Japanese cooperative industrial relations because in the sense that the most important characteristics of postwar Japanese industrial relations, including seniority wages, job security as permanent employment, and the abolition of status discrimination between staff and worker, were all realized through the councils and struggles. First of all, Japanese workers gained a new wage structure which determined wages based on age, need, standards of living, prices, and inflation through the labour offensive of 1946–7. This was called the Densan-style wage structure, after the victory of the Electric Power Industry Worker's Union (Densan) in its struggle with management. It did not take long for the Densan wage structure to spread throughout Japan. After significant labour defeats in the early 1950s, management regained considerable authority and flexibility in the determination of wages. Yet the essential part of the Densan wage structure was maintained, and its most important function was that it established not only the postwar seniority wage structure but also a base for permanent job security and the abolition of status discrimination, as we will see later.

The Densan wage structure was formed to seek livable minimum levels for workers of entry-level age at a 'base-wage (*kihon-kyu*)', and to try to ensure continued living wages by insisting on the priority of age, seniority, and family size in subsequent raises. The Densan structure, therefore, reduced the significance of piecework and incentive-pay schemes, which had flourished in prewar Japan. Because of this emphasis upon seniority, it became advantageous for workers to stay in a company as long as possible. And because of the concept of 'base-wage', an adoption of monthly payments for workers quickly spread instead of the hourly or daily payments system which had predominated in the prewar period. The monthly payments gradually wiped out the obvious status gap represented by the monthly versus hourly salary system and between white- and blue-collar workers. In addition, the frequent base-ups for living wages keyed to the triple-digit inflation diminished the wide income gaps between white- and blue-collar workers and created the background for the abolition of status discrimination.

Job security was as important as wages in the postwar union movement. In the chaotic and inflationary postwar economy, Japanese companies, which had placed emphasis on the management ideology of paternal care before the end of the war, resumed mass dismissals and millions lost their jobs. The unions put themselves on the line in defence of jobs. Andrew Gordon points out two major historical reasons for this: slow development of national industrial unions and of an effective public-welfare system.[42] For an individual whose pay was linked in some measure to his seniority and status with a firm, firing not only took away a job, but it condemned him to lower wages with his next employer, because poorly developed industrial unions did not secure his seniority and rank. In addition, as Japan lacked an effective public-welfare system, the threat of unemployment was literally a threat to survival. Therefore, the unions fiercely defended their members' job security. Through the chaotic battles in 1946, several unions, such as at Ishikawajima Shipbuilding and Kobe Steel, won 'no-dismissal' promises from the management. With the beginning of the consolidation drive of firms and Dodge's deflationary policy in 1949, firms no longer kept excessive workforces and began to dismiss their employees. The battles for the defence of jobs were fierce and more protracted than ever. The unions, however, lost every major battle in 1950, but confrontations were prolonged and unions continued to place job security high on their list of priorities. Managers began to realize that labour peace was a better choice. In the 1950s, managers and unions established a set of rules concerning job security; as Gordon explains, companies began to think it better to choose growth 'by modernizing and expanding with the workers on hand, rather than firing those with obsolete skills and hiring cheaper, younger workers, even if this meant retraining the expensive adults'.[43]

Abolition of status discrimination was another epoch-making incident in Japanese labour history. As mentioned above, the Densan wage structure diminished the wide income gap between white- and blue-collar and established a monthly salary payment even for blue-collar workers. This was the beginning of the abolition of status discrimination. In addition, the unions, initially separated between white- and blue-collar, merged into unified unions during the labour offensives of 1946 and 1947, and fought together against mass dismissals and plant shutdowns. According to Okouchi Kazuo's detailed study, in 1947, 320 (80.7 per cent) out of 397 postwar unions studied were unified.[44] Throughout the labour offensive, 'unity of workers and staff' and 'abolition of the status system' were the two most prevalent slogans of the union movement.

The unified unions were considered by labour leaders as a means to attain uniform treatment of all employees. By 1948, the unions demanded the use of the very neutral term, 'employees' union', rather than staff or workers' union. The Densan wage structure and the abolition of status discrimination resulted in a single rank system which consisted of functional classification ladders, typically moving from apprentice, operative, foreman, supervisor, section chief, to division chief. In reality, however, the abolition of the status system which had dominated the prewar shopfloor was not the end to all hierarchy, and brought other dimensions of status such as educational background and seniority, and it was on these that the new wage structure calculation was mainly based. Nevertheless, the abolition of visible status discrimination was important, because it created a more egalitarian social and economic order.

As we have examined above, Japanese managers and workers established enterprise unions with job security, seniority wages, and equal treatment of staff and workers through serious struggles. It is no exaggeration to say that the competitiveness of the Japanese manufacturing sector has been built upon that pattern of industrial relations. That is because the rapid introduction of new innovations and incremental innovations (*kaizen*) through quality control circles and the cooperative efforts of engineers could not have been realized without those labour practices and the atmosphere of equality. The enterprise unions that emerged by 1950 were not craft or trade organizations. They were designed to defend jobs at a company. So long as jobs were secured, unions did not oppose the introduction of new innovations. Under job security contracts with unions, managers had to transfer or retrain workers when they introduced new innovations. The enterprise unions and job security, thus, enabled Japanese firms to introduce new innovations and made workers commit themselves to the quality control circle movement.[45] Also, the equal treatment given staff and workers established a base for cooperative efforts for better quality and lower costs. Thus, enterprise unions and Japanese labour practices created in the postwar period, prepared the ground for the high economic growth in the late 1950s and 1960s based on a rapid introduction of new innovations and incremental improvement of production technology by staff and workers. In the prewar era, in order to keep skilled workers, several large corporations had adopted seniority wages and long-term employment. We cannot deny that some continuous effects of these labour practices had an impact on postwar labour relations. As we have shown, however, the prewar seniority wage and long-term employment systems were completely different from those created in the postwar period. There were neither unions nor equal treatment between white- and blue-collar workers in the prewar period. Long-term employment, seniority wages and company unions were all postwar products of protracted struggles between management and labour.

Before we summarize the arguments of this chapter, let's look at a concrete example of the creation of an enterprise union in the postwar period.

9.2.4 The Case of Kawasaki Heavy Industries' Steel Division

As early as December 1945, with the encouragement of SCAP's labour policy, several unions were formed in Kawasaki Heavy Industries (KHI). In KHI's Steel Division, workers and staff formed the Fukiai Labour Union and the Fukiai Staff Union respectively. During the chaotic period of 1946, many leftist organizers supported by the Sanbetsu sneaked into the company and organized a radical union movement and labour offensive. Responding to the labour offensive in the late 1946, the management offered 40 per cent and 30 per cent wage increases for staff and workers in January 1947. The unions in KHI, except the unified Steel Factory Union which had been created by merging the Fukiai Labour and Staff Unions in May 1946, agreed to the company's offer, since SCAP and the Japanese government had begun clamping down on radical unions. On 31 January 1947, SCAP ordered a stop to the planned general strike by Sanbetsu and Sodomei thus warning the radical union movement.

However, the Steel Factory Union in KHI, refusing the company's offer, decided to strike on 31 March. The Hyogo Local Police Office intervened, since it regarded the strike as violating SCAP's directive of 31 January. It was ordered that the strike cease within four days. Because of this intervention and oppression, the union leaders and workers were frustrated and became more radical. In the middle of the serious inflation of December 1947, the unions of KHI demanded three major concessions: a minimum wage and new compensations for industrial accidents, a paid holiday, and a new retirement allowance. Trying to consolidate its management foundation, the company counter-offered with a more moderate revision of the payment schedule, desiring a peaceful settlement with the unions. Again, the frustrated Steel Factory Union blocked a peaceful agreement, while the other unions agreed to come to the table with the company. Insisting on the fulfilment of their three demands, the Steel Factory Union declared a sole struggle against the company. Director Nishiyama Yataro, who had been in charge of KHI's Steel Division, thought that the Union was beyond control and that management had to fight to establish its authority. The confrontation with the union was the first test the newly promoted managers had to face. The Steel Factory Union brought the case to the Kobe Local Labour Committee to be mediated. Nishiyama, however, refused any mediation in this case. Faced with the company's refusal, the union decided to start a strike and production control in April 1948. This was the so-called '1948 Kawasaki Strike'.

The leftist leaders, increasingly radicalized, expelled moderate members from the union's top organ and started a piston 24-hour strike. The company decided to lock out workers and stopped any payroll on 8 May, and the union then declared an unlimited strike on 13 May. While the struggle continued the union and its workers faced triple-digit inflation and a food shortage. Criticism of the radical union leaders gradually emerged. Particularly after the union put KHI's labour department head under factory arrest and violently attacked him, moderate workers became sceptical of the union. On 17 April, 244 members of the Fukiai staff left the union and formed a new Fukiai Staff Union. This was the beginning of a split in the union. Foremen and workers with titles and the workers at the food and restaurant section also left the union and formed their own moderate unions respectively in the middle of May. Two violent struggles between the radical union members and the new moderate unions occurred. On 18 May, when the union, lacking food, attacked the KHI food warehouse and stole some foodstuffs, the management sued the union and dismissed 27 radical leaders. In the following days, 2500 out of 3000 steel workers withdrew from the union and formed the Fukiai Factory Union, as a 'second union'. Only 500 workers stayed in the radical union.

The company reopened the factory with help from the second union on 23 May and started production. On 23 June, the first union brought the case to the Kobe Local Court to investigate. The company and the new second union asked the Kobe Local Labour Committee to mediate the case. After a month-long investigation, the Committee reached its conclusions.[47]

(1) the company had to hire all members of the first union except for 6 leaders who had been prosecuted, and the 27 members who had already been dismissed were to be treated as voluntary retirees;
(2) the company had to pay the first union members the same amount of bonus which had been paid to the second union members;
(3) the company had to pay 700 yen per day in lockout compensation;
(4) the first union had to agree to the company's offer of 21 March and to refrain from any hostile activity.

Thus the so-called '1948 strike' ended on 7 July. After the struggle, the company and the unions began to establish a cooperative relationship through peaceful measures, and by the middle of the 1950s a unified enterprise union was established at the newly established Kawasaki Steel. Without the fierce confrontation and struggle of 1948, improved relations between the management and workers in Kawasaki would not have been possible. Nishiyama, the first president of Kawasaki Steel, recalled, 'Since the end of the struggle [in 1948], the enterprise union has grown healthy and management and labour have begun to understand each other and to cooperate in the company's development.'[48] Nishiyama gained self-confidence as president from having the union problem settled, and with support from the newly established union he carried out his bold plan to build the integrated works in Chiba.[49] The newly-established Kawasaki's enterprise union supported Nishiyama's decision and cooperated with the company in transferring 4274 workers from Kobe to Chiba by 1963.[50]

In other companies in various industries, labour relations followed a similar pattern. The serious confrontations of the late 1940s thus created cooperative industrial relations in Japan.

↳ serious confrontations of late 1940 created cooperative industrial relations in Japan

9.3 CONCLUSION

As we have examined above, the postwar reforms initiated by SCAP were crucial to the creation of Japanese competitiveness in the postwar period. Essentially, the dissolution of big business, the severing of old personnel ties by the economic purge, and the introduction of a democratic labour movement played a significant role in the creation of competitive industries, new managerial leaders, and cooperative industrial relations.

In the steel industry, as we have seen, the dissolution of the Japan Steel Corporation was the first and major step toward creating an oligopolistic structure in the industry. The economic purge removed four or five top executives from every company and promoted younger and more educated professional managers to the positions of top management. The introduction of the democratic labour movement and the legal protection of workers' rights promoted the formation of the more than 18 000 unions with five million members within a year or two.

These fundamental reforms were a shock to industry. However, they did not automatically bring about a competitive industry, innovative top management, and a cooperative labour union. The breakup of Japan Steel was important, but the establishment of Kawasaki Steel and its entry to integrated production was more important in initiating the fierce oligopolistic competition of the Japanese steel industry. The economic purge brought a great opportunity for newly promoted top managers, but the reason why they were able to manage their companies during such difficult times was that they were all well-trained professional managers and had accumulated their managerial and technological expertise through operational experiences before and during the war. In addition, the newly promoted presidents gained self-confidence from the experience of having serious confrontations with labour unions and having them settled. It was they who initiated bold expansion strategies that realized an unprecedented high economic growth in the 1960s.

SCAP's encouragement of the labour union movement released the long oppressed energy of Japanese workers and facilitated democratic unionization after the war. Furthermore, the Japanese union movement went beyond wages and worker organization to support communist revolution in February 1947. However, the emergence of Japanese cooperative labour relations was guaranteed neither by SCAP's encouragement nor by Japanese cultural preference. The Japanese cooperative enterprise union based on lifetime employment and seniority wages was created through severe confrontation and struggle. Postwar managers and workers learned through the bitter struggles in the 1940s and 50s that it was better to cooperate than to confront.

External reforms worked only when the objects of reform were able to exploit the opportunities they presented. The dynamic interaction between external postwar reforms and internal motivations thus can only explain the essence of the Japanese experience of economic reform.

Notes

* The author would like to thank Chen Chien Heng and David Gross for their helpful comments and research.

1. For the dissolution of the Zaibatsu, see Hadley (1970).
2. Uekusa Masu also points out the importance of the dissolution and the need for a detailed study: Uekusa (1979).
3. Inside the Yawata Works, Imaizumi Kaichiro, the chief engineer of the steelmaking section, had been critical of inefficiency of the state-owned steel works, while several economists and private managers were sceptical of the state-owned system. On the establishment of Japan Steel, see Yonekura (1990) ch. 5.
4. 'The Sixty-Fourth Diet Record', in *Nihon Seitetsu Kabushiki Kaisha Seiritsu Shiryo-shu*, vol. 1 (Internal Documents on the Establishment of the Japan Steel Corporation, 1936) p. 21.
5. Nakai Reisaku, the first president of Japan Steel, recalled how radically the company changed after privatization and how he had to manage it efficiently. See Nakai (1956).
6. See Yonekura (1990) chs 5–8.
7. Kawasaki's decision was innovative in three ways: (i) it pioneered the

first path for integrated production among non-integrated producers and created the base of the postwar competitive oligopolistic structure; (ii) it built a state-of-the-art seacoast steel plant which became a worldwide model of the modern steel plant with large-scale production; and (iii) it pioneered the over-borrowing pattern of capital procurement which would characterize the Japanese corporate finance system during the high economic growth era. See Yonekura (1991) pp. 211–17.

8. Hadley (1970) pp. 84–8.
9. Ibid, pp. 89–90.
10. Noda (1966) pp. 233–4.
11. 'Behind the Japanese Purge – American Military Rivalries', *Newsweek*, 27 January 1947.
12. Hadlev (1970) p. 95.
13. Ibid, p. 92.
14. Noda (1966) p. 235.
15. Yoshino (1968) p. 87.
16. Ibid, p. 90.
17. Wakimura (1983).
18. On Toyoda and Watanabe, see Nihon Seitetsu Kabushiki Kaisha-shi Henshu Iinkai (ed.) (1959).
19. See Nihon Kokan Kabushiki Kaisha Rokuju-nenshi Hensan Iinkai (ed.) (1972).
20. On Itani, see Kyuju-nen Shoshi Henshu Iinkai (ed.) (1986).
21. Sumitomo Kinzoku Kogyo (ed.) (1974).
22. On Tamiya and Asada, see Shinko Goju-nenshi Hensan Iinkai (ed.) (1954).
23. Tekko Shinbun-sha (ed.) (1973).
24. Nagano (1980).
25. Kawada (1980) p. 471.
26. Tekko Shinbun-sha (ed.) (1971) p. 298.
27. Yonekura (1991) pp. 214–17.
28. Tekko Shinbun-sha (ed.) (1971) pp. 150–62.
    Nishiyama won the Hattori Prize, a prestigious prize, in 1918 and established his reputation as 'the king of the open hearth furnace' in the industry.
29. Tekko Shinbun-sha (ed.) (1971) p. 397.
30. See OECD Reviews of Manpower and Social Policy (1972); Abegglen (1984) pp. 88–9; and Kenney and Florida (1988).
31. Interview at GM corporate office, 30 July 1986.
32. See Gordon (1985).
33. Tsuda (1983).
34. Moore (1983) pp. 62–7.
35. Ibid, p. 13.
36. Urabe and Omura (1983) pp. 63–4.
37. See Moore (1983) chs 2, 3 and 4.
38. Ibid, pp. 48–56, and Gordon (1985) p. 332.
39. Takashina (1985) pp. 16–17.
40. Urabe and Omura (1983) pp. 69–73.
41. Gordon (1985) p. 345.

42. Ibid, pp. 362–3.
43. Ibid, p. 390.
44. Okouchi (ed.) (1956) p. 92.
45. For these incremental innovations at the Japanese factory, see Nonaka and Yonekura (1983) and Yonekura (1987).
46. Historical facts are based on Kawasaki Seitetsu Kabushiki Kaisha Shashi Henshu Iinkai (ed.) (1976) pp. 507–17, and Daiyamondo-sha (ed.) (1964) pp. 21–5.
47. Tekko Shinbun-sha (ed.) (1973) pp. 351–2.
48. Daiyamondo-sha (ed.) (1964) p. 25.
49. The managers promoted after the purge gained strong self-confidence from the experience of the early conflicts with unions and the overcoming of these problems. Several examples are introduced by Miyajima (1991).
50. Kawasaki Seitetsu Kabushiki Kaisha Shashi Hensan Iinkai (ed.) (1976) pp. 517–18.

    Although in Japanese practice the family name precedes the given name, the names are inverted to normal English order in this book except for the text and notes in this chapter.

References

Abegglen, James (1984), *The Strategy of Japanese Business* (Cambridge, MA: Ballinger Publishing Company).

Daiyamondo-sha (ed.) (1964) *Rekishi o Tsukuru Hitobito-Kawasaki Seitetsu Shacho Nishiyama Yataro – Tetsu Zukuri Kaisha Zukuri* (Biography of Nishiyama Yataro – President of Kawasaki Steel Inc.) (Tokyo: Daiyamondo-sha).

Gordon, Andrew (1985) *The Evolution of Labor Relations in Japan: Heavy Industry, 1853–1955* (Cambridge, MA: Harvard University Press).

Hadley, Eleanor (1970) *Antitrust in Japan* (Princeton: Princeton University Press).

Kawada, Shige (1980) *Watakushi no Rirekisho* (My Memoir), (Tokyo: Nihonkeizai Shinbun-sha).

Kawasaki Seitetsu Kabushiki Kaisha Shashi Henson Iinkai (ed.) (1976) *Kawasaki Seitetsu Niyugo-nenshi* (A 25-Year History of Kawasaki Steel), (Kobe: Kawasaki Seitetsu Kabushiki Kaisha).

Kenney, Martin, and Richard Florida (1988) 'Beyond Mass Production: Production and the Labor Process in Japan', *Politics & Society*, vol. 16, no. 1 (New York: New York University Press).

Kyuju-nen Shoshi Henshu Iinkai (ed.) (1986) *Kyuju-nen no Ayumi: Kawasaki Jyukogyo-shoshi* (A 90-Year History of KHI), (Tokyo: Daiyamondo-sha).

Miyajima, Hideaki (1991) 'Zaikai Tsuiho to Shin-keieisha no Tojo' (The Economic Purge and New Managers), *Will*, July (Tokyo: Chuo Koron-sha).

Moore, Joe (1983) *Japanese Workers and the Struggle for Power, 1945–1947* (Madison: The University of Wisconsin Press).

Nagano, Shigeo (1980) *Watakushi no Rirekisho* (My Memoir), (Tokyo: Nihonkeizai Shinbun-sha).

Nakai, Reisaku (1956) *Tetsu to Watashi: Hanseiki no Kaiso* (Steel and Me: A Memoir of My Life), (Tokyo: Tekko to Kinzoku-sha).

Newsweek, 'Behind the Japanese Purge – American Military Rivalries', 27 January 1947

Nihon Kokan Kabushiki Kaisha Rokuju-nenshi Hensan Iinkai (ed.) (1972) *Nihon Kokan Kabushiki Kaisha Rokuju-nenshi* (A 60-Year History of NKK), (Tokyo: Nihon Kokan Kabushiki Kaisha).

Nihon Seitetsu Kabushiki Kaisha-shi Henshu Iinkai (ed.) (1959) *Nihon Seitetsu Kabushiki Kaisha-shi* (A History of the Japan Steel Corporation), (Tokyo: Nihon Seitetsu Kabushiki Kaisha-shi Henshu Iinkai).

'The Sixty-Fourth Diet Record', in *Nihon Seitetsu Kabushiki Kaisha Seiritsu Shiryo-shu*, vol. 1 (Internal Documents on the Establishment of the Japan Steel Corporation, 1936).

Noda, Kazuo (1966) 'Postwar Japanese Executives', in Ryutaro Komiya (ed.), *Postwar Economic Growth in Japan* (Robert S. Ozaki, trans.), (Berkeley: University of California Press).

Nonaka, Ikujiro and Seiichiro Yonekura (1983) 'Gurupu Dainamikusu no Inobeshon: Soshiki Gakushu Toshiteno JK Katsudo' (Innovation for Group Dynamics; JK Activity as Organizational Learning at Nippon Steel), *Shogaku Kenkyu*, vol. 25 (Tokyo: Hitotsubashi University).

OECD Reviews of Manpower and Social Policy (1972) *Manpower Policy in Japan* (Paris: OECD).

Okouchi, Kazuo (ed.) (1956) *Rodo Kumiai no Seisei to Soshiki* (A History and Organization of Unions), (Tokyo: University of Tokyo Press).

Shinko Goju-nenshi Hensan Iinkai (ed.) (1954) *Shinko Goju-nenshi* (A 50-Year History of Kobe Steel), (Kobe: Shinko Goju-nenshi Hensan Iinkai).

Sumitomo Kinzoku Kogyo (ed.) (1974) *Kasuga Hiromu Tsuikairoku* (Reminiscence of Kasuga Hiromu), (Osaka: Sumitomo Kinzoku Kogyo Kabushiki Kaisha).

Takashina, Akira (ed.) (1985) *Shogen Sengo Rodokumiai Undoshi* (Interviews for a History of the Labour Movement in the Postwar Period), (Tokyo: Toyo Keizai Shinpo-sha).

Tekko Shinbun-sha (ed.) (1971) *Tekko Kyojin-den: Nishiyama Yataro* (A Biography of Nishiyama Yataro), (Tokyo: Tekko Shinbun-sha).

Tekko Shinbun-sha (ed.) (1973) *Tekko Kyojin-den: Miki Takashi* (A Biography of Miki Takashi), (Tokyo: Tekko Shinbun-sha).

Tsuda, Masumi (1983) 'Sengo Keiei to Roshi Kankei' (Postwar Management and Industrial Relations), *Hitotsubashi Business Review*, vol. 31, no. 2 (Tokyo: Chikura Shobo).

Uekusa, Masu (1979) 'Senryoka no Kigyo Bunkatsu' (Corporate Dissolutions in the Occupation Era), in Takafusa Nakamura (ed.), *Senryoki Nihon no Keizai to Seiji* (Economy and Politics in the Occupation Era), (Tokyo: University of Tokyo Press).

Urabe, Kuniyoshi and Kihei Omura (1983) *Nihonteki Roshi Kankei no Tankyu* (An Exploration of Japanese Industrial Relations), (Tokyo: Chuo Keizai-sha).

Wakimura, Yoshitaro (1983) 'Sengo Keiei-shi no Shuppatsuten: Zaibatsu Kaitai' (Dissolution of the Zaibatsu), *Hitotsubashi Business Review*, vol. 31, no. 2 (Tokyo: Chikura Shobo).

Yonekura, Seiichiro (1987) 'Recognizing Potential in Innovation', Institute of Business Research Discussion Paper no. 132 (Tokyo: Hitotsubashi University).

Yonekura, Seiichiro (1990) 'The Japanese Iron and Steel Industry: Continuity and Discontinuity, 1850–1970', (Ph.D. Diss., Harvard Univ.).

Yonekura, Seiichiro (1991) 'The Postwar Japanese Iron and Steel Industry: Continuity and Discontinuity', in Etsuo Abe and Yoshitaka Suzuki (eds), *Changing Patterns of International Rivalry: Some Lessons from the Steel Industry* (Tokyo: University of Tokyo Press).

Yoshino, Michael (1968) *The Japanese Managerial System: Tradition and Innovation* (Cambridge, MA: The MIT Press).

Part III

The Role of the Government in the Postwar Growth Process

10 National Economic Independence and the Rationalization of Industry

Yoshie Yonezawa

The primary objective of this chapter is to examine the ways in which the rationalization of major industries in postwar Japan contributed to the resurgence of economic independence. Particular emphasis is placed on the period between the end of the so-called Dodge Line and the beginning of rapid economic growth. The industrial reconstruction carried out under SCAP (Supreme Commander for the Allied Powers) control and the rationalization of industries that occurred after the dissolution of SCAP controls are investigated as well as the significance of government policy toward industrial rationalization.

Economic historians have left us with voluminous material on this period in the history of the modern Japanese economy. Drawing in many respects on this rich heritage, this chapter tries to show how the hostile control of trade by SCAP distorted industrial reconstruction and how the obsessive concern for the external balance on the part of the Japanese government hindered industrial rationalization. However, in spite of this distortion and hindrance, the Japanese were, in the end, able to reconstruct and rationalize their industries as a whole and achieve national economic independence.

This chapter reconfirms the view that Japan's development was aided by four circumstances. First, the occupation policies of SCAP shifted from hostility to appeasement in the period of economic reconstruction, reflecting the advent of the Cold War. Second, American aid for reconstruction and the economic boom brought about by the Korean War served to cushion Japanese companies in the initial phase of industrial rationalization. Third, the fact that Japan was a small and less developed country meant that the government could adopt a strategic industrial adjustment policy based on a mercantilistic trade policy. The final and most crucial circumstance was that the Second World War had not been so long and destructive that economic behaviour based on capitalistic market principles had not been completely wiped out of the collective Japanese memory.

In the first section we overview the macro features of the supply-side development of the national economy and characterize the phase during which economic independence was secured from a historical perspective. In the second section, we examine how the major manufacturing industries were reconstructed and rationalized. In the final section, we explore the impact that a series of governmental measures had on industrial reconstruction and rationalization.

10.1 NATIONAL ECONOMIC INDEPENDENCE

In this section we overview the historical macroeconomic process in which Japan regained her economic independence while still occupied by the Allied Forces. During this period Japan regained national sovereignty and established the infrastructure necessary for the so-called rapid economic growth era of the 1960s. This overview makes explicit the Achilles' heel of the Japanese economy, shows how crucial international trade has been to economic growth, and outlines the factors responsible for maintaining workers' incentives and enterprise vitality.

10.1.1 Independence

In order to outline the broader macroeconomic process of independence we need to first clarify the meaning of 'national economic independence' as an economic concept. Dr Joseph Dodge, whose policy prescription for rescuing the Japanese economy from serious stagflation is referred to as the Dodge Line, once said that the Japanese economy was walking on stilts: one of the stilts being American aid to the Japanese government, and the other, fiscal subsidies provided to companies by the Japanese government. The Japanese economy was still dependent on these two stilts almost five years after the end of the Second World War, even though the government had made sincere efforts to reconstruct and transform the economy utilizing the policy formula outlined by SCAP.

In this paper, we define economic independence as a state without these two stilts. In other words, it refers to the situation where not only the government but also private sector can conduct economic activity without relying on subsidies or foreign aid.

In his paper on current Soviet economic reforms, Nordhaus (1990) points out that reform requires market discipline, government budget discipline and other crucial conditions in order to succeed. In other words, households, firms and even governments must balance their budgets in order to avoid bankruptcy in the long run. This definition of economic discipline is in line with the definition of economic independence mentioned above. In short, if national economic independence is to be achieved, it is absolutely essential to enforce an economic discipline which respects severe budget constraints.

Mundell (1962) has provided us with the most widely used criteria for the assessment of national economic condition: external and internal balances. Conventionally, it is understood these two balances are thought worthwhile in the short run because accumulation of net external debt and persistent stagflation may destabilize the political environment in which economic activities are normally conducted. This concept assumes short-run macroeconomic conditions and is premised on economic discipline and the independence of citizens and governments. A long-term external and internal imbalance would imply a decline in individual economic discipline and the loss of national economic independence. Therefore, these two criteria, particularly external balance, are more useful in assessing the long-term rather than short-term economic conditions of a nation. In addition, by definition, transitional external deficits will make up for a shortage of national savings. If external deficits contribute to a nation's capital formation for economic development, they can also, in the long run, bring forth external surpluses to repay the external debt. Thus, if we merely focus attention on the short-term external balance rather than the long-term one, we will lose the opportunity to increase mutual economic gains.

10.1.2 Supply Side of the National Economy

Energy Constraints

In 1945, the year of Japan's unconditional surrender, the average GNP fell to half of that of the previous year. However, in spite of a phenomenal hyper-inflation, unstable growth and population pressures, the Japanese people were able to gradually improve their economic condition in terms of per capita GNP. From 1950 to 1955, average GNP was the same as that achieved in the period between 1934 and 1936. However, there are two points to note with respect to the reconstruction process. First, reconstruction required painful, long-term efforts lasting from five to ten years. Second, although Japan experienced a growth recession from 13 per cent in 1948 to 2.2 per cent in 1949, per capita GNP itself did not experience a setback. This factor probably encouraged many Japanese, particularly during the years of extreme hardship.

This long-term, steady reconstruction of economic condition does not, when viewed as whole, appear to have been particularly miraculous. Table 10.1 traces GNP, gross capital stocks (capital), total persons employed (labour) and total energy consumption (energy). We can see an interruption in the movement of GNP and capital from 1944 to 1946 due to the lack of data on them in 1945, the year of the Japanese surrender. However, rough estimates of the degree that

Table 10.1 Supply-side of GNP and external dependence

Year	*Real GNP (1934–6 prices)*	*Gross capital (1934–6 prices) (1934–6=100)*	*Employed persons*	*Energy (coal equivalent)*	*Current account (%)*		
					Surplus /GNP	*Export etc. /GNP*	*Import etc. /GNP*
1930	84.8	87.2	93.7	–	0.3	16.9	16.6
31	87.6	89.2	91.8	–	–0.6	15.2	15.8
32	106.7	91.2	92.3	–	–0.1	14.8	14.9
33	93.2	93.8	94.2	–	–0.1	20.1	20.2
34	104.4	96.7	97.5	92.1	–0.3	21.1	21.4
35	107.9	99.9	99.4	100.4	0.9	22.7	21.8
36	87.7	103.4	97.7	107.5	1.0	23.7	22.7
37	123.3	107.0	98.6	119.2	–2.5	23.7	26.2
38	128.5	110.5	99.6	124.2	–2.4	20.0	22.4
39	123.9	114.3	100.6	132.5	0.3	20.2	19.9
1940	114.6	120.3	102.8	143.7	0.1	19.5	19.4
41	124.2	128.2	103.1	136.3	–2.3	13.6	15.9
42	123.6	134.9	103.2	135.9	–2.0	9.3	11.2
43	125.2	143.2	102.5	133.1	–1.4	7.7	9.1
44	119.4	151.3	100.6	114.5	–0.5	5.3	5.8
45	–	–	84.4	57.0	–	–	–
46	64.6	120.4	98.6	60.2	–4.0	1.1	5.1
47	71.0	124.8	105.5	71.2	–4.1	2.1	6.3
48	82.7	129.9	109.5	86.2	–4.1	3.0	7.2
49	85.9	135.0	114.1	89.0	–3.3	6.4	9.7

Table 10.1 Supply-side of GNP and external dependence

Year	Real GNP (1934–6 prices)	Gross capital (1934–6 prices) (1934–6=100)	Employed persons	Energy (coal equivalent)	Current account (%) Surplus /GNP	Export etc. /GNP	Import etc. /GNP
1950	96.4	139.8	113.1	104.8	2.7	11.9	9.2
51	112.1	145.4	114.6	120.5	3.8	16.7	12.8
52	124.0	151.6	118.0	125.5	–1.1	12.6	11.5
53	132.0	158.7	124.6	138.7	–1.1	11.2	12.3
54	139.7	167.6	125.4	139.7	–0.4	10.9	11.3
55	152.0	174.9	129.4	152.2	0.9	11.4	10.5
56	163.2	183.9	132.0	171.9	–0.2	12.2	12.4
57	175.2	195.9	135.5	183.9	–1.9	12.0	14.0
58	185.0	209.9	136.0	180.8	1.5	11.4	10.0
59	201.5	224.7	137.2	207.9	1.1	11.8	10.8
1960	228.3	244.9	140.4	241.6	0.4	11.5	11.1

Note: The authorized and/or official statistics for 'capital' between 1941 and 1949 are not available. Here, we estimate it by using the data for gross domestic capital formation at current prices and the capital goods prices as deflator.

Sources: Ohkawa, Shinohara and Umemura (eds), *Choki Keizai Tokei: Suikei to Bunseki*, 1, 2, 3 (Estimates of Long-term Economic Statistics since 1868, vols 1, 2, 3); Somu-cho Tokei-kyoku, *Nihon Choki Tokei*, 1, 3 (Statistics Bureau, Management and Coordination Agency, Historical Statistics of Japan, vols 1, 3); Toyo Keizai Shimpo-sha, *Kanketsu Kokusei Soran*, 1 (The Comprehensive Statistics of Japan for the Showa Era, vol. 1); Nihon Ginko, *Nihon Ginko 100 Nen-shi: Shiryo-hen* (The Bank of Japan, A Hundred-Year History of the Bank of Japan: Data and Statistics) 1986; Rodo-sho, *Rodo Tokei Nempo* (The Ministry of Labour, The Yearbook of Labour Statistics).

each variable fell between 1944 and 1946 are as follows; GNP at 46 per cent; capital at 20 per cent; labour at 2 per cent and energy at 47 per cent. In view of this supply-shock and the development since then, it is generally considered that critically the recovery of the Japanese economy in this period was dependent on the availability of energy.

External Dependence and Balance

International trade and financial transactions extend the limitations of domestic market size and push up the ceiling of resource endowment constraints. In this sense, a nation's potential for growth and improvement of living standards is ultimately dependent on the transactions it has with other countries. However, the economic benefits derived from international interdependence are achieved within inter-temporal external budget constraints. In other words, a nation must adjust its domestic economic conditions in order to maintain its external balance in the long run. Without doing this the country will suffer from an external debt problem and will have to give up a degree of autonomy in the management of its national economy.

Until Japan forced herself into closing her economy to trade with the rest of the world by triggering the war with the Allied Powers, her dependence on external trade had risen to around 20 per cent in terms of GNP. Even under the restraints imposed by Occupation policies, trade expanded rapidly as Japan imported the food and raw materials essential to the maintenance of an acceptable standard of living and stable levels of industrial production. Naturally, imports exceeded exports, a consequence of the fact that the national consumption of foods for survival and basic requirements of industrial goods exceeded production levels. This, of course, was itself a result of the shortage of materials and the limited number of exportable products in Japan at that time. Japan recorded high current account deficits in the balance of payments until 1950: 4 per cent of GNP in 1946, 4.1 per cent in 1947–8 and 3.3 per cent in 1949 as can be seen in Table 10.1.

In the immediate postwar period it would have been almost impossible for Japan to have carried out normal business activities with other countries, most of whom would have liked to have retaliated against Japan by demanding reparations. Thus, Japan would not have been able to import the food and materials vital to her economic reconstruction without the aid that was provided by the US beginning in 1946.

In early 1948, the apparent antagonism between the USSR and the US resulted in a change in the SCAP's policy stance from that of hostility to that of appeasement. As if in concert with the change in attitude toward Japan on the part of the Western world, that year the Japanese government established the institutional framework necessary for the introduction of foreign capital. One of the objectives of this arrangement was to moderate the external constraints that the balance of payments would have on the Japanese economy once Japan could no longer expect or depend on foreign aid. In fact, American aid for Japanese imports had already fallen to an extremely low level by 1950. Moreover, the Special Procurement Order induced by the Korean War(1950–2) resulted in a windfall external surplus which provided the preliminary condition for relieving Japan of its dependence on foreign aid.

Soon after, the Japanese government put into effect economic policies that would ensure that the economy would not fall into the plight of external debt accumulation. As a result, the domestic economic boom was cooled by various measures (excluding for exchange rate realignment) whenever the balance of payments tended toward a deficit situation. The Japanese economy after 1950 was able to overcome external constraints on its independence.

10.1.3 Major Players in the Supply-Side of the National Economy

The effectiveness of such policy measures is dependent on the degree of faith that the public has in the government and on the government's ability to provide appropriate policy guidance. Such guidance includes stimulating an incentive for labour to work and entrepreneurs to take risks. The former factor is of considerable importance in a country confronting the kind of crises that Japan had to endure during the painful period before the economy stabilized. Here, we review how the Japanese government created a situation of mutual trust with the major players, that is, the workers and firms, in the supply-side of this democratic policy and capitalistic economy.

As a defeated nation, Japan had to transform her politico-economic system according to the American model: New Deal principles were emphasized in the pre-Dodge Line and free market principles after the Dodge Line. Although the economic policies developed by SCAP and based upon American experiences with the New Deal have been evaluated negatively,[1] the introduction of land reform, the dissolution of the Zaibatsu, the enactment of the Labour Union Law (Rodo Kumiai-ho) at the end of 1945, and the official announcement of the New Constitution all served to constrain unfair vested-interests and gave many people with low bargaining power considerable opportunities and channels to seek their interests. In addition, the so-called safety-nets, including the Public Assistance Law (Seikatsu Hogo-ho) enacted in 1946 and the 1947 Law on the Benefits and Insurance for the Unemployed (Shitsugyo Hoken-ho) are important to note even though the institutions in place were insufficient to adequately protect workers' living conditions. At any rate, a series of institutional reforms aimed at farmers, corporations and labour which were based on the American ideal of fairness, seem to have resulted in a considerable amount of public trust in government.

Workers' Attitudes

The wider the gap between the expectation for higher wages which is brought about by idealistic institutional reforms and the actual rates at which companies pay workers, the more serious labour disputes are. On the other hand, as Kindleberger (1982) stresses, people's collective memory affects their behaviour for many decades. According to Table 10.2, if we judge the degree of severity of labour disputes in terms of workers involved and man-days lost, then it is clear that between 1952 and 1955 Japanese workers left radicalism behind and began to support milder and more stable movements. This was to last until 1960.

Table 10.2 Supply-side players

Year	*Real wage (manufacturing) (1934–6=100)*	*Unemployment rate (%)*	*Workers involved /dispute (1934–6=100)*	*Man-days lost /dispute (1934–6=100)*	*Profitability (net profit/ paid-in-capital, %)*		*Discount rate %*
					All industries	*Manufacturing*	
1930	96.1	5.2	152.4	298.1	12.8	4.4	6.8
31	100.9	5.9	114.4	251.0	–	4.9	7.5
32	98.3	6.9	101.1	175.5	6.6	8.4	6.6
33	99.6	5.7	111.9	127.5	9.0	14.1	6.1
34	101.7	5.0	114.2	146.5	10.4	15.1	5.4
35	99.7	4.7	101.0	101.2	12.4	16.2	5.3
36	98.6	4.4	85.4	51.8	12.7	16.2	5.0
37	101.1	3.8	182.7	104.5	13.9	17.4	4.9
38	105.7	3.1	96.2	24.3	14.2	17.4	4.7
39	112.8	2.3	208.3	19.7	14.8	17.8	4.6
1940	94.3	–	136.6	46.5	14.6	16.7	4.7
41	90.8	–	94.1	–	13.4	14.6	4.5
42	76.9	–	97.5	–	13.3	14.2	4.5
43	75.8	–	64.5	–	12.7	13.2	4.5
44	–	–	61.6	–	–	–	4.5
45	–	–	1168.9	–	–	–	4.7
46	–	4.0	5380.6	4283.7	–	–	5.6
47	39.6	1.1	7756.5	3060.1	–	–	7.5
48	63.4	0.7	8048.0	2900.2	–	–	10.2
49	88.0	1.0	4252.8	1921.8	–	–	9.9
1950	116.1	1.2	2871.4	2320.3	33.3	41.4	9.5
51	128.2	1.1	4321.2	3189.5	94.4	124.0	9.5
52	142.1	1.2	5431.5	7689.6	43.0	51.4	9.3
53	152.1	1.1	4840.4	2107.5	31.8	44.7	9.3
54	154.4	1.5	3842.6	1934.8	21.7	27.1	9.3
55	154.2	1.6	5066.6	1621.2	23.8	26.6	8.9

Table 10.2 *continued*

Year	Real wage (manufacturing) (1934–6=100)	Unemploy-ment rate (%)	Workers involved /dispute (1934–6=100)	Man-days lost /dispute (1934–6=100)	Profitability (net profit/ paid-in-capital, %) All industries	Manufacturing	Discount rate %
56	164.4	1.7	4609.6	2157.2	29.1	33.3	8.4
57	167.9	1.4	5716.1	2123.5	23.2	27.8	8.9
58	163.6	1.4	6206.0	2042.1	14.1	17.1	8.4
59	175.6	1.5	4981.1	2215.6	22.5	29.5	8.2
1960	183.1	1.1	5689.3	1390.4	24.6	31.2	8.1

Sources: Somu-cho Tokei-kyoku, *Nihon Choki Tokei*, 1, 3 (Statistics Bureau, Management and Coordination Agency, Historical Statistics of Japan, vols 1, 3); Toyo Keizai Shinpo-sha, *Kanketsu Kokusei Soran*, 1 (The Comprehensive Statistics of Japan for the Showa Era, vol. 1); Nihon Ginko, *Nihon Ginko 100 Nen-shi: Shiryo-hen* (The Bank of Japan, A Hundred-Year History of the Bank of Japan: Data and Statistics) 1986; Rodo-sho, *Rodo Tokei Nenpo* (The Ministry of Labour, The Yearbook of Labour Statistics).

This characteristics of labour disputes in the postwar years preceding 1955 seems to have been influenced not only by the economic conditions of this period but also by those in the prewar years. The average real wage of workers in manufacturing industries had already begun to fall at the beginning of the Second World War, and by 1947 was only 40 per cent of the 1934–6 level (hereafter called the prewar level). Fortunately, wages were rapidly improved after the war, and in 1952 were 42.1 per cent higher than the average for the prewar period. Additionally, in the postwar period workers had less reason to worry about unemployment. While the average rate of unemployment in the 1930s was about 5 per cent in the 1950s it was less than 2 per cent (although in 1946 it reached 4 per cent as a result of frictional unemployment).

Companies' Vitality

Fuelled by the desire for profit, firms serve as the engines of the capitalistic market economy. As such, they are organized and managed by individuals who have both entrepreneurial skill and benefit from fair and free competition in the market. It is this freedom to independently manage one's company and to accept responsibility for bankruptcy that results in enterprise vitality. Unfortunately, in the immediate postwar period such business conditions were controlled by SCAP through the Dodge Line. Although SCAP failed to control many negative aspects of the postwar economy, such as the black market and hyper-inflation, they succeeded in transforming the institutional and legal framework in favour of fair business and free competition. This was accomplished by abolishing the Zaibatsu in 1946 and through the implementation of deconcentration through the enactment of the Anti-Monopoly Law (Dokusen Kinshi-ho) in 1947. In fact, concentration ratios in the major industries were considerably low in those years.[2]

At any rate, it is almost impossible for any company to manage its business activities without being able to make its own economic calculations. This was particularly the case in postwar Japan, which had both an uncertain institutional framework and a currency which had lost its fundamental function. More than anything else, the reparations issue was the major area of uncertainty confronting industry in the period before 1948 when SCAP policies remained hostile. Under conditions where normal market mechanisms could not operate, the Japanese government had to try to sustain the industrial production crucial to the reconstruction and stabilization of the economy. With that objective, the government mobilized funds and man-power and channelled these to firms in strategic industries. However, as a consequence, many of the companies receiving government subsidies lost management discipline and industrial efficiency.

Established in 1949, the Dodge Line was an important turning point because it forced Japanese firms and the government to re-establish efficiency and discipline in management. Although business freedom had returned as a result of the dissolution of economic controls, the disciplinary fiscal and financial policies set out in the Dodge Line had forced the government, many firms and labour to suffer considerably. Thus, the rationalization of company management and industrial activities became the top priorities for individuals and the government. The profit motive alone proved insufficient to carrying out this tough task. However, most Japanese firms were able to overcome their plight by making the best of the temporary economic boom resulting from the war which broke out in Korea in 1950. The abnormally high rate of profitability shown in Table 10.2 (124 per cent in 1951) is evidence of this fact. Although Japanese companies Japanese companies had the wisdom not to miss a once-in-a-lifetime opportunity, it is doubtful whether the Japanese economy and Japanese companies could have succeeded in achieving economic independence and rationalization without the boom brought about by this war.

10.2 INDUSTRIAL RATIONALIZATION

The primary aim of this section is to review the process and policies of industrial rationalization in the post Second World War period. In order to underscore the significance of the industrial rationalization carried out between 1950 and 1955, we first touch upon the reconstruction processes of key Japanese industries under the so-called Priority Production System (Keisha Seisan Hoshiki) before the Dodge Line was put into effect. Next, we review the price performances, productivity and profitability of those industries after the Dodge Line. Finally, we explore how firms in these industries secured their independence from the government by reducing dependence on the government in financing investment.

Generally speaking, all aspects of a firm in any given industry have to be rationalized if the firm is to compete with other firms and survive in domestic and overseas markets. Therefore, the rationalization of a given industry is itself merely the aggregation of each firm's own efforts at rationalization as it responds to market signals and policy measures. On the other hand, if we focus on the supply-side of a national economy and recognize that certain externalities between industries distort it, then it becomes clear that policy intervention is needed to correct such distortions. Accordingly, we should note that there are two definitions of industrial rationalization: the rationalization of all activities necessary to increasing the companies' profitability, and the rationalization of all firm responses that contribute to the improvement of the supply-side of the national economy.

10.2.1 The Painful Process of Industrial Reconstruction

During the period of reconstruction most Japanese had to endure seriously lowered living standards. The production levels of consumer goods had begun to fall as soon as Japan went into war with the US in 1941, and had fallen to about 30 per cent of the prewar level by 1945, the year the war ended. As shown in Table 10.3, this was an inescapable burden for a nation at war. While Japan had the heavy and chemical industrial bases required for producing the arms necessary for modern warfare, they had to produce these under closed economic conditions and with a limited resource endowment. The demilitarization of the industrial structure soon after the war and the enforcement of various Occupation policies drastically reduced the production of investment and capital goods in 1945. However,

Table 10.3 Production index (1934–6=100)

Year	*All industries*	*Investment goods*	*Capital goods*	*Consumer goods*	*Producer goods*	*Coal, lignite*	*Iron and steel*	*Chemical*	*Textile*	*Machinery*
1930	74.1	90.7	101.9	79.8	58.3	81.6	48.6	48.1	64.8	103.5
31	66.9	69.8	79.2	77.1	56.6	72.8	42.9	48.1	68.6	72.4
32	70.5	66.3	67.9	82.6	65.1	72.9	51.4	62.3	74.4	62.1
33	86.7	90.7	96.2	92.2	77.1	84.4	71.4	70.8	85.1	93.1
34	92.2	94.2	96.2	96.3	87.4	93.3	85.7	82.1	93.8	93.1
35	97.6	94.2	90.6	99.1	99.4	98.1	100.0	99.1	99.6	93.1
36	110.2	111.6	113.2	104.6	113.1	108.6	114.3	118.9	106.7	113.8
37	128.3	143.0	152.8	115.6	126.9	117.6	131.4	135.9	121.5	155.2
38	133.7	153.5	169.8	114.2	132.0	126.5	151.4	155.7	100.2	175.9
39	146.4	184.9	209.4	117.0	142.3	133.0	165.7	167.0	100.2	217.3
1940	153.6	223.3	254.7	111.5	142.3	146.4	168.6	164.2	90.5	258.6
41	159.0	251.2	294.4	96.3	144.0	147.0	174.3	164.2	73.5	300.0
42	155.4	254.7	305.7	88.1	137.1	141.9	182.9	135.9	58.0	310.4
43	157.2	275.6	334.0	71.6	140.6	149.1	205.7	118.9	38.0	341.4
44	159.0	317.4	390.6	52.3	135.4	141.5	191.4	107.5	20.3	403.5
45	70.5	139.5	169.8	27.5	56.6	80.4	68.6	45.3	7.7	165.5
46	30.7	45.3	45.3	27.5	29.1	55.3	22.9	25.5	12.9	51.7
47	38.0	55.8	50.9	31.7	39.4	73.7	28.6	36.8	17.4	62.1
48	50.6	80.2	84.9	37.2	51.4	90.6	48.6	48.1	19.7	93.1
49	65.1	101.2	107.6	49.5	66.9	101.1	85.7	65.1	26.4	113.8
1950	79.5	108.1	107.6	60.6	85.7	101.8	120.0	90.6	37.4	124.1
51	106.6	170.9	175.5	78.4	109.7	114.6	160.0	118.9	53.2	196.6
52	115.7	170.9	175.5	88.1	120.0	114.8	162.9	133.0	60.6	206.9
53	139.2	202.3	220.8	114.2	140.6	123.0	194.3	164.2	72.8	258.6
54	150.0	219.8	243.4	126.6	150.9	113.0	197.1	189.6	78.9	289.7
55	162.7	219.8	237.7	143.1	162.9	112.2	220.0	217.9	88.3	300.0
56	198.8	289.5	339.6	162.4	205.7	123.1	268.6	263.2	105.0	434.5
57	233.1	373.3	469.8	188.5	229.7	136.7	308.6	311.3	116.0	600.0
58	229.5	352.3	424.5	202.3	217.7	131.3	291.4	328.3	103.4	579.4
59	274.7	411.6	498.1	235.3	272.6	124.9	388.6	367.9	120.5	744.9
1960	341.6	547.7	690.6	269.7	342.9	134.7	511.4	444.3	142.4	1034.6

[illegible] The Fiscal History of the Showa Era: Statistics, vol. 19).

production of these had already reached its limit in the previous years, heavily determined as it was by the availability of materials, that is, producer goods. Table 10.3 reveals that the production of producer goods had already lost its expansionary potential by 1944.

The Japanese did not achieve the standard of living attained in the prewar period until after attaining political independence. Although the production of consumer goods lagged behind that of investment and capital goods, the steady increase in the production of consumer goods made it possible to maintain public confidence. On the other hand, the sectors producing the investment goods which were later to lead the Japanese economy, had returned to prewar production levels by 1950. This rapid revival and the progress made by these industries thereafter was possible because companies were able to use equipment which had been developed during the war but that had escaped damage during the air bombings and avoided the fate of other equipment which was demanded as reparations payments after the war by the Far Eastern Commission of the Allied Nations. While there were some positive aspects in the process of industrial reconstruction, it still took five painful years to return to the prewar production levels of all industries aggregated, and even so many industries remained inefficient .

Industries such as coal, iron and steel, fertilizers, textiles, electricity, and shipping were regarded as sectors vital to the reconstruction and independence of the Japanese economy. In the following section, we examine four of these: coal, iron and steel, fertilizers and textiles. The coal industry was the dominant supplier of primary energy to the Japanese economy. The iron and steel industry, which had played an important role in military production, became the major provider of the basic materials required by Japan's modern industries. At the same time, chemical fertilizers were needed to raise agricultural productivity in order to feed the Japanese public. Likewise, the textile industry was important not only in providing clothing for the Japanese people but also as an efficient earner of foreign currency. As such, the textile industry was considered a leading candidate for government support.

The Priority Production System

In Section 10.1 we supported the view that Japanese economic activities were largely determined by the availability of energy. The two major energy sources for production were coal, and by the early 1960s, hydroelectric power. Although the demand for hydroelectric power gradually increased, more than half of the energy demand was satisfied by the coal mining industry. Coal was an important raw material for industrial production and an important fuel source for the transportation of goods. Thus, domestic coal was particularly crucial to the reconstruction and independence of the Japanese economy in the early stages of the postwar period.

While coal production remained high it was based on an extremely vulnerable system. During the war a vast amount of labour had been rapidly mobilized in order to keep production levels high. But the coal industry operated under a declining labour productivity resulting from the use of antiquated equipment and the shortage of materials such as steel and cement. In addition, worker morale and skill levels could not help but be low: about 40 per cent of coalminers were forced labourers drafted mainly from Korea, Japan, and China. After 1946, when these workers were liberated and were able to return to their homes and began to deal with their feelings about the harsh treatment they received during the war, it became difficult to begin the rebuilding of the coal industry.[3]

Fortunately, compared with the low levels of production experienced by other industries in the immediate postwar period, the coal industry actually fared well. However, the speed at which the coal industry returned to prewar production levels was slower than that of other industries. Even though the coal industry had regained prewar levels by 1950, it did not continue to grow at the same pace as other industries thereafter.

The first priority of the pre-Dodge Line industrial policy was to achieve the monthly coal production levels outlined by the government, representatives from companies and learned persons. However, the slow rise in the production of coal led to a slowdown in the production of steel, cement and fertilizers.

At the end of 1946 the government introduced the so-called Priority Production System which recognized the inter-industrial relationship between coal, steel and fertilizers. Above all, this system emphasized the interdependence between coal and steel. It was determined that it was necessary to secure the expansion of both industries under the severely controlled and closed economy and to alleviate the constraints on the balance of payments. The preferential treatment given to large numbers of workers in the coal mining industry initially attracted additional workers. In fact, their number far exceeded the peak attained during the war. At the same time, extensive subsidies to the firms concerned helped to improve production conditions and contributed to increased labour productivity. As result of these two factors, the coal industry was able to achieve the quantitative objectives outlined under this system, though at a slower pace than anticipated. What about the case of the iron and steel industry?

The changing pattern of production in this industry was the most drastic among the four industries outlined here. The severe decline and the low level of production experienced in 1945 and 1946 were mostly due to reductions in coal-input to this industry, itself the result of the institution of an emergency rationing of basic necessities by the government. What factors, then, led to the rapid recovery attained thereafter?

This industry consists of the two sectors: pig iron and crude steels-(ingot and steel). While both sectors rely on the infusion of coal, each also requires other sector-specific materials for production. For example, the production of pig iron is not possible without the input of iron ore, and the availability of heavy oil. In addition to the preferential allocation of coal under the Priority Production System, the import of heavy oil and iron ore permitted by SCAP in 1947 and 1948 led to a critical acceleration of production by this industry. The expansionary power of the iron and steel industry was so strong that, even though the economy as a whole experienced deflation in reaction to the Dodge Line in 1949, the industry itself recorded much higher growth rates for production than the manufacturing sector as a whole.

The industry was able to first overcome resource bottlenecks when, as a result of the change in policy stance of the Occupation authorities in 1948, companies were able to import crucial resources. The introduction of the Priority Production System, outlined above, also proved of considerable benefit to the industry. Prior to 1948 SCAP stance toward this industry had been to limit production capacity to a level in line with the availability of domestic coal and iron ore.[4] In addition, before Japan achieved political independence, the industry was confronted by uncertainties with respect to the possible requisitioning of equipment for reparations. This was the case even though the list of equipment demanded as reparations payments had been gradually revised by SCAP and later *de facto* abolished. (About 75 per cent of the equipment necessary for the production of steel would have been taken away if the first report on reparations had been implemented.)[5]

10.2.2 After the Dodge Line

One of the goals of the Dodge Line was to encourage Japanese firms to establish efficient management methods and to conduct industrial activities independent of government subsidies. It was thought that if companies did this, then they would be able to compete with respect to price and quality in the world market under a reasonable level of exchange rate. It was also assumed that they would gain a level of profitability commensurate with that of other companies. In order to achieve this goal under the free market conditions that existed after the dissolution of economic controls, the firms in key industries had to rationalize their production and management systems. Likewise, the government also had to establish an institutional environment which would encourage companies to rationalize. Of course, ultimately it is the law of the survival of the fittest which decides who will be the losers in a given industry. However, if domestic and global macroeconomic conditions are favourable, the losers may not remain losers for long, as they can more easily find new opportunities in other areas.

The Dodge Depression and the Korean War Boom

Industrial controls were successively abolished in the two-year period after the Dodge Line was established in May 1949. Most firms wanted to start investing in the renovation of aging equipment and the introduction of equipment incorporating modern technologies. However, macroeconomic conditions and policy circumstances, including a severe deflation and tight fiscal-financial measures induced by an austere budget, made it hard to adopt this type of rationalization. Thus, companies had to pursue rationalization by closing unprofitable establishments and firing excess workers. Such moves were made possible by subsidies provided for the recovery of production. In addition, American styles of business management, including quality-control, operation-control and human-resource-management, were also introduced following their active promotion by SCAP.[6] These efforts were regarded as the necessary prerequisites to rationalization.

The Korean War gave momentum to these efforts at industrial rationalization in two regards. First, the demand created by special procurements and the global demand for goods induced by this war led to expanded Japanese exports. This not only resolved the problem of excess supply but also led to increased investments in equipment in order to produce further supplies. During this phase most firms achieved stability and enjoyed a surprisingly high profitability. Second, with the end of this boom the Japanese began to have doubts about the international competitiveness of their industries. As a result, from 1950 through 1960 many companies began to recognize in earnest the importance of rationalization and began to make serious efforts to achieve this objective. What were the results of these rationalization efforts?

Price, Productivity and Profitability

In order to expand exports, a firm has to offer goods that are both cheaper and of a higher quality than goods from other countries. Here, we examine the long-term price-competitiveness of key Japanese industries.

In Table 10.4 we can find a common pattern in the movement of Japanese prices relative to those of the US. With the exceptions of cotton yarn and ammonium sulphate, the price-competitiveness of key Japanese industries drastically declined from 1950 to 1951, but by 1955 these industries had regained their original position. Unfortunately, there was little improvement in price-competitiveness during the latter half of the 1950s. On the other hand, if we focus on absolute levels of relative prices, the following products were foreign currency earners: cotton yarn, cotton fabrics, ammonium sulphate and bar steel. However, the problem of the high prices of coal and iron could not be solved during the time of rationalization.

The improvement of productivity was a necessary condition for a firm wanting to reduce production costs so that it could remain price-competitive in both global and domestic markets. Here, we review the productivity performances of key industries in terms of physical productivity (labour hours or persons per unit required to produce a product). As shown in Table 10.5, the ranking of industries in terms of the degree of productivity improvement for the period between 1950 and 1955 is as follows: cotton yarn, ammonium sulphate, coal and blast furnaces. However, as of 1960, reflecting the speed at which each industry improved productivity, the ranking changed as follows; ammonium sulphate, cotton yarn, blast furnaces and coal.

While the ammonium sulphate industry experienced a smooth increase in productivity during this period, the coal industry did not fare as well. This is to be expected given the fact that the coal industry was confronted by the natural constraints of a limited coal endow-

Table 10.4 Comparative price of Japanese goods (US=100)

Year	*Cotton yarn*	*Cotton fabrics*	*Pig iron*	*Bar steel*
1950	142.9	79.3	60.0	78.6
51	127.7	134.3	154.8	166.9
52	97.6	115.3	157.8	166.9
53	105.0	100.5	138.8	127.7
54	83.6	86.9	122.3	121.2
55	84.0	83.6	114.9	107.5
56	87.7	95.8	133.6	121.2
57	79.7	91.4	143.8	115.1
58	78.6	81.3	118.0	82.4
59	71.0	82.7	111.9	89.9
60	63.9	78.9	111.9	89.9
Year	*Steel plate (thick)*	*Steel plate (thin)*	*Ammonium sulphate*	*Coal (coking)*
1950	78.1	96.3	129.6	159.2
51	187.7	262.3	92.0	295.0
52	187.7	220.7	119.2	217.6
53	142.1	203.2	114.1	215.5
54	136.7	179.8	113.5	211.1
55	118.5	157.7	110.6	172.1
56	141.4	171.1	118.4	151.6
57	139.6	162.6	151.7	159.8
58	110.0	134.4	114.1	165.6
59	120.1	139.6	97.1	158.4
60	120.1	139.6	106.3	171.8

Source: Okura-sho, *Zaisei Kin'yu Tokei Geppo* (Ministry of Finance, Monthly Bulletin of Financial Statistics) no. 21, 1951; nos 24, 27, 31, 1952; nos 34, 37, 40, 1953; nos 43, 47, 50, 1954; nos 54, 58, 1955; nos 62, 67, 1956; nos 72, 75, 78, 1957; nos 82, 90, 1958; no. 94, 1959; nos 104, 107, 113, 117, 1960. Data refer to June of each year.

ment. In addition, coal-industry labour unions were so radical that industrial relations were considerably unstable and not conducive to improvements in industrial productivity.

The periods during which the cotton-yarn and the iron and steel industries showed a distinct improvement in productivity were the early half of the 1950s and the latter 1950s respectively. The fact that Japan had to limit the export of textiles and steel in response to American demands during the 1960s is evidence of the success of the

Table 10.5 Productivity (required working hours per unit, 1950=100)

Year	*Cotton yarn*	*Ammonium sulphate*	*Iron & steel (blast furnace)*	*Coal*
1946	213.1	–	–	202.4
47	172.7	175.9	357.0	179.7
48	174.5	169.2	207.4	151.4
49	133.5	132.4	141.4	120.4
1950	100.0	100.0	100.0	100.0
51	100.3	90.2	83.5	91.0
52	64.6	67.6	89.5	92.5
53	55.0	61.0	73.1	83.7
54	45.9	52.6	72.0	78.4
55	43.2	49.3	65.3	64.1
56	39.4	43.7	60.2	59.8
57	37.7	39.5	55.6	57.1
58	40.7	34.1	52.7	70.4
59	38.4	30.5	41.8	68.2
1960	36.9	26.3	36.9	59.1
61	34.8	24.7	31.2	47.9
62	35.5	21.1	27.5	39.0
63	32.7	18.3	24.0	31.7
64	30.9	15.6	19.9	30.5
65	29.1	13.8	18.0	29.5

Notes: (1) The labour productivity of the coal industry is measured in terms of persons engaged per unit of production.
(2) The measurement standard for the productivity of the ammonium sulphate industry was changed between 1951 and 1952.

Source: Rodo-sho, *Rodo Seisansei Tokei Chosa Shiryo* (Ministry of Labour, Statistics on Labour Productivity: Report) 1966.

productivity improvements made during the 1950s. Such improvements made it possible for these industries to become powerful exporters in the 1960s.

At any rate, for the firms in the industries concerned, the ultimate objective of rationalization was to attain profit levels comparable to those of other industries. Above we outlined how most Japanese companies were able to enjoy extraordinary profits by taking advantage of the business opportunities offered by the Korean War. This was also true for the key industries discussed here. After the economic boom resulting from the Korean War, profits fell to more normal levels, as shown in Table 10.6(a). However, it is clear that the profit

Table 10.6 (a) Profitability (1948–60) (net profit/net worth, %)

Year	*Mining*	*Textiles*	*Chemical*	*Iron & steel*	*Machinery*
1948	83.1	35.0	13.1	–	6.7
49	56.1	21.2	29.9	–	19.5
1950	21.8	28.9	15.7	–	1.5
51	20.8	32.7	24.0	–	15.7
52	17.1	10.9	9.8	–	13.5
53	9.3	10.2	10.5	4.5	11.3
54	6.4	6.5	9.6	2.2	5.5
55	5.1	3.2	8.8	0.7	7.5
56	8.7	8.3	10.3	6.4	7.1
57	7.7	8.7	9.7	9.3	12.2
58	4.1	3.8	6.8	4.5	10.7
59	9.5	8.1	7.9	6.5	12.5
1960	5.9	9.2	14.5	10.2	16.2

Source: Okura-sho, *Zaisei Kin'yu Tokei Geppo* (Ministry of Finance, Monthly Bulletin of Financial Statistics) nos 4, 12, 1950; nos 23, 25, 29, 1952; nos 33, 38, 1953; nos 42, 48, 1954; nos 52, 56, 1955; nos 61, 66, 1956; nos 70, 76, 1957; nos 81, 87, 1958; nos 92, 97, 1959; nos 102, 108, 1960; nos 114, 120, 1961.

Table 10.6 (b) Profitability (1960–74) (net profit/owned capital %)

Year	*Mining*	*Textiles*	*Chemical*	*Iron & steel*	*Machinery*
1960	6.3	14.9	12.4	15.5	19.5
61	2.2	11.7	10.8	12.6	21.0
62	2.2	5.9	9.5	2.4	18.5
63	3.5	9.5	12.3	8.0	12.0
64	4.3	6.2	11.1	7.6	12.1
65	4.4	3.7	9.6	3.9	7.7
66	4.7	5.3	12.0	15.0	9.8
67	5.6	13.2	15.6	17.6	18.5
68	3.1	11.2	15.3	13.9	22.4
69	8.2	13.6	17.7	21.4	23.2
1970	–10.2	13.8	14.8	17.2	20.1
71	–3.6	5.7	8.3	1.3	12.3
72	3.9	10.2	10.0	11.4	10.7
73	15.5	28.6	20.2	27.7	17.2
74	0.6	–10.1	14.4	17.7	14.1

Source: Okura-sho, *Hojin Kigyo Tokei: Nenpo Soran* (Financial Statements of Corporations: Collected Annual Report) 1976.

levels of the iron and steel industry were significantly lower than those of other industries until 1957, although it is difficult to measure the profitability of this industry before 1952 due to the lack of data.

Most of the firms outlined above were able to become profitable as a result of the economies of scale brought about by rationalization efforts in the late 1950s. During the First Rationalization Plan (1951–5) they were able to modernize their equipment through investments supported by government measures. These efforts and steps taken under the next Rationalization Plan (1956–60) resulted in a steep rise in the production of major items after the mid-1950s and in the remarkable reduction in the unit production cost after 1957.[7]

Finally, we would like to review the profitability of key industries during the rapid growth era and to compare the profit-performance of the iron and steel industry with that of the machinery industry. This is of particular interest because both industries were given high priority in the industrial policies of the late 1950s. It is also useful in exploring the historical meaning of the rationalization policies presented in detail below. Table 10.6(b) shows that the coal industry was not able to overcome the constraints of a limited natural resource endowment. On the other hand, the table reveals that the iron and steel industry finally became competitive with the machinery industry in the late 1960s. Incidentally, it must be noted that the extremely high level of profit rate immediately after the war is partly owing to the statistical reason; value of net worth was not yet adjusted for inflation.

Two Stilts and Two Cushions

As stated above, the goal of the Dodge Line was to force the Japanese government to become independent of American aid and Japanese firms to become independent of financial and fiscal subsidies as quickly as possible. The numerous proposals concerning the requisitioning of industrial machinery for reparations payments were gradually modified and eventually abolished. At the same time, these proposals can be regarded as 'negative aid' in the form of pressure against the defeated and occupied Japan. The US government continued to help Japan secure her people from starvation and disease and to reconstruct her economy through the provision of generous long-term loans, aid such as that provided by the programmes for Government and Relief in Occupied Areas (1946–51) and Economic Rehabilitation in Occupied Areas (1949–51). American aid lessened the impact that the balance of payments and the lack of foreign currency had on the import of foodstuffs, fertilizer, oil, cotton and

Table 10.7 Foreign supports for trade (%)

Year	*The US aids /import*	*The special procurement /export* Total	Merchandise	Service
1946	63.1	–	–	–
47	77.2	–	–	–
48	67.5	–	–	–
49	59.1	–	–	–
1950	37.1	18.2	13.8	48.1
51	8.1	16.5	18.8	12.6
52	0.3	14.7	15.9	13.0
53	–	20.3	20.7	19.6
54	–	10.0	6.5	17.4
55	–	6.4	3.3	15.1
56	–	5.0	2.8	11.6
57	–	6.2	4.6	11.2
58	–	3.9	2.3	9.6
59	–	3.7	2.6	8.0
1960	–	3.2	2.3	6.7

Source: Okura-sho, *Showa Zaisei-shi: 19, Tokei* (Ministry of Finance, The Fiscal History of the Showa Era: Statistics, vol. 19) 1978.

iron ore. Just how tall was this stilt? The share of imports covered by financial aid during the immediate postwar period is shown in Table 10.7. However, the dependence on foreign aid declined rapidly after 1949, reflecting the success of Dodge Line policies introduced that year.

The other stilt was the government subsidies provided by the Reconstruction Finance Bank (Fukko Kin'yu Kinko) (1947–62) to key industries (mainly the coal industry). As a whole, the degree of financial dependence on such subsidies was considerably high, as shown in Table 10.8. Although subsidies for equipment contributed to some extent to the recovery of industrial production, they simultaneously produced inflationary pressure on the economy as a result of the Bank of Japan's practice of underwriting the bank's bonds. However, the drastic curtailment of government subsidies that resulted from the Dodge Line forced companies to become independent as quickly as possible.

The Dodge deflation, other circumstances which made exports difficult such as the introduction of the \$1=¥360 exchange rate, the

Table 10.8 Financial dependence on Government and foreign sources (%)

Year	*The government's share*							*The share of US counter-part fund*	*The foreigners' share*	
	Total net external flow of funds	*Flow of equipment funds*						*Total net external flow of funds*	*Flow of total net investment*	*Flow of equipment funds*
		Total	*Textiles*	*Chemicals*	*Machinery*	*Iron and steel*	*Coal*			
1947	33.1	–	–	–	–	–	–	–	–	–
48	15.3	–	–	–	–	–	–	–	–	–
49	–0.6	–	–	–	–	–	–	1.8	–	–
1950	–3.1	–	–	–	–	–	–	5.6	0.2	–
51	1.5	–	–	–	–	–	–	5.7	0.7	–
52	2.6	8.1	16.3	18.9	18.1	19.5	26.5	5.0	1.6	–
53	7.8	21.9	23.3	14.3	10.5	14.8	36.1	0.1	1.9	–
54	16.3	24.4	15.9	8.9	14.0	3.1	7.5	–	1.1	–
55	11.1	22.0	15.0	9.4	14.9	2.3	34.8	–	2.8	–
56	5.0	9.6	8.7	5.5	9.2	6.7	36.3	–	2.6	–
57	6.1	11.4	17.0	6.7	11.9	7.6	34.7	–	2.7	1.7
58	7.3	12.8	13.9	9.2	10.8	4.9	26.7	–	6.0	7.2
59	6.4	11.7	16.2	9.8	8.2	3.4	34.1	–	2.6	5.2
1960	5.5	8.7	10.6	5.0	6.1	2.9	44.3	–	2.6	3.8

Sources: Okura-sho, *Showa Zaisei-shi: 19, Tokei* (Ministry of Finance, The Fiscal History of the Showa Era: vol. 19, Statistics) 1978. Nihon Ginko, *Keizai Tokei Nenpo* (Bank of Japan, Economic Statistics Annual).

devaluation of the pound sterling, and the withdrawal of the two stilts mentioned above, brought forth two fears with respect to the availability of foreign currency and funds for business operations and for investment in rationalization. Fortunately, the US provided financial aid as a part of the Counterpart Funds of US aid, although the management of this aid was under the strict control of SCAP (Table 10.8). Furthermore, the special procurement that resulted from the Korean War mitigated the fears that the government had regarding the availability of foreign currency and the possibility that some firms might remain idle (Table 10.7). The figures in Table 10.7 reveal the extent to which US aid and the Korean War served to cushion the Japanese economy and Japanese industries against the possibility of economic collapse and bankruptcy.

10.2.3 Financial Independence

With the end of the economic boom brought about by the Korean War and the return of national sovereignty, most firms began to make serious efforts at rationalization. The Japanese government, too, could no longer expect substantial foreign aid. Although most companies had been able to accumulate reserve funds from the extraordinary profits they made during the Korean War, these funds were not sufficient to carry out serious rationalization measures. The primary means to achieve rationalization was to introduce new equipment, technologies and know-how. It was hoped that such measures would result in competitiveness in the domestic and overseas markets and managerial independence.

On the other hand, once Japan regained her political independence the Japanese government was able to formulate Japanese economic institutions and policies in accordance with her own national interests. This free hand in the formation of economic policy would not have been productive if the government had not had enough money to put them in place. Although the Japanese government could no longer depend on aid from the US, they were able to record continual fiscal surpluses in the special account of the US's Counterpart Fund. They were also able to accumulate most of the funds that were previously loaned out by the Reconstruction Finance Bank. This was made possible by the austere budget constraint on the fiscal balance imposed by the Dodge Line.

Here, we evaluate the degree of financial independence that Japanese firms in the industries concerned had from their government. Table 10.8 reveals three interesting facts with respect to these firms. First, they were largely independent of loans from government financial institutions especially after 1955. Second, they could expect government financial institutions, particularly the Japan Development Bank (Nihon Kaihatsu Ginko) (1951–), to lend them funds for equipment investment. Finally, financial dependence increased in the initial phase of industrial rationalization, from 1952 to 1954. The latter two conditions would not have been possible without the surplus in the government budget outlined above. In the latter part of the 1950s, the government's share of industrial financing stabilized at around 5 per cent for total funds and 10 per cent for equipment funds. Thus, as they left the initial period of rationalization behind them, Japanese firms were able to attain financial independence from the government.

Of course, if we examine individual industries we get a different picture from that presented in Table 10.8. The coal industry, for example, is exceptional because it was so much dependent on the government for funds. The textile industry also had a much higher level of financial dependence than the industrial average, a situation which did not decline definitively. In the 1950s, the major sector of the textile industry, cotton yarn and fabrics, consisted largely of small- and medium-sized firms with limited finances. The Small Business Finance Corporation (Chushokigyo Kin'yu Koko) (1953–) was responsible for providing funds to these firms. As mentioned above, the coal industry had its own inherent limitations as an industry dependent on a poorly endowed natural resource, while the cotton textile industry had a low credit rating resulting from the fact that the industry consisted of small- and medium-size firms with volatile earnings.

We cannot overlook the role that foreign capital played in this process.[8] Foreign capital was considerably attractive to Japanese companies. It was much more expensive to procure capital from domestic financial sources than it was from US and British financial markets, as shown in Table 10.9. Under the Foreign Exchange and Foreign Trade Control Law (Gaikoku Kawase oyobi Gaikoku Boeki Kanri-ho) (1949–) and the Foreign Investment Law (Gaishi-ho) (1950–), the Japanese government permitted the import of foreign investment capital, based on the following criteria. First, the introduction of foreign funds would contribute to an improvement in the balance of payments; second, it would help strengthen crucial industries and public utilities; third, it was necessary in order to be able to renew contracts for technological assistance in strategic industries and public utilities. Initially, the first criterion was considered of

Table 10.9 Comparison of interest rates (%)

		Japan (Oct. 1952)	USA (Aug. 1952)	UK (Aug. 1952)
Official discount rate		5.84	1.75	4.00
Private bank	Loan	6.21	1.75	3.50
	Discount	7.67	2.31	3.00
	Call	3.65	2.57	2.25
	TD	5.00	2.50	2.00
Securities yield	GB	5.50	2.70	4.30
	TB	5.48	1.87	2.46
	CD	9.02	3.18	4.93
	Share	7.78	5.37	6.47

Notes: TD: Time deposit
GB: Medium/long term government bond
TB: Treasury bill
CD: Corporate debenture

Source: Okura-sho, *Zaisei Kin'yu Tokei Geppo* (Ministry of Finance, Monthly Bulletin of Financial Statistics) no. 32, 1952.

primary importance to the maintenance of the independence of the Japanese economy. Later, however, these regulations became more flexible as the economic progress and international competitiveness of major Japanese industries was strengthened.

Comparing column 1 with column 10 in Table 10.8, it becomes clear that the foreign capital that entered Japan made up for the falling share of lending by government financial institutions after 1954. In particular, key industries such as iron and steel, and chemicals and machinery, which became leading industries in the decades to follow, and public utilities such as electric power and transportation, which provide the infrastructure for the economy, were able to enjoy preferential treatment in the procurement of foreign funds for equipment investment. Even if other Japanese firms had hoped to reduce their financial dependence on government institutions by importing foreign capital, it was almost impossible to do so under the selection system described above.

The ability to earn foreign currency through exports was regarded as an effective means to achieve economic independence. Of course, it was hoped that Japanese firms would be able to export without any help from the government. However, the international competitiveness of key Japanese industries was quite uncertain, as is revealed in the comparison of US and Japanese prices. Products processed from domestic steel were expensive on the international market because domestic iron and steel production relied on domestic coal which was mined at tremendous cost. These products had trouble becoming price-competitive on the world market.

The Export Bank of Japan (1951–2) and the Export-Import Bank of Japan (Nihon Yushutsunyu Ginko) (1952–) made up for this handicap by providing loans for the export of heavy machineries such as vessels, rolling stock, electrical power plants, textile machinery and steel products. The ratio of the average lending approved by the EX-IM Bank for the export of these products to the value of export in the 1950s is as follows: 69.7 per cent for vessels, 33.2 per cent for rolling stock, 49.1 per cent for electrical power plants, and 26.4 per cent for textile machinery. On the whole, however, such financial assistance appears limited when compared with the total value of exports. The average ratio of total export credits to the total value of exports was 4.5 per cent.

10.3 GOVERNMENT ROLE IN THE RATIONALIZATION PROCESS

We begin this section with a brief review of the institutional aspects of the so-called Industrial Rationalization Policy ((Sangyo Gorika Seisaku) IRP). This is followed by an overview of the government's attitudes and positions regarding the formation and implementation of IRP. Finally, we examine the significance of IRP in the rationalization process, relying on the reviews provided in the preceding two sections and on the influential discussions on IRP by leading economists.

10.3.1 Legal Framework of IRP[9]

One of the first steps taken under the IRP was the elimination of the negative heritage of the Priority Production System, particularly the problem of high-priced coal and steel. Following the guidelines recommended by the Industrial Rationalization Council (Sangyo Gorika Shingikai) (1949–64), the government adopted 'Measures for Rationalizing the Steel and Coal Mining Industries' as a Cabinet Resolution in 1950. As a consequence of the Council's more comprehensive report, 'Methods for Rationalizing Our Industries' announced in 1951, IRP was given legal authority by the enactment of the Enterprise Rationalization Promotion Law (Kigyo Gorika Sokushin-ho) in 1952. The following plans were introduced in concert with this law: the First Rationalization Plan of the Steel Industry (1951–5) (later succeeded by the Second Rationalization Plan (1956–60) and the Third Rationalization Plan (1961–5)), the Three Years' Rationalization Plan for the Coal Mining Industry and the Law on Temporary Measures for Coal Mining Industry Rationalization (Sekitan Kogyo Gorika Rinji Sochi-ho) (1956–62).

The Enterprise Rationalization Promotion Law provided the legal framework for the rationalization of companies in specific industries. This law suggested that the following methods would be effective in the promotion of enterprise rationalization: technological improvement, modernization of equipment, improvement of roads and ports, raising the efficiency in the use of materials and generative powers and the introduction of management autonomy in small- and medium-sized enterprises. As a result of this law, the government was given the power to guide and provide recommendations to designated companies using the above-mentioned methods, and to grant tax reductions.

Initially companies from 32 industries,[10] including coal, steel, electric power and shipping (all of which also benefited from preferential financing from the Japan Development Bank) were designated as corporations which would benefit from the special depreciation on investments for specific equipment. The number of industries so designated was later extended to fifty. Enterprises in these industries were given preferential treatment in the financing of loans, the rationing of foreign currency, the import of advanced technology, and the provision of tax allowances. However, these companies had to achieve normal profitability and had to submit to close monitoring and investigation by the government in order to enjoy preferential treatment.

What were the criteria adopted by the government in selecting an industry as a designated one?[11] The criteria for designation were as follows; (i) the industry had to be a 'basic' industry and a bottleneck in the industrial structure; (ii) it had to have particular significance in terms of production, export, and contribution to other industries and to import-substitution; (iii) the production increases or the cost reductions achieved by the rationalization of the industry concerned had to be considerably high; (iv) the industry had to produce exportable goods with high earning power and had to be able to offer these goods at internationally competitive prices through the introduction of new equipment; (v) the rationalization and modernization of the industry were deemed urgent; (vi) the industry had a considerable amount of equipment that needed to be modernized immediately and urgently; (vii) the industry had a high potentiality for the modernization of its equipment or had proved the capacity for this.

The priority attached to IRP finally became so high that the Anti-Monopoly Law, which had been introduced by SCAP in order to democratize Japanese industrial organization, was modified to 'rationalize' the relationships between companies in a given industry. Later the so-called depression cartels and rationalization cartels were also legitimized. In addition, several temporary acts and administrative recommendations exempted the following industries from the Anti-Monopoly Law: machinery, electronics, textiles, silk, coal, ammonium sulphate, paper, steel, petroleum oil, etc. The small- and medium-sized enterprises and the trading companies also had protective laws enacted for them: the Small Enterprises Organization Law (Chushokigyo Dantai Soshiki-ho) (1952–) and the Export-Import Transactions Law (Yushutsunyu Torihiki-ho) (1952–) respectively.

10.3.2 Government Standpoint

Professor Komiya (1988) suggests that 'the dregs of prewar and wartime economic thinking with their emphasis on wartime economic controls and planning' were incorporated into the industrial policy in the era of economic reconstruction and independence. Considering the Priority Production System, the criteria used to designate industries which would benefit from the Enterprise Rationalization Promotion Law and the successive introduction of acts to exempt industries from the Anti-Monopoly Law, we cannot help but agree with Komiya's observation. However, we should note that the government also gave high priority to the free market economy and the limits of economic control in a capitalist economy.

In November 1945, the minister of the Commerce and Industry outlined the principal goal behind industrial reconstruction: to abolish or simplify control laws and organizations so as to make the transfer to a free economic system as soon as possible.[12] Recognizing that even wartime economic controls had become nominal once black markets began to flourish during the last phase of the war and the early postwar period, the government couldn't help but follow the public's *laissez-faire* attitude. The government did this even though

SCAP had already proposed the introduction of economic controls to handle the chaos resulting from the collapse of the wartime regime in September.

What about the IRP? Discussions on industrial rationalization had begun as early as 1948, one year before the Dodge Line was implemented. The government's attitude towards IRP went something like this. In the prewar period IRP was used to modify the principle of free competition in the market and to place national economic interest above that of the interests of individual firms. Postwar IRP, however, regarded the firms' efforts to rationalize as a priority, and aimed to assist these efforts, and to induce firms to move in the desirable direction from the point of view of the national economy.

10.3.3 Feasibility of Alternatives

As Professors Harada and Kosai (1987) point out, the eight-year period between the Sino-Japanese War and the end of the Second World War was too short to wipe out profit-seeking behaviour, particularly the entrepreneurship that had been cultivated in the Japanese mind over a long period of time. SCAP's radical democratization of economic and political institutions following American ideals liberated the spiritual energy driving Japanese firms. If one has confidence in Japanese entrepreneurial abilities, then the theoretical appropriateness of the industrial policies undertaken in the period of economic chaos become questionable. Komiya, referring to the West German experience with respect to the setting of exchange rates and their reliance on market functions to solving industrial bottlenecks, begs this question.

From the standpoint of economic policy implementation, Kosai (1989) presents several alternative macro-policy measures which might have been more effective in achieving economic independence (i.e. external balance). However, he also recognizes that the government's observation with the $1=¥360 exchange rate and the difficulties in balancing the government's budget placed practical constraints on the ability to implement these macro measures. He also takes into consideration the institutional immaturity of Japanese capital markets and the pecuniary external economic effects that the coal and steel industries had on other key industries in the era of reconstruction and independence. Finally he examines the benefits of trade in a dynamic perspective and concludes that IRP was economically rational.

Komiya (1988), however, remains sceptical of IRP even under

chaotic economic conditions and argues that Kosai's trusts in market function results in an overly favourable appraisal of the significance of IRP, although he has some reservations with respect to the case of the coal industry. Komiya often cites the numerous durable consumer goods, including radios, TVs, etc. as examples of goods which were successfully exported without relying on government assistance. On the other hand, Kosai verifies through statistical analysis that IRP succeeded in the case of industries with economies of scale such as iron and steel and chemical fertilizers. All of these industries became leading Japanese exporters.

Let us suggest a scenario which takes into account the relationships between production and the availability of materials and energy resources, and productivity improvements due to the import of capital, technologies and know-how from abroad at more favourable prices than those available in the domestic market. In other words, if the Japanese economy had been more open in regard to the trade of goods, technology, and capital, the degree of the government's involvement in the rationalization process through IRP would have been smaller because the business discipline in world markets would have more efficiently guided Japanese industrial activities. In fact, IRP measures worked against this scenario as is shown in the explanation of the legal features of IRP.

In order to understand the mercantilistic trade measures incorporated into IRP, we have to review the well-known policy debate on the role of international trade in national economic development and independence. That is, we need to examine the debate carried out in the early 1950s between those supporting trade dependence and those who were for autarkic development. The proponents of the former position, believers in the free market, argued that Japanese economic independence would be determined by trade. They derived this argument from the theoretical examinations and historical experiences of Japan and other nations. This proposition is based upon the belief that all countries have solved their own unique difficulties by relying on world markets. Planning and/or control-oriented economists, on the other hand, doubted the practical validity of trade-dependent economic development and independence. They based their argument on the fragmented and unstable realities of world markets at that time, which they argued could not sustain free trade. Thus, the proponents of this view placed priority on the development of domestic resources following a government plan.[13]

Most Japanese firms could not break the limit of resource

availability at reasonable cost and had difficulty in finding market outlets for their exportable goods. This occurred because many nations were still hostile toward Japanese companies, even though the American government had already softened its stance one year before the IRP was implemented. In addition, Japan had not yet recovered her currency convertibility in the world market. Consequently, while the Japanese government recognized the theoretical significance of foreign trade to national economic development they also recognized the reality of the chaotic state of world markets which was working against free and open trade. The government thus felt that it was not possible to opt for free and open trade. The greatest barrier to a quick and smooth transition to free trade and an open economy was the government's fear of national bankruptcy due to an external debt which was no longer controllable by the government.[14] Given this attitude and an exchange rate of \$1=¥360, it is clear that the free trade alternative was quite limited.

Lessons from IRP

The IRP is considered to have been largely successful. However, it also left a negative heritage. Companies that failed to rationalize their industrial activities tended to ask for financial and legal aid from the government. The cases of coal and textile industries are examples of this.

Leading economists of the younger generation[15] focus on Japanese industrial policy and try to come up with prescriptions for developing countries suffering from mounting external debts, for the Eastern European countries and the former Soviet countries which are currently implementing economic reforms without first having established economic systems based on market mechanisms, and for the advanced economies which are losing their domestic manufacturing bases. These economists note the strategic aspects of industrial policy, particularly measures for the active promotion of those industries having economies of scale and those emphasizing exports rather than import-substitution. They have also proven that strategic policies are important for industry and trade in imperfect markets. However, there is a fundamental problem in recommending the adoption of such industrial policy and they frankly admit this. If all governments in the world adopt this kind of strategic policy, they will fall into the so-called 'prisoner's dilemma' and will no longer be able to guarantee the success of such policies.

Japan was lucky. She was a small economy and a developing nation. Even though her government adopted a 'mercantilistic' IRP, the developed countries were not threatened by it.

Notes

1. Cohen (1949, pp. 418–19) doubts the General's and Japanese government employees' competencies as economists.
2. See table 35 in Nakamura (1985, 2nd edn, p. 152), and table 4.11 in Miyazaki and Itoh (1989, p. 208).
3. See table 8 in Arisawa (1949, p. 95).
4. See Iida, Ohashi and Kuroiwa (1969, p. 394).
5. See table 3 in Inaba (1947, p. 21).
6. See Tsusho Sangyo-sho (1972, p. 280).
7. See Iida, Ohashi and Kuroiwa (1969, pp. 434–6), and fig. 11.1 and table III in Yamawaki (1989, pp. 282–5).
8. This part draws on Tsusho Sangyo-sho (1972, pp. 237–43).
9. This part draws on Tsusho Sangyo-sho (1972, part I).
10. The following industries were designated: 26 manufacturers (silk, dyeing, fibre board, chemical fertilizer, soda, carbide, tar, intermediate dye, oil and fat (animal and plant), intermediate synthetic drugs and medicine, refined petroleum, fire-proof brick, pig iron, steel and rolled steel, casted steel, forged steel, smelted non-ferrous metal, rolled non-ferrous metal, turbines and boilers for power generating, metal-cutting machinery, bearing and steel balls, power generators, wire and cable, electric machinery for communication, cars, steel vessels, rolling stock). Other industries included whaling, mining of metallic mineral, coal and sulphide ore, construction of electric power facilities and international shipping. See Tsusho Sangyo-sho (1972, pp. 214–15).
11. This part draws on Tsusho Sangyo-sho (1972, pp. 207–24).
12. This part draws on Tsusho Sangyo-sho (1985, vol. 2, pp. 17–26).
13. The policy debate over trade dependence versus autarkic development has been referred to by Professor Kosai on numerous occasions. See Kosai (1989, pp. 28–9), Harada and Kosai (1987, pp. 126–30) and Kosai (1981, pp. 88–9).
14. Kosai judges the characteristic of this policy debate on the development path taken by the Japanese economy in the 1950s as that between those who were pro-free market and free trade and those who were for a controlled autarkic economy. He sees this as a controversy over the optimal degree of international dependence or government interference. However, the Japanese government fundamentally recognized the significance of a policy which followed market principles. This is confirmed by the stance of the Minister of Commerce and Industry toward industrial policy referred above. Thus, the reason why the Japanese government adopted a mercantilistic IRP is more persuasively explained by other factors. Nakamura (1980, pp. 99–100) points out that Japanese economic

policy was excessively concerned with the external balance until the 1960s.

15. For examples, see Krugman (1986) and Itoh, Kiyono, Okuno and Suzumura (1988). Shinohara (1986) praises their theoretical studies as proof of the relevance of his opinion and proposals regarding the industrial policies of postwar Japan.

References

Arisawa, Hiromi (1949) 'Senji Sengo no Kogyo oyobi Kogyo Seisaku' (Wartime and Postwar Industries and Industrial Policy), in *Tokyo Daigaku Keizaigakubu Soritsu 30 Shunen Kinen Ronbun-shu Dai 2 Bu* (The Collected Papers for the 30th Anniversary of the Founding of the Department of Economics, University of Tokyo) (Tokyo: Yuhikaku).

Cohen, J. B. (1949) *Japan's Economy in War and Reconstruction* (Minneapolis: University of Minnesota Press).

Harada, Yutaka and Yutaka Kosai (1987) *Nihon Keizai: Hatten no Biggu-Geemu* (The Big Game in Japanese Economic Development) (Tokyo: Toyo Keizai Shinpo-sha).

Iida, Kenichi, Shuji Ohashi and Toshio Kuroiwa (1969) *Gendai Nihon Sangyo Hattatsu-shi (IV) Tekko* (The Modern History of Japanese Industry (IV) Iron and Steel) (Tokyo: Kojun-sha).

Inaba, Shuzo (1947) *Nihon Keizai no Genjitsu* (The Current State of the Japanese Economy) (Tokyo: Taihei Shobo).

Itoh, Motoshige, Kazuharu Kiyono, Masahiro Okuno and Kotaro Suzumura (1988), *Sangyo Seisaku no Keizai Bunseki* (Economic Analysis of Industrial Policy) (Tokyo: University of Tokyo Press).

Kanamori, Hisao, Miyohei Shinohara *et al.* (1981) *Nihon Keizai Jiten* (The Encyclopedia of the Japanese Economy) (Tokyo: Nihon Keizai Shinbun-sha).

Keizai Kikaku-cho (Economic Planning Agency) (1957), *Sengo Keizai-shi: Sokan Hen* (Postwar Economic History: Survey) (Tokyo: Okura-sho Insatsu-kyoku).

Keizai Kikaku-cho (Economic Planning Agency) (1976), *Gendai Nihon Keizai no Tenkai* (The Economic Development of Modern Japan) (Tokyo: Okura-sho Insatsu-kyoku).

Kindleberger, C. P. (1982) 'Collective Memory vs. Rational Expectations: Some Historical Puzzles in Macro-Economic Behavior', in *Economic Essays in Honour of J. H. Gelting*, ed. by S. Andersen and K. Laurse et al. (Copenhagen: Danish Economic Association).

Komiya, Ryutaro (1988) 'Introduction', in Komiya, Okuno and Suzumura (1988).

Komiya, Ryutaro, Masahiro Okuno and Kotaro Suzumura (eds.) (1988) *Industrial Policy of Japan* (Tokyo: Academic Press Japan). Translation of *Nihon no Sangyo Seisaku* (Tokyo: University of Tokyo Press, 1984).

Kosai, Yutaka (1981), *Kodo Seicho no Jidai* (The Era of High Economic

Growth) (Tokyo: Nihon Hyoron-sha). Translated as *The Era of High-Speed Growth* (Tokyo: University of Tokyo Press, 1986).

Kosai, Yutaka (1988) 'The Reconstruction Era', in Komiya, Okuno and Suzumura (1988).

Kosai, Yutaka (1989) 'Kodo Seicho he no Shuppatsu' (Take-off to the Era of High Economic Growth), in Nakamura (1989a).

Krugman, P. R. (ed.) (1986) *Strategic Trade Policy and the New International Economics* (Cambridge, Mass.: MIT press).

Lipton, D. and Jeffery Sachs (1990) 'Creating a Market Economy in Eastern Europe: The Case of Poland', *Brookings Papers on Economic Activity*, 1, pp. 75–145.

Miyazaki, Masayasu and Osamu Itoh (1989) 'Senji Sengo no Sangyo to Kigyo' (The Industry and Firm in the Wartime and Postwar Periods), in Nakamura (1989a).

Miwa, Ryoichi (1989) 'Sengo Minshuka to Keizai Saiken' (The Democratization and Economic Reconstruction of the Postwar Periods), in Nakamura (1989a).

Mundell, R. A. (1962) 'The Appropriate Use of Monetary and Fiscal Policy under Fixed Exchange Rate', *IMF Staff Papers*, pp. 70–9, March.

Nakamura, Takafusa (1980) *Nihon Keizai: Sono Seicho to Kozo* (The Japanese Economy: Growth and Structure) (Tokyo: University of Tokyo Press). Translated as *The Postwar Japanese Economy* (Tokyo: University of Tokyo Press, 1981).

Nakamura, Takafusa (1974) *Nihon no Keizai Tosei* (Economic Control in Japan) (Tokyo: Nihon Keizai Shinbun-sha).

Nakamura, Takafusa (ed.) (1989a) *Nihon Keizai-shi* (The Japanese Economic History), vol. 7 (Tokyo: Iwanami Shoten).

Nakamura, Takafusa (1989b) 'Gaisetsu: 1937–54' (An Overview: 1934–54), in Nakamura (ed.) (1989a).

Nihon Kaihatsu Ginko (The Japan Development Bank) (1963) *Nihon Kaihatsu Ginko 10 Nen-shi* (Ten-Year History of The Japan Development Bank) (Tokyo: Nihon Kaihatsu Ginko).

Nihon Yushutsunyu Ginko (The Export-Import Bank of Japan) (1963) *10 Nen no Ayumi* (Ten-Year History of the Export-Import Bank of Japan) (Tokyo: Nihon Yushutsunyu Ginko).

Nordhaus, W. D. (1990) 'Soviet Economic Reform: The Longest Road', *Brookings Papers on Economic Activity*, 1, pp. 287–318.

Okura-sho (Ministry of Finance) (1983) *Showa Zaisei-shi* (The Fiscal History of the Showa Era), vol. 13 (Tokyo: Toyo Keizai Shinpo-sha).

Rodo Sogishi Kenkyu Kai Hen (The Study Group of Labor Disputes, ed.) (1991) *Nihon no Rodo Sogi: 1945–80 Nen* (The Labour Disputes of Japan: 1945–80) (Tokyo: University of Tokyo Press).

Sachs, J. D. (1987) 'Trade and Exchange Rate Policies' in *Growth-Oriented Adjustment Programs*, ed. by V. Carbo, M. Goldstein and M. Kahn (IMF and the World Bank).

Shakai Seisaku Gakkai (1978) 'Gorika to Rodosha Kaikyu' (Rationalization and Workers' Class), in *Shakai Seisaku Gakkai Nenpo* (Annual Report of The Social Policy Society of Japan) (Tokyo: Ochanomizu Shobo).

Shinohara, Miyohei (1986) 'Shohyo Nihon no Sangyo Seisaku' (Book review

'Industrial Policy of Japan') *Economic Studies Quarterly*, vol. 37, no. 1, pp. 88–90.

Tsusho Sangyo-sho (Ministry of International Trade and Industry) (1972) *Shoko Seisaku-shi: Sangyo Gorika (2)* (History of Industry and Commerce: Industrial Rationalization (2)), vol. 10 (Tokyo: Tsusho Sangyo Chosa-kai).

Tsusho Sangyo-sho (Ministry of International Trade and Industry) (1985) *Shoko Seisaku-shi: Sosetsu (2)* (History of Industry and Commerce: Overview (2)), vol. 2 (Tokyo: Tsusho Sangyo Chosa-kai).

Yamawaki, Hideki (1989) 'The Steel Industry', in Komiya, Okuno and Suzumura (1988).

11 Technology Importation: Japan's Postwar Experience

Akira Goto

11.1 INTRODUCTION

The purpose of this chapter is to describe the process of technology importation by the Japanese manufacturing industry since the Second World War as well as to discuss its salient features and the factors behind successful technology transfer.

It is widely believed that postwar Japan imported many advanced technologies and used them effectively to upgrade its industrial level; importation of technology is seen as one of the most important factors behind its rapid economic growth. This policy was also centred in the years after the Meiji Restoration in 1867, when Japan entered its first major push toward modernization. The Tokugawa era governments (1603–1868) imposed isolation on the country from 1639 and restricted foreign trade to that with the Chinese and Dutch nations alone. Though information on the advanced science and technology of the West was provided by the Dutch and came to play a certain role afterwards, their influx was nevertheless restricted until the end of this period.

The end of isolation in 1854 and the establishment of non-feudal central government after the Meiji Restoration prompted the Japanese government and industry to begin importing advanced foreign technology and work to catch up with Western countries economically and militarily. Imported technologies played the major role in the provision of national infrastructures as well as in the private sector. Foreign engineers were hired, students were sent abroad, advanced machinery was imported, licensing agreements were signed. The economy entered a period of continuous growth at the end of the nineteenth century, and imported technology was a major reason for economic success.

The Second World War forced Japan once again into technological isolation. Before and during the war, Japan increased the allocation of resources to research and development to fill the void. Despite these efforts, the technological gap with Western countries widened due to the country's isolation. Thus, when the Second World War ended, Japan found itself lagging far behind. The process of 'catching up and forging ahead' began again.[1] First, Japan imported the 'backlog' of technologies developed overseas before and during the war. Then, as the economy recovered from the war's devastation and started to grow at exceptionally high rates, new technologies that were as yet little used even in developed countries began to be imported.

Intense competition and the high rate of demand growth prompted firms to search for superior technology, often in overseas markets. If a firm succeeded in acquiring state-of-the-art technology, it could profit greatly. If it failed to do so, it could be driven from the market place. The technological base created before and during the Second World War, together with high, long-term investment in research and development thereafter, created a base for this process of selection, absorption, adaptation, implementation and diffusion of advanced technology. In short, strong pressures from the market and the existence of a technology base were the major factors behind active and successful technology transfer.

The Japanese government intervened in this process in several ways. The government permitted certain selected firms to use scarce foreign currency to purchase technology from abroad. In some cases, it intervened in the negotiation process for technology agreements between foreign firms and Japanese firms to ensure that Japanese firms could obtain technology on favourable terms.

In addition to policies that dealt directly with technology, other policies, notably trade policy and that concerning foreign investment in Japan, had a major impact on this process. Although restrictions have been gradually liberalized, exports to and direct investment in Japan were made difficult in many ways in the 1950s and 1960s. Thus, the only possible way for foreign firms with superior technology to exploit their advantages was to sell the technology. The consequences of this policy are complicated and must be examined from various angles.

The goals of the government policy on technology were not simple. Of course, it seems obvious that the goal of the government, notably the Ministry of International Trade and Industry (Tsusho Sangyosho: MITI), was to promote domestic industry. However, there are various avenues by which to pursue this goal, and it was not obvious which one was best. It was also true that there were other objectives which could not be ignored, such as the protection of small firms. Often, these policy considerations and goals contradicted each other. Implementation and effects of the government policies again cannot be described in simple terms.

The organization of this chapter is as follows. In the following section, the process and the trends of technology importation in post Second World War Japan is examined. The third section discusses some of the major features of this process. The fourth provides some brief concluding remarks.

11.2 THE PROCESS OF TECHNOLOGY IMPORTATION

11.2.1 Initial Conditions

From a technological point of view, there are two reasons why the Second World War was important in creating the conditions for active importation of foreign technology to Japan. First, it left a large technology gap. Since the late nineteenth century, the Japanese economy had been growing steadily. Imported technology played a major role in this process. Aided by indigenous technology and a well-developed education system, imported technology was used effectively to create Japan's own technology base and to promote economic growth. Some manufacturing firms were approaching the technological frontier and had started to produce world-class products. These include firms in the shipbuilding, steel, aircraft, and electrical machinery industries. However, even these industries where the Japan's technological gap had been narrowed the most, still depended heavily on imported technology. And they continued to import major technologies even after the outbreak of the Sino-Japanese War in 1937.

The Second World War forced Japan into technological isolation. Japan tried to fill the technological void with increased domestic R&D (research and development), but these efforts brought little success. Thus, when the war ended, Japan found itself lagging far behind the technological levels attained in Western industry. In addition, there were a number of industries such as petro-chemicals and electric appliances, in which Japan was a complete newcomer. Japan faced a huge 'backlog' of technologies to be imported.

The second effect of the war on subsequent technological developments in Japan was the inheritance of the key 'heavy' industries such as shipbuilding, steel, machinery and chemicals, the development of which had been given top priority by the wartime state. These industries were much favoured in terms of resource allocation during wartime. Consumer goods industries, notably textiles, were forced to convert to the production of military-related goods. Thus, the percentage manufacturing production provided by of heavy industry (machinery, metal, and chemicals) production rose from 33.9 per cent in 1931 to 79 per cent in 1944.[2]

Needless to say, this push reflected the desperate war effort, and a substantial proportion of production facilities were hastily and poorly constructed and of little use after the war. However, it is also true that when the war ended, Japan was left with large amounts of heavy industry plant and equipment. Between 60 and 100 per cent of heavy industries' plant and equipment survived the Allied Forces bombings.[3] In addition, there were large numbers of workers who had the experience, if not all the necessary skills, of working in these plants.

As mentioned above, the R&D effort was much increased during the war. According to one estimate, which should be taken as only a rough indicator, the percentage of R&D in GNP went from 0.22 per cent in 1930 to 1 per cent by 1942. There were 1214 research organizations employing 49 560 staff and spending 886 million yen (current price) in 1942.[4] After the war, Japanese military spending was virtually eliminated, and the resources accumulated in the heavy industry were converted to produce civilian goods. Thus, the Second World War left Japan with a widened technology gap, and, at the same time, the resource base to fill it.

11.2.2 The Process of Technology Importation

Technology is essentially knowledge, or information, and it travels in many forms. It can be embodied in a person. Foreign engineers bring and teach advanced technology, and the Japanese go and acquire it abroad. Technology also may be embodied in machinery and equipment. Through their use in the production process, cost reduction may be achieved or new products may be produced. In addition, the advanced technologies which created the new machinery and equipment can be learned. By taking machines apart, it is possible to learn about new materials or new components used in their construction.

This practice is known as reverse engineering and is widely used in the developing countries, as well as among competing firms in the developed countries.

Another channel of technology transfer is the purchase of technology and technological services. Included in this category are various kinds of technology agreements including licensing agreements, hiring consultants, and the purchase of blueprints and other materials. To be precise, licensing is the sale of the legal rights to use a technology. In some cases, a firm must have a licensing agreement and pay royalties to use a technology only because another company patented that technology earlier. In such cases technology licensing does not necessarily mean technology transfer.

Foreign direct investment is another important channel of technology transfer. Foreign firms often bring new ways of doing business to host countries. These might include not only new technologies but also new management and marketing techniques and production and inventory control methods. Such advances will eventually be diffused to local firms. It is often the case that foreign direct investment takes the form of a joint venture with a local firm or firms, sometimes because of restrictions imposed by the local government. These restrictions are designed to encourage transfer of technology to local partner firms, as well as to avoid foreign control of domestic industries.

There are other channels through which technology may be transferred, including academic and trade journals, exhibitions, and trade shows. Increasingly, multinational corporations are operating research laboratories worldwide, and intra-firm, international technology transfer is growing. Overseas laboratories are often created to carry out the research necessary to adapt products to local conditions and to monitor the R&D activities of local firms and research institutions. Gradually, they develop global R&D networks, integrating the R&D resources of various countries.

Among these channels, direct investment in Japan was severely restricted until gradual liberalization began in the late 1960s and early 1970s. There were several exceptions, however. One is foreign-owned firms that were established in the prewar years. In addition, during the 1956–63 period when the so-called yen-based investment system was adopted, several foreign firms established operations in the Japanese market.[5] These included IBM, Esso (Exxon), Mobil, Nestle, Olivetti, and NCR, among others. These firms brought new technology and new ways of doing business to Japan. However, they were exceptions and, until liberalization began, direct foreign investment in Japan was limited and in fact grew little even with liberalization.

Other channels for technology transfer were extensively used, however. Imported machinery and equipment played a critical role in leading industries in improving the product quality and productivity. The automobile industry used imported machine tools and robots, the steel industry imported converters and rolling machines, electric utilities imported generators, and so forth. Domestic machinery and equipment manufacturers tried to learn from the imported machinery and equipment so as eventually to begin domestic manufacture.

Japanese firms eagerly sought technological agreements with US and European firms. Most automobile manufacturers with Toyota Motor Corporation (Toyota Jidosha) the major exception had some such technological agreements with Western manufacturers.[6] The major electric machinery manufacturers, Toshiba Corporation, Mitsubishi Electric Corporation (Mitsubishi Denki), and Fuji Electric Company, Ltd. (Fuji Denki), each had extensive technological agreements with GE, Westinghouse, and Siemens, respectively. The steel industry introduced the revolutionary LD converter process pioneered by an Austrian firm. The textile manufacturers eagerly sought technological agreements with Western firms concerning the production of new synthetic fibres with US and European firms. Again, the list of these agreements is extremely long. Under their terms, Japanese firms obtained patent licenses and know-how. It was often the case that foreign engineers were invited for advice and instruction.

Consultants, mostly from the US, were often used to help modernize the production process. For example, Nissan Motor Company, Ltd. (Nissan Jidosha) hired US consultants to help with plans for their advanced Oppama plant, which was completed in 1961.[7]

The purchase of blueprints was also common. There were some interesting cases where Japanese firms bought title to inventions or ideas, which had been developed only at the laboratory level. One well known case is the purchase of a mid-to-low-density polyethylene production process by Mitsui Petrochemical Industries, Ltd. (Mitsui Sekiyu Kagaku Kogyo) from a German scientist. Mitsui was said to have paid 1.2 million dollars for two notebooks of experiment data, and it eventually built a plant based on these data (Ekonomisuto, 1934).

Japanese firms routinely sent their top engineers abroad to investigate promising technology. Trade associations and institutions like the Japan Productivity Center (Nihon Seisansei-honbu) often organized 'missions' to study technological trends and learn business practices.

Thus, in the 1950s and 1960s, Japan acquired advanced foreign technology by many routes, but not via direct foreign investment. It is important to note here the diversity of channels through which technology was transferred. It is often the case that discussions on technology transfer or importation are based on the technology balance of payments statistics, which essentially covers payments and receipts for patent licence, know-how, and associated expenses. However, as the above discussion suggests, only a part of the actual flow of technological knowledge is captured by these statistics. Learning through reverse engineering for instance, is not in such figures. Nor is learning through journals, trips and 'missions' included. And judging from various case studies, these methods played an important role in the process of learning advanced technology by Japanese firms in the postwar years. Especially, those industries and firms which started to grow in the early postwar years upgraded their technology via reverse engineering, the accumulation of minor technological improvements and other measures. This sort of strategy seems also to characterize the newly industrialized countries. As quantitative measures and well-defined statistics do not account for technology transfer through these channels, we must remember that the technological balance of payments statistics data is but a part of the whole story of technology transfer. In particular, we should not put too much emphasis on the significance of the major high-technology importation agreements.

11.2.3 Trends in Technology Importation

In this subsection, we examine the trends in technology importation in postwar Japan using the technology balance of payments statistics with the caveat mentioned above. Figure 11.1 shows trends in the number of new technical agreements between Japanese and foreign firms, and payments for patent licences, know-how, and associated expenses. The number of agreements varies with yearly economic conditions of and with the progress of technology importation liberalization. However, after remaining rather stable at about 200–300 per year, the number of agreements started to increase steadily from 1958 until 1973, when the first oil crisis hit the Japanese economy. The number of agreements increased more than tenfold during this period.

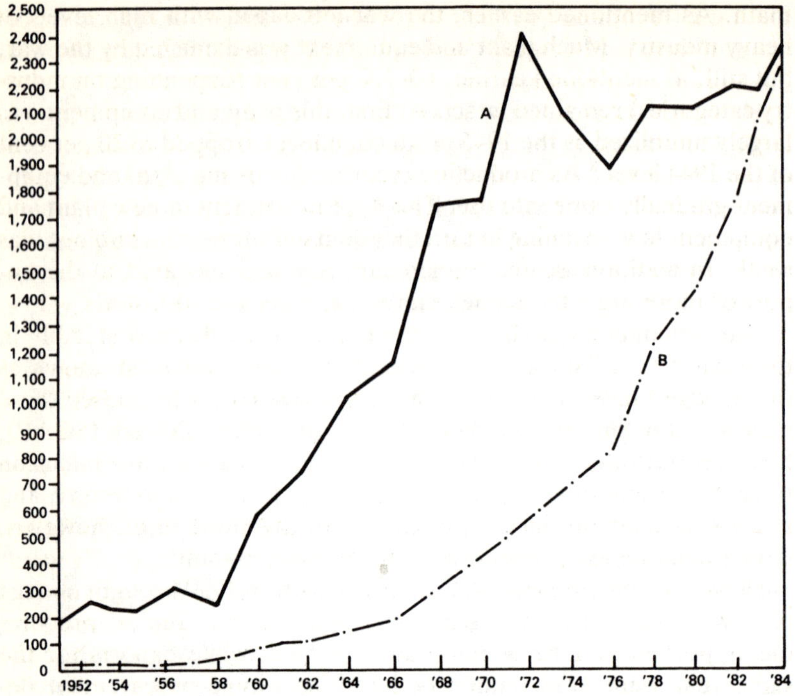

Figure 11.1 Number of new technical agreements and payments for technology imports, 1954–84

A: Number of new technical agreements.
B: Payments for technology imports (million dollars).

Source: Kagaku Gijutsu-cho (Science and Technology Agency) *Gaikoku Gijutsu Donyu Nenji Hokoku* (Annual Report on the Import of Foreign Technology), each year.

Expenditure levels grew steadily and almost exponentially. This rather smooth, exponential growth-path, in contrast to the irregular growth of agreements numbers, is due to the fact that most agreements required Japanese firms to pay running royalties for long periods of time (typically about ten years). Such long-term commitments mean that expenditure changes were small relative to total annual expenses.

That technology importation patterns were relatively stagnant until the mid-1950s reflects the economic conditions of the War's aftermath. As mentioned earlier, the war left Japan with high levels of heavy industry. Much plant and equipment was damaged by the war, but still, as mentioned earlier, 60–100 per cent (depending on industry categories) remained intact. At first, this plant and equipment was largely unutilized as the 1946 production level dropped to 20 per cent of the 1944 level.[8] As production recovered, existing plant and equipment gradually came into use. This kept investment in new plant and equipment low, meaning in turn that demand for new technology was weak. In addition, scarce foreign currency was allocated to the import of more urgently needed materials, fuels and foodstuffs.

The economy gradually recovered and started to grow steadily in the early 1950s. The severe measures to counter inflation known as the 'Dodge Line', named after the Detroit banker who drafted these measures for Supreme Commander for the Allied Powers (SCAP), had been introduced in 1949. These measures called for a balanced budget and abolition of subsidies, forcing firms to modernize and streamline their production processes. In the short term, however, strong deflationary pressure was put on the economy.

However, the outbreak of the Korean War in 1950 brought a surge of new procurement contracts for Japanese firms. Special procurements peaked in 1952 at 824 million dollars, while exports for the same year were 1273 million dollars.[9] This huge procurement demand proved more than enough to offset the deflationary pressure of the Dodge Line. Efforts by firms to modernize their production to survive without government subsidies, financed by increasing savings, and the sudden pump in demand due to the Korean War, helped Japan onto the steady growth path.

Still, in the early 1950s, increased production was largely achieved through activation of unused plant and equipment rather than by new investments. At the same time, the demand for consumer durables and 'luxuries' was still very small. The demand for new technology thus remained rather weak even though the economy had entered high growth.

In the late 1950s, the demand for new plant and equipment started to grow rapidly as the economy surpassed the prewar peak and high growth continued. Private sector investment in plant and equipment grew 39 per cent in 1956 and 25 per cent in 1957. On the consumer side, rising incomes created strong demand for automobiles, electrical appliances and other consumer durables. These new conditions induced strong demand for technology in the late 1950s. In addition, as the schedule for gradual trade liberalization was announced, firms

Table 11.1 Distribution of Japanese technology import agreements, by type of industry, 1949–65 and 1965–72 (per cent)

Industry	*1949–65*	*1965–72*
Non-electrical machinery	26.3	25.5
Electrical machinery	22.2	15.7
Chemicals	15.4	15.3
Iron and steel	6.0	3.4
Transport machinery	5.7	5.0
Textiles and fabrics	4.4	6.5
Metal products	3.1	3.1
Precision instruments	2.4	2.9
Ceramics	2.0	2.4
Petroleum and coal	1.6	2.5
Construction	1.2	1.0
Food processing	0.7	2.3
Other	9.0	14.4

Sources: 1949–65 data: Kagaku Gijutsu-cho (Science and Technology Agency), *Gaikoku Gijutsu Donyu Nenji hokoku* (Annual Report on the Import of Foreign Technology), 1970; 1965–72 data: Kagaku Gijutsu-cho, *Kagaku Gijutsu Hakusho* (White Paper on Science and Technology), 1974, p. 288. Taken from Peck and Tamura, (1976) p. 539.

experienced new pressure to upgrade their production processes and technology levels to compete with foreign firms. This concern also encouraged firms to seek superior technology abroad.

The rapid increase in technology importation from 1958 was accompanied by several qualitative changes. First, as can be seen from Table 11.1, non-electrical machinery (engines, machine tools, and other industrial machinery), electrical machinery and chemicals consistently have been the three largest technology importing industries throughout the postwar period. However, the shares of electrical machinery and iron and steel dropped sharply from the 1945–65 period to the 1965–72 period, possibly reflecting the rising technological level of these industries.

The second change was the growing proportion of technology importation related to the production of consumer goods. According to Ozawa (1974), technological agreements for consumer goods increased much faster than average during the 1963–71 period. Imports of technology for such goods as air conditioners, colour-television sets, leisure products, cosmetics and dress designs increased in the late 1960s. This changing pattern reflects a change in government policy: in the 1950s, policy encouraged the importation of technology that contributes to the 'reconstruction of industries' and discouraged that for 'luxuries', but these policies were gradually relaxed. However, it must be noted that the most important reason for the change lies not in the revision of government policy, but in demand changes due to rising income.

Per capita real GNP reached its prewar peak in 1955, and in the latter half of the 1950s GNP grew about 8 per cent annually. In the 1960s, the annual growth rate surpassed 10 per cent. Investment demand likewise grew rapidly, and demand for consumer durables and 'luxuries' rose explosively. From the standpoint of preserving balance of payments, it was better to import technology and design and manufacture such goods domestically than to import them. At any rate, the balance of payments consideration became less pressing as exports grew. Thus, rapid economic growth created the demand for consumer durables and luxuries, in turn creating demand for the technology used to produce them.

The third change concerned the terms of technology importation. According to Peck (1976), the price Japanese firms paid for technology increased as government restrictions on its importation were removed. The implication here is that with the restrictions the government intervened in the process of technology importation and tried to limit competition among Japanese firms that might drive up the price of technology. A well-known case that illustrates this point is the importation of the LD process by the steel industry, where MITI made arrangements for Japanese firms so that they would not bid up the price of this important technology.[10] In other cases, MITI selected limited numbers of firms and allowed them to use foreign currency. Thus, the sellers of technology did not have the opportunity to make Japanese firms compete against each other and bid up the price of technology. Peck (1976) shows that the percentage of agreements with high running royalty rates increased after the major liberalization of 1968. Lynn (1982) estimates that US producers paid much higher royalty rates to import the same LD converter technology purchased by Japanese steel producers under MITI's guidance, even after taking into account the unexpectedly high rate of increase of production by Japanese producers.

These arguments and estimates suggest that government intervention suppressed the price of foreign technology when its importation was restricted. However, it should be noted that the steel industry's case was rather exceptional. There were few cases where industry-wide arrangements were so successfully achieved.[11] In another famous case of technology importation, about thirty Japanese firms approached the Italian firm that invented polypropelene, a synthetic fiber, to buy the technology, thus giving the Italian maker the upper hand. Apparently, the effectiveness of government intervention to keep the price of technology low varied from case to case, depending on the conditions of the market for each technology. Though intervention helped to lower the price of technology in a number of cases, its overall effectiveness is difficult to estimate.[12]

Negotiations on technology importation involve not only price but other factors as well. Technology sellers often attach various conditions to the sale. These include territorial restrictions imposed on the sale of goods that were manufactured with the imported technology; restrictions on the improvement of the imported technology; and cross-licensing, which has much grown in importance. In the late 1960s, the proportion of agreements with such restrictions increased. For instance, number of agreements that required cross-licensing grew from 3 in 1965 to 37 in 1968.[13] Although the percentage of this type of agreement was still very small in 1968 (about 2 per cent of the total), government officials were concerned that technology importation would become more difficult if Japanese firms did not develop their own technology to offer in return. The agreements with sales territory restrictions also multiplied during the late 1960s and into the 1970s. The percentage of agreements that prohibited technology-importing Japanese firms from exporting goods manufactured with the imported technology increased from 10.1 per cent in 1968 to 30.9 per cent in 1974.[14] This trend also alarmed Japanese firms as well as government officials since it reduced export potential.

The fourth change was the decrease in importation of new technology that had never been imported into Japan. According to the Science and Technology Agency (Kagaku Gijutsu-cho: STA), new technology represented 65 per cent of imported technology in 1963, but only 30 per cent in 1968.[15] The 1969 White Paper of the STA declared that importation of major technologies developed in the West during and after the war was over.

11.3 ROLE OF MARKET MECHANISM AND GOVERNMENT INTERVENTION IN TECHNOLOGY IMPORTATION

The very active and successful importation of advanced technology by Japanese firms can be explained in various ways. The most important factor was, we believe, a strong profit incentive. If a firm was successful in importing advanced technology, it could enjoy high rates of return. If it failed, it might well be driven out of the market. This 'invisible hand and hidden foot' of the market compelled Japanese firms to search for advanced technology. Also important were the ability of Japanese firms to utilize the imported technology, as well as the favourable world environment in which technology was transferred. The Japanese government shaped and intervened in this process in many ways.

11.3.1 Growing Markets and Intense Competition

As mentioned earlier, the number of new technology agreements started to grow rapidly at the end of the 1950s. Following the drastic measures of the 'Dodge Line' to control inflation and the outbreak of the Korean War and the resultant jump in demand, the economy started to grow at 8 per cent per year in the early 1950s. Still, investment in plant and equipment by the private sector was only about 10 per cent of GNP during the first half of the decade, while household demand, mostly directed towards necessities, grew rapidly.

In the mid-1950s, investment in plant and equipment also began to increase, pulled by rapid growth and the changing structure of demand. The plant and equipment inherited from the war, such as old steel mills, became obsolete and insufficient to meet new needs. The changing demand structure created new industries which required new investment. It should be noted that this rapidly expanding market for manufactured goods was difficult to penetrate for many foreign firms at least until the mid-1960s. In 1959, the trade liberalization ratio was only 26 per cent, meaning only 26 per cent of the total value of imports was automatically allowed to enter the country. The trade liberalization proceeded swiftly and the ratio reached 70 per cent at the end of 1961. Subsequently, the importation of steel was liberalized in 1961, automobiles in 1965 and computers in 1971. However, the share of imports did not grow quickly in many manufactured goods markets. The liberalization of direct foreign investment in

Japan followed in the late 1960s and the 1970s. Again, however, the market share of foreign-owned firms remained low. Thus Japanese firms were faced with a fast-growing domestic market and with a world market which was also growing, if at levels less than those in Japan. This growth in turn created strong demand for plant and equipment, while the rapid increase in investment in plant and equipment boosted demand for advanced technology. There was expansion by existing firms as well as new entries into existing industries such as steel, and all sought plant and equipment embodying best practices in the world at that time. New industries have also emerged, such as in petrochemicals and electrical appliances. The automobile industry, although existing before the war but limited mainly to producing taxicabs and military vehicles, might also be considered a new industry. These new industries required new investment and new technology on a massive scale.

Thus the growing demand for consumer goods, together with limited foreign competition, led to strong demand by domestic firms for investment in plant and equipment, as well as advanced technology. This, in turn, enabled the introduction of new goods and cost reductions, further increasing final demand. Under these conditions, the profits of Japanese firms grew. As Odaka (1989) shows, the profit rate of the non-financial private sector more than doubled from 1955 to 1970. And in many cases, investment meant the importation of advanced technology.

There have been many cases that illustrate the high return on investment in imported technology and plant and equipment. Nissan, Japan's second largest automobile manufacturer, made technology agreements with the British car producer Austin in 1952. At first, it was a knock-down operation where Nissan simply assembled parts provided by Austin, with the technological help also provided by the British company. According to a Nissan executive at that time, the company quickly sold all the cars they assembled at one million yen per car, with a 200 thousand yen profit per car.[16]

Another example of profitable technology importation was the case of Toray Industries, Inc. Toray (then Toyo Rayon) obtained licensing agreements from DuPont covering the technology to manufacture nylon in 1951. The licence fee Toray paid to DuPont was three million dollars (1.08 billion yen) in initial payments plus 3 per cent of sales up to five million pounds of production per year. The initial payment alone exceeded Toray's equity capital, which was 750 million yen at that time. But Toray's profit was enormous. After two years of large losses, nylon brought Toray 500 million yen of profit in the first half of fiscal 1953 alone, and it steadily grew afterwards as demand increased rapidly. Until the entry of a second firm in 1955, Toray was the only producer of nylon in Japan. This allowed Toray to quickly recover its huge investment in technology importation. A third firm entered as late as 1963. As a result, the demand for nylon grew rapidly from the late 1950s while the number of firms remained at two. Toray's profit/sales ratio for its nylon division was over 10 per cent during this duopoly period.

Thus, rapidly growing markets for manufactured goods, which were often difficult for foreign firms to penetrate, carried strong incentives for investment in plant and equipment as well as technology.

While the market provided handsome rewards to firms for upgrading technology, intense competition punished them if they failed to do so. The so-called 'Economic Democratization Policy' administered by Supreme Commander for the Allied Powers (SCAP) broke up pre-war Zaibatsu, large conglomerates, and large independent firms. Many dominant firms in various industries, such as Japan Steel Corporation (Nippon Seitetsu), Mitsubishi Heavy Industries, Ltd. (Mitsubishi Jukogyo), and Oji Paper Company, Ltd. (Oji Seishi) were split into several firms. The Anti-Monopoly Law (Dokusen Kinshi-ho) was also introduced. Modelled after the US Antitrust Law, it had several unique provisions, such as the prohibition of holding companies, and was more stringent in many ways than the original. Even though the number of firms that were actually broken up was smaller than intended, and some eventually merged again, and the law's enforcement was sometimes not very active, these policy measures helped to create a competitive market structure and the policy tools to maintain it.

More important, rapidly growing markets induced new entries, further increasing competition. Well-known examples include Sony Corporation and Honda Motor Company, Ltd. (Honda Giken Kogyo). In steel, aluminium, and petrochemicals, the number of firms increased and in many cases surpassed firm numbers in the US where markets were much larger. In some cases, existing firms and the government tried to discourage further entry, citing the waste caused by 'duplicate investment' and 'excessive competition' and stressing the importance of economies of scale. These efforts met with little success.

Even though the actual share of imports in manufactured goods and foreign direct investment into Japan did not increase quickly after liberalization of trade and investment, liberalization did pressure domestic firms to upgrade their technology further to be competitive with the much larger firms of the US and Europe. In addition, partly due to the Japanese governments concern over the balance of payments, Japanese firms intensified their efforts to export.

Thus, although actual foreign competition in the domestic market might not have been intense, domestic firms were exposed to the intense competition among themselves, the prospect of forthcoming competition with foreign firms in the domestic market, and actual competition with foreign firms in the world market. They were under strong competitive pressure to upgrade their technology. The importation of advanced technology was one of the most important strategic options available to Japanese firms.

11.3.2 Absorptive Capacity

The incentives provided by the market mechanism are a necessary condition for active technology importation. The sufficient condition is the existence of the capability to select, import, adapt, and implement the technology. In order to be able to exploit the advantage of being backward by using the existing technologies developed by advanced countries, a country cannot be too backward. The capability to use advanced technology is often called absorptive capacity. As mentioned earlier, Japan inherited a rather strong technology base, and further investment in R&D and education not only promoted Japan's indigenous innovation but also helped in the efficient use of imported technology. Its absorptive capacity was thus unusually high.

Comprehensive R&D expenditure statistics are not available to the early postwar years. According to the Science and Technology Agency estimates that date back to 1953, it seems that R&D expenditure began to grow rapidly in the latter half of the 1950s.[17] From 1955 to 1961 it grew more than 20 per cent per year. As a per cent of national income, it grew from 0.84 per cent in 1955 to 1.73 per cent in 1961.

The increase in R&D expenditures in the latter half of the 1950s coincides with the increase in technology importation, which began in 1958. Overall, domestic R&D and technology importation grew together over time. It was also true that firms and industries that spent large R&D expenditures imported technology actively as well. In other words, the industry or firm that actively imports technology also spends on R&D actively. There are many possible explanations for this relationship. One is that where or when technology is advancing rapidly, both domestic R&D and the opportunity to import technology likely increase. When there is rapid technological progress in electronics, for example, firms carry out their own R&D and at the same time trade their technology. Another possible explanation is that sellers of technology often require not only payment but also technology in return. Thus in order to buy technology, a firm must have its own technology to offer. This necessity forces technology-importing firms to do their own R&D.

While these explanations seems to explain the relationship at least partially, they also have problems. For instance, according to Blumenthal (1979), the significant positive relationship between domestic R&D and technology importation exists only in a limited number of countries. Thus the technological opportunity explanation alone is insufficient. As to the second explanation, the number of technology importation contracts in Japan with cross-licensing clauses is rather small, although it has been increasing rapidly. In 1965, there were only 3, in 1968, 37, and in 1982, 98.

A more important basis of this relationship may be that even though the technology gap was wide, Japan did not import technology via foreign direct investment, even though this route was often the fastest most and direct means of technology transfer. Rather, Japan imported the technology alone. Thus importing firms had to carry out their own additional R&D to adapt the imported technology to commercial use.[18] In addition, there were a number of cases where Japan imported technologies as yet untested commercially, exemplified by the case of Mitsui Petrochemical's importation of the mid-to-low-density polyethylene production process mentioned earlier. In the cases of transistors and VCRs, Japanese firms imported military or other non-commercial technology, and adapted it to manufacture household products. This process of adaptation required domestic R&D expenditures and creativity.

To put it another way, the very existence of Japan's technology base and active R&D enabled the importation of technology alone. And the imported technology, in turn, helped to enhance the technology base and to induce further R&D. Domestic R&D and technology importation both expanded through this process.

11.3.3 Government Policy

As mentioned in the previous sections, the strong profit incentives to import advanced technology and the technological capability to use it were the important factors behind the active importation of technology by Japan. This is not to say, however, that government policy did not influence the process of technology importation in many ways.

There were four sets of government policies that directly affected the process. The first was government control of commercial imports, based on the Foreign Exchange and Foreign Trade Control Law (Gaikoku Kawase oyobi Gaikoku Boeki Kanri-ho) of 1949 and the Foreign Investment Law (Gaishi-ho) of 1950. The importation of technology usually requires payment in foreign currency. When the duration of a technology importation contract exceeded one year, the purchased technology was treated as an asset from the accounting point of view and regulated under the Foreign Investment Law. When a contract was for less than one year, it was treated as current transaction and regulated under the Foreign Exchange and Foreign Trade Control Law. The first type, the more prevalent, was called 'ko-shu', or type A technology, while the latter was called, 'otsu-shu', or type B. In principle, each application to import technology was to be reviewed by the Foreign Investment Board (Gaishi-Shingikai), except for technologies that cost little and could be imported with the Bank of Japan's approval. In any case, screening was largely carried out via consultation with government ministries, particularly the Ministry of International Trade and Industry.

The restrictions on technology importation were gradually liberalized, and the number of technologies whose importation was subject to review decreased rapidly.[19] Major liberalization measures were implemented in 1961, 1968, and 1972. The 1968 liberalization was especially important. It meant that the importation of technology costing less than 50 thousand dollars was approved automatically, except for contracts that included cross-licensing agreements, that involved a foreign parent firm and its subsidiary in Japan, or that were related to seven designated areas of technology: arms, ammunition, aircraft, space, computers, nuclear energy, and petrochemicals. These exceptions, as well as technologies costing more than 50 thousand dollars, were still subject to ministry review. Finally, in 1980, the two principal laws were consolidated into the Foreign Exchange and Foreign Trade Control Law. Henceforth, all technology importation was liberalized except for twelve designated technologies, and even in these, importation was liberalized for all technologies costing less than 100 million yen.

Where the importation of technology was not liberalized, especially before 1968 liberalization, the government could influence technology choice to import and also which firm would import it. As mentioned earlier, Toray was allowed to import the DuPont's nylon manufacturing technology. The textile industry was seen as one of Japan's most important industries because its output was of vital importance for daily life, and because it had great export potential. Toray was chosen because it had the necessary technological capability to commercialize the process, as it had been experimenting with nylon before the agreement with DuPont.

Several selection criteria existed, but they were rather vague and changed over time. In the 1950s, the balance of payments consideration was emphasized, along with so-called 'important' industries and public utilities. It was not clear which industries were considered 'important', but they seem to have included capital goods industries, industries with high export potential, and those related to the production of basic necessities, such as the fertilizer and textile industries. The logic was that imported technology should contribute to improving the balance of payments by reducing imports or eventually increasing exports, and help also to promote the important industries for the reconstruction of the nation. In the 1950s, it is important to remember that the foreign currency reserves necessary to buy technology abroad remained scarce. Thus the applicant firm was obliged to demonstrate how the technology it hoped to import would contribute to improving the balance of payments as well as furthering the 'reconstruction of the nation'. It also had to show that it was capable of understanding and implementing the technology and successfully manufacturing and marketing the final product.

In the early 1960s, these requirements were gradually dropped as the economy grew and the balance of payments improved. Firms were no longer required to prove the importance of their intended imports to the balance of payments. It became possible also to import such 'unimportant' technologies such as golfwear designs. The 1961 criteria for reviewing applications included the following: (i) the imported technology should not deter the development of indigenous technology; (ii) the imported technology should not disrupt the existing 'order' of industry; (iii) the imported technology should not cause difficulties for small firms; (iv) the importing firm should be technologically and financially capable of using the technology. Again, these were rather vague criteria and could be interpreted in many ways.

The significance and implications of these case-by-case reviews of technology importation and the criteria applied to them can be summarized as follows. According to Ozaki (1972) and Peck (1976), the balance of payments consideration was unimportant, even irrelevant, because the size of payment for technology was very small. Ozaki estimated the percentage of royalty payments for type A technology of Japan's total foreign exchange payments for imports and non-trade transactions to be 0.8 per cent in 1955 and 1.8 per cent in 1960. Ozaki and Peck argue that the savings of foreign exchange to be gained by restricting technology importation was very small at best, and therefore concern over the balance of payments could not justify case-by-case review. Instead, they believe there was some hidden motive, such as the reduction of royalty rates.

It seems to be true that the balance of payments concern has been overly emphasized in explaining governmental review and intervention. On the other hand, it remained true that balance of payments was the overriding concern of policy-makers until the late 1960s, as it was the limiting factor of economic growth of Japan. During this period, the economic boom increased imports and worsened Japan's balance of payments position. For unclear reasons, the devaluation of the yen was not an option. The Bank of Japan was thus forced to raise the discount rate to slow the economy and reduce imports in order to improve the balance of payments. Economic growth would have been stronger if the balance of payments ceiling could have been raised. Under these conditions, improving the balance of payments position was of the greatest concern, although each effort to do so may have appeared small. Nonetheless, we must stress that the reduction of foreign exchange payments through limiting technology importation was not an important part of Japan's economic strategy. The important point was the reduction in imports of manufactured goods or raw materials, as well as the increase in exports through promoting domestic industry, in part via the importation of advanced technology.

The next question is whether the government was capable of choosing the best technology and the best company to improve the balance of payments, and whether its choice differed from that of the market. Such questions are difficult to answer conclusively. It is often argued that government had superior information gathering and processing abilities, especially in the early postwar years. However, there were cases where the government made poor decisions because of incompetence or out of political motive. One widely known error is reported by Trezise (1976). According to Trezise, the Sony Corporation had to wait almost two years to get approval to import transistor technology, because a MITI official concluded that Sony, then a small start-up firm, lacked the skills to develop an untried technology. It is impossible to draw definite conclusions from anecdotal evidence, but we can say that government intervention is not without costs and there is no reason to believe, *a priori*, that government makes fewer mistakes than the market. This is also true with the important industry criterion. There is no reason to believe that government is more capable and willing to choose the important industry for the welfare of the nation than is the market.

Another question is whether government intervention actually changed the overall pattern of technology importation. The Sony case suggests that despite red tape and delays, small start-up firms could eventually get approval. In the case of nylon, Toray got the approval first and was practically guaranteed the monopoly position until the second firm got similar approval. But after delay, other firms also managed to get approval. The same argument applies to the important industry criterion. In the 1950s, demand for capital goods and necessities such as food and clothing was strong, while that for luxuries remained weak. Therefore, the demand for technology related to so-called important industries was strong. The net incremental effect of government review based on this criteria may not have been significant.

Other criteria, namely the protection of domestic technology and preservation of the existing industrial order, were difficult to enforce in many cases because they contradicted the overriding concern of the government, the promotion of domestic industry. The criterion to protect domestic technology reflected the view that the development of domestic, indigenous technology should be promoted to avoid overdependence on foreign technology. This concern reflects in part the controversy over the grand strategy of economic reconstruction. One group advocated an essentially free trade approach, while others proposed a more self-sufficient, if not autarkic, approach. In the case of technology, however, conflict was almost non-existent because foreign technology was so far advanced and there were few domestic technologies to protect. The consensus was that it was important to promote domestic industry's importation of advanced technology while at the same time encouraging domestic R&D. An interesting example here is the importation of synthetic fibre technology. When this technology began to be imported in the 1950s, there was concern that this trend might jeopardize the development by Japanese manufacturers of their own synthetic fibres, which was then in its early stages. In other words, the importation of foreign technology might nip the bud of domestic, indigenous technology. However, imported fibre technology brought huge benefits to consumers and profits to importing firms. Importing advanced technology was better, at least in these terms, than restricting it in order to protect and promote domestic technology. Indeed, importation of advanced technology was often a necessary step to upgrade domestic technology.

Also unclear is the impact of the criterion to protect the existing 'industrial order'. What this criterion was intended to prevent was market dominance by a firm which had imported advanced technology, and also situations where an imported technology radically changed the product or production process and threatened the viability of small-parts or components manufacturers. There were in fact cases where the government arranged that all major manufacturers had access to advanced foreign technology, as in the case of the steel industry and imported LD converter technology. There have also been instances where the government has tried to create balance between firms by giving import permission to each, as in the case of synthetic fibre. Here, when one firm was given permission to import the technology for one synthetic fibre, its competitor was permitted to import another technology for another fibre. In this way, the government has at times tried to prevent abrupt changes of market share, which could have been caused by the import of a new technology. On the other hand, it seems that there were few cases where technology importation was prevented on the grounds that it might drive small firms from the market.[20]

Thus there is insufficient evidence to judge the significance and effectiveness of this 'industrial order' criterion. However, it is evident that through the 1950s and 1960s, the changes in market share and firm turnover were drastic as the economy grew rapidly and demand structure and technology underwent fundamental change. Thus, even though there were cases where government tried to protect the status quo, change was inevitable. The government's overriding concern was to promote domestic industry, and the importation of advanced technology was essential to this process in many cases. Thus when the importation of some important new technology threatened existing market structures the government usually did not prevent importation but compensated in other ways, such as through subsidies, to those affected.

The arguments above suggest that government oversight of technology importation seems to have had minimal impact on the overall pattern of technology importation. The technologies to be imported were in the end imported and firms that wanted to import imported anyway.

However, from the individual firm's standpoint, government intervention has been significant. In the case of nylon technology, Toray, with its prior experience with nylon production, might have been a successful early importer had the government not intervened. But it remains true that the government did not give other firms permission to import nylon technology for several years afterward, meaning huge monopoly profits for Toray during the interim. There is also the case of the steel industry's introduction of BOF technology and the industry-wide technology-sharing arrangement to that was orchestrated by MITI, as we have seen. Under this arrangement, firms that had known of the technology and were experimenting prior to the agreement were denied the opportunity to gain a technological advantage, albeit a short term one, over competitors. As Peck (1976) notes, 'In a fast growing economy it can be of importance whether government policy delays or speeds up the use of a particular technology by only three or four years'.

The above discussion also suggests that the government review system under vague criteria provided bureaucrats with strong powers over the private sector. Whether a firm could win permission to import important technology before its competitors was one of the most significant factors behind firm profits. This review system seems to have led to certain undesirable features of government–industry relationships, which continued in part even after technology importation was liberalized.

The second set of policies that affected the process of technology importation was the preferential tax measures used to encourage technology importation.[21] Two types of tax measures were included. The first was introduced in 1953 to reduce the tax withholdings on payments made to foreign corporations in exchange for imported technology. The second was to promote technology importation by allowing tariff exemptions on certain machines necessary for economic development but not produced domestically. These tax exemptions were designed to help technology-importing firms to reduce their tax burdens and upgrade their technological bases. Both measures were introduced in the early 1950s; tax savings due to these measures peaked in 1961 at 9.9 billion yen. These measures were abolished in the mid-1960s, as the emphasis of technology policy shifted from technology development through importation to technology development through domestic R&D.

The third policy affecting technology importation was the review of international technological agreements by the Fair Trade Commission

(Kosei Torihiki-iinkai: FTC). If foreign firms licensed technology to Japanese firms on conditions that were considered to be unreasonable restraints of trade or unfair trade practices, the FTC requested revisions in contract conditions or voided the agreements. Conditions which might be considered as violations of the Anti-Monopoly Law included: restrictions by licensor on export price, quantity, geographical area or buyer of the product which was manufactured using the technology in question; grant back clause mandating the licensee to provide the adapted, improved technology based on the originally licensed technology to licensor; and restrictions that dealt with competing technologies or products of the licensor. The FTC also strove to prevent 'excessive' royalties from being demanded by licensors. There was no such review system for agreements between Japanese firms. While FTC intervention on these grounds was intended to prevent unfair trade practices, it also acted to enhance the bargaining position of Japanese firms *vis-à-vis* foreign firms when Japanese firms negotiated licensing agreements.

In contrast to the above-mentioned policies which were directly related to the process of technology importation, there were various other policies which affected technology importation indirectly. For instance, various financial incentives like tax breaks and low-interest loans for investment in plant and equipment also encouraged technology importation. Further, macro policy to stimulate growth also helped to create strong demand for advanced technology. Indeed, creating an environment that was conducive to the introduction of new technology was the most important factor for successful technology importation. All policies that helped to do so were important in this sense.

Policies on trade and foreign investment in Japan had a more profound impact on technology importation. As described in other chapters in this book, trade liberalization started in the early 1960s and foreign investment liberalization in the late 1960s. However, even with the onset of liberalization, the foreign firms' penetration of the Japanese manufacturing market has remained rather low. As mentioned earlier, foreign firms with advanced technology sold the technology to Japanese firms rather than building plants or selling the floral goods manufactured with the technology, as it was difficult and/or costly to pursue other options. Japanese firms were thus able to obtain technology and sell the final products in the fast-growing domestic market. Needless to say, these policies entailed welfare costs, as they limited foreign competition and capital, although it is true that intense competition among domestic firms and the high savings ratio after the 1950s compensated these to a significant degree.

11.3.4 World Environment

Technology importation, like other forms of international trade, became active only under a politically stable world environment. After the Second World War, the worldwide political situation was stable because of, rather than despite, the cold war. The so-called Pax Americana, or Pax Russo-Americana, prevailed. International trade increased rapidly as the world economy grew, and this, in turn, further accelerated growth of trade. The IMF (International Monetary Fund) and GATT (General Agreement on Tariffs and Trade) provided the institutional framework for this process. The Paris Convention and WIPO (World Intellectual Property Rights Organization) played important roles for technology trade. Under these circumstances, international trade in technology also grew rapidly. From 1960 to 1965, the payments for technology importation by Japan, France and West Germany combined grew 180 per cent. In 1960, Japan paid 94.9 million dollars, France 90.8 million dollars, and West Germany 127.5 million dollars. In 1965, the amounts were 167.0, 213.0 and 195.2, respectively.[22] It appears that these countries also imported technology at least as actively as Japan. Actually, there was a large flow of technology from the US to Europe and Japan in the postwar period. The political and economic environment of this period was favourable to world trade including trade in technology at least within the capitalist economy block. Japan's active technology importation should be considered in this context.

11.4 CONCLUSION

As an economy develops, the growth and changing structure of demand for goods generate demand for advanced technology. In turn, the introduction of advanced technology furthers growth. This cyclical process characterizes most high-growth economies. Advanced technology is often available only from foreign markets, but the process of acquiring advanced technology from abroad is not like shopping for food at the supermarket. It requires deliberate effort on the part of the buyer and the right environmental conditions as well.

Notes

1. See M. Abramovitz, 'Catching Up, Forging Ahead, and Falling Behind', *Journal of Economic History*, 56 (June 1986) pp. 385–406.
2. See Miyazaki and Ito (1989).
3. *Ibid*.
4. See Hiroshige (1973).
5. See Komiya (1972).
6. Toyota was also negotiating technological agreements with Ford. However, they did not materialize because the US government restricted foreign investment and the sending of engineers abroad after the Korean War broke out. See Inoki (1989).
7. See Ekonomisuto (1984). The case-studies of technology importation in this chapter are largely taken from this book.
8. See Miyazaki and Ito (1989).
9. See Nakamura (1989).
10. See Lynn (1982).
11. The importation of technology for television was made under somewhat similar arrangements at the latter stage of importation. See Kogyo Gijutsu-in (1964).
12. According to Tsusho Sangyo-sho (1989), MITI intervened in about 40 per cent of the technology importation contracts of the 1950s to change the contract terms such as price and contract length. This slows that MITI extensively intervened in the negotiation process in the 1950s.
13. See *Gaikoku Gijutsu Donyu Nenji Hokoku* (Annual Report on the Import of Foreign Technology) each year.
14. See Tsusho Sangyo-sho (Ministry of International Trade and Industry), 1989 see note 11.
15. Kagaku Gijutsu-cho (Science and Technology Agency), *Kagaku Gijutsu Hakusho* (White Paper on Science and Technology) (1969).
16. Ekonomisuto (1984).
17. Kagaku Gijutsu-cho (Science and Technology Agency), *Kagaku Gijutsu Hakusho* (White Paper on Science and Technology) each year.
18. As to the two aspects of R&D, namely, to create new knowledge and to create the knowledge base to absorb new knowledge, see Cohen and Levinthal (1989).
19. For an excellent discussion of this process, see Sekiguchi (1986).
20. Tsusho Sangyo-sho (1989) reports cases where small firms protested at the importation of technology by larger firms. However, the number of such cases seems to be small relative to the total number of cases of technology importation.
21. See Goto and Wakasugi (1988).
22. As mentioned earlier, the technology balance of payments figures capture only a part of the entire technology transfer process.

References

Blumenthal, Tuvia (1979) 'A Note on the Relationship between Domestic Research and Development and Imports of Technology', *Economic Development and Cultural Change*, vol. 27, pp. 303–6.

Cohen, Wesley M. and Daniel A. Levinthal (1989) 'Innovation and Learning: The Two Faces of R&D', *Economic Journal*, vol. 99.

Ekonomisuto (1984) *Shogen Kodo Seicho-ki no Nihon* (Testimony on Japan in the High Growth Era) (Tokyo: Mainichi Shinbun-sha).

Goto, Akira and Ryuhei Wakasugi (1988) 'Technology Policy', in *Industrial Policy of Japan*, ed. by Ryutaro Komiya, Masahiro Okuno and Kotaro Suzumura (Tokyo: University of Tokyo Press). Translation of *Nihon no Sangyo Seisaku* (Tokyo: University of Tokyo Press, 1984).

Hiroshige, Toru (1973) *Kagaku no Shakai-shi* (Social History of Science) (Tokyo: Chuo Koron-sha).

Inoki, Takenori (1989) 'Seicho no Kiseki: 1' (Path of Growth: 1), in *Nihon Keizai-shi*, vol. 8, ed. by Yasukichi Yasuba and Takenori Inoki (Tokyo: Iwanami Shoten).

Kogyo Gijutsu-in (Agency of Industrial Science and Technology) (1964) *Gijutsu Kakushin to Nihon no Kogyo* (Technological Innovation and Japan's Manufacturing Industry) (Tokyo: Nikkan Kogyo Shinbun-sha).

Komiya, Ryutaro (1972) 'Direct Foreign Investment in Postwar Japan', in *Direct Foreign Investment in Asia and the Pacific*, ed. by Peter Drysdale (Toronto: University of Toronto Press).

Lynn, Leonard H. (1982) *How Japan Innovates* (Boulder: Westview Press).

Miyazaki, Masayasu and Osamu Ito (1989) 'Senji Sengo no Sangyo to Kigyo' (Industry and Firm in the Wartime and Postwar Period), in *Nihon Keizai-shi*, vol. 7, ed. by Takafusa Nakamura (Tokyo: Iwanami Shoten).

Nakamura, Takafusa (1989) 'Gaisetu 1937–1954' (Overview 1937–54), in *Nihon Keizai-shi*, vol. 7, ed. Takafusa Nakamura (Tokyo: Iwanami Shoten).

Odagiri, Hiroyuki and Akira Goto (forthcoming) 'The Japanese System of Innovation: Past, Present and Future', in *National Systems of Innovation*, ed. by Richard Nelson (Oxford: Oxford University Press).

Odaka, Konosuke (1989) 'Seicho no Kiseki: 2' (Path of Growth: 2), in *Nihon Keizai-shi*, vol. 8, ed. by Yasukichi Yasuba and Takenori Inoki (Tokyo: Iwanami Shoten).

Ozaki, Robert S. (1972) *The Control of Imports and Foreign Capital in Japan* (New York: Praeger).

Ozawa, Terutomo (1974) *Japan's Technological Challenge to the West, 1950–1974* (Cambridge, Mass.: MIT Press).

Peck, Merton J. (1976) (with Shuji Tamura) 'Technology', in *Asia's New Giant*, ed. by Hugh Patrick and Henry Rosovsky (Washington: Brookings Institution).

Peck, Merton J. and Akira Goto (1981) 'Technology and Economic Growth: The Case of Japan', *Research Policy*, vol. 10.

Sekiguchi, Sueo (1986) 'Gijutsu Yunyu-sha toshiteno Nihon' (Japan as a Technology Importer), in *Chokusetsu Toshi to Gijutsu Iten*, ed. by Sueo

Sekiguchi and Tran Van Tho (Tokyo: Japan Center for Economic Research).

Trezise, Phillip (1976) (with Yukio Suzuki) 'Politics, Government, and Economic Growth in Japan', in *Asia's New Giant*, ed. by Hugh Patrick and Henry Rosovsky (Washington: Brookings Institution).

Tsusho Sangyo-sho (Ministry of International Trade and Industry) (1989) *Tsusho Sangyo Seisaku-shi* (History of Policies on International Trade and Industry), vol. 5 (Tokyo: Tsusho Sangyo Chosa-kai).

12 The Role of Economic Planning in Japan

Takao Komine

12.1 INTRODUCTION

Many arguments have been made with respect to Japanese economic planning, each reflecting different lines of inquiry. Perceptions vary between not only foreign and Japanese observers, but also Japanese economists and the officials in charge of economic planning.

I will try to clarify the positive role played by economic planning in Japan and outline its limitations as well. First, I would like to raise two important questions concerning Japanese economic planning in order to lay out the main concerns of this chapter.

12.1.1 To What Extent Did Economic Planning Contribute to Successful Economic Development in Postwar Japan?

Many foreign observers in particular argue that economic planning has played an important role in bringing about the remarkable economic successes of the postwar period. It is true that the Japanese government has maintained a system of long-term economic planning which is rather unique among industrialized countries with free markets. In the West, only France and Sweden rely on indicative economic planning similar to that of Japan. Other countries, including Germany, Great Britain and Canada, also have long-term economic plans; however, these cover rather limited areas such as expenditure projections and do not include any economic policy statements. Furthermore, many overseas observers tend to have notion that in Japan the government and private sector maintain close relationship to achieve common economic goals. It is only natural that such observers conclude that it was Japan's unique planning system that brought about a unique economic development.

On the other hand, many economists in Japan argue that the Japanese economic plan is only a decoration. The results of economic performance have often differed from those projected in the plan, and economic policy measures have not necessarily been implemented in the manner outlined in the plan. Consequently, these economists place relatively less emphasis on economic planning as an explanatory variable.

I share the view that the Japanese economic plan did not contribute to postwar economic performance nearly as much as overseas observers have suggested. Postwar economic performance was a result of a number of factors. Both independent and policy factors at the macro and micro level have contributed to development, economic planning representing only one of the factors at the macro level. Independent factors at the macro level, including a high savings and investment rate and changes in the industrial structure contributed much to development. Even without planning, the Japanese economy would have out-performanced other industrialized countries.

However, this observation does not mean that planning was meaningless. Clearly, Japanese economic plan has played an important role in many areas, some of which will be described in this chapter.

12.1.2 Is the Japanese Experience in Economic Planning of Relevance to the Former Centrally Planned Economies?

The characteristics of the Japanese economic plan were particular to the stage of development of the Japanese economy. This is an important point when we consider whether the Japanese planning experience is relevant to other countries, especially the Central and Eastern European countries currently trying to make the shift from centrally planned to market-oriented economies.

In order to consider possible relevance, we must first understand the characteristics of the Japanese economic planning system. In order to do this, it is best to divide the postwar period into two phases.

The first phase of economic planning is the period of stabilization immediately after the war, from 1946 to 1955. Economic planning was imperative during this period, as the government tried directly to control economic activities and prices. This was for Japan a period of reconstruction, of efforts made to transform and stabilize the devastated Japanese economy. Mining and manufacturing production had been fallen 70 per cent from production levels of the 1934–36 period. Inflation skyrocketed, with prices soaring 200 per cent in the first half of 1946.

At this time, the Japanese government drew up an economic plan which was similar to the economic plans of the centrally planned countries. Economic reconstruction would have been impossible through a free market system. In addition to hyper-inflation, many markets were beset with huge gaps between pent-up demand and limited supplies of goods. There was no alternative but to control resource allocation and prices. To implement economic controls, the Economic Stabilization Board (Keizai Antei-honbu: ESB) and the Price Administration Agency (Bukka-cho) were established.

The second phase is the period after 1955 until the present. After achieving economic stability, controls were abolished in many areas and replaced with markets. The characteristics of economic planning during this second period are completely different from those in the first phase. They became indicative plans which outline basic economic policy and provide guidelines, not directives, for the economy.

What follows is a detailed description of the economic plans during these two phases.

12.2 JAPANESE ECONOMIC PLANNING IN THE PERIOD OF RECONSTRUCTION

From 1947 to early 1950s the Japanese government implemented an economic plan in order to directly control the economy. The Economic Stabilization Board (ESB) played a central role in making and implementing this plan.

12.2.1 The Rationing Process

The Economic Stabilization Board was established in 1946 with a power base that was far superior to that of any other agency concerned with economic policy. The ESB was most importantly charged with implementing government controls on prices and production. The Ordinance to Establish an Economic Stabilization Board (Keizai Antei-honbu-rei) states 'under the control of the Prime Minister, the ESB shall make emergency plans for stabilizing the production and distribution of commodities, labour, prices, finance, trade, etc. and shall coordinate, supervise and promote the policies of other ministries and agencies'.[1]

The rationing procedure is a good example of how the government planned and implemented such controls. Rationing procedures were authorized by the Temporary Law for Adjusting the Demand and Supply of Materials (Rinji Busshi Jukyu Chosei-ho), the Rules on Procedures for Allocation of Designated Products (Shitei Seisan Shizai Wariate-kisoku) and the Rules on Procedures for Rationing Goods (Shitei Haikyu Busshi Haikyu Tetsuzuki Kisoku).

Many important raw materials such as coal and steel were put under rationing systems. The Ministry concerned calculated users' demands and submitted total demand figures to the ESB. The ESB then calculated total demand and supply for the coming quarter and allocated materials on a sector-by-sector basis. Based on this quarterly plan, the appropriate Ministry issued each user with a ration certificate.

It is important to remember that from their outset, direct economic controls were intended to be temporary. When the ESB was established, the Supreme Commander for the Allied Powers (SCAP) specified that it would be a temporary organization specifically designed to cope with the economic crisis. Almost every Japanese participant recognized that direct control was a poor means of resource allocation and that it should be used only in emergency situations. As increased production gradually brought a greater supply of goods onto the market, problems with excess demand were eased. Government controls were gradually dismantled, and the ESB was dissolved in 1952.

12.2.2 Economic Information Supplied by the ESB

The ESB played another important role – that of supplying detailed and reliable economic information to the public. It was understood that one of its duties would be to generate economic statistics that would enhance the rational, scientific basis of economic policy-making. There were three important developments at the ESB regarding this role. First, the Board released a document entitled 'The Real State of the National Economy' (*Keizai Jisso Hokoku-sho*). This report revealed that all three sectors of the domestic economy, government, business and consumers, were experiencing deficits. It called upon the Japanese people to endure temporary poverty but to be optimistic about future economic recovery.[2]

This document signalled a change in the attitude of policy-makers. Previously, they had tended to make decisions without providing any background information to the public. But this document attempted to make public the actual state of the economy and asked for the support and cooperation of all citizens. The general reaction to the report was very favourable and the Board was asked by the Diet to release such reports at least once a year. Since then, the Annual Economic Report (*Nenji Keizai Hokoku*) – generally referred to as the Economic White Paper (*Keizai Hakusho*) – has been published every year. This report is widely read and is one of the most important documents for understanding the economic situation of Japan today.

Second, the ESB conducted a survey of war damage and publicized its results in 1948 and 1949. The survey targetted three areas of damage – that to human life, national wealth and productive capacity.

Third, the ESB worked to compile basic economic statistics. In 1953, the first report on the Japanese GNP (Kokumin Shotoku Hakusho) was published, estimating GNP from 1946 to 1951. In 1948, per capita GNP was 100 dollars, which put Japan 42nd on a list of 70 countries. By 1989, per capita GNP had become 23 463 dollars, the third highest in the world.

One of the basic conditions for economic development is public confidence in its government and economic policies. To win this support, the government must among other things provide detailed and reliable economic information. The ESB played an important role in carrying out this function.

12.3 ECONOMIC PLANNING IN A MARKET ECONOMY

The ESB was dissolved in July 1952 and the Economic Deliberation Agency (Keizai Shingi-cho) was established in its place. This Agency was replaced by the Economic Planning Agency (Keizai Kikaku-cho) in 1955, charged with the creation and implementation of long-term economic plans.

12.3.1 Basic Characteristics of Japanese Economic Planning after 1955

In December 1955, the 'Five-Year Plan for Economic Self-Support' was adopted as the first official long-term economic plan. While long-term economic planning has continued, they are carried out today in the context of a market economy. Their character and objectives are thus completely different from those of centrally planned economies.

In Japan, allocation of economic resources is basically determined by markets. Thus, the government's ability to control the economy is limited. Japanese economic planning is today referred to as 'indicative planning'; in other words, the government merely 'indicates' the general direction of economic development, not the details within it.

It was made clear from the outset that the Japanese economic plan was only to supplement the market mechanism. The foreword of the 'Five-Year Plan for Economic Self-Support' states:

> This economic plan is to be implemented in an economic system based on the free activities and initiatives of individuals and private companies. In recognition of the principle that government regulation should be minimal, the achievement of the objectives stated in the economic plan is highly dependent upon the appreciation and effort of the Japanese people themselves.[3]

Recently, the economic plan 'Economic Management within a Global Context' released in 1988, similarly states:

> Given that the Japanese economy is basically market-driven, no economic plan can be expected minutely to define and control every sector of the economy and society or to compel implementation of its projections. Rather, the basic role of economic planning in Japan is (1) to present a forecast for the way the economy ought and can develop; (2) to point out the basic directions that the government should follow in implementing its medium- and long-term economic policy management as well as to identify the priority policy objectives and means; and (3) to provide basic guidelines for household and corporate decisions.[4]

12.3.2 Main Features of Economic Plans after 1955

There are three main components to Japanese economic plans. The first part is a general description of economic conditions and government economic policy objectives. This is followed by a detailed description of government economic policies to be implemented in the period covered by the plan. Finally, a quantitative forecast of main economic indicators is provided.

The first part of each economic plan is designed to clarify long-term policy objectives. Japanese postwar economic plans can be classified into five categories according to their objectives (Table 12.1).

Table 12.1 Selected features of economic plans in Japan

Name of plan	*Name of plan (Japanese)*	*Date published and Cabinet at the time of plan approval*	*Planning period (FY)*	*Aims*
Five-Year Plan for Economic Self-Support	Keizai Jiritu Go -kanen Keikaku	Dec. 1955 Hatoyama	1956–60	Self-support of the economy Full employment
New Long-Range Economic Plan	Shin Choki Keizai Keikaku	Dec. 1957 Kishi	1958–62	Maximization of growth, Improvement of national living standards Full employment
National Income Doubling Plan	Kokumin Shotoku Baizo Keikaku	Dec. 1960 Ikeda	1961–70	do.
Medium-Term Economic Plan	Chuki Keizai Keikaku	Jan. 1965 Sato	1964–68	Rectifying imbalances
Economic and Social Development Plan	Keizai Shakai Hatten Keikaku	March 1967 Sato	1967–71	Balanced and steady economic development
New Economic and Social Development Plan	Shin Keizai Shakai Hatten Keikaku	April 1970 Sato	1970–75	Construction of admirable society through balanced economic growth
Basic Economic and Social Plan	Keizai Shakai Kihon Keikaku	Feb. 1973 Tanaka	1973–77	Promotion of national welfare Promotion of international cooperation

continued on p. 312

Table 12.1 continued

Name of plan	*Name of plan (Japanese)*	*Date published and Cabinet at the time of plan approval*	*Planning period (FY)*	*Aims*
Economic Plan for the Second Half of the 1970s	Showa Goju Nendai Zenki Keizai Keikaku	May 1976 Miki	1976–80	Realization of a richer national life and stable development of the economy
New Economic and Social Development Seven-Year Plan	Shin Keizai Shakai Nana-kanen Keikaku	Aug. 1979 Ohira	1979–85	Shift to a stable growth path Enrichment of quality of national life Contribution to the development of the international economic community
Outlook and Guidelines of Economy and Society in the 1980s	Hachiju Nendai Keizai Shakai no Tenbo to Shishin	Aug. 1983 Nakasone	1983–90	Formation of peaceful and stable international relations, creation of an economy and society full of vitality Ensuring a secure and affluent people's life
Economic Management within a Global Context	Sekai to Tomoni Ikiru Nihon	May 1988 Takeshita	1988–92	Reducing the massive external imbalance and contributing to a better world Creating diverse lifestyles and better quality of life, Promoting balanced economic and social development nationwide

Source: Keizai Kikaku-cho (Economic Planning Agency), *Economic Planning in Japan*.

The first category includes plans concerned with recovery from the damage of the Second World War and the achievement of a self-supporting economy. The 'Economic Rehabilitation Plan (Keizai Fukko Keikaku)' (which was drafted in 1949 but not officially approved by the government) and the 'Five-Year Plan for Economic Self-Support' (1955) fall into this category.

The second category includes plans aimed at achieving a high growth rate. The 'New Long-Range Economic Plan' (1957) and the 'National Income Doubling Plan' (1960) belong to this category.

The third category of economic plans reflect an emphasis on balanced economic growth and social development. The idea of the welfare state was introduced into these plans and the government started to use the word 'social' in the title. The 'Economic and Social Development Plan' (1967) and the 'Basic Economic and Social Plan' (1973) are in this category.

The fourth category covers plans which aimed to return Japan to a path of stable growth after the oil crises of 1973 and 1979. With virtually total dependence on foreign oil, the Japanese economy suffered from high rates of inflation, a balance of payment deficit and a severe down-turn in business after each oil shock. The annual growth rate fell from around 10 per cent to around 4 to 5 per cent. Moreover, the financial situation of the government worsened as a result of reduced tax proceeds and increased public spending to stimulate the economy. The main goal of economic policy during this period was to secure stable growth and to reestablish sound public finance.

The 'Economic Plan for the Second Half of the 1970s' (1976) tried to show how economic policy programmes would help the country recover from severe inflation and recession after the first oil crisis. Likewise the 'New Economic and Social Development Seven-Year Plan' (1979) outlined programmes for recovery after the second oil crisis. In this plan, a general consumption tax was proposed in order to reduce the budget deficit. However, the new tax drew public opposition and the ruling Liberal Democratic Party (Jiyu Minshu-to: LDP) did poorly in the subsequent election in 1979. Thereafter, the government changed its strategy and started to pursue a balanced budget through not tax increases but spending cuts. 'Outlook and Guidelines of Economy and Society in the 1980s' (1983) made administrative and fiscal reform one of its highest priorities.

Finally, recent plans such as 'Economic Management within a Global Context' (1988) gives highest priority to international prob-

Table 12.2 The change in policy objectives

	Five-year plan for economic self support (1955)	*New long-range economic plan (1957)*	*National income doubling plan (1960)*	*Medium-term economic plan (1965)*	*Economic and social development plan (1967)*	*New economic and social development plan (1970)*
Economic growth	Economic independence without US aid.	Higher economic growth rate. Higher accumulation of capital.	Double per-capita GNP in 10 years.	Stable growth. Correct dis-equilibrium caused by high growth.	Balanced economic growth.	Balanced growth with manageable balance of payments situation.
Employment	Offer employment opportunity to increasing population.	Absorb excess labor in agriculture and small business.	Rectify low wage and dual economic structure problem.	Efficient use of labour force.	Efficient use of labour force.	
Prices		Price stability of fundamental materials such as coal and electricity.	Cope with monopol-istic corporate behaviour.	Reduce Inflation.	Cut inflation.	Cope with wage, income and productivity problems.
Industries	Move from light to heavy industries. Strengthen industrial infrastructure. Increase production of staple foods.	Stronger industrial structure by promoting heavy and chemical industries.	Stronger industrial structure by promoting high value-added industries. Industri-alize Pacific Belt area.	Modernize low-pro-ductivity sectors such as agriculture, small busi-ness and dis-tribution. Stronger industrial structure.	Strengthen industrial foundation to cope with capital liberaliza-tion. Develop-ment of indigenous technology.	Promote information-intensive and high-value-added industries. Promote information-oriented economy.
International economy	Strengthen export com-petitiveness.	Promote exports.	Economic coopera-tion with developing countries.	Higher inter-national status and trans-formation to open economy. Promote exports and liberalize imports.	Liberaliza-tion of capital tran-sactions.	Contribute to international economic society. Active promotion of trade and investment liberalization.
Social	Restrain consumption and promote savings.	Eliminate poverty and illness. Stable life for low-income families.	Promote social security system. Higher consump-tion both in quality and quantity.	Promote social welfare system. Stabilize land prices.	Promote social develop-ment.	Promote consumer protection. Build better pension system.

continued on p. 316

Table 12.2 Continued

	Basic economic and social plan (1973)	*Economic plan for the second half of the 1970s (1976)*	*New economic and social development seven-year plan (1979)*	*Outlook and guidelines of economy and society in the 1980s (1983)*	*Economic management within a global context (1988)*
Economic growth	Internally and externally balanced growth.	Transform from high growth to stable economy.	Domestic demand-led economic growth.	New growth path sustained by information and knowledge-intensive industry.	Domestic demand-led growth.
Employment	Promote a five-day workweek.	Secure full employment.	Secure full employment. Promote employment of elderly.	Secure full employment.	Shorten working hours (1880 hours a year by 1992).
Prices	Prevent inflation.	Control inflation by taking money supply fully into account.	Stabilize prices by adequate demand control.	Maintain price stability.	Narrow the disparity between Japanese and international prices.
Industries	Promote knowledge-intensive industries.	Promote technology-intensive industries. Transfer to resource-saving and environment-protective structure.	Promote knowledge-intensive industries in line with international harmonization and securing employment.	Promote knowledge and software-intensive industrial structure.	Industrial restructuring to make economy more compatible with the world economy.
International economy	Development assistance of 1% of GNP. Secure fundamental balance of payments.	Cooperation and contribution for world economic development.	Prevent trade friction. Development assistance through enhancing human resources.	Build economy and society open to the world.	Contribute to the world by expanding imports, strengthening economic cooperation and recycling surplus capital.
Social	Create better environmental conditions. Improve pension system.	Improve social security system.	Build Japanese-style welfare state. Build rural-urban state.	Cope with 80 years life-style.	Create a life-style in which the individual can enjoy a better quality of life.

continued on p. 317

Table 12.2 Continued

	Five-year plan for economic self support (1955)	*New long-range economic plan (1957)*	*National income doubling plan (1960)*	*Medium-term economic plan (1965)*	*Economic and social development plan (1967)*	*New economic and social development plan (1970)*
Others		Development of atomic energy. Better economic statistics.	Shift from solid energy to liquid energy. Cope with environmental pollution. Promote social investment.	Cheap and stable supply of energy. Issue no government bonds.	Maintain sound budgetary conditions. Reduce cyclical fluctuation in finance.	Stronger anti-cyclical budgetary process. Rationalization of finance and government management.

lems. In the middle of the 1980s, the Japanese current account surplus became so large that it was difficult to maintain harmonious relationships with the rest of the world. The first 'Maekawa Report' released in 1986 suggested the urgency of transforming Japan's export-led economic structure into a domestic demand-led one. Reflecting this change, the latest plan emphasizes the reduction of the massive external imbalance and contributions to the world economy. It also projects that during the period covered by the plan, Japan will experience a moderate growth led by domestic demand and proposes changes in Japan's economic structure which would simultaneously reduce the external imbalance and improve the quality of national life. The plan makes various policy recommendations such as deregulation of distribution system and import restriction, the reduction of working hours, and the promotion of direct foreign investment.

12.3.3 A Change in Policy Objectives

The Japanese economic plan outlines how the government intends to handle the national economy from a long-term perspective. The economic policies described in the plan represent an official commitment on the part of the government. Without exception the plans are adopted by the cabinet.

Table 12.2 shows how policy objectives have changed over time. On the basis of the table, it can be said that the Japanese economic plan has succeeded in outlining appropriate, long-term policies which

Table 12.2 Continued

	Basic economic and social plan (1973)	*Economic plan for the second half of the 1970s (1976)*	*New economic and social development seven-year plan (1979)*	*Outlook and guidelines of economy and society in the 1980s (1983)*	*Economic management within a global context (1988)*
Others	Cope with growth limit caused by environment and energy. Implement technology assessment.	Promote economic security. Stable supply of resources and energy.	Introduce general consumption tax. End deficit financing bonds within 7 years.	Revise government management and finance. End deficit financing bonds within 8 years.	Promote administrative reform. Promote deregulation. Move facilities out of Tokyo.

have been flexible enough to accommodate economic and social changes.

For example, government policy in general has shifted from an emphasis on economic growth to an emphasis on welfare problems and international cooperation. Recent problems such as environmental pollution and the need to strengthen social welfare system were promptly reflected in the economic plan.

Long-term changes in the industrial structure have also been taken into account in the plans, including the shift from an industrial structure based on heavy and chemical industries to one based on high value-added, knowledge-intensive industries. Table 12.3 compares projected changes in the industrial structure with actual results. The 'National Income Doubling Plan' (1960) projected high rates of production growth for heavy and chemical industries. It projected that the average annual growth rate of production for heavy and chemical industries at 13.2 per cent in the period from 1959 to 1970. This was somewhat higher than the 11.3 per cent projected for manufacturing as a whole. During this period in fact, the growth rate of total manufacturing production was 14.8 per cent while that for the heavy and chemical industries was 18.3 per cent. The plan underestimated total production growth, although it correctly projected a relatively higher growth rate for the heavy and chemical industries. The 'Economic Plan for the Second Half of the 1970s' predicted relative increases in production for technology-intensive industries such as those producing machinery products. In this plan, the pro-

Table 12.3(a) Projection of industrial structure of 'National Income Doubling Plan' and results (average annual growth rate, 1959–70, %)

	Projected	*Actual*
Manufacturing	11.3	14.8
Heavy and chemical industry	13.2	18.3
Iron and steel	10.4	16.8
Non-ferrous metal	9.1	14.6
Machinery	14.6	19.8
Chemical products	11.9	15.1
Petroleum and coal products	11.9	18.5
Light industry and others	7.4	9.6
Ceramic, stone and clay products	9.9	12.3
Rubber products	10.4	11.5
Leather products	5.3	10.8
Pulp and paper products	7.1	12.1
Lumber and wood products	3.4	9.1
Food products	5.9	5.5
Tobacco products	3.2	8.3

Note: Projected figures based on 1955 prices. Actual figures based on 1970 prices.

Source: Somu-cho (Management and Coordination Agency), *Sangyo Renkan-hyo* (Input-Output Table of Japan) 1991

Table 12.3(b) Projection of industrial structure of 'Economic Plan for the Second Half of the 1970s' and results (average annual growth rate, 1975–80, %)

	Projected	*Actual*
Total	7.8	4.6
Primary industry	1.7	0.1
Secondary industry	8.8	5.3
Mining	4.6	3.6
Manufacturing	9.2	5.3
Chemical products	9.0	3.3
Metal products	6.8	4.7
Machinery	10.7	9.3
Others	8.7	3.5
Construction	7.2	3.7
Tertiary industry	6.7	4.9
Transport and telecommunication	5.6	3.7
Utility industry	7.8	5.3
Other services	6.8	5.0

Note: Projected figures based on 1970 prices. Actual figures based on 1985 prices.

Source: Somu-cho (Management and Coordination Agency), *Sangyo Renkan-hyo* (Input-Output Table of Japan), 1991.

jected average annual growth rate of production was 7.8 per cent for overall industrial production and 10.7 per cent for the machinery industry. In fact, overall production increased by 4.6 per cent while the increase for machinery industry was 9.3 per cent.

12.3.4 Economic Projections in the Plan

Japanese economic plans have also made public long-term economic projections of key economic indicators.

In particular, the economic plans of the 1950s and 1960s included numerous detailed projections. The first official economic plan – the 'Five-Year Plan for Economic Self Support' (1955) – contained forecasts of GNP and its components, agricultural production, employment by industry, the national budget, and source and use of funds by industry. The 'National Income Doubling Plan', adopted in 1960, included forecasts of population, demand and industrial components of GNP, employment structure by industry, the balance between investment and savings, budget revenues and expenditures, balance of payments, and labour productivity.

In those days, the main goal of economic planning was to secure a foundation for industrial activity and to achieve high economic growth. In order to draw up the policies necessary to achieve these objectives, detailed quantitative analysis of demand and supply conditions was indispensible to economic progress.

However, economic plans from the 1970s on have included fewer detailed projections. The 'New Economic and Social Development Seven-Year Plan' (1979), for example, presented just a few projections such as demand and income components of GNP and government finance. The 'Outlook and Guidelines of Economy and Society in the 1980s', adopted in 1983, contained forecasts for few indicators – GNP growth, unemployment, and the rate of inflation. Moreover these projections were offered with caution. For instance, the 'New Economic and Social Development Seven Year Plan' stated: 'The economic environment, especially the oil situation, is likely to fluctuate, and we can draw various kinds of economic scenarios. The projection presented in this plan is just one possible scenario which might occur under specific conditions. It is quite possible that we will have large discrepancies between projected and actual figures.'[5] 'Economic Management within a Global Context', (1988) similarly notes: 'Given the very considerable unpredictability of domestic and international developments, however, the following figures should be understood as rough estimates with considerable leeway on either side.'[6]

There are several reasons for the shift from detailed to simple projections and that from frankness to caution. First, the focus of planning shifted from economic growth to broaden social concerns. Second, economic forecasting has become more difficult because the economic environment, especially international variables such as the oil price and exchange rate, began to fluctuate considerably. Third, the government was unable to present a detailed economic outlook that was consistent with what was presented in the plan. The 'Outlook and Guidelines of Economy and Society in the 1980s' (1983) showed the government's intention to end its dependence on deficit-financing government bonds, to revise the external imbalances, and to realize domestic demand-led economic growth. However, the government couldn't present projections in which all of these policy objectives could be consistently realized.

12.3.5 The Economic Plan and the Actual Economy

It is often argued that in Japan, government and business cooperate in order to set economic priorities and achieve certain economic objectives, and that economic plans have been the institutional framework that has made this cooperation possible.

However, I believe that planning has had less strong influence on the economy than has been suggested. The policies outlined in the plans have not necessarily been implemented, and there are always discrepancies between projections and actual economic performance. Some have in fact argued that these problems mean that planning has been nothing more than window-dressing.

It is not surprising that the economy does not perform exactly as the economic plan has projected. Supply and demand are determined through the interaction of producers and consumers in the marketplace. The government cannot directly control these exchanges. Moreover, unpredictable economic fluctuations may have repercussions for the economy as a whole. Clearly, there is no way to guarantee that economic projections outlined in economic planning will correctly coincide with actual economic performance (Table 12.4).

It is often argued that while the macroeconomic projections in the economic plan are meant to serve as guidelines for the private sector, the government is responsible for implementing the economic policies included in the plans. However, these policies have not always

Table 12.4 Comparison between projected and actual economic performance

Name of plan	*Date published and cabinet at the time of plan approval*	*Planning period (FY)*	*Projection in the plan and actual performance*			
			Average annual growth rate of real GNP (%)	*Unemployment rate in final year (%)*	*Average annual rise in consumer prices (%)*	*External balance (Current accounts) at the final year (US$ 100 million)*
Five-Year Plan for	Dec. 1955	1956–60	4.9	1.0	–	0
Economic Self-Support	Hatoyama		9.1	1.5	1.8	–0.1
New Long-Range Economic	Dec. 1957	1958–62	6.5	–	–	1.8
Plan	Kishi		10.0	1.3	3.4	–0.2
National Income Doubling	Dec. 1960	1961–70	7.8	–	–	1.8
Plan	Ikeda		10.3	1.2	5.7	23.5
Medium-Term Economic	Jan. 1965	1964–68	8.1	–	approx. 2.5	0
Plan	Sato		10.4	1.1	5.0	14.7
Economic and Social	March 1967	1967–71	8.2	–	approx. 3	14.5
Development Plan	Sato		10.1	1.3	5.7	63.2
New Economic and Social	April 1970	1970–75	10.6	–	4.4	35
Development Plan	Sato		5.1	1.9	11.1	1.3
Basic Economic and	Feb. 1973	1973–77	9.4	–	4% level	59
Social Plan	Tanaka		3.5	2.1	12.9	140.0
Economic Plan for the	May 1976	1976–80	a little over 6	1.3% level	6% level	approx. 40
Second Half of the 1970s	Miki		4.9	2.1	6.4	–70.1
New Economic and Social Development	Aug. 1979	1979–85	approx. 5.7	approx. 1.7	approx. 5	Roughly basic accounts balanced
Seven-Year Plan	Ohira		4.1	2.6	3.6	550
Outlook and Guidelines	Aug. 1983	1983–90	approx. 4	approx. 2	approx. 3	Internationally
of Economy and Society	Nokasone		4.5 (FY. 1983–89)	2.2 (FY. 1989)	1.4 (FY. 1983–89)	harmonious balance
in the 1980s						
Economic Management	May 1988	1988–92				
within a Global Context	Takeshita		approx. 3.75	approx. 2.5	approx. 1.5	
			5.2 (FY. 1988–89)	2.2 (FY. 1989)	1.8 (FY. 1988–89)	

Note: Average annual growth rates of real GNP are based on the SNA (System of National Accounts) at CY 1980 price.
Top figures: projected.
Bottom figures: actual.

Source: Keizai Kikaku-cho (Economic Planning Agency), *Economic Planning in Japan*.

been implemented. This does not mean that the Japanese economic plan is just a decoration. There are several reasons why it is often difficult to implement planned economic policies.

First, there is no central organization to implement the economic plan. The Economic Planning Agency plays a central role in drafting the plan, but its implementation is highly dependent on each responsible Ministry or Agency. The Economic Planning Agency cannot force the ministries to implement the policies as stated in the plan.

Second, the budgetary system is not subject to or in keeping with long-term economic planning. Instead, the budget must be approved by the Diet every year. The government's commitment to its expenditures is thus limited to a one-year period. Though the economic plan may include planning for long-term public investment, but implementation is not guaranteed due to restrictions inherent in the budgetary process.

12.3.6 Flexibility of Japanese Economic Planning

Long-term economic planning in a market economy is confronted with a dilemma. On the one hand, its policies should be implemented and its objectives pursued. However, in an interdependent world economy, it is almost impossible to predict long-term economic development. Thus it becomes necessary to revise policy objectives and measures according to changes in the economic and social environment.

The Japanese economic plan covers five to ten years. The average period has been 6.6 years. However, no plan completed its terms. As Table 12.1 shows, the Japanese government has adopted eleven economic plans over 36 years. None of these plans has ever been completed.

Some critics therefore argue that the government has not worked hard enough to implement policy measures outlined in economic plans. To my mind, however, this frequent replacement shows the flexibility of Japanese economic planning. Continual revision of economic plans is necessary to cope with an unpredictable environment as well as changing public preferences.

Perhaps Japanese economic planning is better regarded a kind of rolling plan. Officially, the government has eleven separate plans. However, each plan was based on previous efforts and aimed at filling the gaps between stated objectives and results achieved.

12.4 ECONOMIC PLANNING IN THE JAPANESE ECONOMY

What role has economic planning played in Japan? The 1965 report of the Economic Council's Committee to Study Basic Issues in Economic Planning (chaired by Kazushi Ohkawa) highlights three significant functions.[7]

12.4.1 Three Roles of Japanese Economic Planning

The Committee pointed out three roles of economic planning in Japan.

First is the educational and informational role fulfilled by economic forecasting. In the economic plan, the government provides an overview of its outlook for the economy, which is consistent with its economy policy stance. Private companies are then better able to formulate their own long-term plans.

Japanese private companies trust government projections and make their own long-term plans based on them. This is not because of a traditional close relationship between government and private enterprise. It is because the government tries to take business trends into account in the planning process so that final projections released are not far from the general consensus held by private enterprises.

To confirm this point, we can show that the growth rates projected in the economic plans are consistent with what is called the adaptive formation of expectations. In other words, current expectations for the next period are formed in part based on the difference between former expectations and actual results. For instance, when we compare the projected growth rate and that achieved, we find that the projected rate lies somewhere between the former projected rate and the actual rate (Figure 12.1). In other words, if the actual rate is higher than the projected one, the next projected rate is also higher than the previous projected rate, but lower than the actual rate in the previous period. However, the two plans adopted in the 1980s carried growth rate projections which were not consistent with the above-mentioned hypothesis and fell short of actual outcomes. There are several reasons for this change: (i) people's interests have shifted from economic growth to social problems; (ii) the government was reluctant to include an optimistic growth projection which would stimulate demand for government expenditures; (iii) it was believed

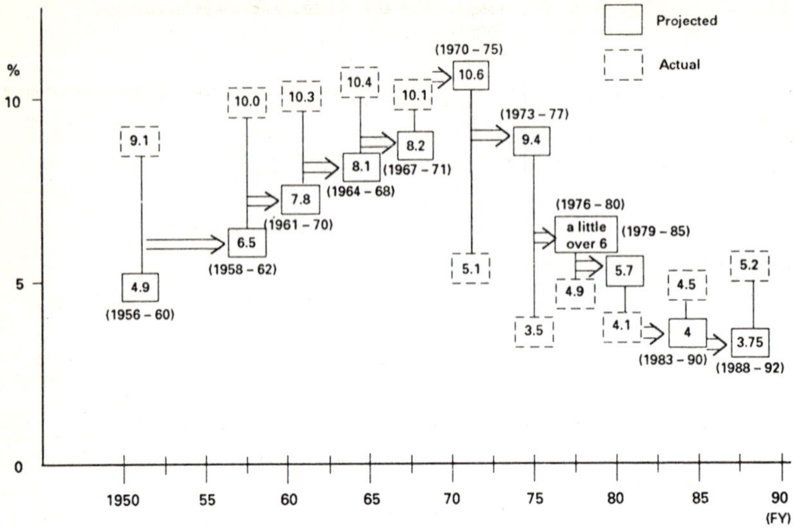

Figure 12.1 Relationship between projected and actual growth rate

that growth rates would fall because of external shocks such as the second oil crisis and the yen's appreciation.

The second role of economic planning is the statement of long-term policy commitments. Every plan includes an expenditures programme to be carried out by the government. As such, the plan is a statement of the administration's long-range goals.

The third role relates to the planning process. There are two ways to evaluate the usefulness of economic planning. One is to do so with reference to economic outcomes and to judge whether economic planning helped realize them. Another is to evaluate the plan-making process itself. In my view, the importance of Japanese economic planning is in the processing and formulation of the plan. Through the planning process, all economic actors, both public and private, constituting national economy are able to share the same information. I will discuss this point below.

12.4.2 Planning Process in Japan

There are three main steps to finalize an economic plan. First, the Prime Minister requests the Economic Council (Keizai Shingikai), an advisory committee to the Prime Minister, to draft a new economic

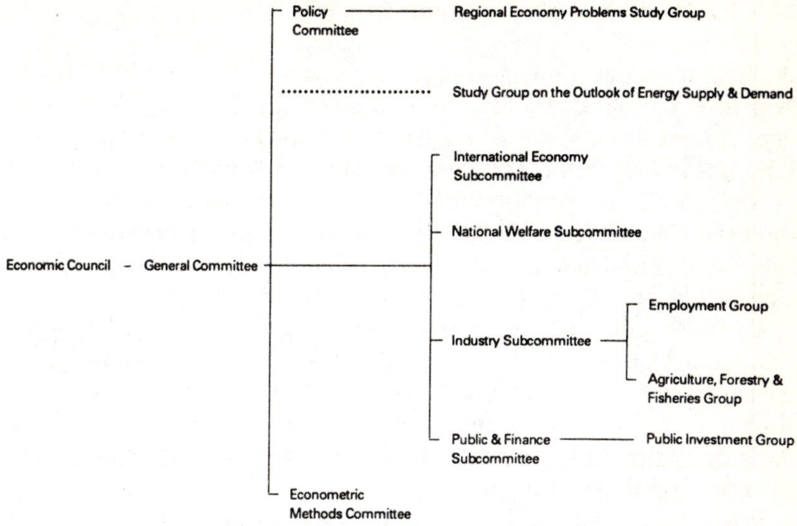

Figure 12.2 Organization of the Economic Council for the 'New Economic and Social Development Seven-year Plan'

Source: Keizai Kikaku-cho (Economic Planning Agency), *Economic Planning in Japan*.

plan. Typically, the Prime Minister indicates only the general purpose of a plan, leaving the details for later discussions.

Second, the Economic Council proceeds to discuss various economic matters and submits a draft of the new plan to the government. This process generally takes from several months to a year. The Economic Council is composed of learned and experienced persons from diverse backgrounds including academics, business, labour, the press and government service. When drafting the economic plan, the Council appoints additional temporary members. In all, more than 200 individuals participate in the drafting process. Figure 12.2 shows the organization of the Economic Council at the time of drafting the 'New Economic and Social Development Seven-year Plan' (1979).

Finally, the Cabinet adopts the draft, and it becomes the official economic plan of the government. Typically, the original draft is approved by the Cabinet without any changes.

12.4.3 The Role of the Economic Council

An important question arises when we consider this process. That is, how is it possible that a draft composed by the Council, an independent committee consisting of private individuals, becomes the official long-term plan of the government? Does this mean that a private group sets the course for long-term economic management? If so, then the Council has considerably broader and greater powers than the Cabinet or Diet. Alternatively, some argue that the Council is simply a puppet controlled by the government.

To address this question we should take into account the Economic Planning Agency, which acts as a coordinator in the plan-making process. On the one hand, the Agency prepares discussion materials for the Council based on member requests. On the other hand, the Agency works to form a consensus among the many departments and agencies in the government.

When the Economic Planning Agency distributes the draft economic plan to all departments and agencies, it receives more than one thousand comments. These comments are discussed and compromises reached. Masahiko Aoki (1981) has hypothesised that each department and agency acts as an 'agent' of an interest group in the society in the planning process. He argues that negotiations among various departments and agencies are regarded as a kind of social bargaining. Based on my experience participating in the planning process, I believe that this is a reasonable hypothesis. We can regard that each member of the Economic Council is as an 'agent' as well as being a private individual. When 'Economic Management within a Global Context' was drafted in 1988, the Economic Council consisted of eight representatives of industry (electric power, construction, electronics, steel, clothing, automobiles, banks and securities), three representatives of labour unions, five academics, one member of a consumers' group, one journalist, and eight former government officials. Labour representatives, for example, participate in the planning process by making policy requests which will benefit labour. After policies have been decided, labour is persuaded to accept the draft.

We can say that in Japan social bargaining is implemented efficiently in the process of drafting the economic plan.

As a result, when the draft is finally submitted to the government, its contents have already been approved by all government organizations. It is wrong to regard the Council as having more power than the Cabinet or the Diet, but it is equally wrong to dismiss it as a puppet.

12.4.4 Information-Sharing in the Planning Process

We can also view economic planning as an information-sharing process.

First, the basic policy stance of the Prime Minister is made public through economic planning. One of the most important roles of the economic plan is to show the long-term economic vision held by the Prime Minister. When a new Prime Minister is nominated, he must come up with new economic targets and policies in a new economic plan. Prime Minister Ikeda drew up the 'National Income Doubling Plan' (1960) officially to show his intention to pursue his campaign promise to double average wages in ten years. Prime Minister Sato came up with the 'Economic and Social Development Plan' in 1967 to express his views on social development. Likewise, Prime Minister Ohira proposed his 'New Economic and Social Development Seven-year Plan' in 1979 in order to implement his 'Rural City Plan' (Den-en Toshi Koso).

The feasibility of each Prime Minister's agenda was reviewed through the planning process by the government and the Economic Council and a more realistic policy package was made public in the form of an economic plan.

Second, information is shared by private companies and the government. In the economic plan, long-term economic projections for the economy's growth rate, industrial structure and the labour market situation are presented.

Of course, the projections in the economic plan are just guidelines. Still, many argue that setting guidelines improves economic growth through so-called announcement effects. Kazuo Sato (1990) explains this effect as follows: when the government forecasts a certain level of economic growth, private companies believe that the growth rate is guaranteed through the use of policy instruments. They set their own targets based on this projection. In the process of setting targets, the officially projected growth rate is taken to be the bottom line of growth, and they try to do better. Consequently, the growth rate achieved turns out to be better than the projection proposed in the economic plan.

Why has the Japanese government so succeeded in gaining the confidence from the private sector? To understand this relationship, we must first that much information is exchanged between the government and private business before plan guidelines are set. When we think about these guidelines, we tend to regard them as government products which are simply handed down to private business. But such notions are wrong. There is a two-way flow of information between the government and private business and a give-and-take attitude on both sides. The government tries to gather information about the actual state of each industry, and private business tries to understand macroeconomic conditions. Thus when guidelines are finally formulated, their basic thrust is already clear to private business.

We must also recall that the Japanese government maintained a so-called time-consistent economic policy by including long-term policy commitments in the economic plan. Blanchard and Fisher (1989) argue that a government which promise long-term commitment to carrying out a policy will produce a better outcome than one which implement economic policies from short-term point of view. Sharing of information and time-consistent economic policy result in private sector confidence in government economic management, stable, long-term expectations and as well as savings and investment behaviour oriented to a long-term perspective.

12.5 CONCLUSION

In conclusion, I would like to answer two questions raised at the beginning of this chapter.

First, how much as Japanese economic planning contributed to the successful economic development occurring in the postwar period?

It is doubtful that economic planning was the main factor in Japanese economic success. The Japanese economy would have been successful without economic planning.

However, economic planning has served as an important institutional framework for managing the national economy in the following manner. First, it compiled important economic information such as long-term economic projections and future direction of economic policies. Second, in the process of planning, economic information was shared by various parties and social bargaining was implemented efficiently. Such information-sharing encouraged confidence in the government and its economic policies.

The second question is whether the Japanese economic planning experience is relevant to the former centrally planned economies.

Naturally, the government and people of each country must develop an economic management system appropriate to their country's stage of economic development.

Here I can only say that with regard to transformation from a centrally planned to a market economy, the Japanese experience between 1945 and 1955 may be suggestive. During the early postwar period, the Japanese government tried to directly control the demand and supply of important materials. At the same time, it tried to make people understand economic conditions by supplying detailed information.

To build an efficient economic management system after the transformation period, the Japanese experience after 1955 may also serve as a useful reference. Japan's experience suggests that economic planning has only a limited role in a market economy. However, it can effectively function as an important institutional framework connecting the government and private economic agents.

Notes

1. Article 1 of the Ordinance to Establish an Economic Stabilization Board (Keizai Antei-honbu-rei).
2. The Economic Stabilization Board (Keizai Antei-honbu), 'Real State of the National Economy' (*Keizai Jisso Hokoku-sho*), June 1947.
3. Foreword by Saburo Okita for the Comprehensive Report on 'Five-Year Plan for Economic Self-Support' (Keizai Jiritsu Go-kanen Keikaku), Jan. 1956.
4. Economic Planning Agency (Keizai Kikaku-cho), 'Economic Management within a Global Context' (Sekai to Tomoni Ikiru Nihon), May 1988, ch. 10, section 1, 'The Plan's Nature and Role'.
5. Economic Planning Agency (Keizai Kikaku-cho), 'New Economic and Social Development Seven-Year Plan' (Shin Keizai Shakai Hatten Nana ka-nen Keikaku), Aug. 1979, Foreword for Reference Material 1, 'The Economic Outlook of F.Y. 1985'.
6. Economic Planning Agency (Keizai Kikaku-cho), Economic Management within a Global Context (Sekaito Tomoni Ikiru Nihon), May 1988, ch. 9, 'The Economy during Restructuring'.
7. Economic Council (Keizai Shingikai), 'Report of Basic Problems of Economic Plan Committee' (Keizai Keikaku Kihon-mondai Kenkyukai Hokoku), 1969.

References

Aoki, Masahiko (1981) 'Keizai Keikaku no Kino Saiko' (Re-thinking the Role of Economic Planning), in *Keizaigaku no Atarashii Nagare* (New Trend in Economics), ed. by Yasusuke Murakami and Koichi Hamada (Tokyo: Toyo Keizai Shinpo-sha).

Blanchard, Oliver Jean and Stanley Fisher (1989) *Lectures on Macroeconomics* (Cambridge, Mass.: MIT Press).

Blumenthal, Tuvia and Chung H. Lee (1985) 'Development Strategies of Japan and the Republic of Korea: A Comparative Study', *The Developing Economies*, September.

Hayashi, Yujiro (1957) *Nihon no Keizai Keikaku* (Japan's Economic Plans) (Tokyo: Toyo Keizai Shinpo-sha).

Keizai Shingikai (Economic Council) (ed.) (1969) *Nihon no Keizai Keikaku* (Japan's Economic Planning).

Keizai Kikaku-cho (Economic Planning Agency) (1988) 'Sengo Keizai Fukko to Keizai Antei-honbu' (Postwar Economic Recovery and the Economic Stabilization Board), mimeo.

Keizai Kikaku-cho (Economic Planning Agency) (1990), *Economic Planning in Japan*, mimeo.

Sato, Kazuo (1990) 'Indicative Planning in Japan', *Journal of Comparative Economics*, vol. 14.

Murrel, Peter (1990) 'Result-Oriented and Process-Oriented Evaluations of Indicative Planning', *Journal of Comparative Economics*, vol. 14.

13 Trade and Capital Liberalization Policies in Postwar Japan

Toru Nakakita

13.1 INTRODUCTION

This chapter has three main aims. First, it outlines the broad process in which international trade and capital liberalization policies were designed and implemented in the postwar period. Second, it analyses this policy framework and its underlying concepts from a theoretical standpoint. Third, it assesses the consequences of reform from a contemporary viewpoint. While the main focus is on international trade policy from the end of the high-growth period, where relevant, policies related to the importation of foreign capital and technology are also touched upon.

Throughout the chapter, several questions with respect to the nature of the postwar economy and Japan's role in an increasingly interdependent global economy are addressed. In particular, as we make a chronological analysis of three important periods in the postwar Japanese economy – the demobilization period, the period of high growth and the current era of internationalization – we seek to answer the following questions: How was Japan able to expand the scope of its private-sector activities and reconstruct its economy following the postwar commercial blockade? How did Japan gain membership to GATT and the IMF and become accepted into the world community? How did Japan improve an industrial and trade structure initially centring on chemical and heavy industries? Finally, what problems does Japan face at present, given the increasing integration of the world economy?

Before beginning our analysis, however, it is perhaps helpful to outline the three major elements of postwar economic development: trade liberalization, capital liberalization and global interdependency. These three elements developed in successive waves.

Through trade liberalization the private sector was able to expand the scope of its economic activities while the nation regained its membership in international society, growing increasingly interdependent with the rest of the world. This process began in a piecemeal fashion: starting with the commercial blockade immediately after the war, it expanded over time as sovereign rights were gradually transferred from the Supreme Commander for the Allied Powers (SCAP) to the Japanese government. The private sector gained further initiative after the setting of a single exchange rate.

In the 1950s, when import restrictions and controls on technological imports were put into place to cope with a shortage of foreign currency, intense competition and the continuous improvement in productivity through innovation resulted. This also made it possible to alleviate the problems created by overpopulation and food shortages. Such developments led to the establishment of the pro-trade argument that Japan, endowed with scant natural resources and a large population, could survive only through the expansion of international trade, while endeavouring to modernize and reform its industrial structure in a flexible way.

Trade liberalization was most actively pursued in the early part of the 1960s in parallel with the high growth policy of the Ikeda cabinet. This policy stance led to the promotion of Japan's status in such international organizations as the International Monetary Fund (IMF) and General Agreement on Tariffs and Trade (GATT), a sharpening of the competitiveness of Japan's exporting industries and, in due course, a growing trade surplus. However, as the 1970s drew near, Japan's enthusiasm for opening its markets rapidly waned, and residual import restrictions that were in violation of GATT regulations remained unchanged. The tendency for Japan to react to pressures from abroad in a passive and untimely manner increased.

When the issue of capital liberalization came to the fore in the latter part of the 1960s, Japan's attitude was characterized by exclusiveness and a deep feeling that such liberalization was harmful to Japan. Liberalization proceeded in stages, pushed by mounting outside pressure, but consistently lacked strong leadership. The delay in capital liberalization contributed to the strengthening of the domestic industrial base, particularly among exporting industries, such as automobiles and electronics. However, it engendered an insular image of Japan abroad.

During the 1980s, Japan rose to the status of economic superpower, and pressures on its markets became even stronger as the global economy became more interdependent. The scope of market opening measures has gone beyond the traditional areas of commodities and services and now includes human exchanges, information, financing, and technology. These developments increasingly blur the line between international and domestic issues, and require a more active promotion of free trade principles and the further opening of its markets on the part of Japan. Likewise, as its relations with East Asian countries continue to expand, Japan is urged to contribute to their economic development by increasing the imports of manufactured goods from these countries.

13.2 THE DEMOBILIZATION PERIOD (1945–54, 1955–60)

The so-called period of demobilization stretches from Japan's defeat in 1945 to the start of the rapid economic growth that began in 1960. This period can be further divided into two sub-periods, that is, the periods before and after 1955. The period before 1955 can be characterized as a time of suspended commerce. Major issues in this period were the reopening of private sector trade, the establishment of a single exchange rate and membership in GATT and the IMF. The latter period, which is characterized as a period of economic recovery and reconstruction, served as a bridge to the period of high economic growth in the 1960s, and was the take-off period for the Japanese economy. As exemplified by the commonly heard phrase, 'the postwar period is over', during the demobilization period economic activities expanded far beyond prewar levels. But in the beginning imports outpaced exports in volume, and Japan suffered from a chronic shortage of foreign currency. A mercantalist trade policy was therefore implemented, and in order to maintain a positive international balance of trade, strict import controls were enforced by means of foreign currency allocation.

13.2.1 Defeat and the Reopening of Foreign Trade

(a) The Beginning of the Occupation: Suspension of Trade

After Japan's defeat in the war, the right to determine important economic activities fell under the strict and direct controls of SCAP. This restriction was stipulated in Article 11 of the Potsdam Declaration and other related documents including the US Administrative Policy vis-a-vis Japan which stated that, without prior permission by the SCAP, no commodities nor products would be allowed to be exported or imported.

As a result, only those imports necessary for the maintenance of a minimum standard of living and social order in the occupied territory were permitted. The basic policy was to export commodities to finance imports. Economic recovery was not one of the immediate goals of the Occupation Forces in Japan; rather, they emphasized democratization and demobilization. Consequently, Japanese trade fell far below prewar levels. For example, in terms of accumulated value, during the period between October 1945 and December 1946, food and cotton accounted for about 90.4 per cent of total imports, while silk and cotton products accounted for 60.2 per cent of total exports. As a result of this situation, Japan continued its extremely heavy dependence on US aid.

Trade mechanisms were managed by the government. Acting under the supervision of occupation forces, the Japanese government purchased goods for export from domestic manufacturers and then exported them. At the same time, the government received goods imported by the occupation forces and distributed them among domestic manufacturers.

The GHQ (General Headquarters) was the primary agent in such foreign trade, and although, the official domestic enforcement agency was the Board of Trade (Boeki-cho), various subordinate groups also were involved in the actual implementation of such trade. Thus, foreign trade activities came under the dual management of the occupation administration and the Japanese government.

This management structure resulted in a great deal of abuse and misuse. First, because of the one-sided representation of the government by the occupation forces in trade contracts, traders were not allowed to engage directly in transactions, nor receive first-hand information on the world market, etc. This resulted in what came to be known as 'blind' trade. Conditions were often coercive and unfair; stockpiles of goods were not sold abroad, and claims could not be made against defective goods imported from abroad through the occupation forces.

Second, the settlement of accounts and the management of foreign reserves were also under the authority of SCAP. While the Occupation administration determined the dollar prices of export goods, it was the Board of Trade (Boeki-cho) that acquired such items from manufacturers at official prices and exported them, paying for them in yen from the Trade Fund Special Account (Boeki Shikin Tokubetsu Kaikei). The official prices were determined by the Price Control Ordinance (Bukka Tosei-rei) and consequently set with no regard to international prices. The conversion factors that were used as standards bore no relationship to the actual value of the goods. Consequently, a system of multiple exchange rates was put into place (Table 13.1). Account settlements were conducted under the authority of the Occupation forces according to the availability of foreign currencies, while domestic settlements were carried out at official prices. Both operations were conducted independently of one another.

This system of multiple exchange rates virtually amounted to a financial subsidy. During this period, Japan's foreign trade balance was in the red, so it was only natural to expect that the yen accounts would be in the black. In fact, there was a deficit in the yen account. Due to the multiple exchange rate system, goods were exported at relatively low prices in dollars terms, whereas imported goods were subject to fairly low yen prices. The government financed the resulting imbalance, thus registering an enormous deficit in the Trade Fund Special Account. This effectively meant setting a high exchange rate for imported goods, while lower rates were applied to goods for export. The multiple exchange rates system served to check price hikes and supported export industries. However, a great discrepancy between exchange rates for imports and exports resulted. The discrepancy was as high as 400 yen even within groups of exported goods, as is shown in Table 13.1, with caustic soda being 200 yen and glass sheet 600 yen, for example. This led to a massive distortion in resource allocations.

From 1947 to the first half of 1949, these financial subsidies were used by Japanese authorities for price adjustment purposes. These subsidies comprised one-quarter of total General Government Expenditure and constituted a heavy financial burden. In addition, the Trade Fund Special Account was in the red, so US aid had to be allocated to finance this deficit. The exchange system was gradually streamlined among given product groups. In order to eliminate these subsidies, arrest inflationary pressures and bring the Japanese economy in line with the rest of the world, it became imperative for the government to strengthen efforts to rationalize the economy.

Table 13.1 Exchange rates for major traded goods (as of 31 January 1949) (yen per dollar)

Imported goods	
Pig iron	67
Lauan (timber)	77
Cotton for domestic use	80
for export	250
Potassic fertilizer	82
Salt	103
Leather, wool	120
Iron ore	125
Raw rubber, phosphate rock	154
Wheat	165
Sugar	177
Cooking coal	178
B type heavy oil	284
Chemicals	200–350
Exported goods	
Caustic soda	200
Iron bars	240
Cotton yarn	250
Cotton cloth	250–420
Staple fibre and rayon, woollen yarn, and canned goods	300
Silk fabrics	300–420
Coal, cement	320
Wood	320–420
Tea	330
Woollen fabrics	350
Raw silk	420
Automobiles	430
Dyes, steel ships	500
Bicycles	510
Radio sets	550
Animal hides	580
Porcelains, glass sheet, mirrors, and celluloid products	600

Note: Import dollar prices were calculated using the CIF, while FOB prices were used for export dollar prices. The statistics for fabrics are those issued on 1 February.

Source: Keizai Antei-honbu (Economic Stabilization Board) *Keizai Hakuzho* (Economic White Paper), 1949.

(b) Partial Demobilization of State-Controlled Trade

Around the end of 1947, gradual changes were made in occupation policies. The focus shifted from demilitarization and democratization to economic reconstruction and a return to the world market. SCAP now sought to speed up Japan's recovery as much as possible and turn it into a bulwark against the spread of communism in Asia. Hence the importance of exports as a mean to attain economic recovery grew, and the resumption of private sector trade and the streamlining of trade procedures were considered concrete measures for promoting the expansion of exports.

In August 1947, private sector trade was partially reopened, but only on the export side. Although the Board of Trade was still the contracting party on the Japanese side, it did allow direct negotiations and dealings between buyers. Thus, company representatives as well as individual buyers began to visit Japan. Nonetheless, private importing was completely banned until 1950.

(c) Establishment of a Single Exchange-Rate System

Once private trade resumed, it soon surpassed that of government trade. In May 1948, business transactions were extended to a significantly wider range of products (Table 13.2), and as transactions with foreign traders progressed, it was increasingly felt that the lack of a link between the yen and foreign currencies made trade transactions difficult. Exchange rates varied according to the products concerned and were distorted by subsidies. Hence, they did not reflect genuine production costs. This meant that traders could benefit from transfer pricing and the arbitrage of different products. At the same time, the Japanese government hoped to eradicate rampant inflation by reducing subsidies. These circumstances, resulted in demands for the introduction of a single exchange rate.[1]

In the spring of 1948 the Young mission, headed by Ralph Young of the US Federal Reserve Board, came to Japan and recommended the establishment of a single exchange rate of 270–330 yen to the US dollar as a step in resolving the economic crisis and bringing about economic reform. But SCAP argued that priority should be given to strengthening the domestic economy, and the proposal was not adopted. Later, under special orders of the US President, Joseph Dodge came to Japan and suggested transferring some of SCAP's authority to the Japanese government. He placed great importance

Table 13.2 Percent of private sector trade in Japan's total exports (based on yen value)

1947	Sep	3.0	1948	Jan	13.0	May	55.0
	Oct	13.0		Feb	31.0	Jun	46.0
	Nov	8.0		Mar	30.0	Jul	54.0
	Dec	11.0		Apr	29.0		

Source: Tsusho Sangyo-sho (Ministry of International Trade and Industry) *Tsusho Sangyo Seisaku-shi* (History of Policies on International Trade and Industry), vol. 4, 1990.

on the establishment of a stable foundation for economic recovery in Japan based on three principles: the support of an 'overbalanced' budget which created fiscal surpluses; the abolition of subsidies to offset price differentials; and the stabilization of foreign exchange rates. Based on these principles, he instituted a policy whose goal it was to actively achieve a strictly balanced budget, based on an exchange rate of ¥360 to the US dollar, which went into effect on 25 April 1949.

The changeover from a regulated, planned economy to a free market economy was accomplished virtually overnight. It is true, however, that on the manufacturing and trade sides, there remained a number of controls, such as those over the allocation of foreign currency, but these were lifted in the early 1960s. The transition in industrial management based on the ¥360 rate, left the Japanese economy exposed to the rough seas of free competition. The exchange rate set at US$1 = ¥360 lasted for 22 years, or until the 'Nixon shock' of August 1971, which forced the revaluation of the yen to ¥308 once the Smithsonian Agreement went into effect in December 1971.

In light of the fact that the Young Report of 1948 had suggested setting the rate at ¥330 to the dollar, the actual rate of US$1 = ¥360 set one year later meant that the yen had a lower value than originally recommended. However, there is some disagreement over whether the ¥360 rate was relatively high, too low or right on target.

The dominant view (supported by Komiya, Kojima, Fujino and Ueda) is that the yen was overvalued, and contributed to import substitution of Japanese industries. Ueda (1985) estimated import and export equations and, based on the assumption of IS balance at full employment and capital mobility came up with an equilibrium rate of ¥600 to the US dollar. Fujino (1988) asserts that 'the purchasing power parity (PPP) of Japan's tradables in 1955, regardless of whether one looks at relative or absolute PPP, should have meant the establishment of a US$1 = ¥450–490 rate. Thus, the ¥360 rate was an overvaluation of the yen'.

In contrast, Shinohara (1989) argues that in 1949 the relative PPP rate (based on 1939 standards) should have been ¥277 to the dollar, the real exchange rate being undervalued by about 20 per cent. He also points out that even if one uses calculations based on the 1973 real equilibrium rate, the ¥360 rate was still approximately 20 per cent undervalued, and that this provided the foundation for export-led growth in postwar Japan.

13.2.2 Framework for 'Industrial Policy'

(a) Import Restrictions as Protectionist Measures

After the establishment of the single exchange rate in 1949, the basic framework for trade and capital transactions was put into place. In December 1949, the Foreign Exchange and Foreign Trade Control Law (Gaikoku Kawase oyobi Gaikoku Boeki Kanri-ho) was enacted, and based on this Law, import and export trade control ordinances were introduced. While the private sector was permitted to import goods relatively freely, foreign exchange activities were still under the control of the government, and the allocation of foreign currency was strictly enforced. Therefore, the Foreign Exchange Law was a ban in principle, with some exceptions being permitted, and was based on institutional relations and practices that had existed before the war.

In 1949 Japan still suffered from a chronic shortage of foreign currency, and it was not until the early 1950s that the Japanese economy attained full employment. Once business was given the opportunity to import and export freely, the international balance of payments went into deficit. Therefore, in order to maintain the external balance, the government had to introduce measures to control imports.

In this regard, however, policy instruments such as tariffs and import controls differ little from each other except that the latter creates rents for import licence holders and increases misallocation of resources if monopolistic power prevails in the domestic market. The Ministry of Finance (Okura-sho: MOF) had the power to decide currency allocation based on supply-and-demand estimates provided by other ministries. The MOF chose to control the settlement of international trade by allocating foreign currency and implementing import controls rather than simply introducing tariffs.[2]

By distributing foreign currency to important industrial sectors, the government attempted to nurture specific domestic industries. Protectionist measures such as the introduction of import controls favoured such domestic industries as machine tools, iron and steel, and automobiles, while priority was given to purchasing the most modern machines, technology and raw materials to be used in the production of exportable items. Allocation was based on export volumes, facilities, market share, etc. Thus, the policy decisions of the government with respect to foreign currency allocation greatly influenced corporate behaviour at this time.[3]

The foreign currency budget, which served as the basis for currency allocation, was no more than a semi-annual estimate of foreign currency payments. No legal requirements for public disclosure were attached to this budget nor was approval required by the Diet. The Ministry of International Trade and Industry (Tsusho Sangyo-sho: MITI) formulated supply-and-demand estimates for various commodities based on its contacts with the relevant industry associations. Based on these estimates, the required volume of import was calculated and then multiplied by the unit import price. This resulted in a fairly precise prediction of import value. It was therefore assumed that import controls could be effectively implemented through the utilization of market information gathered by a government-industry network that had been established in the prewar period.

(b) Foreign Direct Investment in Japan and the Introduction of Technology

The basic policy stance with respect to direct investment in Japan was established in the 1950 Foreign Investment Law (Gaishi-ho). This Law was amended on an *ad hoc* basis and was strictly enforced.

Between 1956 and 1963, yen-based foreign enterprises were allowed to set up operations in Japan, but the establishment of wholly-owned subsidiaries by foreign corporations was allowed only on condition that returns from investments and liquidations would not be transferred to the corporations' home countries. There was particularly active foreign investment in the oil, machinery and chemical industries. Many of the Japanese subsidiaries of leading world enterprises such as Esso, Olivetti and Hoechst, which are still active in Japan, were at this time already reaching 100 per cent foreign ownership.[4]

The technology gap between Japan and the West was very wide at this time. Companies that were able to successfully introduce technology from overseas gained an advantage in domestic competition, and consequently the introduction of foreign technology was an important aspect of competition. MITI placed priority on the importation of advanced technology that could be used in the improvement of productivity and the rationalization of industry. Through administrative guidance (*gyosei shido*) MITI helped companies to negotiate, with a view that the industry could reduce patent fees and that MITI could supervise the diffusion of imported technology.

However, this is not to say that the criteria for importing technology were written in stone. A great deal of discretion was permitted in the implementation of such regulations. Financial assistance was given for the purchase of certain officially designated, high-quality Western goods. But such assistance was provided only for the purchase of machines to be used as prototypes for the domestic manufacture of equivalent machinery. In fact, the trial manufacture of such products in Japan was also subsidized.

In this manner, the postwar Japanese government was quite flexible in granting permission for the import of technology that would help strengthen productivity, but direct foreign investment that might result in foreign participation in the management of Japanese enterprises was prohibited as a general rule in order to protect domestic entrepreneurs. These restrictions on capital investment by foreign companies were in strong contrast to the warm reception and tax exemptions given by some countries in postwar Europe, such as Italy and the Benelux countries, although France and other nations had restrictions similar to those in Japan.

Thus, Japan's postwar trade and industrial policies were based on two protectionist measures: foreign exchange controls which limited foreign capital investment and the import of raw materials, and the Foreign Investment Law which promoted the importation of technology.

The above trade policies were coordinated with domestic manufacturing policies, such as the laws concerning the promotion of specific industries and tax deductions for certain industries. The outbreak of the Korean War in 1950 and the American special procurements that followed pulled Japan out of the recession. In particular, industrial production and investment dramatically surged to meet the demand of US troops deployed in Korea. These developments had a major impact on the formulation of Japan's policy framework during the latter half of the 1950s.

(c) The Trade vs. Domestic Development Argument

As the nation strove towards rapid economic recovery, it was natural that economists and policy-makers were engaged in an intense debate over appropriate policy adjustments. On one hand, a case for domestic development was forwarded by prominent economists such as Arisawa (1950) and Tsuru, who argued that while international trade was important, the nation should be wary of becoming overly dependent on the promotion of foreign trade. They based their argument on certain conditions existing at that time: an inadequate external demand, a volatile world situation characterized by East-West conflict, progress in production technologies in Asia, and the concentration of wealth in the US. Such conditions, they argued, mandated that high priority should be given to the development of domestic industries. In their view, only through domestic development could the nation attain a higher standard of living.

On the other hand, pro-traders such as Nakayama (1953) and others argued that Japan's economy would be bolstered by the expansion of external trade. As exemplified by the experience of Britain after the Industrial Revolution, the only way for Japan, an island nation with poor natural resources and a large population, to sustain its existence would be through the promotion of international trade. The fact that Japan was able to achieve rapid economic development from the Meiji period on, despite unfavourable initial conditions, demonstrated its superior ability to absorb foreign technologies. Thus, Japan should aim to develop through an expansion of its trade with the rest of the world.

In short, an expansion in exports would bring about economic recovery. However, the essence of this pro-trade argument is not necessarily in line with current notions of free trade. Essentially, the pro-trade view advocated in the 1950s was that economic development should be promoted through the expansion of exports based on the theory of dynamic comparative advantage. In the end, the pro-traders won but as such policies had a strong mercantilist bent, and because they resulted in a slowing of import liberalization, they became a major source of overseas trade friction in later years.

The reconstruction of Japan's export business was considered so urgent that there was a general feeling of 'export or die'. One important issue at the time was how to assure a steady supply of cheap raw materials, as bottlenecks occurred all too frequently. It was also felt that the domestic supply-side had to be strengthened for the sake of economic reconstruction. There was strong argument for the maintenance of foreign currency reserves as well as the acquisition of sufficient foreign currency to eliminate such bottlenecks. Even after the Japanese trade balance went into the black in the latter half of the 1960s, the government continued to rely on these policy measures. Naturally, this played a major role in slowing the liberalization of trade and capital and the revaluation of the yen in later years.

The fear of external deficits and the stubborn avoidance of borrowing are also apparent. Theoretically, had trade deficits become a problem, Japan would have had two equally valid options: draining foreign reserves or expanding overseas financing. The basic mindset of those in power, however, was that it was better to expend foreign currency reserves than to accept loans from abroad. This can be interpreted as an expression of their intention to avoid losing a free hand in the economy as a result of an inability to pay overseas debts.[5]

With the opportunities stemming from the outbreak of the Korean War in 1950, Japan's export, production, investment, and employment all increased rapidly, and a strong base for high economic growth was established. The inflow of foreign currency as a result of special procurements made by the US during the Korean War was especially effective in freeing Japan from the restrictions of international trade. In 1951 the Economic White Paper (*Keizai Hakusho*) declared 'the postwar period is now over'.

From 1955 to 1960 Japanese exports increased at an annual rate of 14 per cent in volume terms, and the growth rate continued to rise in the succeeding five years when trade liberalization was substantially carried out. Looking at the composition of exports, the shift from light industrial goods, such as foodstuffs and textiles to heavy industrial goods, such as machines, chemicals, and metals, was particularly striking (Table 13.3). Japan became internationally competitive based mainly on its heavy and chemical industries. Foreign currency restraints gradually relaxed as a result of the progress brought about by the pursuit of the heavy industrialization that also became the driving force in growth.

13.2.3 The Problem of GATT Membership

Given the above-mentioned domestic arrangements, the greatest problem for Japan was gaining membership in GATT (General

Table 13.3 Change in value of major export goods

	A	*B*	*C*	*D*	*E*	*F*	*G*	*H*
1950/55	18.2	21.9	11.8	44.2	15.1	–	28.7	–
1955/60	14.1	14.7	10.3	17.7	6.6	4.8	24.4	99.4
1960/65	17.9	2.6	5.7	28.1	28.3	31.6	31.7	38.0
1965/70	15.1	6.8	7.1	22.9	13.3	12.7	21.4	41.1
1970/75	9.9	–7.8	0.9	6.4	8.9	10.8	15.0	19.8
1975/80	9.2	4.3	0.4	1.7	4.1	0.2	12.7	17.4
1980/85	7.2	–5.3	2.9	4.6	0.9	0.9	6.1	4.3
1985/90	2.9	–2.1	–4.7	7.4	–8.5	–1.0	3.6	–0.3

Note: A = Total; B = Foodstuffs; C = Textiles; D = Chemicals; E = Non-ferrous metals and metals; F = Iron and steel; G = Machinery and equipment; H = Automobiles.
Each figure shows annual growth rate based on volume indexes.

Sources: Tsuruta (1982), and extrapolations (from 1980) based on Okura-sho (Ministry of Finance) *Gaikoku Boeki Gaikyo* (The Summary Report, Trade of Japan).

Agreement on Tariffs and Trade). GATT membership was important symbolically as it showed that Japan had once again become a member of the international community. It was also an important step in the broadening of Japan's export frontiers: no longer could Japan practise trade under unfair conditions – it now had to participate in international trade based on non-discriminatory principles.

Beginning in late 1947 and early 1948, the United States actively supported the establishment of Japan as a trading nation, while advocating Japan as an anti-communist stronghold amidst the turbulence of the cold war. The Reciprocal Trade Agreements Act was extended in June 1954 and provided the legal foundation for the opening of tariff negotiations that were the precondition for Japan's entry into GATT.

However, European countries, especially Great Britain, were strongly opposed to Japan's membership in GATT. Their opposition was rooted in Japan's prewar policy, particularly its policy after the 1931 gold embargo. Taking advantage of the undervalued yen, Japan's exports to Western nations and British colonies greatly expanded. Politically, Japan's troop movement overseas, symbolized by the Manchurian Incident of 1931, helped reinforce the impression overseas that Japan was not interested in preserving international order and would not abide by international rules. The dominant thinking in the West was that dumping was possible due to low wages and poor working conditions in Japan. In addition, Britain attempted to prevent Japan's postwar return to the international community by speaking out against Japan's membership in international organizations such as the ILO (Patterson, 1966).

In October 1952, Japan applied for GATT membership but, due to European opposition, was not accepted. Japan finally became a provisional member in October 1953. Although this allowed Japan the right to air its views, it could not vote nor participate in tariff negotiations.

Full membership came in September 1955, after which the rights and duties of GATT membership applied to Japan in regard to economic relations with other member countries, except for those Contracting Parties invoking Article 35.

Article 35 enabled those countries with strong reservations about Japan's membership in GATT as a Contracting Party to nullify Japan's entry into GATT. With Britain at the forefront, 14 of the 34 members at that time, including France, Belgium, Australia, New Zealand, and Cuba invoked the Article.

Japan immediately called for the retraction of Article 35 in the General Assembly held in October of the same year. In subsequent years, Japanese diplomacy concentrated its efforts on this objective. The first step toward the recision of Article 35 was taken in response to Japan's growing ties with Asian and South American countries. Japan had to promote import liberalization in the earlier part of the 1960s, but as attitudes towards Japan gradually improved several nations signed treaties with Japan, including the Japan–France Commercial Treaty, the Japan–Britain Treaty on Commerce and Navigation, and the 1963 Japan–Australia Commercial Agreement Protocol. These countries then promised to retract Article 35.

However, Japan had to accept safeguard clauses, import restrictions by the West and promise to implement voluntary export restraints. After Article 35 was rescinded, Japan had to deal with quantitative restrictions (QR) placed on Japanese exports. Hence, even today negative perceptions of Japan by European seem to remain fundamentally unchanged.

13.3 THE PERIOD OF HIGH GROWTH (1960–70)

Against the backdrop of a favourable international environment, Japan achieved a high level of economic growth as well as a high degree of industrialization. Based on the Bretton Woods System, world trade volume increased greatly, and the US, with its effective demand expanding as a consequence of the New Economics, increased its economic influence around the world. The prices of primary commodities, such as crude oil and iron ore, continued to fall. From 1960 to 1968, the Japanese economy realized an average 10.2 per cent growth in real GDP, and heavy industries, such as steel, chemicals, and heavy electrical equipment, continued to increase their share in the industrial structure. The expansion of Japanese manufactured exports gave strength to demands from abroad for Japan to liberalize its trade, and trade and capital were eventually liberalized. Furthermore, Japan's position in international organizations such as GATT and the IMF was visibly upgraded during this period.

13.3.1 Substantial Progress in Trade Liberalization (Promotion to Article 11 and Article 8 Positions)

(a) Background for Trade Liberalization

Ever since its entry into GATT in 1955, Japan had been an Article 12 country (a country permitted to impose import restrictions for balance of payments reasons). But with the expansion of manufactured exports and a favourable trade balance, Japan could no longer avoid being designated an Article 11 country, or a country which, in principle, is not allowed to implement import restrictions for balance of payments reasons.

Pressure to open the Japanese market mounted sharply toward the end of the 1950s. Initially, such pressure came from the US, which, beginning in 1958, began to experience a reversal in its trade balance. Certain sectors of American industry, such as textiles, increasingly lost their ability to compete with Europe, Japan, and some parts of Asia.

In light of this change, the US requested that other member nations liberalize their import markets. At the General Assembly held in Tokyo in October 1959, the US Undersecretary of State,

Douglas Dillon, stressed that 'there is no longer any justification for import restrictions on goods from dollar areas because of trade balance difficulties', and threatened that the US was prepared to resort to retaliatory measures if Japan did not abolish its strict import restrictions.

During this period progress was made in restoring currency convertibility in Europe. As Europe's economic recovery progressed, exports expanded, and their trade accounts improved. In February 1961, West Germany, Italy, and Britain became GATT Article 11 countries and were obliged to abolish import restrictions.

In contrast, Japan's liberalization ratio was only 16 per cent when it joined the GATT, and even in 1959 the ratio hovered around 26 per cent.[6] Furthermore, Japan still had strict exchange controls based on its foreign currency allocation system. This sparked strong criticism from the US and others, and pressure was put on Japan to liberalize imports.

(b) Import Liberalization Policies under the Ikeda Cabinet

In June 1960, the Ikeda Cabinet decided on a 'Trade and Capital Liberalization Plan', which set the framework for succeeding import liberalization policies. The plan was designed to raise the liberalization ratio from 41 per cent in April of that year to 80 per cent within three years. It was thought that if the liberalization of oil and coal was possible, it could be brought up to 90 per cent.

During that period, the liberalization of imports meant simply the substitution of import controls with import tariffs. The import duty burden rate went up substantially after 1960 (Table 13.4). Each item was categorized according to the timing of its liberalization. The time period of implementation could be divided into four phases: (i) immediate application, (ii) applicable within three years, (iii) applicable after three years, (iv) non-applicable. The rate of tariff for each item depended on the timing of its liberalization.

More specifically, whereas the duty rates on industrial materials were substantially lowered, the rate of tariffs imposed on agricultural products (powdered low-fat milk, butter, beans, etc.) and on manufactured products (machine tools, etc.) were raised.

To help cushion the impact of import liberalization, the tariff quota system as well as reclassification of items were introduced.

As mentioned above, liberalization was carried out in phases. During the first half of the liberalization process, the plan of liber-

Table 13.4 Customs duty burden rates of developed nations

	Japan	*US*	*EC*	*West Germany*	*France*	*Italy*
1956	3.2	5.4	–	7.1	5.6	8.1
1960	6.6	7.5	–	6.6	5.5	7.6
1965	7.3	6.8	–	4.1	6.2	6.8
1970	6.9	5.7	7.4	5.9	5.8	7.5
1975	2.9	3.6	5.0	4.1	3.0	(2.8)
1980	2.6	3.1	2.6	(4.0)	(2.3)	(1.8)
1985	2.6	3.6	2.7	–	–	–
1988	3.4	3.8	3.9	–	–	–

Note: Customs duty burden rate is defined as the ratio of tariff revenues to total import values (or to import values of taxed commodities).

Source: Komiya (1988), p. 181, and further supplemented Original data from Okura-sho (Ministry of Finance), *Zaisei Kin'yu Tokei Geppo* (Monthly Bulletin of Financial Statistics).

alization listed products to be liberalized. As time progressed, only products not to be liberalized came to be listed and the tempo quickened, particularly after 1963.

Amidst this general import liberalization, Japan's liberalization of oil imports was especially important, reducing the degree of dependence on domestically produced coal, while increasing the import of crude oil, particularly during the world oil exploration boom in the 1960s. By liberalizing oil imports, Japan set itself on a course of high growth, fuelled by a large supply of cheap energy from overseas. Pro-trade policy had become firmly established.

It was necessary to substantially raise the duties on oil in order to protect the 'setting-sun' domestic coal industry, but as this would lead to a large increase in energy costs throughout Japanese industry, it proved to be a major road block to full-scale heavy industrialization. After a long debate, crude oil imports were finally liberalized, but duties on crude oil were simultaneously raised to lessen the price differential between imported crude oil and domestic coal.

As Japan's petroleum imports increased, domestic coal production was rationalized and declined thereafter. The 1973 petroleum import volume had, by 1955 standards, increased 28 times, and the percentage of total primary energy consumption that it occupied went from 20 per cent in 1955 to 80 per cent in 1973.

(c) *The Significance of Import Liberalization*

While the liberalization of trade was driven by strong pressure from abroad, the Ikeda Cabinet that had put forth the 'National Income Doubling Plan (Kokumin Shotoku Baizo Keikaku)' reacted positively to the pressure. The liberalization plan was a reflection of the strong determination to gear the economy towards a more open system. Ikeda argued that if Japan wished to join the ranks of advanced nations, and if there was to be any hope for the long-term development of Japan in the international community, then liberalization policies were just as vital as high-growth policies.

There was, however, a sense of insecurity and deeply rooted opposition to the liberalization of imports in the business community. Those in political, business, and bureaucratic circles who had become accustomed to the protectionism that had lasted for a 30-year period beginning with the blockade initiated in 1931 and continuing through the war, defeat and afterwards, strongly feared that a massive flow of cheap, high-quality foreign products would deal a deadly blow to domestic industries. However, in the autumn of 1961 strong pressure to liberalize came from the IMF authorities, and liberalization plans were put into effect a year ahead of schedule. As a result, liberalization proceeded at high speed, and by August 1963 the liberalization ratio had reached 92 per cent.

With the realization of import liberalization, a full-fledged return to international society was made possible, and the framework for entry into the rank of advanced nations was set. In February 1962, Japan was promoted to GATT Article 11 status, and in April 1964 became an IMF Article 8 country and joined the Organization for Economic Cooperation and Development (OECD). Because the foreign currency allocation system was found to be in violation of Article 8 of the IMF agreement, it was abolished.

The opportunities afforded by trade liberalization contributed to domestic competition. Companies in the major industrial sectors rushed to complete mass production systems, and there was more active investment in production facilities. These efforts resulted in an expansion of the domestic market and were the driving force behind continued productivity improvements.

Thus, Japan's import liberalization greatly expanded in the first half of the 1960s. This trend gained further impetus with the tariff reduction resulting from Japan's participation in the GATT Kennedy Round in the mid-1960s. However, the liberalization of the import of

Table 13.5 Change in residual import restrictions[1]

	Total	(A)	(B)	Major items of import liberalization
1964	123	–	–	Sorghum, lemons, lead and zinc ores, ammonium sulphate, colour TVs, bulldozers
1965	122	–	–	Passengers cars
1966	124[2]	–	–	Powdered cocoa, man-made filaments
1968	121	53	68	Cosmetics, alloy tools
1969	118	50	68	Glass, industrial sewing machines
1970	90	35	55	Wine, margarine, typewriters, boilers, machine tools, dynamos, penicillin
1971	40	12	28	Whisky, black tea, pork
1972	33[3]	9	24	Ham and bacons
1973	31	8	23	Dates, high-quality calculating machines
1974	29	7	22	Malt, integrated circuit
1975	27	5	22	Computers, peripheral equipment and components
1986	23	1	22	Animal skins, its processed products
1989	21	1	20[4]	Processed cheese, tomato
1990	17	1	16[5]	Non-aromatic juice, fruit puree and its paste, preparations of beef, canned pineapples
1991	15	1	14[5]	Beef, oranges
1992	14	1	13[5]	Orange juice

[1] Items such as rice (which is subject to the staple food control system), monopoly goods, and arms and ammunition are excluded, since they are exempt from obligatory import liberalization under the GATT.
[2] Because of reclassifications in May 1966, the number of items changed.
[3] Because of reclassifications in April 1972, the number of items changed.
[4] Classification was based on the four-digit CCN until 1987. However, since 1988 the four-digit base HS has been in use, the number of items has not been publicly available except through MITI reports.
[5] This number excludes partial liberalization of saccharid.
(A) = manufactured goods, (B) = agricultural goods.

Sources: Tsusho Sangyo-sho (Ministry of International Trade and Industry), *Tsusho Hakusho* (White Paper on MITI), various years; and other MITI documents.

synthetic fibres, machine tools, passenger cars, and computers was postponed until after 1965. The liberalization of items such as agricultural products was also delayed (Table 13.5).

13.3.2 Progress in Capital Liberalization

(a) General Background of Capital Liberalization

Entry in the OECD in 1964 brought with it responsibility for carrying out capital liberalization. At the time Japan obtained membership, it held reservations on 18 of 37 items of the OECD liberalization code, this number being as large as that of Spain. European countries had begun to implement capital liberalization more than ten years earlier but as there was no visible progress in Japan's liberalization of its capital, outside pressure mounted.

Beginning in 1965, Japan began to show trade surpluses with the US and the following year showed a surplus in global trade. Because of this, the OECD in its periodic examination urged Japan to remove these reservations, and the US began to make more strident requests for Japan to carry out capital liberalization. In the 1965 Fourth Meeting of the Japan–US Committee on Trade and Economic Affairs, for example, capital liberalization was an important issue and its activation was strongly urged.

At that time, with the exception of the views of a few scholars, the dominant attitude with respect to capital liberalization, particularly among business and bureaucratic circles, as well as the mass media, was that Japan should take steps to avoid an 'invasion' by foreign enterprises that were overwhelmingly superior in capital and technology (the 'Second Coming of the Black Ships' argument). It was argued that Japan should push for the reorganization of domestic industry and exploit economies of scale to improve the international competitiveness of Japanese firms against the technological superiority of the US.

Komiya (1967a,b), however, argued that foreign direct investment is the transfer of managerial resources across national borders, and that the essence of the problem was, properly speaking, the growth of firms and their entry into markets. Consequently, he argued that in those areas with future development possibilities that were not yet fully exploited firms should aggressively and actively pursue market entry. He disagreed with the proposition that administrative guidance should be used to limit the market power of foreign firms, and instead emphasized that the correct application, based on non-discriminatory principles, of the Anti-Monopoly Law (Dokusen Kinshi-ho) would be sufficient to cope with the situation.

Nevertheless, the great majority of people focused their energies on raising the ratio of Japanese-owned capital, devising methods for stabilizing stockholdings and encouraging an amalgamation of large domestic corporations as a means of preventing takeovers.

(b) Liberalization of Direct Investment in Japan

In July 1967, the Cabinet outlined its 'Fundamental Policy towards the Liberalization of Direct Investment in Japan'. Thirty-three industries were categorized as Number I industries (up to 50 per cent foreign capital participation permitted) and 17 were designated as Number II industries (permission for 100 per cent foreign capital ownership). This represented, a step towards partial liberalization and the removal of extensive restrictions.

In the same vein, the Second and Third Liberalizations (March 1969 and September 1970 respectively) were carried out in stages. Under these liberalizations, industries such as the automobile industry were allowed up to 100 per cent foreign ownership. The Fourth Liberalization, which took place in August 1971, took a new form as it included a 'negative list' indicating those industries which were not yet liberalized. Nonetheless, strong dissatisfaction was expressed by the US because the computer industry was excluded from liberalization.

In May 1973 after the Fifth Liberalization was launched, only five non-liberalized industries remained and limitations on ownership by foreign firms had been put to an end. As far as the computer industry was concerned, 50 per cent ownership was permitted from August 1974, and by December 1975, it was completely liberalized. This meant that capital liberalization had been completed in ten years.

In December 1980, a new foreign exchange law was enacted. Under this law foreign exchange transactions were liberalized in principle, and the basic emphasis shifted from the 'prohibition of foreign transactions with exceptions' to 'freedom of transactions with exceptions'.

(c) The Significance of Capital Liberalization

What significance and impact did foreign exchange controls on inward direct investment and subsequent capital liberalization have on the Japanese economy?

First, Japan's import restrictions were designed to protect infant industries. In cases like Japan's where a large domestic market exists, production costs are expected to decline sharply once domestic production gets into full swing under the protection of import restrictions. The private sector is also expected to be strongly motivated to expand production and sustain itself even after import restrictions are lifted.

Table 13.6 shows a comparison of two industries: automobiles and computers. Both industries had already strengthened their domestic production bases to a large extent, and, after liberalization was

Table 13.6 Trade and capital liberalization

(1) Automobiles

	(A)	*(B)*	
1960	4.2		Import liberalization of buses and trucks (previously, import quotas with 40% tariff rates)
1965	14.5	40(35)	*Import liberalization of passenger cars*
1967		↓	Completion of the GATT Kennedy Round
1968		↓	US–Japan automobile negotiations
1969		36(17)	Business tie-up between Mitsubishi and Chrysler
		↓	Cabinet decision on the capital liberalization of automobiles beginning in Oct. 1971
1970	20.5	20(17)	Decision on advancing the timing of capital liberalization to the spring of 1971
		↓	
		↓	Business tie-ups with Toyo-Kogyo and Ford, Isuzu and GM
		↓	
1971		10(10)	*Capital liberalization (up to 50% ownership)*
		↓	Import liberalization of automobile engines
1975	40.0	↓	Complete capital liberalization of automobile industry
1978	50.9	0(0)	

Note: (A) and (B) show the export ratios and tariff rates for passenger cars, respectively. The figures in brackets denote the tariff rates on large-sized cars.

(2) Computers and integrated circuits

	(C)	*(D)*	
1971	–	3	Capital liberalization of the IC industry (up to 50%)
1972	–	3	Import liberalization of peripheral equipment, excluding memory chips and terminals
1973	2	3	Import liberalization of ICs for less than 200 elements
1974	5	4	Import liberalization of ICs for more than 200 elements
			Complete capital liberalization of IC industry
			Capital liberalization of computers (up to 50% ownership)
1975	11	6	*Complete capital liberalization of computer industry*
			Import liberalization of computers, memories, and terminals
1976	12	7	*Complete capital liberalization of the software industry*
1979	28	7	Balance of trade for semiconductors becomes positive
1980	32	10	
1981	29	15	Balance of trade for computers becomes positive
1982	34	21	Tariffs on semiconductors lowered (bilaterally with US)
1985	32	33	Removal of tariffs on semiconductors (bilaterally with US)

Note: (C) and (D) denote the export ratios for semiconductors and computers, respectively.

launched, were able to rapidly expand their exports to become major exporting industries. The industrial policy followed by MITI sought to delay liberalization as much as possible amidst growing pressures. While providing a grace period to the industries concerned, MITI tried to create a consensus on the timing of liberalization. To this extent, it may be argued that MITI played a role in nurturing domestic industry by limiting imports.

Nevertheless, it should be recognized that the protection of domestic industries cannot account for every case of postwar economic development in major industries. There are numerous cases where firms gained a competitive edge on their own, such as in the electronics industry (colour TVs, audiovisual machines, VTRs) and other machinery industries (communications equipment, and robots). Conversely, industries such as petrochemicals and aluminium could not improve their competitiveness, in spite of heavy government protection. The rice industry is an example of outright failure to grow. This demonstrates the crucial importance of basic factors such as the spirit of entrepreneurship, a stable supply of imported technology and its appropriate application, the availability of a large skilled labour force. Therefore, government policy merely supplemented these factors, playing an auxiliary role.[7]

Second, the postponement of liberalization seems to have helped strengthen domestic industries, but it also led to a worsening of international economic relations. The protracted liberalization of strategic industries, such as computers and passenger cars, by such measures as limiting foreign ownership to 50 per cent or cross-holding of company stocks, has given rise to the present-day image of Japan as an exclusive country. Had even a few multinational companies been permitted to enter the Japanese market earlier overseas operations could have actively been carried out with the Japanese market as a bulwark, thus alleviating the economic frictions of today.

Third, with the progress in capital liberalization, MITI's power to intervene and control private sector activities declined. Toward the end of the 1960s, when the criticisms against the gigantic merger of Yawata Steel Corporation (Yawata Seitetsu) and Fuji Steel Corporation (Fuji Seitetsu) in 1968, and the problem of environmental pollution, came to the fore, this authoritative style of administration came to a dead stop. The idea of encouraging international competitiveness solely based on economies of scale also gradually receded. Instead, industrial policy was now geared towards supporting market mechanisms. Under these circumstances, MITI has sought out a new role by attaching more importance to private sector initiatives, providing recommendations, and assessing prospects and suggesting directions.

13.4 THE INTERNATIONALIZATION OF THE JAPANESE ECONOMY AND THE RISING ECONOMIC SUPERPOWER (1976–80, 1980–90)

In the late 1970s and early 1980s, when Japan's share in the world GNP was reaching approximately 10 per cent, a small-economy mentality was no longer based on reality. During this period, a series of dramatic events shook the world trading system, including the collapse of the Bretton Woods System, two oil shocks, and the worldwide spread of stagflation. Despite these crises, the Japanese economy was able to continue to grow by conserving energy, improving productivity growth through quality control, and moving towards a higher value-added and more information-oriented industrial structure. Its macroeconomy maintained high performance and its role in the world economy steadily increased.

Meanwhile trade relations with the US and European countries increasingly worsened and Japan's policy-makers were forced to concentrate their efforts on the resolution of trade friction. Despite moves to introduce voluntary export restraints and to further open its market, Japan's trade surpluses, particularly that with the US, continued to grow globally. The fact that in Japan liberalization proceeded only as a consequence of outside pressure provoked strong criticism. Given the ongoing trend towards the integration of the world economy, strong leadership commensurate with Japan's economic strength was now badly needed.

13.4.1 The Revaluation of the Yen and the Progress of Import Liberalization

After Japan began to ease up on efforts to liberalize trade and capital policies in the late 1960s, its trade surplus grew sharply, foreign reserves continued to increase, and the authorities were finally freed from foreign reserve constraints.

Despite these trends, Japan maintained high tariffs for many imported items, including passenger cars, computers and other manufactured products. Residual import restrictions had been placed on as many as 121 product categories as of 1968 (Table 13.5).

To cope with its growing trade deficits with Japan, the US government requested the holding of trade negotiations with Japan, aimed at the removal of import restrictions. As a result of ongoing trade negotiations, and mounting pressures from outside, Japan's import restrictions, mainly those on manufactured products, steadily declined in number. The liberalization of Japan's outward direct investment was launched in 1968, and continued until the completion of the fourth liberalization in 1972.

Despite these efforts, Japan's accelerating trade surpluses could not be arrested. In 1969 monetary policy was tightened to check inflationary pressures, leading to increased trade surpluses. In retrospect, and according to the policy assignment theory, exchange rates should have been manipulated to correct the fundamental disequilibrium in the balance of payments. But in government and business circles, even discussion of changes in the exchange rate was taboo. Therefore, in order to avoid upward revaluation, the government attempted to cope with circumstances by lowering import tariff rates, expanding the size of import quotas, and improving the generalized system for preferences (GSP).

In August 1971, US President Nixon announced the New Economic Programme, which included the suspension of the convertibility of the US dollar into gold, the imposition of import surcharges, and other macroeconomic policy measures designed to contain US domestic inflation. This move pushed the world economy into a period of managed floating exchange rates, marking the end of the Bretton Woods System. Nixon's announcement came as a shock to the Japanese business community, which had been prepared to defend to the death the ¥360 rate. In December of that year, the Smithsonian Accord was reached, setting a new exchange rate of ¥308 to the dollar. Because this new exchange rate was difficult to sustain, it was finally discarded in February 1973, and a full-fledged floating system was introduced.

13.4.2 The Oil Crises and the Conversion of the Industrial Structure

The two oil crises had a strong impact on the Japanese economy, particularly on the heavy and chemical industries, which had greatly depended on imported oil during the period of high growth. However, Japan responded by introducing stringent measures, practising energy and resource conservation and carrying out thorough rationalization. These measures resulted in a sharp decline in energy inputs in manufacturing industries and eventually reduced the volume of imported crude oil.[8]

Accordingly, the Japanese economy began to rely more on higher value-added industries, particularly automobiles, electronics, machine tools and other processing and assembling industries. This was due largely to a technological advancement taking place on the shop-floor, including total quality control (TQC), automation, and electronic manufacturing techniques. In the meantime, heavy industrial sectors, including aluminium, cement, and paper and pulp, lost their competitive edge with the ascendancy of the Asian Newly Industrializing Economies (ANIEs). Adjustment policy measures were implemented for 'structurally depressed industries'; including the coordinated scrapping of excess production capacities, the creation of a special guarantee fund, and the formation of cartels among such industries. Internationally, voluntary export restraints were requested of neighbouring countries in East Asia, and tariff quotas were introduced for aluminium, but there were no outright protective measures introduced. The guidelines drawn up by the OECD for positive adjustment policy (PAP) were essentially followed, though certain difficulties were encountered.

The Japanese economy recovered from the damage caused by the oil crises, and in the 1980s, as the price of crude oil fell, its economic position was further strengthened. After the late 1970s, Japan's manufactured exports to European countries increased noticeably, and this led to serious trade frictions with the European Community (EC).

It was in this environment that Japan participated actively in the GATT Tokyo Round which began in September 1973. This Round coincided with a slow-down of the world economy affected by the oil crisis, making negotiations difficult. For its part, however, Japan offered to implement an average 50 per cent reduction of its tariffs for industrial products, to expedite the implementation of this reduction and agreed to various codes related to non-tariff barriers.

Despite these efforts, protectionism gained momentum. Restraints were resorted to one after the other in such products as colour TVs, passenger cars, VTRs, etc. These restrictive measures were introduced as temporary measures, but once applied, they not only remained, but were intensified each time they were renewed.

13.4.3 American Protectionism and the Further Opening of Japanese Markets

In the first half of the 1980s, protectionism gained momentum, especially in the US Congress. The American government introduced the concept of 'fair trade', and thereby shifted the focus from 'equal opportunity' to 'equal results'. Accordingly, the focus of the demands on Japan shifted from import controls to improved access to the Japanese market and guarantees of import expansion.

Import expansion guarantees provided for a certain market share on a reciprocal basis, and in cases where this commitment was not adhered to, the US threatened to enforce the 'Super 301' of the 1988 Omnibus Trade Act which states that trading partners can be forced to open their market by retaliatory actions.

However, such pressure was applied in order to remove import restrictions, including non-tariff barriers (such as distribution problems and *keiretsu*), as well as high tariff rates.[9] The Market-Oriented Sector-Selective (MOSS) approach to Japan that began in 1985 was an attempt to examine trade barriers in four areas (telecommunications, pharmaceutical products, medical and electric equipment, and forest products) and to negotiate away those barriers deemed unnecessary based on the principle of reciprocity. The Japan–US Structural Impediments Initiative (SII) that began in September 1989 had similar aims and discussions centered on major issues such as *keiretsu* and exclusive business practices.

13.4.4 New Concerns in Opening Japan's Market

With the exception of the period during the two oil crises, Japan's balance of payments continued to show an enormous surplus, and its share of world GNP increased from 6 per cent in 1970 to 11.8 per cent in 1986. In addition, while Japan became the world's largest creditor nation in 1985, the US became the world's largest debtor nation. Moreover, with the progress in detente, the Soviet Union seemed less and less a potential enemy, while Japan was increasingly viewed as a serious competition to American interests.

The 1986 Maekawa Report (formally, the Report prepared by the Advisory Group on Economic Structural Adjustment for International Harmony) argued that the expanding current account surplus was dangerous, and recommended the correction of this trend as a middle-term policy target. For Japan, which had made the

Table 13.7 Ratio of manufactured imports to nominal GDP

	Japan	*US*	*Canada*	*W. Germany*	*France*	*UK*	*Italy*
1975	2.4	3.4	15.5	10.3	9.0	12.2	8.0
1980	3.0	4.8	17.1	13.3	11.7	15.0	10.9
1985	3.0	6.4	19.1	15.6	12.8	16.6	11.0
1989	3.7	7.2	18.6	17.1	16.2	18.9	12.2

Source: Nihon Boeki Shinko-kai (JETRO), 'Trends in Japan's Manufactured Imports', 1990.

strengthening of its international competitiveness its primary policy objective, throughout the postwar period, this represented an historical change in fundamental policy.[10]

By the end of the Tokyo Round in April 1979, the average Japanese tariff rate was one of the lowest among the developed nations and accordingly by 1985 the customs tariff burden ratio had declined to around 2.5 per cent (Table 13.4).[11] Further, Japan actively acceded to GATT codes for government procurement and other codes.

As of April 1991, residual import restrictions remained on 15 items (Table 13.5). In the mining and manufacturing industry the only item with restrictions is coal. Thus, the focus from here on will be on the reduction of import restrictions on agricultural products including rice and wheat.

Presently, the prime target of criticism is the closed nature of business practices inside Japan, examples being the complicated distribution system, *keiretsu*, collusion within domestic industries, and other informal non-tariff barriers. However, this 'exclusiveness' also includes such things as the subcontracting system and the lifetime employment system, which are justifiable from the standpoint of establishing long-term transactional relationships.

Nonetheless, if one examines the import penetration ratio of Japan, it becomes clear that Japanese rates are far below those of European countries, and are much lower than those in the US. (Table 13.7). The existence of large price differentials between domestic and overseas prices was also pointed out in the SII meetings. Likewise, it cannot be denied that there are extremely complicated import procedures, as well as rules and customs regarding services, certification, standards, and financing.

Other problems to be addressed include transparency in decision process and the streamlining of procedures including administrative guidance. Given the higher degree of global interdependency today, uniformity in international rules and coordination between nations on antimonopoly laws, M&A, and financial dealings are necessary.

13.4.5 Economic Globalization and the Free Trading System

In the latter half of the 1980s, the globalization of Japanese firms progressed dramatically. After the large appreciation of the yen following the Plaza Accord in September 1985, Japan's foreign direct investment surged, and Japanese firms became actively engaged in foreign operations. Accordingly, interrelationships developed among national economies, and Japan's import of manufactured goods increased. Japan's trade and production structures are steadily following a pattern of intra-industry trade.

Concerning exports bound for the US, unfilled quotas are on the rise, while local production of automobiles, semiconductors, and machine tools has proceeded rapidly, substituting for direct exports from Japan. The major focus is now shifting toward local production in the US, and even to reversed imports into the Japanese market.

In the meantime, overseas operations by Japanese firms in East Asian countries have contributed to the development of the local economies. This has been welcomed by Asian countries as it augments employment opportunities and technology transfer. There is a *de facto* economic zone evolving out of the initiatives of the private sector. Japan's trade policy can no longer be discussed without considering its developing relations with other Asian countries.

As the globalization of firms progresses, the relative importance of possessing territory and natural resources will decline. In so far as the remittance of interest and principal is guaranteed, the existence of national borders does not matter seriously, meaning that the location of business activity becomes of secondary importance. What is of crucial importance in the age of globalization is the security of market access and the upholding of free trade principles, not the size of territories or population.

13.5 CONCLUSION

In retrospect, Japan's postwar economic prosperity can be attributed to favourable conditions, market forces and, in particular, a liberal trade regime. These factors enabled Japan to attain an impressive rate of productivity growth and a high standard of living despite the nation's physical limitations.

Since the yen's appreciation in 1985, Japan's foreign direct investment has surged and its firms have expanded the range of their activities. In the age of globalization, Japan should promote more actively the principle of free trade by taking initiatives to further open its domestic market. Market-opening measures not only will improve resource allocation by reducing the large gap between domestic and overseas prices, but will also encourage economic development in other countries, particularly in East Asia.

APPENDIX: THE PATH OF TRADE AND CAPITAL LIBERALIZATION IN POSTWAR JAPAN

Year	*Item*
1947 August	Private sector trade reopened
1949 April	Unified exchange rate (US$1=¥360) established
1949 December	Foreign Exchange and Foreign Trade Control Law enacted
1950 June	Outbreak of Korean War
1951 September	San Francisco Peace Treaty signed (takes effect in April 1952)
1953 August	Japan joins IMF
1955 September	Japan gains full membership in GATT (provisional membership from October 1953)
1960 April	Import quotas largely eliminated (Trade and Exchange Liberalization Planning Outline)
1963 February	Japan communicates to GATT its accession to GATT Article 11
1964 April	Japan becomes IMF Article 8 country (abolition of foreign exchange budget, enacting of tariff quota system) Japan joins the OECD
1964 May	Opening of the Kennedy Round (closes in June 1967)
1964 October	Import Liberalization reaches 92.8 per cent
1967 July	First Capital Liberalization (100 per cent – 17 industries, 50 per cent – 33 industries)
1968 June	Expansion of liberalization of technology imports
1968 July	First round of tariff reductions (1910 items) in line with the GATT Kennedy Round
1969 March	Second Capital Liberalization (100 per cent – 44 industries, 50 per cent – 160 industries)
1969 October	Decision to liberalize remaining import quotas on 55 items (to be carried out by December 1971)

1970 September	Third Capital Liberalization (100 per cent – 77 industries, 50 per cent – 447 industries)
1971 April	Capital Liberalization of automotive industry
1971 August	Announcement of new American trade policies ('Nixon shock')
	Fourth Capital Liberalization (100 per cent – 228 industries, 50 per cent – all but 7 industries)
1971 December	Smithsonian Agreement (US$1=¥308)
1972 July	Liberalization of technology imports
1973 February	Yen moved to a floating exchange rate system
1973 May	Fifth Capital Liberalization (in principle 100 per cent in all but 5 industries)
1973 October	The First Oil Crisis (The Fourth Arab-Israeli War)
1974 August	50 per cent Capital Liberalization of computer industry
1974 December	100 per cent capital liberalization of IC industry, 50 per cent capital liberalization of information processing industry
1975 February	Opening of the Tokyo Round (closes in December 1979)
1975 June	Capital liberalization of distribution industry
1980 December	New Foreign Exchange Law enacted (liberalization in principle of current and capital transactions)
1986 January	Removal of tariffs on 146 agricultural products and 1703 manufactured products
1989 April	Liberalization of tariffs on 1004 manufactured products
1991 April	Liberalization of imports of beef, oranges
1992 April	Liberalization of orange juice imports

Notes

1. For an analysis of the problems of setting a single exchange rate and its impact on trade from the standpoint of currency convertibility, see McKinnon (1979) chs 1 and 2.
2. One possible reason for this preference was that in order to attain such short-term policy targets as external balances, currency allocations were more effective and it could be implemented more flexibly. In contrast, altering tariffs and subsidies in response to short-term fluctuations in external balances would require the approval of the Diet, a much more cumbersome and less flexible procedure.
3. In actuality, this applies to the foreign currency allocation system (FA) and the automatic foreign currency allocation system (AFA). There was another system, the automatic approval system (AA). The import value under these three systems was responsible for more than half of Japan's total imports during the period 1954–60.
4. Although IBM was not a yen-based enterprise, it was already permitted

by 1950 to set up a wholly-owned subsidiary in Japan. This was thought to be primarily due to IBM's overwhelming monopoly on the basic technology for computers.

5. From the Meiji period on, the Japanese government has taken a cautious attitude towards the introduction of foreign capital. It was thought then that foreign borrowing would result in the increase of outside influence, thus limiting Japan's freedom of manouver. However, this fear disappeared after the Russo-Japanese War, and excessive foreign bond issuance led to a rapidly growing foreign debt. By the beginning of the First World War in 1914, Japan's foreign debt had reached US$ 1.95 billion, and the debt service ratio surged to 36.9 per cent. With increased business opportunities in foreign markets due to the outbreak of the First World War, Japan managed to escape the dangers of an accumulated foreign debt (Harada and Kosai, 1987).

   Given the historical background, postwar Japan has consistently pursued economic development without excessive reliance on foreign borrowing.

   Nevertheless, it should be noted that under the Ashida Cabinet (March to October 1948), a plan to actively introduce foreign capital was seriously considered. Under that plan the transfer of profit and principal to an enterprise's home country would have been guaranteed on a non-discriminatory basis. This cabinet had come to power on the platform that the overall economic crisis should be overcome through the introduction of foreign capital. Soon afterwards, however, the US occupation policy began to shift. Namely, it was argued that excessive economic reforms might have an adverse impact on Japan's economy, thereby hampering its economic reconstruction. As a result, the plan considered by the Ashida Cabinet was abandoned (Miyazaki, 1987).
6. The liberalization ratio is defined as the ratio of liberalized import values (that is, free imports plus imports with tariffs imposed) to total import value. However, this ratio has not been released since 1972, when the figure reached almost 95 per cent.
7. For studies based on this concept, see Komiya (1988), Ito *et al.* (1988) and others. However, this point seems to entail further empirical examination.
8. Using 1973 as the base year with a GNP value at 100, Japan's real GNP for 1988 grew by 76 per cent, while imported crude oil decreased by more than 30 per cent in the same period, meaning that its energy inputs required for producing a unit of GNP declined more than 60 per cent.
9. However, if the principle of reciprocity were to work in a negative way, this principle is likely to amount to protectionism. A prime example was the US–Japan agreement on semiconductors, out of which arose serious friction over whether or not Japan guaranteed a 20 per cent share of the Japanese market for US semiconductors. For an argument emphasizing the dual aspects of reciprocity, see Cline (1982).
10. However, strong opposition has been expressed to some of the ideas suggested by the Maekawa Report, in particular, that Japan should reduce its surplus in the current account to the level of one per cent of its nominal GNP (Komiya, 1988).

11. The customs tariff burden ratio began to surge again after 1985 (Table 13.4). This is not only because the *ad valorem* tax rate for imported oil has gone up as a result of declining oil prices, but also because the manufactured import ratio has risen in recent years (tariff rates for manufactured goods are relatively higher than those for industrial materials).

References

Arisawa, Hiromi (1950) *Sai-Gunbi no Keizaigaku* (Economics of Rearmament) (Tokyo: Nihon Hyoron-sha).

Cline, William (1982) *Reciprocity: a New Approach to World Trade Policy?* (Washington: Institute for International Economics).

Fujino, Shozaburo (1988) 'Japan's Current Account in the Postwar Period', *Keizai Kenkyu*, vol. 39, no. 2, pp. 97–108.

Hagiwara, Toru (1972) *Nihon Gaiko-shi* (The History of Japan's Diplomacy), vol. 30, (Tokyo: Kajima Kenkyu-sho Shuppankai).

Harada, Yutaka and Yutaka Kosai (1987) *Nihon Keizai: Hatten no Biggu Geemu* (The Japanese Economy: The Big Game of Economic Development) (Tokyo: Toyo Keizai Shinpo-sha).

Ito, Motoshige, Kazuharu Kiyono, Masahiro Okuno and Kotaro Suzumura (1988) *Sangyo Seisaku no Keizai Bunseki* (Economic Analysis of Industrial Policy) (Tokyo: University of Tokyo Press).

Johnson, Chalmers (1982) *MITI and the Japanese Miracle: The Growth of Industrial Policy* (Stanford, California: Stanford University Press).

Keizai Kikaku-cho (Economic Planning Agency) (1962) *Sengo Keizai-shi: Boeki-Kokusai Shushi-hen* (The Economic History of Postwar Japan: Trade and Balance of Payments) (Tokyo: Okura-sho Insatsu-kyoku).

Keizai Kikaku-cho (Economic Planning Agency) (1960) *Boeki Kawase Jiyuka Keikaku Taiko* (The Outline of the Trade and Exchange Liberalization Plan).

Keizai Kikaku-cho (Economic Planning Agency) (1986) *Maekawa Hokoku* (Report by the Advisory Group of Economic Structural Adjustment for International Harmony).

Komiya, Ryutaro (1967a) 'Shihon Jiyuka no Keizai Gaku' (Economics of Capital Liberalization), *Ekonomisuto*, July 25.

Komiya, Ryutaro (1967b) *Kokusai Keizai Gaku Kenkyu* (Studies on International Economics) (Tokyo: Iwanami Shoten).

Komiya, Ryutaro (1988) *Gendai Nihon Keizai* (Contemporary Japanese Economy) (Tokyo: University of Tokyo Press).

Kosai, Yutaka (1981) *Kodo Seicho no Jidai* (Tokyo: Nihon Hyoron-sha). Translated as *The Era of High-Speed Growth* (Tokyo: University of Tokyo Press, 1986).

Kosai, Yutaka (1989) 'Kodo Seicho heno Shuppatsu' (Setting off towards High Growth), in *Nihon Keizai-shi*, vol. 7, ed. by Takafusa Nakamura (Tokyo: Iwanami Shoten).

Krugman, Paul (1990) *Rethinking International Trade* (Cambridge, Mass.: MIT Press).

McKinnon, Ronald I. (1979) *Money in International Exchange: The Convertible Currency System* (Oxford: Oxford University Press).

Miyazaki, Masayasu (1987) 'Ashida Naikaku-ki no Gaishi Donyu Mondai' (The Introduction of Foreign Capital under the Ashida Cabinet), *Shinshu Daigaku Kyoiku Gakubu Kiyo*, no. 61, pp. 85–97.

Nakayama, Ichiro (1953) *Nihon Keizai no Kao* (The Face of the Japanese Economy) (Tokyo: Nihon Hyoron Shinsha).

Oka, Shigeo (1964) *Sengo Nihon no Kanzei Seisaku* (Japan's Tariff Policy in the Postwar Period) (Tokyo: Nihon Hyoron-sha).

Okita, Saburo (1961) *Keizai Seisaku to Kokusai Kankei: Boeki Jiyuka no Haikei* (Economic Policy and International Relations: The Background of Trade Liberalization) (Tokyo: Nihon Hyoron-sha).

Patterson, Gardner (1966) *Discrimination in International Trade, The Policy Issues 1945–1965* (Princeton: Princeton University Press).

Penrose, Edith (1959) *The Theory of the Growth of the Firm* (Oxford: Blackwell).

Shinohara, Miyohei (1989) 'Yushutsu Gata Seicho to Kawase Reto: Sairon' (The Export-led Growth and Exchange Rates: Restatement), *Keizai Kenkyu*, vol. 40, no. 3.

Tsuruta, Toshimasa (1982) *Sengo Nihon no Sangyo Seisaku* (Japan's Industrial Policy in the Postwar Period) (Tokyo: Nihon Keizai Shinbun-sha).

Tsusho Sangyo-sho (Ministry of International Trade and Industry) (1989–), *Tsusho Sangyo Seisaku-shi* (History of Policies on International Trade and Industry, various volumes (Tokyo: Tsusho Sangyo Chosa-kai).

Uchino, Tatsuro (1987) *Sengo Nihon Keizai-shi* (The Economic History of Postwar Japan) (Tokyo: Kodan-sha).

Ueda, Kazuo (1985) 'Sengo Nihon no Keijo Shushi to Koeki Joken' (Current Account and Terms of Trade in Postwar Japan), a paper presented to Zushi Conference.

14 Deregulation and Protectionism in Japanese Agriculture

Toshihiko Kawagoe*

14.1 INTRODUCTION

Agriculture is one of the most heavily regulated sectors in the Japanese economy. The Price mechanism has not yet functioned well in many agricultural products' markets owing to strict government control. Although various agricultural regulations dating to the Second World War have been gradually removed, the basic structure of the regulations has been maintained over the postwar period. Indeed government intervention grew during the period of high economic growth, resulting in a protection level among the highest in the world. Ironically, in spite of the heavy regulation which was intended to protect the sector, Japanese agriculture has continuously declined and deteriorated. The number of full-time farms and workers has decreased, but the production structure of agriculture has changed little.

The purpose of this chapter is to review the process of agricultural policies over the postwar period and to identify the cause of failed structural adjustment in relation to agricultural protectionism. After a brief preparatory discussion of Japanese agriculture in the next section, section 14.3 reviews the structural policies of agriculture and investigates how agricultural policies in Japan came to a deadlock. Section 14.4 analyzes the evolution of the protection policies, referring to rice policies over the postwar period as a typical example of the market distortion. The consequences of postwar agricultural policies are summarized in section 14.5 as a concluding statement.

14.2 AGRICULTURE IN POSTWAR JAPAN

14.2.1 An Overview of Agriculture

The Japanese archipelago is located in temperate monsoon Asia and bounds the northern edge of the rice growing region. Annual rainfall is 1000 to 2000 mm with an average temperature of 10 to 15 degrees centigrade and is characterized by hot and humid summer seasons and cold winter seasons. Agricultural land – including arable land, orchards and permanent pastures – occupies only 14 per cent of total land area, whereas forested land accounts for 66 per cent. Population density is high at 329.3 per square kilometre. Agricultural land area per capita is only 0.044 hectares, which is one of the lowest levels among the industrial countries. For example, it is one-fifth that of the former West German Federal Republic and only one-fortieth that of the United States (FAO, 1987).

Rice cultivation was a suitable farming system feeding the densely populated country and rice has been the most important food staple for the Japanese. Thus, Japanese agriculture has heavily relied on rice production and most farm producers have been rice-growing peasants. Livestock was introduced relatively recently. In 1960, rice and livestock occupied 47 and 15 per cent of the total agricultural output, respectively. During the past three decades, although the share of rice dropped gradually, it still occupied about 30 per cent in 1988. Livestock's share increased to 27 per cent over the same period. (JMAFF(c)).

From the Meiji Restoration in 1869 until the Second World War, the number of farms in Japan had remained roughly constant at a level of 5.5 million and the agricultural land area totalled about 6 million hectares. Half of agricultural land was wet paddy fields, while the rest was cultivated under upland conditions. After the War, both the number of farms and agricultural land area have slightly decreased, owing to out-migration of farmers into the industrial sector and the conversion of land to residential property and industrial use. In 1989, there were 4.2 million farm households holding 5.3 million hectares of agricultural land. Accordingly, the average farm size has been very small – only 1.09 hectares in 1941 and 1.26 hectares in 1989. These farms are basically operated as family farms, mainly based on family labour.

From the early stages of Japan's economic development until the mid-1910s, labour was relatively abundant and land was the major constraint on agricultural production. Efforts to agricultural development were geared to facilitating the substitution of labour for land. Then, as wage rates rose owing to increased labour demand from the non-agricultural sector, the direction of development was shifted toward labour-saving route, while raising land productivity through progress of biological technology, represented by seed improvements with intensive application of fertilizers (Kawagoe, Otsuka and Hayami, 1986).[1]

This development process has been sustained under a well installed infrastructure. A public agricultural research and extension system was already established by the end of the nineteenth century. An industrial sector capable of supplying modern inputs, such as fertilizer and chemicals, has also developed. Improvement of the transportation network ensured extensive marketing in the domestic markets and facilitated commercialization of peasant production.

Over the course of economic development, the relative position of the agricultural sector declines because the income elasticity of food demand is lower than that of manufactured commodities. In Japan, agriculture's share of total GDP dropped from 13 per cent in 1960 to 1.9 per cent in 1989. The share of the agricultural labour force declined from 26.8 per cent in 1960 to 6.6 per cent in 1989. The relative decline of agriculture has also occurred on the demand side of farm products. Engel's coefficient, food expenses divided by household disposal income, has declined from 35.2 per cent to 24 per cent during the same period.

Moreover, Japanese dietary patterns changed drastically over the postwar period. As per capita income grows, demand for protein-rich food, such as meat and dairy products, tends to increase. In Japan, a shift from the traditional diet based on rice and fish to more diversified consumption patterns, including meats, dairy products and wheat-based foods, has occurred. Although rice has remained the major staple food in the Japanese diet, annual per capita consumption has declined continuously since 1962, when it reached the peak of 118 kg, to 70 kg in 1989.[2] On the other hand, per capita consumption of protein-rich food, such as meat and dairy products, has increased quickly throughout the period.[3]

14.2.2 Protectionism of Japanese Agriculture

It is often pointed out that Japanese agriculture is heavily protected and food prices in Japan are higher than in other countries. For example, the rice price is four times higher than that in the United States and seven times higher than the export price of Thailand.[4] Japanese border policies on agricultural commodities, such as import quotas on oranges and beef, virtual import ban on rice, and various other non-tariff trade barriers, have been severely criticized as unfair trade practices in the arena of international trade negotiations. Indeed, major grains, beef and dairy products are more heavily protected in Japan than in the European Community. The level of protection for all commodities in Japan was more than two times higher than that of the EC in 1980. By the mid-1950s, however, the level of overall protection in Japan was lower than in the European Community (Anderson *et al.*, 1986, p. 27). Japan's protection level has been raised over the past three decades, owing to the steady decline in the comparative advantage of the agricultural sector during the period of high economic growth.

However, Japan has also become one of the largest importers of agricultural commodities in the world. During the past several decades, Japan has continuously expanded its imports, while decreasing self-sufficiency in major food staples, such as wheat, barley and coarse grains. In 1960, 40 per cent of wheat and 20 per cent of coarse grains were was still produced domestically. By 1980, the self-sufficiency rate of wheat had declined to 10 per cent and that of coarse grains dropped to nil (JMAFF (a)). The only exception is rice, where almost total self-sufficiency has been maintained throughout the period. As a result of the relative decline of domestic production, the self-sufficiency rate of total food supply measured on a calorie basis declined from 79 per cent in 1960 to 48 per cent in 1989 (Table 14.1). As shown in the table, this tendency contrasts with that of other industrial countries, such as former West Germany and the Netherlands, where self-sufficiency rates were raised over the past three decades.

Why was agricultural protection strengthened in Japan, while at the same time its domestic markets were opened and its food self-sufficiency declined? The failure of agricultural policies over the postwar period resulted in the protectionism and inefficiency of Japanese agriculture. A strictly regulated land market hampered modernization of the agrarian structure, and the sector's comparative advantage was lost quickly during the period of high economic growth. The market for rice, Japan's most important crop, has been distorted by government intervention, which has also hampered the restructuring of agriculture along more productive lines. These distortions will be examined in the following sections.

Table 14.1 Comparisons of food self-sufficiency rate of total food supply on a calorie basis among developed countries, 1960–85

	1960	*1970*	*1980*	*1985*
Japan	79	60	53	48[a]
Germany, FR	–	66	92	93
The Netherlands	–	71	104	98
UK	–	48	74	77
USA	–	115	134	127

[a] Figure in 1989.

Source: JMAFF, *Shokuryo Jukyu Hyo* (Food Balance Sheets).

14.3 FAILURE OF STRUCTURAL POLICIES

Japanese agriculture has been traditionally shouldered by a peasantry comprised of a large number of small family farms. This characteristic, inherited from the feudal Tokugawa era (the seventeenth century to the midnineteenth century), has been strengthened during the period of modern economic growth since the Meiji Restoration. Labour-intensive and land-saving technologies have been pursued, and the highly intensive nature of agricultural production based on irrigated rice culture has been elaborated.

14.3.1 Land Reform and Agricultural Land Law[5]

Before the Second World War, half of all agricultural land was cultivated by small tenant farmers. Most tenant-cultivated land was owned by small-sized landowners. Tenants typically paid nearly half of their product as land rent to landlords. Poverty in rural areas was a root cause of the social unrest in prewar Japan. Since the 1920s, government deflationary policies and the world depression pushed down agricultural prices and farm income, causing a serious agricultural crisis. Tenancy disputes became a common phenomenon in rural areas.

After the devastation caused by the war, the country faced starvation. Major policy targets at this time were to democratize the rural community and to increase agricultural production, especially rice, to overcome severe food shortage in the country. Drastic land reform was carried out from 1946 to 1950 under strong guidance from Supreme Commander for the Allied Powers (SCAP) of the occupation

Table 14.2 Chronological summary of the structural policies of Japanese agriculture

Year		*Major land policies*
1946–50	Land reform	Transfer of farmland from landlords to tenant farmers
1952	Agricultural Land Law	(Protection of cultivators) Strengthen tenantry rights Control of land rent Restriction of farmland conversion Restriction of landlordism
1961	Agricultural Basic Law	(Aim to establish viable farms through farm size expansion and productivity increase) Promotion of mechanization and group farming.
1962	Agricultural Land Law (amendment)	Removal of farm-size ceiling on land ownership
1970	Agricultural Land Law (amendment)	Freedom to terminate long-term land lease contract (more than 10 years)
1975	Agricultural Development Law (amendment)	(Farmland utilization programme) Freedom for short-term land lease contract under farmland utilization programme
1980	Farmland Utilization Promotion Law; Agricultural Land Law (amendment)	Freedom of short-term land lease contract through mediation of village headman; Freedom of land lease contract in kind or of share tenancy

forces (Table 14.2). All tenanted land owned by absentee landlords and the portion of village landlords' land which exceeded one hectare were compulsorily purchased by the state and sold to their tenant farmers. The land price paid to landlords was reduced to a negligible level by rapid inflation since purchase price was fixed at 1945 price levels. As a result of the reform, most farmland under tenancy came into cultivators' hands.

As discussed in Chapter 8 of this volume, major factors behind the success of the drastic land reform included the existence of the superior power of SCAP, and also the fact that landlord power had already been undermined by various wartime regulations on land. The land reform brought about more equal assets and income distributions among farmers, which contributed to the democratization and social stability of the rural society in Japan. Thus, the reform was

Table 14.3 Changes in the number of farms by operational land area and average farm size in Japan, 1941–89

Year	Number of farms (thousands)					Average farm size (ha)
	Total	*Less than 0.5 ha*	*0.5 to 1.0 ha*	*1.0 to 2.0 ha*	*Larger than 2.0 ha*	
1941	5410	1810	1620	1460	520	1.09
1955	6040	2330	1970	1380	360	0.94
1960	6060	2320	1920	1430	390	1.00
1970	5340	2020	1610	1290	420	1.09
1980	4660	1940	1310	990	420	1.17
1989	4190	1690	1170	890	440	1.26

Sources: JMAFF, *Noringyo Census* (Census of Agriculture and Forestry); *Kochi oyobi Sakutsuke Menseki Tokei* (Statistics of Arable Land and Area Planted); *Nogyo Chosa* (Agricultural Survey).

a success in terms of its political objective. However, it should be noted that the reform did not change the basic structure of agricultural production. The land reform transferred land ownership from landlords to tillers of the soil. Small tenant farmers became small owner cultivators without any significant change in average farm size. Because of the land reform, in fact, average farm size slightly declined from 1.09 hectares in 1941 to 0.94 hectares in 1955 (Table 14.3).

In order to secure the results of land reform and prevent the revival of landlordism, the Agricultural Land Law (Nochi-ho) was enacted in 1952. Under the law, land rent was strictly controlled at a very low level and tenantry rights were much strengthened to protect cultivators. It became almost impossible for landowners to evict the few remaining tenants from their cultivating land. The legal maximum on farmland holdings was set at 3 hectares (12 hectares in Hokkaido prefecture). Absentee ownership was not allowed. Land could be traded at market prices as long as the purchaser's land holdings did not exceed the limits. However, only farmers cultivating more than 0.3 hectares (2 hectares in Hokkaido) were allowed to purchase the farmland. Transactions of farmland were subject to the assent of the Village Agricultural Committee. Landownership and use has been frozen in the conditions in which it emerged from the land reform (Dore, 1959, p. 198). The land reform and the Agricultural Land Law thus set the basic structure of Japanese agriculture for the postwar period.

STOP

By the mid-1950s the Japanese economy had recovered from the wartime devastation and entered the period of high economic growth. The comparative advantage of agriculture began to decline quickly and the income gap between farm and non-farm sectors widened. Food consumption patterns also began to change. Modernization of the industrial structure of agriculture was required. In 1961, the Agricultural Basic Law (Nogyo Kihon-ho) was enacted, setting a new basic plan for agricultural policies. The new policy aimed to increase agricultural income through the improvement of agricultural productivity. For this purpose, agrarian structure needed to be improved through the expansion of farm size and mechanization. Diversification, especially through the introduction of livestock, was recommended, as the structure of food demand changed. Traditional peasantry farming had to be turned into modern entrepreneurial farms, called viable farms (*Jiritsu Keiei Noka*), which could keep up with the transition of the Japanese economy. Viable farms are defined as family farms which have sufficient farmland holdings for full-time operation and which can generate income comparable to that of non-farm households. (Article 15, the Agricultural Basic Law). The policy aimed to establish as much as possible viable farms. It also intended to promote cooperative farming. Besides the enactment of the Agricultural Basic Law, various policy measure were taken for supporting the law. An agricultural infrastructure improvement project was begun in 1961. A credit system for farmers, supporting their efforts to modernize management, was also introduced.[6]

Soon afterward, another important change came with the amendment of the Agricultural Land Law in 1962, in which the upper limits of farmland holdings was relaxed. The government intended that farm size expansion should be attained only through the purchases of farmland or opening new land. The strict regulation on land tenancy was not relaxed to prevent any reappearance of landlordism. In this respect, structural policies under the Agricultural Basic Law contradicted the land policies set up during land reform. The former emphasized economic efficiency in agricultural production, while the latter emphasized equity in rural communities.

14.3.2 Failure of Structural Policies

In spite of the government's efforts, the objective of the Agricultural Basic Law could not be realized. During the first decade under the Basic Law in the 1960s, no apparent change of farm size distribution was observed. Throughout the 1960s, the number of farms with operational land sizes larger than two hectares increased from 390 000 to 420 000, a number which remained fewer than in the prewar period. Average farm size increased minimally, from 1.00 to 1.09 hectares (Table 14.3). As a result, only 6.6 per cent of the farms were defined as viable in 1970. Why did farm size remain so small? The major reason was the sharp increase in part-time farming. During the period of high economic growth, construction of highways, factories and housing was booming and provided many employment opportunities for farmers as construction workers. Development of transport networks made it easier for farmers to commute to jobs in the cities. Non-farm employment opportunities thus increased rapidly in rural areas.

A large number of workers was drawn from agriculture to the non-farm sector. During the period from 1960 to 1989, the number of workers mainly engaged in agriculture decline nearly one-third, while this decrease was compensated by an increase in the number of workers supplementally engaged in farming (Table 14.4). The number of part-time farms increased sharply, especially in type II category, where more than half income derives from off-farm sources. Just after the war, more than half of all farmers were engaged in full-time farming, while only 16 per cent were in the type II part-time farmers. When the structural policies under the Agricultural Basic Law were initiated, full-time, type I and type II farms each constituted roughly one-third of total farmers. The share of type II part-time farms increased rapidly to 50 per cent in 1970, reaching 72 per cent by 1989. On the other hand, the share of full-time farms decreased to 14 per cent by 1989. While the total number of farms decreased slowly owing to an increase in part-time farms, arable land area also decreased slightly due to a conversion of farmland to non-farm purposes. As a result, average farm size increased at slow rates. Thus, structural adjustment of Japanese agriculture through farm size expansion, a key objective of the Agricultural Basic Law, was not realized. Part-time farmers have not sold their farmland and the agrarian structure has not changed throughout the period.

Ironically, however, part-time farming enables farm households to earn income comparable to that of non-farm households. Until the beginning of the 1960s, average income per farm household member was about 30 per cent lower than that of the average non-farm household member. This disparity has been narrowed and the former

Table 14.4 Changes in agricultural labour force, number of farms and arable land area in Japan, 1946–89

	1946	*1960*	*1970*	*1980*	*1989*
Workers engaged in agriculture[a] (thousands)					
Mainly engaged[b]	16 320	14 540	10 250	6 970	5 970
Supplementary[c] engaged	2 170	3 120	5 220	5 570	5 090
Total	18 490	17 660	15 470	12 540	11 060
Farms (thousands)					
Full-time	3 270	2 080	830	620	600
Part-time I[d]	1 680	2 040	1 800	1 000	570
Part-time II[e]	950	1 940	2 710	3 040	3 020
Total	5 910	6 060	5 340	4 660	4 190
Arable land (thousand ha)	5 320	6 070	5 800	5 460	5 280

[a] Farm household members above 16 years old who engage in farming any amount of time.
[b] Engaged in farming more than in other economic activities.
[c] Engaged in farming less than in other economic activities.
[d] Farms with farm income larger than off-farm income.
[e] Farms with farm income smaller than off-farm income.

Sources: JMAFF, *Noringyo Census* (Census of Agriculture and Forestry); *Nogyo Chosa* (Agricultural Survey); *Kochi oyobi Sakutsuke Menseki Tokei* (Statistics of Arable Land and Area Planted).

exceeded the latter by the mid-1970s (Table 14.5). Meanwhile, the share of off-farm income in total farm household income increased from 50 per cent in 1960 to 67 per cent in 1970 and nearly 90 per cent in 1988.

Two underlying conditions help to explain the dominance of part-time farming. First, progress in mechanization drastically reduced required labour input for farm operation. This tendency was especially prominent in rice cultivation, the most dominant sector of Japanese agriculture. Second, the rice price has been supported at a very high level under the Food Control System, with the government promising to purchase all rice that farmers produce. These technological and economic conditions have enabled small farmers to produce rice while engaging in off-farm jobs.

Table 14.5 Comparisons of income between farm households and urban workers' households in Japan, 1960–88

	1960	*1970*	*1980*	*1988*
	(thousand yen per household member)			
Farm household income:				
Farm income	39	110	234	234
	(50)[b]	(33)	(19)	(13)
Off-farm income[a]	40	220	1039	1509
	(50)	(67)	(81)	(87)
Total (1)	79	330	1273	1743
	(100)	(100)	(100)	(100)
Urban worker household income (2)	115	358	1111	1546
Relative income, % (1)/(2)	68	92	115	113

[a] Off-farm income includes pensions and other private grants.
[b] Percentage share of each income sources are shown in parentheses.

Source: JMAFF, *Nogyo Hakusho Fuzoku Tokei Hyo* (Statistical Appendix to the Agricultural White Paper).

The technological change which facilitated part-time farming in rice cultivation was the diffusion of power tillers. Before the introduction of power tillers, farm operation was largely based on manual labour and draft animals. Although some machines such as threshers and water-lifting pumps had been in use since before the Second World War, the most arduous tasks, such as land preparation for rice cultivation, required labour of young male workers. With the introduction of power tillers, women and old people were able to keep farming, since the manual labour of male could be replaced by the machines.[7] As a result, young and middle-aged males in farm households tend to engage in non-farm economic activities. In correspondence to the increase part-time farming, the number of power tillers increased at an explosive rate during the 1960s (Figure 14.1).

14.3.3 Farm Mechanization and Scale Economies

Since the late 1960s, Japanese agriculture has entered a new stage of farm mechanization. Until that time, farm operations were only partially mechanized, leaving several tasks such as transplanting and harvesting to manual labour. As shown in Figure 14.1, the diffusion

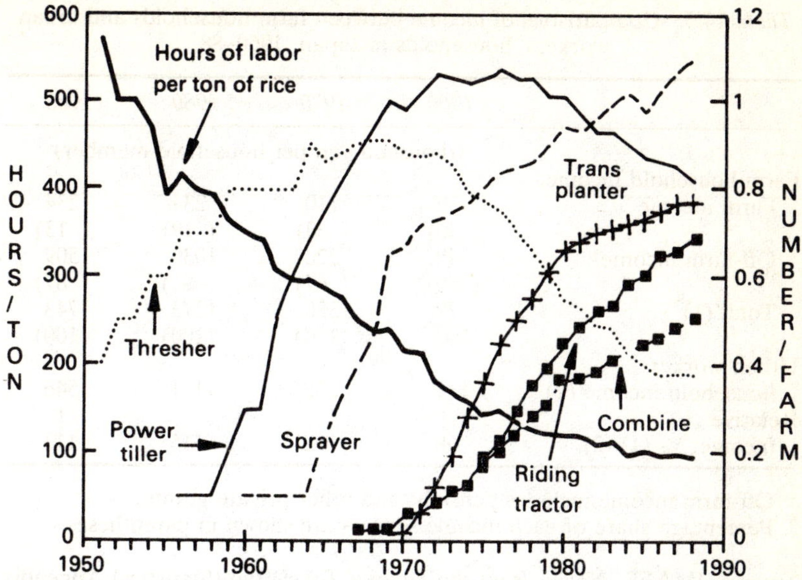

Figure 14.1 Farm mechanization in Japanese agriculture, 1951–88
Note: The number of machines per farm = average number of machines per farm owned by rice producing farms.

Source: JMAFF, *Kome oyobi Mugirui no Seisanhi* (Production Costs of Rice, Wheat and Barley).

of power tillers and threshers reached saturation by the end of the 1960s. Meanwhile, these small machines began to be replaced by medium-scale machinery such as riding tractors and combines. Rice transplanters were invented and became widespread at this time. The whole process of rice farming has been mechanized. These mechanization processes seem to have been continuous, judging from the steady decreases in labour input per ton of rice over the postwar years (Figure 14.1). However, medium-scale mechanization differs in that increasing returns to scale of farm operations can be observed. When non-farm wage rates rose, labour flowed from agriculture to the non-agricultural sector. Labour absorption by the non-agricultural sector has pushed the farm wage rate up and thus encouraged progress in mechanization, but this can only be employed economically through expansion of farm size and greater entrepreneurial abilities.

Farm mechanization using medium- or large-size machinery is characterized by increasing returns to scale because it needs a large

Table 14.6 Comparison of rice production costs in Japan by farm size, 1955–88

Farm size (ha)	*Index of production cost per kg (below 0.3 ha = 100)*				
	1955	*1960*	*1970*	*1980*	*1988*
Total costs:					
Below 0.3	100	100	100	100	100
0.3 to 0.5	104	106	95	94	94
1.0 to 1.5	98	96	80	76	75
2.0 to 3.0	90	93	73	66	70
Above 3.0	96	88	78	61	61
Labour costs:					
Below 0.3	100	100	100	100	100
0.3 to 0.5	101	106	98	92	90
1.0 to 1.5	92	91	79	66	61
2.0 to 3.0	74	83	64	50	51
Above 3.0	73	77	67	42	41
Machinery costs:					
Below 0.3	100	100	100	100	100
0.3 to 0.5	139	135	104	102	96
1.0 to 1.5	157	146	91	83	80
2.0 to 3.0	144	137	75	67	66
Above 3.0	144	121	72	58	56
Scale elasticity[a]:	1.08	1.10	1.18	1.30	1.32[b]

[a] Scale elasticity is the inverse of cost elasticity (b) with respect to output (Q), which was estimated from the cost function, $\ln C = a + b \ln Q$. See Hayami and Kawagoe (1989) for the details.
[b] Figure in 1984.

Source: JMAFF, *Kome oyobi Mugirui no Seisanhi* (Production Costs of Rice, Wheat and Barley).

farm unit to operate the machinery efficiently. The effect of mechanization on decreasing average cost in relation to farm size is shown in Table 14.6. Until the 1960s, compared to small farms, large farms spent less on labour but more on machinery per unit of rice output, and there was no apparent difference in total cost between the different farm size classes. Medium-scale machinery has been introduced, however, the costs of both labour and machinery have been lower for large farms than for small farms. Strong economies of scale with respect to output were evident in the 1980s. The dominance of small-scale part-time farming in Japan could have been undermined by the progress of the mechanization.

The economies of scale associated with the mechanization in Japan does not mean that an optimum farm size for the most efficient use of the medium-scale machinery would be no larger than the average farm size in Europe. It should be noted, however, that the optimum farm size in Japan would much exceed the present average. The large gap represents an adjustment lag created by institutional rigidities in the land market (Hayami and Kawagoe, 1989).

14.3.4 Prospects for Agricultural Adjustment

Deregulation in 1962 was not very effective in stimulating the land market. The nationwide construction boom at that time raised farmers' expectations of windfall gains from conversion of their land for alternative use, thereby increasing incentives to hold on to land until some lucrative opportunity might arise (Hayami and Kawagoe, 1989). Actually, land prices rose quickly, at a rate higher even than the return on land from farm production (Hayami, 1988, p. 86). Thus the government's expectation that farm size could be expanded through purchase of farmland was not realized.

In order to overcome these difficulties the government opened the way to expansion of farm size through land leasing. The Agricultural Land Law was amended in 1970, enabling long-term leasing for periods of more than ten years to be terminated automatically. Several exemption clauses were introduced for short-term leasing of paddy-land during the winter season. Strict rent control was relaxed. However, landowners remained unwilling to lease out their land for fear of losing it to their tenants. Partly originating in the land reform period, the idea of farm tenancy in Japan continues to suffer from image problems. Various other regulations were relaxed during the 1970s. In 1975, the Agricultural Development Law (Noshi-ho) was amended to legalize land leasing for less than ten years, subject to agreement by the villagers who participated in a village-level farm utilization programme. In 1980, the Farmland Utilization Promotion Law (Noyochi Riyo Zoshin-ho) exempted from the Land Law short-term contracts mediated by village authorities. Under such contracts, the leased land is returned automatically to landowners upon termination of the contract period.

Although many regulations on the land rental market have been significantly relaxed, the prospects for farm-size expansion via land leasing remain limited. According to the 1985 Census of Agriculture, leased-land was only 7.5 per cent of the total cultivated area. This figure was far lower than that in Western Europe and North America, where 20 to 50 per cent of farmland is leased.

Large-scale tenant farming is still rare in Japan. And most tenant farmers lease fragmented plots of land from different landowners, making difficult the efficient utilization of medium-scale machinery. Small farms have tried to seek scale economies through joint utilization of machinery or sub-contracting of farm operations to machinery owners. However, inefficiencies persist in the use of large machinery on small farm units. Regulations on land tenure, though relaxed gradually, have been a major institutional impediment for increasing farm scale in Japan.

14.4 PROTECTION POLICIES IN DISARRAY

Since the comparative advantage of agriculture has disappeared over the process of high economic growth, various protection policies for the agricultural sector have been introduced in addition to the structural policies of the Agricultural Basic Law. As discussed previously, structural policy objectives have not been achieved, and at the same time protectionist policies have gradually become strengthened under strong pressure from the highly organized farmers, resulting in protection levels among the highest in the world.

14.4.1 Means of Agricultural Protection

Agricultural protection policies are designed to increase farmers' income through government intervention in various stages of economic activities, such as farm production, marketing and trade. Although numerous types of protection measures have been introduced, they may be classified into three categories: price support of agricultural output, trade restrictions on agricultural commodities, and subsidies to agricultural inputs.

Many agricultural commodities benefit from direct price support by the government. Rice, wheat and barley are strictly controlled by the government under the Food Control Law (Shokuryo Kanri-ho) with domestic prices supported at very high levels. Dairy products, silk, sugar, and other goods are also under price support and their markets are controlled by monopolistic, semi-governmental institutions. A wide variety of subsidies are distributed to the agricultural sector, accounting for 80 per cent of the total agricultural budget in 1984 (Hayami, 1988, p. 57).

Moreover, imports of many agricultural commodities are restricted under various forms of border protection. The most notorious protection measures in Japanese trade policies have been import quotas, which are violations of GATT rules. In 1962 the number of commodities under import quotas was 81, but was gradually reduced to 28 in 1971 and to 22 in 1974. Since then, although several commodities under quotas have been partially liberalized, the number of commodities under quotas remained at 22 until recently. Oranges and beef restrictions in particular were criticized by Japan's trade partners as a symbol of unfair trade practices. Under strong pressure from abroad, the government decided to lift quotas on oranges, beef and several other commodities as of 1991.[8] The quotas were replaced by tariffs.

State-trading is another major protection measure. Since state trading itself does not violate GATT rules, it is heavily used in Japan to protect major staple foods, such as rice, wheat and barley. However, overly strict restrictions on rice trade have come under attack in multilateral trade negotiations. Indeed, rice policies are one of the most serious cases of protectionism in Japan, with price support, border protection, and subsidies. Complicated regulatory structure is extensively integrated and form a basis for Japanese agricultural policies.

14.4.2 Rice Policies and the Food Control Law

Rice occupies an overwhelmingly important position in Japanese agriculture. Gross output from rice production occupied 47 per cent of total farm output in 1960 and 29 per cent in 1988. Thus rice policies inevitably become critical issues in Japanese politics. In order to understand the mechanisms of agricultural protection in Japan, a review of the rice policies over the postwar period may prove helpful. The evolution of major rice policies is chronologically summarized in Table 14.7. Conditions of the rice market are also shown in the table.

Before the Second World War, Japan constantly imported rice from Korea and Taiwan and occasionally from South East Asia. During the progress of the war on the Asian Continent in the late 1930s, the conditions of the domestic rice market gradually worsened. In 1939, severe drought hit Korea and western Japan, inaugurating what was to become a decade of food shortages. The

Table 14.7 Chronological summary of the rice policies in Japan

Year	*Condition of rice market*	*Major rice policies*
1939	Severe drought hit Korea and West Japan. Beginning of rice shortage.	Grain Ration Control Law Grain auction markets were closed; licensing of grain marketing agents; government intervention in the market.
1942	Food shortage worsens; queues and black market.	Enactment of Food Control Law All marketing processes and pricing put under direct control; ration of major food items (rice 330g/day).
1945	Severe crop failure.	
1946	Peak of food crisis.	Beginning of forced procurement.
1950	Food shortage continues. Producer price lower than import price.	In order to raise producer price, move to indirect control was proposed, but failed.
1950–2		Removal of direct controls on coarse grains, potato, wheat and barley.
1952–3	Severe crop failure.	In order to procure sufficient amount of rice, producer price raised rapidly. Deficit of Food Control Accounts.
1955	Abundant harvest. Producer price exceeds import price.	
1960–		Costs and income compensation scheme was introduced and producer price was raised drastically. Deficit of Food Control Accounts accumulated under negative margin.
1967–	Abundant harvest continues. Yield increases rapidly. From food shortage to overproduction.	
1969		Liberalization of semi-controlled rice.
1970		Government's old rice stock reached 7.2 million tons.

Table 14.7 Continued

Year	*Condition of rice market*	*Major rice policies*
1971	Paddy land diversion programme started.	Disposal of old rice (Phase 1). Restriction of procurement.
1972		Removal of rationing on rice.
1976	Revival of overproduction.	
1979		Disposal of old rice (Phase 2).
1987		Cut in producer price (5.95%)

Source: JMAFF, *Shokuryo Kanri Tokei Nenpo* (Annual Statistics for Staple Food Control).

government began adopting measures to control the rice market that year with the Grain Ration Control Law (Beikoku Haikyu Tosei-ho), which enabled the government to intervene the market. Auction markets of rice were closed. A licensing system for marketing agents was introduced. Over the course of the war, food shortages in the country worsened due to stagnant domestic production and declining imports. With the enactment of the Food Control Law in 1942 all marketing processes, including the pricing of staple foods, came under direct control by the government. Almost all commodities were under rationing systems. In the case of rice, 330 grams was set as the daily ration per person under the programme. Food supplies were short and queuing at the food shops became the norm. Many necessities were sold on the black market.

When the war ended in 1945, Japan experienced severe crop failures and food import had ceased. The following year saw the peak of the food crisis. In order to procure a sufficient amount of rice for the rationing programme, forced procurement of rice from farmers was implemented. However, the rice price in the black market was 25 times higher than the government purchase price; only 63 per cent of the target was procured by the end of March 1946 (Mochida, 1990, p. 136).

Food shortages continued into the early 1950s. The producer and the consumer prices of rice were set at a lower level than the import price (Figure 14.2). The government purchase price in 1951 was 47 000 yen per ton (brown rice), with the corresponding consumer price set at 44 900 yen the import price was much higher, at 71 800 yen per ton. In order to keep the consumer price at a low level, the

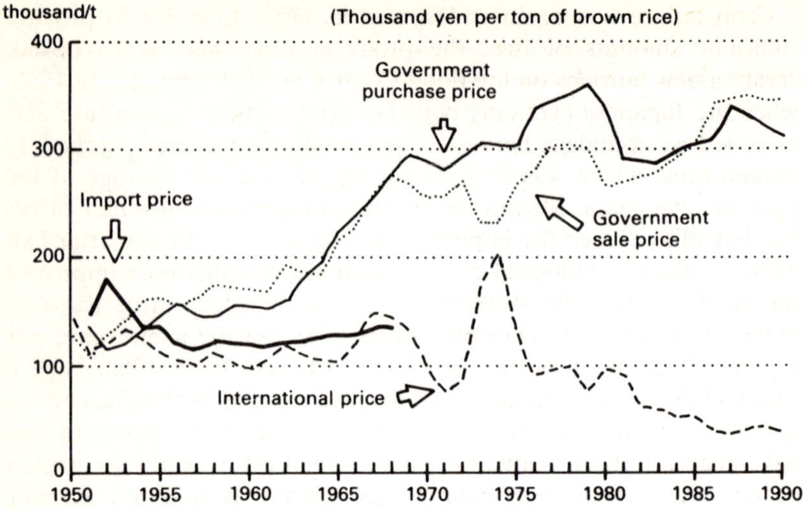

Figure 14.2 Changes in rice prices in Japan, 1950–90
Note: Prices are deflated using a wholesale price index (for all commodities, 1985 = 1). The government purchase price shows prices of previous years for comparison with the sale price. Import price represents the government purchase price from Korea and Taiwan. International price represents FOB in Bangkok (brown rice equivalent milled rice, 5% broken).

Sources: JMAFF, *Shokuryo Kanri Tokei Nenpo* (Annual Statistics for Staple Food Control); Bank of Japan, *Bukka Shisu Nenpo* (Price Indexes Annual); IRRI, *World Rice Statistics 1987*, table 93.

producer price was suppressed. Meanwhile, deregulation had begun for major agricultural commodities under the deflation policy guided by Joseph Dodge (the so-called Dodge Line). Direct controls on potatoes and coarse grain were removed in 1950 and 1951, respectively. In 1952, controls on wheat, barley and naked barley were changed from direct to indirect control based on state trading, whereby the government purchased crops at floor prices.

Deregulation of direct control on rice was considered several times by the ruling party and the bureaucracy. Moving to indirect control meant an increase in producer and consumer prices. However, deregulation was blocked by SCAP, which feared rapid increases in consumer prices. It should be noted that by the 1950s the Food Control System had functioned as consumer protection, because the consumer price was set at a lower level.

Crop failure was again widespread in 1953. In order to procure sufficient amounts of rice, the producer price had to be raised, creating new burdens on the Food Control Special Account. In 1955, when the Japanese economy began to grow rapidly, agriculture also recorded an abundant harvest. Total production of rice reached 12 million tons, which was 35 per cent higher than the average of the previous five years. Meanwhile, both producer and consumer prices had begun to exceed the import price (Figure 14.2). In the latter half of the 1950s, technological development in rice cultivation improved the yield significantly. Accordingly, annual production of 12 to 13 million tons became achievable every year. At the same time, per capita consumption of rice began to decrease from 1962, with a resultant decrease in the domestic demand for rice. Self-sufficiency of rice was fully attained. Since the mid-1950s, domestic prices of rice have been raised far above the international price, while the import of rice was strictly restricted by the monopolistic Food Agency (Shokuryo-cho) under the Food Control Law. Hence, the characteristic of the Food Control System has fundamentally changed from consumer protection to producer protection. Under these conditions, deregulation of rice control means the reduction of producer price, which has been strongly opposed by farmers.

Throughout the 1960s, the income gap between farm and non-farm sectors widened. In order to compensate for this disparity, the government resolved to raise the income obtained from rice production. To this end, the producer price was raised drastically. The Cost and Income Compensation Scheme was introduced in 1960 as a calculating basis of the government purchase price. Under this scheme, the producer price was determined on the basis of average production costs for the previous three years and the labour cost of farmers, which was set as the average wage rate in industry. If the income of the non-farm sector increased, the producer price of rice increased also under this system. However, this system was apparently incompatible with the structural policies under the Agricultural Basic Law. High prices enabled small marginal farms to continue rice production and hence the structural adjustment of Japanese agriculture was limited. Moreover, setting the producer price was highly charged politically. It was increased at rapid rates during the 1960s and 1970s.

It was natural that with the supported producer price set far above the market equilibrium price, production began to exceed demand (Figure 14.3). Excess supply had to be purchased by the government under the Food Control System. The deficit of the Food Control

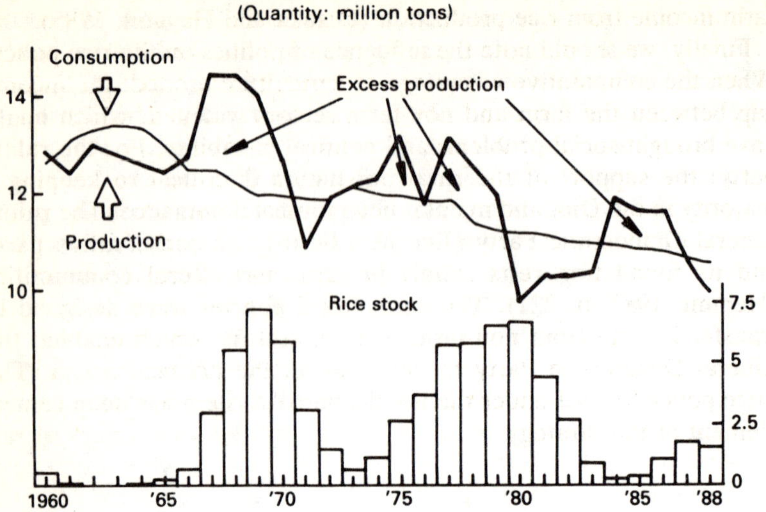

Figure 14.3 Changes in the rice market and government rice stock, 1960–88

Source: JMAFF, *Shokuryo Kanri Tokei Nenpo* (Annual Statistics for Staple Food Control); *Shokuryo Jukyu Hyo* (Food Balance Sheets).

Special Account grew rapidly during the 1960s. In 1970, the stock of old rice held by the government reached 7.2 million tons. The government had to dispose of the old rice stock for feed and industrial use, or for export. The disposal price was very low because the low quality of old rice, carried over period of years. The financial loss resulting from the disposal programme also exacerbated the Account deficit.

In order to reduce the accumulation of surplus rice as well as the Food Control Special Account deficit, several measures have been taken since 1969 to deregulate the Food Control System. Under the Food Control System, all produced rice is sold to the Food Agency through farmers' cooperatives and then sold to wholesalers. In 1969, an alternative marketing channel was introduced, allowing high-quality rice to be sold direct to wholesalers by the cooperatives.[9] Also, in 1972, direct controls on the consumer price and the marketing channel from wholesalers to retailers were lifted. A diversion programme for rice-planted areas was introduced in 1969. The programme pays subsidies to farmers who divert paddy land to other crops. The social cost of rice policies in the mid-1980s ranged between 1700 and 2100 billion yen, amounting to 40 to 70 per cent of total farm income from rice production (Otsuka and Hayami, 1985).

Finally, we should note the influence of politics on the rice policy. When the comparative advantage of agriculture eroded, the income gap between the farm and non-farm sectors widened, which might have brought social problems and political instability. For the ruling party, the support of the rural population is critical to keeping a majority in the Diet and maintaining political dominance. The ruling Liberal Democratic Party (Jiyu Minshu-to) is a conservative party and its foundation rests solidly in rural agricultural communities (Hemmi, 1982, p. 221). The agricultural policies were designed to transfer income from non-farm to farm sectors, which enabled the Liberal Democratic Party to dominate in the political arena. The price policy for rice under the Food Control System has been central element of this strategy.

14.5 CONSEQUENCES OF MARKET DISTORTION

This chapter has reviewed the economic and political aspects of agricultural protection policies, focusing on rice policies during the postwar period. We must stress that the failure of structural policies is closely connected with the rice policies.

The Japanese government has aimed to increase farm sector income through structural policies. Viable farms were expected to earn comparable income to that of non-farm households. Farm size expansion and mechanization were seen as necessary for establishing a modern agricultural sector. However, this vision of modernization has not been realized. One reason may be the land reform, which democratized the rural communities. There is no doubt that the reform contributed to equalizing income and assets distribution in rural society, which contributed to political stability over the postwar period.

From the viewpoint of industrial policy, however, land reform helped to prevent change in the production structure of agriculture. The strict control of farmland under the Agricultural Land Law froze the land market and became a major impediment to structural adjustment of the sector. The industrial structure of agriculture has changed little over the postwar period, supported further by price support of the products which helped to lessen inter-sectoral income gaps. Under such heavy protection, efforts for structural adjustment in agriculture were hampered. With high levels of price supports and a government guarantee to purchase any amount of the produce, producers have little incentive to reduce production costs. And many farms have insisted on producing rice even as consumption patterns have diversified from rice to other crops, resulting in a low level of self-sufficiency of most agricultural commodities other than rice.

Income compensation for the poor is a target of social welfare policies and intervention in market prices should be used as a measure of pure economic policies. However, in many developed countries, including Japan, price policies have been often used to compensate incomes in the agricultural sector. Price support for rice in Japan has been used to increase farm household income. In general, price support uniformly raises the producer price per unit of the product, regardless of farm size or production efficiency. Large farms can sell a large amount of produce and thus generally earn a high household income, while small farms sell small amounts of produce and earn a low income. Moreover, if agricultural production reveals economies of scale, large farms can earn excess profit under price support programme, because their average cost of the production is lower than small farms. Therefore, it is not easy to compensate income of small farms efficiency by means of price policies. Throughout the 1960s and 1970s, the daily income of rice producers exceeded the income of urban workers on average (Table 14.8). However, since the 1970s, large farms whose operational size is larger than 3 hectares have earned much higher income, while small farms with less than 0.3 hectares have earned much lower income. The advantages of scale for large rice growers are apparent when we consider other farm sectors, such as dairy farms and horticultural farms. However, it does not mean the large farms could expand their operation, since the land market was restricted by rigid institutional regulations.

A confusion of policy measures and targets often resulted in inefficiencies and other negative side-effects, owing to distorted markets. Now that the Japanese economy has reached a highly developed stage as one of the most advanced industrial countries, the productivity gap between the agricultural and the industrial sectors has become so great that current policies are becoming unsustainable. The agrarian structure has not modernized to become competitive in the world market. Japanese agriculture faces fundamental choices in the near future.

Table 14.8 Comparisons of daily income between farm producers and urban workers in Japan, 1960–88

	1960	*1970*	*1980*	*1988*
	(yen per worker per day)			
Farm producers:				
Rice grower:				
Large farm (above 3.0 ha)	1 854	4 856	17 308	21 122
Small farm (below 0.3 ha)	981	2 122	4 346	4 568
Average	1 166	3 297	9 427	11 064
Dairy farm				9 871
Horticulture				6 855
Urban worker	847	3 028	10 480	13 824

Sources: JMAFF, *Nogyo Hakusho Fuzoku Tokei Hyo* (Statistical Appendix to the Agricultural White Paper); *Kome oyobi Mugirui no Seisanhi* (Production Costs of Rice, Wheat and Barley).

Notes

* I am grateful for helpful comments and suggestions from Kunio Ohkama, Juro Teranishi and the members of the study project at the Japan Center for Economic Research.

1. Compared with agriculture in the new Continents, where land is abundant, Japanese agriculture has been characterized by its intensive use of agricultural land and labour. This characteristic is reflected in its relatively high land productivity and low labour productivity among industrial countries. Labour productivity in Japan was only one-tenth that of the US, while land productivity was ten times higher (Kawagoe and Hayami, 1983). Japan's low labour productivity is attributed to a low land–labour ratio, i.e., small farm size.
2. Per-capita consumption of rice increased gradually after the Meiji Restoration (1867). In the 1870s, annual consumption was about 100 kg per person, which increased to 130 to 150 kg by the end of the nineteenth century and reached saturation at 170 kg by the mid-1910s. During the period of hunger after the Second World War, consumption was only 100 kg. Over the postwar period, consumption never fully return to the prewar level, owing to changes in dietary patterns.
3. Annual consumption of meats and dairy products increased from 5.0 and 22.3 kg per capita in 1966 to 28.3 and 80.6 kg in 1989, respectively (JMAFF(a)).
4. Wholesale price in the US at the mill-gate in California, US$645.1/metric

ton (high quality), and the export price of Thailand, $310/ton, are compared with wholesale prices in Japan of medium-grade voluntary marketed rice, $2634.3/ton and the government sale rice, $2192.8/ton. These figures are for milled rice at 1990 prices assuming an exchange rate of yen 150 for US $1 (Seisaku Koso Forum, 1990; JMAFF (c)).

5. Landlordism in prewar Japan and the process of the postwar land reform is discussed in Chapter 8 of this volume.
6. Under the government guided loan programme, a credit system based on the Nogyo Kindaika Shikin (Farm Modernization Fund) was introduced in 1961, in which the government subsidized farmers' cooperatives and enabled them to provide loans at low interest to farmers (Egaitsu, Morozumi, and Yoshimura, 1989).
7. The part-time farms, where operations were shouldered by the grandparents and the wife of the household head, became referred to as *san chan nogyo*, which meant farming by grandpa, grandma and mamma.
8. Figures for commodities under the import quotas are calculated based on CCCN 4 digit (JMAFF(b), 1990).
9. The rice, sold directly from farmers' cooperatives to wholesalers, is called *Jishu Ryutsu Mai* (Voluntary Marketed Rice), of which the share has increased rapidly to occupy in 1990 about 70 per cent of the total marketed rice.

References

Anderson, Kym, Yujiro Hayami and Masayoshi Honma (1986) 'The Growth of Agricultural Protection', in *The Political Economy of Agricultural Protection*, ed. by Kym Anderson and Yujiro Hayami (Sydney: Allen & Unwin).

Bank of Japan, *Bukka Shisu Nenpo* (Price Indexes Annual), (Tokyo: Bank of Japan).

Dore, R. P. (1959) *Land Reform in Japan* (London: Oxford University Press).

Egaitsu, Fumio, Kazuo Morozumi and Keisuke Yoshimura (1989) *Agricultural Finance in Japan* (Tokyo: Japan – FAO Association).

FAO (1987) *Production Yearbook* (Rome: UN/Food and Agriculture Organization).

Hayami, Yujiro (1988) *Japanese Agriculture Under Siege: The Political Economy of Agricultural Policies* (London: Macmillan).

Hayami, Yujiro and Toshihiko Kawagoe (1989) 'Farm Mechanization, Scale Economies and Polarization', *Journal of Development Economics*, 31, pp. 221–39.

Hemmi, Kenzo (1982) 'Agriculture and Politics in Japan'. in *U.S.–Japanese Agricultural Trade Relations*, ed. by E. M. Castle and Kenzo Hemmi with S. A. Skillings (Washington, D.C.: Resources for the Future).

IRRI (1988) *World Rice Statistics 1987* (Philippines, Los Baños: International Rice Research Institute).

JMAFF(a) (Japan Ministry of Agriculture, Forestry and Fisheries), *Shokuryo Jukyu Hyo* (Food Balance Sheets).

JMAFF(b), *Pocket Norin Suisan Tokei* (Pocket Book Statistics on Agriculture, Forestry and Fisheries), (Tokyo: Norin Tokei Kyokai).

JMAFF(c) (1990) *Nogyo Hakusho Fuzoku Tokei Hyo* (Statistical Appendix to the Agricultural White Paper), (Tokyo: Norin Tokei Kyokai).

JMAFF(d), *Noringyo Census* (Census of Agriculture and Forestry), (Tokyo: Norin Tokei Kyokai).

JMAFF(e), *Kochi oyobi Sakutsuke Menseki Tokei* (Statistics of Arable Land and Area Planted), (Tokyo: Norin Tokei Kyokai).

JMAFF(f), *Nogyo Chosa* (Agricultural Survey), (Tokyo: Norin Tokei Kyokai).

JMAFF(g), *Kome oyobi Mugirui no Seisanhi* (Production Costs of Rice, Wheat and Barley), (Tokyo: Norin Tokei Kyokai).

JMAFF(h), Food Agency, *Shokuryo Kanri Tokei Nenpo* (Annual Statistics for Staple Food Control), (Tokyo: Food Agency).

Kawagoe, Toshihiko and Yujiro Hayami (1983) 'The Production Structure of World Agriculture: An Intercountry Cross-Section Analysis', *Developing Economies*, 21, pp. 189–206.

Kawagoe, Toshihiko, Keijiro Otsuka and Yujiro Hayami (1986) 'Induced Bias of Technical Change in Agriculture: The United States and Japan, 1880–1980', *Journal of Political Economy*, 94, pp. 523–44.

Kayo, Nobufumi (ed.) (1977) *Kaitei Nihon Nogyo Kiso Tokei* (Basic Statistics on Japanese Agriculture, revised version), (Tokyo: Norin Tokei Kyokai).

Mochida, Keizo (1990) *Nihon no Kome* (Rice in Japan), Chikuma Library 45 (Tokyo: Chikuma Shobo).

Nakamura, Takafusa (1986) *Showa Keizai-shi* (Economic History of the Showa Era), Iwanami Seminar Books 17 (Tokyo: Iwanami Shoten).

Otsuka, Keijiro and Yujiro Hayami (1985) 'Goals and Consequences of Rice Policy in Japan, 1965–80', *American Journal of Agricultural Economics*, 67, pp. 529–38.

Seisaku Koso Forum (Forum for Policy Innovation) (1990) *Toward Tariffication for Opening the Rice Market in Japan: A Design to Promote International Harmony and Domestic Agricultural Development* (Tokyo: Seisaku Koso Forum).

Appendix: Brief Chronology of Major Events Immediately after the War

Events with* occurred outside Japan.

1945	August	End of Second World War
	December	*Bretton Woods agreement to establish IMF and World Bank enacted
1946	February	Emergency Financial Measures (Kin'yu Kinkyu Sochi-rei) introduced and Deposit Freeze enacted
	March	Price Control Ordinance (Bukka Tosei-rei) promulgated
	August	Establishment of Economic Stabilization Board (Keizai Antei-honbu)
	October	Law on Special Measures for Wartime Compensation (Senji Hosho Tokubetu Sochi-ho) enacted
	December	Introduction of Priority Production System (Keisha Seisan Hoshiki: PPS) decided at cabinet meeting
1947	January	Reconstruction Finance Bank (Fukko Kin'yu Kinko: RFB) established
	January	General MacArthur orders the suspension of a general strike scheduled for 1 February
	March	Introduction of Rationing System of Bank Loans (Kin'yu Kikan Yushi-jyunsoku)
	March	New Public Finance Law (Zeisei-ho) promulgated (introduction of balanced budget principle)
	June	*Marshall Plan for reconstruction of Europe announced
	July	Publication of Japan's first Economic White Paper 'A Report on Actual Conditions in the Economy' (Keizai Jisso Hokoku-sho)
	August	Foreign Trade by private sector resumed on a limited scale
	December	Law for the Elimination of Excessive Concentration of Economic Power (Kado Keizairyoku Shuchu Haijo-ho: EECEP) enacted
1948	April	*Berlin Blockade begins
	May	Ralph Young Mission on Yen Exchange Rate visited Japan

	December	Nine-Point Economic Stabilization Program (Keizai Antei Kyu-gensoku) announced
1949	March	Joseph Dodge announces 'Dodge Line' for economic stabilization
	April	Single Yen-doller exchange rate (360 yen per doller) introduced
	August	Report by Shoup Mission on tax reform announced
	October	Reconstruction Finance Bank stops new lending activity
	October	Foreign trade by private sector fully approved (export from December, import from January 1950)
1950	June	*Outbreak of Korean War
	June	Foreign Exchange and Foreign Trade Control Law (Gaikoku Kawase oyobi Gaikoku Boeki Kanri-ho) promulgated and enacted
1951	March	Establishment of Japan Development Bank (Nihon Kaihatsu Ginko)
	September	Japan–US Peace Treaty ratified
1952	May	Membership in IMF and the World Bank approved
1953	July	*Korean Ceasefire Treaty ratified
	October	Membership in GATT approved

Index